THE
TOASTMASTER'S
TREASURE
CHEST

BY THE SAME AUTHORS
HERBERT V. PROCHNOW

BANK CREDIT
DILEMMAS FACING THE NATION
THE FEDERAL RESERVE SYSTEM
WORLD ECONOMIC PROBLEMS AND POLICIES
THE NEW SPEAKER'S TREASURY OF WIT AND WISDOM

HERBERT V. PROCHNOW AND
ROY A. FOULKE

PRACTICAL BANK CREDIT

HERBERT V. PROCHNOW AND
HERBERT V. PROCHNOW, JR.

THE CHANGING WORLD OF BANKING
A DICTIONARY OF WIT, WISDOM AND SATIRE
THE SUCCESSFUL TOASTMASTER
A TREASURY OF HUMOROUS QUOTATIONS
A TREASURE CHEST OF QUOTATIONS FOR ALL OCCASIONS
THE PUBLIC SPEAKER'S TREASURE CHEST

THE TOASTMASTER'S TREASURE CHEST

HERBERT V. PROCHNOW
HERBERT V. PROCHNOW, JR.

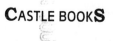

CASTLE BOOKS

This edition published in 2002 by

CASTLE BOOKS

A division of Book Sales, Inc.
114 Northfield Avenue
Edison, New Jersey 08837

This edition published by arrangement with and permission of

HarperCollins Publishers, Inc.
10 East 53rd Street
New York, New York 10022

Library of Congress Cataloging-in-Publications Data

The Toastmaster's treasure chest.

Includes index.
1.   Public speaking—Handbooks, manuals, etc.
2. Wit and humor. 3. Quotations, English. 4. Anecdotes.
5. Proverbs. I. Prochnow, Herbert Victor, DATE.
II. Prochnow, Herbert Victor, 1931-
PN4193.I5T6   1988   082'.02485   87-46167

ISBN: 0-7858-1534-1

Printed in the United States of America

CONTENTS

PREFACE

This book should be helpful to two major groups of persons. First, it is meant for speakers, toastmasters, and those who conduct committee meetings and seminars and lead discussions on civic, professional, and business matters.

Second, the book is for those who read humorous, wise, and inspiring quotations for their own enjoyment and for use in conversation. Appropriate quotations help to make a point convincingly in discussions. They also help to give color, which is essential to interesting conversation.

There are more than seven thousand unusual quotations from over fifteen hundred famous persons, including Bob Hope, Groucho Marx, Helen Hayes, Mark Twain, Oscar Wilde, Benjamin Franklin, Aristotle, Socrates, and Shakespeare.

Many of the quotations are humorous, but there is also a large number reflecting wisdom and inspiration.

The reader may select quotations that will be helpful for a particular event. In addition, there is a comprehensive index to help the reader choose pertinent quotations for any occasion.

Whether one is presiding at a meeting, introducing a speaker, making a speech, giving a few casual remarks, or is engaged in conversation, the quotations of humor, wisdom, and inspiration in this book should help one to speak effectively. In addition to its practical usefulness, the book should also provide many occasions for entertaining reading.

The reader will find the book a valuable reference for many years.

H.V.P.
H.V.P., Jr.

THE
TOASTMASTER'S
TREASURE
CHEST

Charles F. Abbott

1   Business without profit is not business any more than a pickle is a candy.

Goodman Ace

2   I keep reading between the lies.

3   A rule of thumb in the matter of medical advice is to take everything any doctor says with a grain of aspirin.

Jane Ace

4   The chickens have come home to roast.

Marcel Achard

5   Women like silent men. They think they're listening.

Dean Acheson

6   I will undoubtedly have to seek what is happily known as gainful employment, which I am glad to say does not describe holding public office.

Lord Acton

7   Advice to persons about to write history—don't.

8   Power tends to corrupt, and absolute power corrupts absolutely. Great men are almost always bad men.

Cindy Adams

9   Success has made failures of many men.

Franklin Pierce Adams

10   There are plenty of good five-cent cigars in the country. The trouble is they cost a quarter. What this country really needs is a good five-cent nickel.

11   The trouble with this country is that there are too many politicians who believe, with a conviction based on experience, that you can fool all of the people all of the time.

12   I hate the Pollyanna pest
Who says that All is for the Best.

13   If a man keeps his trap shut, the world will beat a path to his door.

14   Accustomed as I am to public speaking, I know the futility of it.

15   Dunking is bad taste but tastes good.

16   Insomniacs don't sleep because they worry about it, and they worry about it because they don't sleep.

17   Middle age occurs when you are too young to take up golf and too old to rush up to the net.

18   You never know what you can do without until you try.

19   Count that day won when, turning on its axis, this earth imposes no additional taxes.

20   Don't tell me what you dreamed last night, for I've been reading Freud.

21   Gosh! I feel like a real good cry!
Life, he says, is a cheat, a fake.
Well, I agree with the grouchy guy—
The best you get is an even break.

22   The best part of the fiction in many novels is the notice that the characters are all purely imaginary.

23   Gentlemen, I love and like you,
Caring little for your I.Q.

Henry Brooks Adams

24   Practical politics consists in ignoring the facts.

25   Nothing in education is so astonishing as the amount of ignorance it accumulates in the form of inert facts.

26   It is impossible to underrate human intelligence—beginning with one's own.

27   Philosophy: unintelligible answers to insoluble problems.

28   Morality is a private and costly luxury.

29   Young men have a passion for regarding their elders as senile.

30   A teacher affects eternity.

James R. Adams

31   Liars are never specific. You even believe a fisherman when he announces the length of his fish in feet and inches. You smile only when he measures his catch with a gesture.

James Truslow Adams

32   There are obviously two educations. One should teach us how to make a living, and the other how to live.

Joey Adams

33   The most popular labor-saving device today is still a husband with money.

34   Nowadays, two can live as cheaply as one large family used to!

35   They tell me he fell in love with a pair of blue eyes—then made the mistake of marrying the whole girl.

36   Bankruptcy is a legal proceeding in which you put your money in your pants pocket and give your coat to your creditors.

John Adams

37   Oh! the wisdom, the foresight and the hindsight and the rightsight and the leftsight, the northsight and the southsight, and the eastsight and the westsight that appeared in that august assembly. [On the U.S. Congress.]

38   My country has in its wisdom contrived for me the most insignificant office that ever the invention of man contrived or his imagination conceived. [On the Vice Presidency.]

John Quincy Adams

39   No English minister has ever been so popular; and the mediocrity of his talents has been one of the principal causes of his success.

40   I smoked tobacco and read Milton at the same time, and from the same motive—to find out what was the recondite charm in them which gave my father so much pleasure. After making myself four or five times sick with smoking, I mastered that accomplishment.... But I did not master Milton.

Joseph Addison

41   Authors have established it as a kind of rule that a man ought to be dull sometimes.

42   Nothing is capable of being well set to music that is not nonsense.

43   A moneylender serves you in the present tense, lends you in the conditional mood, keeps you in the subjunctive, and ruins you in the future.

George Ade

44   Early to bed and early to rise, and you'll meet very few of our best people.

45   "Whom are you?" said he, for he had been to night school.

46   Anybody can win, unless there happens to be a second entry.

47   For parlor use, the vague generality is a lifesaver.

48   The house was more covered with mortgages than with paint.

49   If it were not for the presents, an elopement would be preferable.

50   She was a town-and-country soprano of the kind often used for augmenting the grief at a funeral.

51   After being turned down by numerous publishers, he decided to write for posterity.

52   The music teacher came twice each week to bridge the awful gap between Dorothy and Chopin.

53   She told him it was terrible to hear such things as he told her and to please go ahead.

54   He had been kicked in the head by a mule when young, and believed everything he read in the Sunday papers.

55   My father sent me to an engineering school to prepare me for a literary career.

56   She invariably was first over the fence in the mad pursuit of culture.

57   A good folly is worth whatever you pay for it.

58   A friend who is very near and dear may in time become as useless as a relative.

59   Those dry martinis were too much for me.
Last night I really felt immense,
Today I feel like thirty cents;

It is no time for mirth and laughter
In the cold gray dawn of the morning after.

60   Here's to man, he can afford anything he can get. Here's to woman, she can afford anything she can get a man to get for her.

61   Draw your salary before spending it.

62   He felt like the symptoms on a medicine bottle.

Konrad Adenauer

63   A thick skin is a gift from God.

64   An infallible method of conciliating a tiger is to allow oneself to be devoured.

65   The good Lord set definite limits on man's wisdom, but set no limits on his stupidity—and that's just not fair!

Alfred Adler

66   It is easier to fight for one's principles than to live up to them.

Mortimer Adler

67   The purpose of learning is growth, and our minds, unlike our bodies, can continue growing as we continue to live.

Aesop

68   It is easy to be brave from a safe distance.

69   He that serves God for money will serve the Devil for better wages.

Louis J. R. Agassiz

70   I cannot afford to waste my time making money.

James Agate

71   The English instinctively admire any man who has no talent and is modest about it.

72   To force myself to earn more money, I determined to spend more.

73   I have views on most matters, and am as willing as a politician to change most of them.

74   Long experience has taught me that in England nobody goes to the theatre unless he or she has bronchitis.

Spiro T. Agnew
75   We're sick and tired of having this country run down by a group of phony intellectuals who don't understand what we mean by hard work and patriotism.

Leo Aikman
76   Most of us are umpires at heart; we like to call balls and strikes on somebody else.

Kehlog Albran
77   I have seen the future and it is very much like the present—only longer.

Herm Albright
78   On school chalkboard: A double negative is a no-no.

A. B. Alcott
79   To be ignorant of one's ignorance is the malady of the ignorant.

M. H. Alderson
80   If at first you don't succeed, you're running about average.

Richard Aldington
81   Patriotism is a lively sense of responsibility. Nationalism is a silly cock crowing on its own dunghill.

Alexander the Great
82   I am dying with the help of too many physicians.

Muhammad Ali
83   No one knows what to say in the loser's locker room.

Dante Alighieri
84   There is no greater sorrow than to recall, in misery, the time when we were happy.

Saul Alinsky
85   Once you accept your own death all of a sudden you are free to live. You no longer care about your reputation ... you no longer care except so far as your life can be used tactically—to promote a cause you believe in.

Fred Allen
86   He writes so well he makes me feel like putting my quill back in my goose.

87   What's on your mind, if you will allow the overstatement?

88   The penguin flies backwards because he doesn't care to see where he's going, but wants to see where he's been.

89   A conference is a gathering of important people who singly can do nothing, but together can decide that nothing can be done.

90   He pasted picture postcards around goldfish bowls to make the goldfish think they were going places.

91   Her hat is a creation that will never go out of style; it will just look ridiculous year after year.

92   He was not brought by the stork; he was delivered by a man from the Audubon Society personally.

93   Hollywood is a place where people from Iowa mistake each other for movie stars.

94   If a circus is half as good as it smells, it's a great show.

95   I like long walks, especially when they are taken by people who annoy me.

96   Advertising agency: eighty-five percent confusion and fifteen percent commission.

97   California is a fine place to live in—if you happen to be an orange.

98   I play a musical instrument some, but only for my own amazement.

99   The sky is poor tonight—the moon is down to its last quarter.

100   A celebrity is a person who works hard all his life to become well known, then wears dark glasses to avoid being recognized.

101   Hollywood is no place for the professional comedian—there's too much amateur competition.

102   The American arrives in Paris with a few French phrases he has culled from a conversational guide or picked up from a friend who owns a beret. He speaks the sort of French that is only understood by another American who has also just arrived in Paris.

103   Most of us spend the first six days of each week sowing wild oats, then we go to church on Sunday and pray for a crop failure.

104   A gentleman is any man who wouldn't hit a woman with his hat on.

105   Hush, little bright line, don't you cry,
         You'll be a cliché by and by.

106   If the grass is greener in the other fellow's yard—let him worry about cutting it.

107   I don't want to own anything that won't fit into my coffin.

108   On ships they call them barnacles; in radio they attach themselves to desks and are called vice-presidents.

Grant Allen
109   All men are born free and unequal.

Hervey Allen
110   Every new generation is a fresh invasion of savages.

Marty Allen
111   A study of economics usually reveals that the best time to buy anything is last year.

Woody Allen
112   Most of the time I don't have much fun. The rest of the time I don't have any fun at all.

Peter Altenberg
113   Somebody once asked Anton Bruckner: "Master, how, when, where did you think of the divine motif of your Ninth Symphony?"
    "Well, it was like this. I walked up the Kahlenberg, and when it got hot and I got hungry, I sat down by a little brook and unpacked my Swiss cheese. And just as I opened the greasy paper, that darn tune pops into my head!"

Dr. Walter Alvarez
114   Death keeps taking little bites of me. [Quoting an aging woman.]

Oscar Ameringer
115   Politics is the gentle art of getting votes from the poor and campaign funds from the rich, by promising to protect each from the other.

Lord Amherst
116   In the bad old days ... there were three easy ways of losing money—racing being the quickest, women the pleasantest and farming the most certain.

Idi Amin
117   I do not want to be controlled by any superpower; I myself consider myself the most powerful figure in the world.

118   My people share their money with me and I share my heart with them. That is the right way.

Cleveland Amory
119   You can't make the Duchess of Windsor into Rebecca of Sunnybrook Farm. The facts of life are very stubborn things.

120   The opera is like a husband with a foreign title: expensive to support, hard to understand and therefore a supreme social challenge.

Max Amsterdam
121   Business: the art of extracting money from another man's pocket without resorting to violence.

Anacharsis
122   The market is a place set apart where men may deceive each other.

Brad Anderson
123   I've never heard such corny lyrics, such simpering sentimentality, such repetitious, uninspired melody. Man, we've got a hit on our hands!

Sir Norman Angell
124   The greatest service we can do the Common Man is to abolish him.

Thomas G. Appleton
125   Good Americans, when they die, go to Paris.

Lawrence A. Appley
126   Management is now where the medical profession was when it decided that working in a drug store was not sufficient training to become a doctor.

Marie Aragon
127   We sold our house and are moving into one of those pandemoniums.

John Arbuthnot
128   Biography is one of the new terrors of death.

129   All political parties die at last of swallowing their own lies.

Hannah Arendt
130   The fault is in us.

Pietro Aretino

131   If you want to annoy your neighbors, tell the truth about them.

Aristophanes

132   You cannot make a crab walk straight.

Aristotle

133   Wit is educated insolence.

134   My friends! There are no friends.

Michael Arlen

135   It is amazing how nice people are to you when they know you are going away.

136   She not only expects the worst, but makes the worst of it when it happens.

137   My forebears were successful crooks living on the slopes of Mount Ararat.

Richard Armour

138   It's all right to hold a conversation, but you should let go of it now and then.

139   Workers earn it,
Spendthrifts burn it,
Bankers lend it,
Women spend it,
Forgers fake it,
Taxes take it,
Dying leave it,
Heirs receive it,
Thrifty save it,
Misers crave it,
Robbers seize it,
Rich increase it,
Gamblers lose it . . .
I could use it.

140   That money talks
I'll not deny.
I heard it once;
It said, "Good-bye."

141   Shake and shake
The catsup bottle.
None will come,
And then a lot'll.

142   Of late I appear
        To have reached that stage
        When people look old
        Who are only my age.

143   When all is said and done, we usually wish we had done more and said less.

144   When it comes to eating, you can sometimes help yourself more by helping yourself less.

Neil A. Armstrong
145   That's one small step for man, one giant leap for mankind.

Matthew Arnold
146   Journalism is literature in a hurry.

147   It is hard for a pure and thoughtful man to live in a state of rapture at the spectacle afforded him by his fellow creatures.

Oren Arnold
148   Prayer of the modern American: "Dear God, I pray for patience. And I want it right now!"

Sophie Arnould
149   Oh! the good old days when I was so unhappy.

Raymond Aron
150   What passes for optimism is most often the effect of an intellectual error.

Isaac Asimov
151   If my doctor told me I had only six months to live, I wouldn't brood. I'd type a little faster.

Russell P. Askue
152   If living conditions don't stop improving in this country, we're going to run out of humble beginnings for our great men.

Margot Asquith
153   He could not see a belt without hitting below it. [On Lloyd George.]

John Jacob Astor III
154   The man who has a million dollars is as well off as if he were rich.

Lady Nancy Astor

155   What would we say if men changed the length of their trousers every year?

156   The only thing I like about rich people is their money.

157   I'm an extinct volcano.

158   My vigor, vitality and cheek repel me. I am the kind of a woman I would run from.

Alex Atkinson

159   He had, he said, studied the great philosophers and had therefore come to expect very little in this life, and rather less in the next.

Brooks Atkinson

160   When a pious visitor inquired sweetly, "Henry, have you made your peace with God?" he [Thoreau] replied, "We have never quarrelled."

Clement Attlee

161   I must remind the Right Honourable Gentleman that a monologue is not a decision. [To Winston Churchill.]

Wystan Hugh Auden

162   A professor is one who talks in someone else's sleep.

163   No good opera plot can be sensible, for people do not sing when they are feeling sensible.

164   A poet can write about a man slaying a dragon, but not about a man pushing a button that releases a bomb.

Saint Augustine

165   The playthings of our elders are called business.

Vincent Auriol

166   The work was killing me; they called me out of bed at all hours of the night to receive resignations of prime ministers. [On retirement as president of France.]

Jane Austen

167   I have been a selfish being all my life, in practice, though not in principle.

168   A woman, especially, if she have the misfortune of knowing anything, should conceal it as well as she can.

169   What dreadful hot weather we have! It keeps one in a continual state of inelegance.

Irving Babbitt

170   The American reading his Sunday paper in a state of lazy collapse is perhaps the most perfect symbol of the triumph of quantity over quality. . . . Whole forests are being ground into pulp daily to minister to our triviality.

Lauren Bacall

171   What will it take to get through the year? For starters, I'd suggest health, happiness and sapphires.

Francis Bacon

172   The fly sat upon the axle-tree of the chariot-wheel and said, "What a dust do I raise!"

173   Anger makes dull men witty, but it keeps them poor.

174   God Almighty first planted a garden. And indeed it is the purest of human pleasures.

Arthur ("Bugs") Baer

175   He had insomnia so bad that he couldn't sleep when he was working.

176   She used to diet on any kind of food she could lay her hands on.

177   A good neighbor is a fellow who smiles at you over the back fence but doesn't climb over it.

178   How much would you charge to haunt a house?

179   She was a brunette by birth but a blonde by habit.

180   She's generous to a fault—if it's her own.

181   You can take a boy out of the country but you can't take the country out of a boy.

182   Although it is a far cry from there to here, he laughed all the way.

183   An empty cab drove up, and Sarah Bernhardt got out.

184   Do incubator chickens love their mother?

185   It was so quiet, you could hear a pun drop.

186   A newspaper is a circulating library with high blood pressure.

Walter Bagehot

187   A parliament is nothing less than a big meeting of more or less idle people.

188   An inability to stay quiet is one of the most conspicuous failings of mankind.

189   The great pleasure in life is doing what people say you cannot do.

190   The whole history of civilization is strewn with creeds and institutions which were invaluable at first, and deadly afterwards.

191   There are lies, damned lies, and church statistics.

192   Persecution in intellectual countries produces a superficial conformity, but also underneath an intense, incessant, implacable doubt.

193   Never ascribe to an opponent motives meaner than your own.

194   It was government by discussion that broke the bond of ages and set free the originality of mankind.

195   Poverty is an anomaly to rich people; it is very difficult to make out why people who want dinner do not ring the bell.

196   The reason why so few good books are written is that so few people who can write know anything.

197   Nothing is more unpleasant than a virtuous person with a mean mind.

198   One of the greatest pains to human nature is the pain of a new idea.

199   No great work has ever been produced except after a long interval of still and musing meditation.

200   Everybody at one time or another makes a mistake; but only a fool makes the same mistake twice.

201   A schoolmaster should have an atmosphere of awe, and walk wonderingly, as if he was amazed at being himself.

H. C. Bailey

202   The origin of civilization is man's determination to do nothing for himself which he can get done for him.

James Montgomery Bailey

203   Any young man with good health and a poor appetite can save up money.

204   The dearest object to a married man should be his wife but it is not infrequently her clothes.

Josephine Baker
205   I like Frenchmen very much, because even when they insult you they do it so nicely.

206   The test of good manners is being able to put up with bad ones.

Karle Baker
207   Courage is fear that has said its prayers.

Russell Baker
208   Family solvency is not a felony, but many economists consider it vaguely unpatriotic.

Faith Baldwin
209   She was torn between love and booty.

210   Time is a dressmaker specializing in alterations.

James Baldwin
211   The American ideal is, after all, that everyone should be as much alike as possible.

Stanley Baldwin
212   The intelligent are to the intelligentsia what a gentleman is to a gent.

213   War would end if the dead could return.

Arthur Balfour
214   Nothing matters very much, and few things matter at all.

215   It is unfortunate, considering that enthusiasm moves the world, that so few enthusiasts can be trusted to speak the truth.

Endre Balough
216   The man we call a specialist today was formerly called a man with a one-track mind.

John Baltul
217   Pythagoras said that the whole world was a comedy, of which the philosophers were the spectators.

Honoré de Balzac
218   Friendships last when each friend thinks he has a slight superiority over the other.

219   Money brings everything to you, even your daughters.

220   Bureaucracy is a giant mechanism operated by pygmies.

221   It is necessary to be almost a genius to make a good husband.

222   The man who can govern a woman can govern a nation.

223   When women have made a sheep of a man, they always tell him that he is a lion, with an iron will.

224   Believe everything you hear about the world; nothing is too impossibly bad.

225 ′   The majority of husbands reminds me of an orangutang trying to play the violin.

226   I do not regard a broker as a member of the human race.

John Kendrick Bangs
227   All press agents belong to a club of which Ananias is the honorary president.

Margaret Culkin Banning
228   She never quite leaves her children at home, even when she doesn't take them along.

Sir Frederick G. Banting
229   The one thing I dread is affluence. I have a lovely office now, with pictures on the wall and a swivel chair, and I can't do anything.

Sam Bardell
230   Psychiatrist: a man who asks you a lot of expensive questions your wife asks you for nothing.

Myrtie Barker
231   The idea of strictly minding our own business is moldy rubbish. Who could be so selfish?

Alben Barkley
232   An economist is an unemployed financier with a Phi Beta Kappa key on one end of his watch chain and no watch on the other.

Binnie Barnes
233   He's the kind of bore who's here today and here tomorrow.

James Barnes
234   You can always tell a Harvard man, but you can't tell him much.

P. T. Barnum

235   Every crowd has a silver lining.

236   There's a sucker born every minute.

237   You can fool most of the people most of the time.

238   If I shoot at the sun I may hit a star.

Maurice Barres

239   The politician is an acrobat. He keeps his balance by saying the opposite of what he does.

James Matthew Barrie

240   I know not, sir, whether Bacon wrote the works of Shakespeare, but if he did not it seems to me that he missed the opportunity of his life.

241   When the first baby laughed for the first time, his laugh broke into a million pieces, and they all went skipping about. That was the beginning of fairies.

242   It is not true that woman was made from man's rib; she was really made from his funny bone.

243   Every man who is high up loves to think that he has done it all himself; and the wife smiles, and lets it go at that. It's our only joke. Every woman knows that.

244   I am not young enough to know everything.

245   The printing press is either the greatest blessing or the greatest curse of modern times; one sometimes forgets which.

246   We are all of us failures—at least, the best of us are.

247   The God to whom little boys say their prayers has a face very like their mother's.

248   One's religion is whatever he is most interested in, and yours is Success.

Philip Barry

249   Love: two minds without a single thought.

Ethel Barrymore

250   You grow up the day you have the first real laugh—at yourself.

251   For an actress to be a success she must have the face of Venus, the brains of Minerva, the grace of Terpsichore, the memory of Macaulay, the figure of Juno, and the hide of a rhinoceros.

John Barrymore

252   America is the country where you buy a lifetime supply of aspirin for one dollar, and use it up in two weeks.

253   One of my chief regrets during my years in the theater is that I couldn't sit in the audience and watch me.

254   The way to fight a woman is with your hat—grab it and run.

255   I've read some of your modern free verse and wonder who set it free.

256   A man properly must pay the fiddler. In my case it so happened that a whole symphony orchestra often had to be subsidized.

257   The good die young—because they see it's no use living if you've got to be good.

258   The only reason why a man should pay the least attention to a hat is that it is something one tips to a lady.

259   Paper napkins never return from a laundry—nor love from a trip to the law courts.

260   Speech-making is exactly like childbirth. You are so glad to get it over with.

261   Audiences? No, the plural is impossible. Whether it is in Butte, Montana, or Broadway, it's an audience. The same great hulking monster with four thousand eyes and forty thousand teeth.

Bruce Barton

262   Conceit: God's gift to little men.

263   If advertising encourages people to live beyond their means, so does matrimony.

264   Rumor, that most efficient of press agents.

Bernard Baruch

265   I'm not smart, but I like to observe. Millions saw the apple fall, but Newton was the one who asked why.

266   We can't always cross a bridge until we come to it, but I always like to lay down a pontoon ahead of time.

267   To me, old age is always fifteen years older than I am.

268   During my eighty-seven years I have witnessed a whole succession of technological revolutions. But none of them has done away with the need for character in the individual or the ability to think.

269   Never answer a critic, unless he's right.

270   I am interested in physical medicine because my father was. I am interested in medical research because I believe in it. I am interested in arthritis because I have it.

271   Don't try to buy at the bottom and sell at the top. This can't be done—except by liars.

Jacques Barzun
272   In any assembly the simplest way to stop the transacting of business and split the ranks is to appeal to a principle.

J. L. Basford
273   It requires a strong constitution to withstand repeated attacks of prosperity.

Phyllis Battelle
274   A jay is a bird of the crow family, which can be found in fields and meadows. A jaywalker, on the other hand, is a bird of the Schmoe family who can be found in traffic jams and morgues.

Dr. O. A. Battista
275   You have reached the pinnacle of success as soon as you become uninterested in money, compliments, or publicity.

276   Temptations, unlike opportunities, will always give you a second chance.

277   The average heart specialist can usually check the condition of his patient's heart simply by sending him a bill.

278   Success is defined as luck if it happens to the other fellow—insatiable persistence and hard work if it happens to you.

Charles Baudelaire
279   Life is a hospital, in which every patient is possessed by the desire of changing his bed. One would prefer to suffer near the fire, and another is certain he would get well if he were by the window.

Harry Bauer
280   Hard work never kills anybody who supervises it.

Vicki Baum
281   What I like about Hollywood is that one can get along by knowing two words of English—swell and lousy.

282   Pity is the deadliest feeling that can be offered to a woman.

Anne Baxter
283   I knew her when she didn't know where her next husband was coming from.

Beverley Baxter
284   A great many persons are able to become members of this House without losing their insignificance. [On the British Parliament.]

Philippe de Beaumanoir
285   Women, deceived by men, want to marry them; it is a kind of revenge as good as any other.

Caron de Beaumarchais
286   It is not necessary to understand things in order to argue about them.

Lord Beaverbrook
287   He did not care in which direction the car was traveling, so long as he remained in the driver's seat. [On Lloyd George.]

288   Business is more exciting than any game.

Cesare Beccaria
289   The fault no child ever loses is the one he was most punished for.

Dave Beck
290   I define a recession as when your neighbor loses his job, but a depression is when you lose your own.

Carl Becker
291   No class of Americans, so far as I know, has ever objected . . . to any amount of governmental meddling if it appeared to benefit that particular class.

Henry Becque
292   The defect of equality is that we only desire it with our superiors.

Sir Thomas Beecham
293   The English may not like music, but they absolutely love the noise it makes.

Henry Ward Beecher
294   Next to ingratitude, the most painful thing to bear is gratitude.

295   Selfishness is that detestable vice which no one will forgive in others and no one is without in himself.

296   There are many people who think that Sunday is a sponge to wipe out all the sins of the week.

297   Why is not a rat as good as a rabbit? Why should men eat shrimps and neglect cockroaches?

298   The monkey is an organized sarcasm upon the human race.

299   The difference between perseverance and obstinacy is that one often comes from a strong will, and the other from a strong won't.

300   Never forget what a man says to you when he is angry.

301   No matter who reigns, the merchant reigns.

Lyman Beecher

302   O Lord, grant that we may not despise our rulers; and grant, O Lord, that they may not act so we can't help it.

Max Beerbohm

303   I was a modest, good-humored boy; it is Oxford that has made me insufferable.

304   To give an accurate and exhaustive account of that period would need a far less brilliant pen than mine.

305   I maintain that though you would often in the fifteenth century have heard the snobbish Roman say, in a would-be offhand tone, "I am dining with the Borgias tonight," no Roman ever was able to say, "I dined last night with the Borgias."

306   Nobody ever died of laughter.

307   My gifts are small. I've used them very well and discreetly, never straining them, and the result is that I have made a charming little reputation.

308   You cannot make a man by standing a sheep on its hind legs. But by standing a flock of sheep in that position you can make a crowd of men.

309   To say that a man is vain means merely that he is pleased with the effect he produces on other people. A conceited man is satisfied with the effect he produces on himself.

Alfred Behan

310   Money speaks sense in a language all nations understand.

S. N. Behrman

311   I have had just about all I can take of myself. [At the age of seventy-five.]

312   Having said, from our respective points of view, the worst thing we could say about each other, having uttered the ultimate insult, there's no reason we can't be friends.

313   There are two kinds of people in one's life—people whom one keeps waiting—and the people for whom one waits.

314   Psychoanalysis makes quite simple people feel they're complex.

Francis Albert ("Bee") Behymer

315   Methuselah lived 969 years and all they said about him was that he died. But what was he doing for 969 years? What a story, and all the reporters missed it!

Hilaire Belloc

316   The pleasure politicians take in their limelight pleases me with the sort of pleasure I get when I see a child's eyes gleam over a new toy.

317   She was not really bad at heart,
       But only rather rude and wild;
       She was an aggravating child.

318   They murmured as they took their fees,
       There is no cure for this disease.

319   He who can make a perfect omelette can probably do nothing else.

320   When I am dead, I hope it may be said: "His sins were scarlet, but his books were read."

321   I shoot the Hippopotamus
       With bullets made of platinum,
       Because if I use leaden ones
       His hide is sure to flatten 'em.

Robert Benchley

322   A great many people have come up to me and asked how I managed to get so much done and still look so dissipated.

323   It took me fifteen years to discover I had no talent for writing, but I couldn't give it up because by that time I was too famous.

324   A dog teaches a boy fidelity, perseverance, and to turn around three times before lying down.

325   In America there are two classes of travel—first class, and with children.

326   I do most of my work sitting down; that's where I shine.

327   Drawing on my fine command of language, I said nothing.

328   "Perfectly Scandalous" was one of those plays in which all the actors unfortunately enunciated very clearly.

329   Word has somehow got around that the split infinitive is always wrong. This is of a piece with the outworn notion that it is always wrong to strike a lady.

330   Drinking makes such fools of people, and people are such fools to begin with that it's compounding a felony.

331   If we can develop some way in which a man can doze and still keep from making a monkey of himself, we have removed one of the big obstacles to human happiness in modern civilization.

332   I haven't been abroad in so long that I almost speak English without an accent.

333   A great many people use faulty English without knowing it. Ain't you?

334   Great literature must spring from an upheaval in the author's soul. If that upheaval is not present, then it must come from the works of any other author which happen to be handy and easily adapted.

335   The advantage of keeping family accounts is clear. If you do not keep them, you are uneasily aware of the fact that you are spending more than you are earning. If you do keep them, you know it.

336   There is something about saying "OK" and hanging up the receiver with a bang that kids a man into feeling that he has just pulled off a big deal, even if he has only called the telephone company to find out the correct time.

337   Anyone can do any amount of work, provided it isn't the work he is supposed to be doing at the moment.

Stephen Vincent Benét

338   As for what you're calling hard luck—well, we made New England out of it, that and codfish.

Sir William Gurney Benham

339   The road to ruin is in good repair; the travelers pay the expense of it.

340   When you see a snake, never mind where it came from.

Arnold Bennett

341   It is well, when one is judging a friend, to remember that he is judging you with the same godlike and superior impartiality.

342   Pessimism, when you get used to it, is just as agreeable as optimism.

343   It is only people of small moral stature who have to stand on their dignity.

344   Good taste is better than bad taste, but bad taste is better than no taste at all.

Dan Bennett

345   Repartee: what a person thinks of after he becomes a departee.

346   Most teenagers think that their family circle is composed of squares.

James Gordon Bennett

347   I have made mistakes, but I have never made the mistake of claiming that I never made one.

Jack Benny

348   Before your fortieth birthday keep circulating the story that you're thirty-nine. If people hear it often enough they'll believe it for years.

Robert Hugh Benson

349   It is a tolerable depiction of a bore that he is one who talks about himself when you want to talk about yourself.

350   Youth is a disease that must be borne with patiently! Time, indeed, will cure it.

Jeremy Bentham

351   Lawyers are the only persons in whom ignorance of the law is not punished.

352   Prose is where all the lines but the last go onto the margin. Poetry is where some of them fall short of it.

Edmund Clerihew Bentley

353   John Stuart Mill,
By a mighty effort of will,
Overcame his natural bonhomie
And wrote Principles of Political Economy.

John Bentley
354   Making money is fun, but it's pointless if you don't use the power
it brings.

Nicolas Bentley
355   No news is good news; no journalists is even better.

Bernard Berenson
356   Consistency requires you to be as ignorant today as you were a
year ago.

357   My house, I trust, does express my needs, my tastes and aspirations. It is a library with living rooms attached.

Robert Bergland, Secretary of Agriculture
358   I've never been out of this country but I've been to California.
Does that count?

Ben Bergor
359   It is amazing how quickly the kids learn to drive a car, yet are
unable to understand the lawnmower, snowblower, or vacuum cleaner.

Irving Berlin
360   Listen, kid, take my advice: never hate a song that has sold a
half-million copies!

361   The toughest thing about success is that you've got to keep on
being a success.

Claude Bernard
362   Science increases our power in proportion as it lowers our pride.

Yogi Berra
363   Toots Shor's restaurant is so crowded nobody goes there anymore.

364   If people don't want to come out to the ball park, nobody's going
to stop them.

Eugene P. Bertin
365   The best way to keep teens home is to make home pleasant—and
let the air out of the tires.

366   This summer, one-third of the nation will be ill-housed, ill-
nourished, and ill-clad. Only they call it vacation.

Pierre Berton

367 A Canadian is somebody who knows how to make love in a canoe.

Bruno Bettelheim

368 People always involved in broad issues generally neglect those closest to them. I have seen too many damaged children whose parents were leaders.

Aneurin Bevan

369 We know what happens to people who stay in the middle of the road—they get run over.

370 This second-rate orator trails his tawdry wisps of mist over the parliamentary scene. [On Stanley Baldwin.]

371 He seems determined to make a trumpet sound like a tin whistle. ... He brings to the fierce struggle of politics the tepid ... enthusiasm of a lazy summer afternoon at a cricket match. [On Clement Attlee.]

372 Beneath the sophistication 'of his appearance and manner, he has all the unplumbable stupidities and unawareness of his class and type. [On Sir Anthony Eden.]

373 I have never regarded politics as the arena of morals; it is the arena of interests.

374 The worst thing I can say about democracy is that it has tolerated the Right Honourable Gentleman for four and a half years. [On Neville Chamberlain.]

375 Stand not too near the rich man lest he destroy thee—and not too far away lest he forget thee.

376 Please don't be deterred in the fanatical application of your sterile logic.

377 The mediocrity of his thinking is concealed by the majesty of his language. [On Winston Churchill.]

378 A man [government official] walking backwards with his face to the future.

379 He [Winston Churchill] never spares himself in conversation. He gives himself so generously that hardly anybody else is permitted to give anything in his presence.

Sir William Beveridge

380 ... to avoid the conclusion that economists are persons who earn their living by taking in one another's definitions for mangling.

Hugh M. Beville, Jr.

381   In advertising there is a saying that if you can keep your head while all those around you are losing theirs—then you just don't understand the problem.

Georges Bidault

382   When it comes to laying cards on the table, the Russians never play anything but clubs.

Ambrose Bierce

383   Alliance: in international politics, the union of two thieves that have their hands so deeply inserted into each other's pockets that they cannot safely plunder a third.

384   Bigot: one who is obstinately and zealously attached to an opinion that you do not entertain.

385   Consul: in American politics, a person who, having failed to secure an office from the people, is given one by the Administration, on condition that he leave the country.

386   Conservative: a statesman who is enamoured of existing evils, as distinguished from the Liberal who wishes to replace them with others.

387   Peace: in international affairs, a period of cheating between two periods of fighting.

388   Administration: an ingenious abstraction in politics, designed to receive the kicks and cuffs due to the premier or president.

389   Opposition: in politics, the party that prevents the government from running amuck by hamstringing it.

390   Cynic: a blackguard whose faulty vision sees things as they are, not as they ought to be.

391   Discussion: a method of confirming others in their errors.

392   Egotist: a person of low taste, more interested in himself than in me.

393   The fact that boys are allowed to exist at all is evidence of a remarkable Christian forbearance among men.

394   The gambling known as business looks with austere disfavor upon the business known as gambling.

395   The hardest tumble a man can make is to fall over his own bluff.

396   Here's to woman! Would that we could fall into her arms without falling into her hands.

397   History: an account mostly false, of events unimportant, which are brought about by rulers mostly knaves, and soldiers mostly fools.

398   Hospitality: the virtue which induces us to feed and lodge certain persons who are not in need of food and lodging.

399   A prejudice is a vagrant opinion without visible means of support.

400   Acquaintance: a person whom we know well enough to borrow from, but not well enough to lend to.

401   Faith: belief without evidence in what is told by one who speaks without knowledge, of things without parallel.

402   Acquaintance: a degree of friendship called slight when its object is poor or obscure, and intimate when he is rich or famous.

403   Admiration: our polite recognition of another man's resemblance to ourselves.

404   Armor is the kind of clothing worn by a man whose tailor was a blacksmith.

405   Cabbage: a familiar kitchen-garden vegetable about as large and wise as a man's head.

406   Calamities are of two kinds: misfortune to ourselves, and good fortune to others.

407   Christians and camels receive their burdens kneeling.

408   Positive: being mistaken at the top of one's voice.

409   To apologize is to lay the foundation for a future offense.

410   All are lunatics, but he who can analyze his delusion is called a philosopher.

411   Experience is a revelation in the light of which we renounce our errors of youth for those of age.

412   To the small part of ignorance that we arrange and classify we give the name knowledge.

413   Consult: to seek another's approval of a course already decided on.

414   Philosophy: a route of many roads leading from nowhere to nothing.

415   Patience: a minor form of despair disguised as a virtue.

416   Abstainer: a weak person who yields to the temptation of denying himself a pleasure.

417   Applause: the echo of a platitude.

418   Inventor: a person who makes an ingenious arrangement of wheels, levers and springs, and believes it civilization.

419   Coward: one who in a perilous emergency thinks with his legs.

420   Diaphragm: a muscular partition separating disorders of the chest from disorders of the bowels.

421   When you are ill make haste to forgive your enemies, for you may recover.

422   In the last analysis, ability is commonly found to consist mainly in a high degree of solemnity.

423   Absurdity: a statement or belief manifestly inconsistent with one's own opinion.

424   Alone: in bad company.

425   Architect: one who drafts a plan of your house and plans a draft of your money.

426   Christian: one who believes that the New Testament is a divinely inspired book admirably suited to the spiritual needs of his neighbor.

427   Commendation: the tribute that we pay to achievements that resemble, but do not equal, our own.

428   Consolation: the knowledge that a better man is more unfortunate than yourself.

429   Corporation: an ingenious device for obtaining individual profit without individual responsibility.

430   Dawn: the time when men of reason go to bed.

431   Duty: that which sternly impels us in the direction of profit, along the line of desire.

432   Education: that which discloses to the wise and disguises from the foolish their lack of understanding.

433   Eulogy: praise of a person who has either the advantages of wealth and power, or the consideration to be dead.

434   Fashion: a despot whom the wise ridicule and obey.

435   Hypocrisy: prejudice with a halo.

436   A specialist is one who knows everything about something and nothing about anything else.

437   Patriotism is as fierce as a fever, pitiless as the grave, blind as a stone, and irrational as a headless hen.

438   Quoting: the act of repeating erroneously the words of another.

439   Success is the one unpardonable sin against one's fellows.

440   Ignoramus: a person unacquainted with certain kinds of knowledge familiar to yourself, and having certain other kinds that you know nothing about.

441   Infancy: the period of our lives when, according to Wordsworth, "Heaven lies about us." The world begins lying about us pretty soon afterward.

442   Insurance: an ingenious modern game of chance in which the player is permitted to enjoy the comfortable conviction that he is beating the man who keeps the table.

443   Lawsuit: a machine which you go into as a pig and come out as a sausage.

444   Learning: the kind of ignorance distinguishing the studious.

445   Lecturer: one with his hand in your pocket, his tongue in your ear and his faith in your patience.

446   Liver: a large red organ thoughtfully provided by nature to be bilious with.

447   Longevity: uncommon extension of the fear of death.

448   Mammon: the god of the world's leading religion. His chief temple is in the holy city of New York.

449   Mausoleum: the final and funniest folly of the rich.

450   Mercy: an attribute beloved of detected offenders.

451   Mouth: in man, the gateway to the soul; in woman, the outlet of the heart.

452   Neighbor: one whom we are commanded to love as ourselves, and does all he knows how to make us disobedient.

453   Noise: a stench in the ear. Undomesticated music. The chief product and authenticating sign of civilization.

454   Nominee: a modest gentleman shrinking from the distinction of private life and diligently seeking the honorable obscurity of public office.

455   Notoriety: the fame of one's competitor for public honors.

456   November: the eleventh twelfth of a weariness.

457   Ocean: a body of water occupying about two-thirds of a world made for man—who has no gills.

458   Omen: a sign that something will happen if nothing happens.

459   Opportunity: a favorable occasion for grasping a disappointment.

460   Optimism: the doctrine or belief that everything is beautiful, including what is ugly.

461   Penitent: undergoing or awaiting punishment.

462   In Dr. Johnson's famous dictionary, patriotism is defined as the last resort of a scoundrel. With all due respect to an enlightened but inferior lexicographer I beg to submit that it is the first.

463   Perseverance: a lowly virtue whereby mediocrity achieves an inglorious success.

464   Philanthropist: a rich (and usually bald) old gentleman who has trained himself to grin while his conscience is picking his pocket.

465   Religion: a daughter of Hope and Fear, explaining to Ignorance the nature of the Unknowable.

466   Phonograph: an irritating toy that restores life to dead noises.

467   Platitude: all that is mortal of a departed truth.

468   Politeness: the most acceptable hypocrisy.

469   Politics: a strife of interests masquerading as a contest of principles. The conduct of public affairs for private advantage.

470   Adherent: a follower who has not yet obtained all that he expects to get.

471   Imposter: a rival aspirant to public honors.

472   Very often the quiet fellow has said all he knows.

473   Radicalism: the conservatism of tomorrow injected into the affairs of today.

474   Respectability: the offspring of a liaison between bald head and bank account.

475   You are not permitted to kill a woman who has injured you, but nothing forbids you to reflect that she is growing older every minute. You are avenged 1,440 times a day.

476   Revolution: in politics, an abrupt change in the form of misgovernment.

477   Insurrection: an unsuccessful revolution.

478   Russian: a person with a Caucasian body and a Mongolian soul.

479   Saint: a dead sinner revised and edited.

480   Satire: an obsolete kind of literary composition in which the vices and follies of the author's enemies were expounded with imperfect tenderness.

481   Slang is the speech of him who robs the literary garbage carts on their way to the dumps.

482   Kleptomaniac: a rich thief.

483   Urbanity: the kind of civility that urban observers ascribe to dwellers in all cities but New York.

484   Vote: the instrument and symbol of a free man's power to make a fool of himself and a wreck of his country.

485   Wisdom is a special knowledge in excess of all that is known.

486   Female: one of the opposing, or unfair, sex.

487   Auctioneer: the man who proclaims with a hammer that he has picked a pocket with his tongue.

488   Future: that period of time in which our affairs prosper, our friends are true, and our happiness is assured.

489   Hand: a singular instrument worn at the end of a human arm and commonly thrust into somebody's pocket.

490   The covers of this book are too far apart.

491   Clairvoyant: a person, commonly a woman, who has the power of seeing that which is invisible to her patron—namely, that he is a blockhead.

Josh Billings

492   I honestly believe it iz better tew know nothing than tew know what aint so.

493   No man is so poor that he can't afford to keep one dog, and I've seen them so poor that they could afford to keep three.

494   Adam invented love at first sight, one of the greatest labor-saving machines the world ever saw.

495   Live within your income, even if you have to borrow money to do so.

496   There are two things in this life for which we are never fully prepared, and that is—twins.

497   Never run into debt, not if you can find anything else to run into.

498   The best way to convince a fool that he is wrong is to let him have his own way.

499   Confess your sins to the Lord, and you will be forgiven; confess them to men, and you will be laughed at.

500   A congregation who can't afford to pay a clergyman enough want a missionary more than they do a clergyman.

501   Debt is a trap which man sets and baits himself, and then deliberately gets into.

502   The devil is the father of lies, but he neglected to patent the idea, and the business now suffers from competition.

503   A dog is the only thing on this earth that loves you more than he loves himself.

504   Do not put off till tomorrow what can be enjoyed today.

505   Every man has a perfect right to his opinion, provided it agrees with ours.

506   Experience increases our wisdom but doesn't reduce our follies.

507   Experience is a school where a man learns what a big fool he has been.

508   I never knew an auctioneer to lie, unless it was absolutely necessary.

509   It is the little bits of things that fret and worry us; we can dodge an elephant, but we can't a fly.

510   Laziness is a good deal like money; the more a man has of it the more he seems to want.

511   Man is my brother, and I am nearer related to him through his vices than I am through his virtues.

512   Men ain't apt to get kicked out of good society for being rich.

513   The more humble a man is before God, the more he will be exalted; the more humble he is before man, the more he will get rode roughshod.

514   Never work before breakfast; if you have to work before breakfast, get your breakfast first.

515   Nobody really loves to be cheated, but it does seem as though everyone is anxious to see how near he could come to it.

516   The quickest way to take the starch out of a man who is always blaming himself is to agree with him.

517   Remember the poor—it costs nothing.

518   Self-made men are most always apt to be a little too proud of the job.

519   Silence is one of the hardest arguments to refute.

520   To enjoy a good reputation, give publicly, and steal privately.

521   Take all the fools out of this world, and there wouldn't be any fun or profit living in it.

522   There are but few men who have character enough to lead a life of idleness.

523   When a man comes to me for advice, I find out the kind of advice he wants, and I give it to him.

524   When a man makes up his mind to become a rascal, he should examine himself closely and see if he isn't better constructed for a fool.

525   Woman's influence is powerful, especially when she wants anything.

526   Young man, sit down and keep still; you will have plenty of chances yet to make a fool of yourself before you die.

527   If you want to get a sure crop, and a big yield, sow wild oats.

528   Most men are like eggs, too full of themselves to hold anything else.

529   Some folks are so contrary that if they fell in a river, they'd insist on floating upstream.

530   Money will buy a pretty good dog but it won't buy the wag of his tail.

531   The happiest time in any man's life is when he is in red-hot pursuit of a dollar with a reasonable prospect of overtaking it.

532   The man who ain't got an enemy is really poor.

533   There are people so addicted to exaggeration that they can't tell the truth without lying.

534   If it wasn't for faith, there would be no living in this world; we couldn't even eat hash with any safety.

535   Fame is climbing a greasy pole for ten dollars and ruining trousers worth fifteen dollars.

536   Flattery is like cologne water, to be smelled of, not swallowed.

537   Every man has his follies—and often they are the most interesting things he has got.

538   God save the fools, and don't let them run out, for if it weren't for them, wise men couldn't get a living.

539   The biggest fool in the world hasn't been born yet.

540   Nature never makes any blunders; when she makes a fool she means it.

541   A learned fool is one who has read everything and simply remembered it.

542   Genius ain't anything more than elegant common sense.

543   If a man is right he can't be too radical; if he is wrong, he can't be too conservative.

544   To bring up a child in the way he should go, travel that way yourself once in a while.

545   About the most originality that any writer can hope to achieve honestly is to steal with good judgment.

546   Some folks as they grow older grow wise, but most folks simply grow stubborner.

547   There are people who, if they ever reach heaven, will commence at once looking for their own set.

548   Pity costs nothing, and ain't worth nothing.

549   I never knew a man who lived on hope but what spent his old age at somebody else's expense.

550   Laughing is the sensation of feeling good all over, and showing it principally in one spot.

551   Life consists not in holding good cards but in playing those you do hold well.

552   Love is like measles; you can get it only once, and the later in life it occurs, the tougher it goes.

553   Love is said to be blind, but I know lots of fellows in love who can see twice as much in their sweethearts as I can.

554   When a man gets talking about himself, he seldom fails to be eloquent and often reaches the sublime.

555   The best medicine I know for rheumatism is to thank the Lord it ain't the gout.

556   Metaphysics is the science of proving what we don't understand.

557   Misfortunes and twins never come singly.

558   It is very easy to manage our neighbor's business, but our own sometimes bothers us.

559   Liar: a lawyer with a roving commission.

560   There are two kinds of fools: those who can't change their opinions and those who won't.

561   To establish oneself in the world, one does all one can to seem established there.

562   One of the best temporary cures for pride and affectation is seasickness: a man who wants to vomit never puts on airs.

563   Don't never prophesy, for if you prophesy wrong, nobody will forget it, and if you prophesy right, nobody will remember it.

564   When I was a boy I'd rather be licked twice than postponed once.

565   The man who has learned to reflect has laid by something nice for a wet day.

566   There is only one good substitute for the endearments of a sister, and that is the endearments of some other fellow's sister.

567   Don't despise your poor relations; they may become suddenly rich someday, and then it will be awkward to explain things to them.

568   The hardest sinner in the whole lot to convert is the one who spends half of his time in sinning and the other half in repentance.

569   Most people repent of their sins by thanking God they ain't so wicked as their neighbors.

570   A man is always stronger while he is making a reputation than he is after it is made.

571   The rich should remember that when they reach heaven they will find Lazarus there and have to be polite to him.

572   It ain't so much trouble to get rich as it is to tell when we have got rich.

573   It is much easier to repent of sins that we have committed than to repent of those we intend to commit.

574   Consider the postage stamp: its usefulness consists in the ability to stick to one thing till it gets there.

575   The human mind is full of curiosity but it don't love to be taught.

576   The man who has never been tempted don't know how dishonest he is.

577   Twins: 2 much.

578   It's a wise man who profits by his own experience, but it's a good deal wiser one who lets the rattlesnake bite the other fellow.

579   One-half the troubles of this life can be traced to saying yes too quick, and not saying no soon enough.

580   In youth we run into difficulties, in old age difficulties run into us.

581   I hate to be a kicker, I always long for peace,
But the wheel that does the squeaking,
Is the one that gets the grease.

582   Take the humbug out of this world; and you haven't much left to do business with.

583   Time is money, and many people pay their debts with it.

Jo Bingham
584   Subsidy: a formula for handing you back your own money with a flourish that makes you think it's a gift.

Augustine Birrell
585   That great dustheap called history.

586   Of all odd crazes, the craze to be for ever reading new books is one of the oddest.

587   An ordinary man can ... surround himself with two thousand books ... and thenceforward have at least one place in the world in which it is possible to be happy.

Jim Bishop
588   In her opinion, the seven ages of woman are: baby, infant, junior miss, young woman, young woman, young woman, young woman.

589   The mayor was a man you had to know to dislike.

Otto von Bismarck
590   Be polite; write diplomatically; even in a declaration of war one observes the rules of politeness.

591   You can do anything with children if you only play with them.

592   I have seen three emperors in their nakedness, and the sight was not inspiring.

593   When a man says he approves of something in principle, it means he hasn't the slightest intention of putting it into practice.

Eugene Robert Black
594   I've had diarrhea in forty nations.

Hugo Black
595   When I was forty, my doctor advised me that a man in his forties shouldn't play tennis. I heeded his advice carefully and could hardly wait until I reached fifty to start again.

Peter Black
596   The atmosphere reeked of the delicious odor of unearned money.

John Stuart Blackie
597   Eccentricity is originality without sense.

Judge Blagden
598   A witness cannot give evidence of his age unless he can remember being born.

John Blake
599   The world tolerates conceit from those who are successful, but not from anybody else.

William Blake
600   The eagle never lost so much time as when he submitted to learn of the crow.

Red Blanchard
601   Nowadays they spend $20,000 for a school bus to pick the kids right up at the door so they don't have to walk. They then spend $200,000 for a gym so they can get some exercise.

Marguerite Blessington
602   Love in France is a comedy; in England a tragedy; in Italy an opera seria; and in Germany a melodrama.

Geoffrey Bocca
603   Wit is a treacherous dart. It is perhaps the only weapon with which it is possible to stab oneself in one's own back.

Maxwell Bodenheim

604   H. L. Mencken suffers from the hallucination that he is H. L. Mencken—there is no cure for a disease of that magnitude.

605   Poetry is the impish attempt to paint the color of the wind.

Henry George Bohn

606   Hunger finds no fault with the cookery.

607   One of these days is none of these days.

608   Success makes a fool seem wise.

609   Money is a good servant but a bad master.

Nicolas Boileau-Despreaux

610   A fool always finds one still more foolish to admire him.

611   Money gives an appearance of beauty even to ugliness; but everything becomes frightful with poverty.

Derek Bok

612   If you think education is expensive, try ignorance.

Al Bokiska

613   Do you realize if it weren't for Edison we'd be watching TV by candlelight?

Erma Bombeck

614   Childhood is where "competition" is a baseball game and "responsibility" is a paper route.

Lady Violet Bonham-Carter

615   Sir Stafford has a brilliant mind until it is made up. [Of Sir Stafford Cripps.]

James H. Boren

616   Einstein's theory of relativity, as practiced by Congressmen, simply means getting members of your family on the payroll.

617   I got the bill for my surgery. Now I know what those doctors were wearing masks for.

Jorge Luis Borges

618   You can't measure time in days the way you can money in dollars because every day is different.

619 Of course, in my country [Argentina], most political leaders are, well, not gangsters, but more or less the same kind of thing. No, I mean, people who go in for getting elected, what can you expect of men like that?

Ludwig Borne
620 There are people who take more time to tell a story than it took for it to happen. They are the lords of boredom.

Alan Borovoy
621 In Canada we don't ban demonstrations, we re-route them.

John Collins Bossidy
622 And this is good old Boston,
The home of the bean and the cod,
Where the Lowells talk to the Cabots
And the Cabots talk only to God.

Jim Bouton
623 The older they get the better they were when they were younger.

Christian N. Bovee
624 Next to being witty yourself, the best thing is being able to quote another's wit.

Sir George Ferguson Bowen
625 The rain it raineth on the just
And also on the unjust fella;
But chiefly on the just, because
The unjust steals the just's umbrella.

Dick Bower
626 Don't cross your bridges until you've burned them.

Chester Bowles
627 It is the duty of the liberal to protect and to extend the basic democratic freedoms.

Lord Boyd-Orr
628 Never get up with the lark. Get up only for a lark.

Peg Bracken
629 Why does a slight tax increase cost you two hundred dollars and a substantial tax cut save you thirty cents?

Ben Bradlee

630   News is the first rough draft of history.

Francis Herbert Bradley

631   Everything comes to him who waits—among other things, death.

632   His mind is open; yes, it is so open that nothing is retained; ideas simply pass through him.

633   There are those who so dislike the nude that they find something indecent in the naked truth.

Omar Bradley

634   We have grasped the mystery of the atom and rejected the Sermon on the Mount.

635   I am convinced that the best service a retired general can perform is to turn in his tongue along with his suit, and to mothball his opinions.

636   The world has achieved brilliance without conscience. Ours is a world of nuclear giants and ethical infants.

637   Bravery is the capacity to perform properly even when scared half to death.

Caryl Brahms and S. J. Simon

638   "I am a businessman," said old man Burbage. "What I want is results. So you will pardon me if I speak frankly. The trouble with your plays, Master Will, is that you leave far too many characters alive at the end of them."
"Oh," said Shakespeare.

Johannes Brahms

639   The fact that people do not understand and respect the very best things, such as Mozart's concertos, is what permits men like us to become famous.

Justice Louis Dembitz Brandeis

640   Behind every argument is someone's ignorance.

641   The right to be let alone is the most comprehensive of rights and the right most valued in civilized man.

642   Mere money-making cannot be regarded as the legitimate end . . . since with the conduct of business human happiness or misery is inextricably interwoven.

William Cowper Brann

643   A heretic ... is a fellow who disagrees with you regarding something neither of you knows anything about.

644   No man can be a patriot on an empty stomach.

Robert Brault

645   Most people would rather defend to the death your right to say it than listen to it.

J. Bartlet Brebner

646   Perhaps the most striking thing about Canada is that it is not part of the United States.

Bertolt Brecht

647   Eats first, morals after.

648   What happens to the hole when the cheese is gone?

John Bright

649   Force is not a remedy.

Anthelme Brillat-Savarin

650   The discovery of a new dish does more for human happiness than the discovery of a new star.

David Brinkley

651   Thrift used to be a basic American virtue. Our folklore is full of it. Now the American virtue is to spend money.

Arthur Brisbane

652   The fence around a cemetery is foolish, for those inside can't come out and those outside don't want to get in.

653   Writing good editorials is chiefly telling the people what they think, not what you think.

Steuart Henderson Britt

654   Doing business without advertising is like winking at a girl in the dark. You know what you are doing, but nobody else does.

Dave Broadfoot

655   Canada is a collection of ten provinces with strong governments loosely connected by fear.

Edwin Brock
656   A psychiatrist is a person who owns a couch and charges you for lying on it.

Louis Bromfield
657   I'd like some of it [money] to go where it would undo two great American falsities—that making money is distinguished and important and that motorcars and lavatories have anything to do with what is called civilization.

Jacob Bronowski
658   The world is made of people who never quite get into the first team and who just miss the prizes at the flower show.

Rupert Brooke
659   In Cambridge people rarely smile,
Being urban, squat and packed with guile.

Richard Brooks
660   People in Hollywood can't face the truth in themselves or in others. This town is filled with people who make adventure pictures and who have never left this place. They make religious pictures and they haven't been in a church or a synagogue in years. They make pictures about love and they haven't been in love—ever.

Van Wyck Brooks
661   Earnest people are often people who habitually look on the serious side of things that have no serious side.

662   The American mind, unlike the English, is not formed by books, but as Carl Sandburg once said to me . . . by newspapers and the Bible.

Henry Brougham
663   A lawyer is a learned gentleman who rescues your estate from your enemies and keeps it himself.

664   Education makes a people easy to lead, but difficult to drive; easy to govern, but impossible to enslave.

Heywood Broun
665   A liberal is a man who leaves a room before the fight begins.

666   It is always safe to be dogmatic about tomorrow.

667   Repartee is what you wish you'd said.

668   Appeasers believe that if you keep on throwing steaks to a tiger, the tiger will become a vegetarian.

669   The only real argument for marriage is that it remains the best method for getting acquainted.

670   The swaggering underemphasis of New England.

671   If anyone corrects your pronunciation of a word in a public place, you have every right to punch him in the nose.

672   I see no wisdom in saving up indignation for a rainy day.

Hobart Brown
673   Money doesn't always bring happiness. People with ten million dollars are no happier than people with nine million dollars.

John Mason Brown
674   Reasoning with a child is fine, if you can reach the child's reason without destroying your own.

675   How prophetic L'Enfant was when he laid out Washington as a city that goes around in circles!

T. E. Brown
676   Money is honey, my little sonny,
And a rich man's joke is always funny.

Thomas Brown
677   I do not love thee, Doctor Fell,
The reason why I cannot tell;
But this alone I know full well,
I do not love thee, Doctor Fell.

Sir Thomas Browne
678   The vices we scoff at in others, laugh at us within ourselves.

Robert Browning
679   Fear death?—to feel the fog in my throat,
The mist in my face.

680   Lied is a rough phrase; say he fell from the truth.

William C. Bryant
681   The melancholy days are come, the saddest of the year,
Of wailing winds, and naked woods, and meadows brown and sear.

James Bryce

682   Medicine is the only profession that labours incessantly to destroy the reason for its own existence.

683   The government of cities is the one conspicuous failure of the United States.

Art Buchwald

684   Have you ever seen a candidate talking to a rich person on television?

685   Whether these are the best of times or the worst of times, it's the only time we've got.

Pearl S. Buck

686   People on the whole are very simple-minded in whatever country one finds them. They are so simple as to take literally, more often than not, the things their leaders tell them.

William F. Buckley, Jr.

687   Life can't be all bad when for ten dollars you can buy all the Beethoven sonatas and listen to them for ten years.

J. Fred Bucy

688   Nothing is ever accomplished by a reasonable man.

Henry Cuyler Bunner

689   Shakespeare was a dramatist of note who lived by writing things to quote.

Luther Burbank

690   For those who do not think, it is best at least to rearrange their prejudices once in a while.

Jacob Burckhardt

691   The greatest innovation in the world is the demand for education as a right of man; it is a disguised demand for comfort.

Robert Jones Burdette

692   Don't believe the world owes you a living; the world owes you nothing—it was here first.

693   I shall be so polite to my wife as though she were a perfect stranger.

694   There are two days about which nobody should ever worry, and these are yesterday and tomorrow.

Gelett Burgess

695   My feet, they haul me Round the House,
  They Hoist me up the Stairs;
I only have to steer them, and
  They Ride me Everywheres.

696   With a man, a lie is a last resort; with women, it's First Aid.

697   Bad manners simply indicate that you care a good deal more for the food than for the society at the table.

698   When you're out of luck, speak louder than usual.

699   I never saw a Purple Cow,
I never hope to see one:
But I can tell you anyhow
I'd rather see than be one.

700   If you stop and think about it, you'll realize that three out of four persons do not know exactly what they're doing a large part of the time.

701   I wish that my room had a floor;
I don't so much care for a door,
But this walking around
Without touching the ground
Is getting to be quite a bore!

Edmund Burke

702   The age of chivalry is gone; that of sophisters, economists and calculators has succeeded.

703   Those who have been once intoxicated with power, and have derived any kind of emolument from it, even though but for one year, can never willingly abandon it.

704   We have a degree of delight ... in the real misfortunes and pains of others.

705   The only thing necessary for the triumph of evil is for good men to do nothing.

706   And having looked to Government for bread, on the very first scarcity they will turn and bite the hand that fed them.

Leo J. Burke
707   People who say they sleep like a baby usually don't have one.

Arthur Burns
708   I've always considered writing important. I went through all the stages that economists go through, from jargon to lucidity, and on the way I passed through the sesquipedalian [weakness for using big words] stage.

George Burns
709   Too bad all the people who know how to run the country are busy driving taxi cabs and cutting hair.

Robert Burns
710   Man's inhumanity to man
        Makes countless thousands mourn.

Sir Richard Burton
711   He had every talent save that of using his talents.

Robert Burton
712   Diogenes struck the father when the son swore.

713   They are proud in humility, proud in that they are not proud.

714   A mere madness, to live like a wretch, and die rich.

George Bush
715   A loose cannon on a rolling deck. [On Andrew Young.]

Nicholas Murray Butler
716   An expert is one who knows more and more about less and less.

717   One of the embarrassments of being a gentleman is that you are not permitted to be violent in asserting your rights.

718   America is the best half-educated country in the world.

719   'Tis better to have loved and lost than never to have lost at all.

720   If you follow reason far enough it always leads to conclusions that are contrary to reason.

721   He was born stupid, and greatly increased his birthright.

722   Brigands demand your money or your life; women require both.

Samuel Butler
723   He makes his ignorance pass for reserve, and, like a hunting-nag, leaps over what he cannot get through.

724   Vices, like beasts, are fond of none but those that feed them.

725   Man is the only animal that laughs and has a state legislature.

726   Life is like playing a violin in public and learning the instrument as one goes on.

727   He that complies against his will,
Is of his own opinion still,
Which he may adhere to, yet disown,
For reasons to himself best known.

728   Two heads are better than one, but the man who said that did not know my sisters.

729   Brevity is very good when we are, or are not, understood.

730   I do not mind lying, but I hate inaccuracy.

731   Life is one long process of getting tired.

732   She went up the Nile as far as the first crocodile.

733   All of the animals except man know that the principal business of life is to enjoy it.

734   Any fool can tell the truth, but it requires a man of some sense to know how to lie well.

735   The giraffe must get up at six in the morning if it wants to have its breakfast in its stomach by nine.

736   A hen is only an egg's way of making another egg.

737   If you aim at imperfection, there is some chance of your getting it; whereas if you aim at perfection, there is none.

738   Academic and aristocratic people live in such an uncommon atmosphere that common sense can rarely reach them.

739   The great pleasure of a dog is that you may make a fool of yourself with him, and not only will he not scold you, but he will make a fool of himself, too.

740   It is seldom very hard to do one's duty when one knows what it is, but it is often exceedingly difficult to find this out.

741   Parents are the last people on earth who ought to have children.

742   God cannot alter the past, but historians can.

743   "The Ancient Mariner" would not have taken so well if it had been called "The Old Sailor."

744　　Life is the art of drawing sufficient conclusions from insufficient premises.

745　　An open mind is all very well in its way, but it ought not to be so open that there is no keeping anything in or out of it. It should be capable of shutting its doors sometimes, or it may be found a little drafty.

746　　The money men make lives after them.

747　　Morality is the custom of one's country and the current feeling of one's peers. Cannibalism is moral in a cannibal country.

748　　Some people seem compelled by unkind fate to parental servitude for life. There is no form of penal servitude much worse than this.

749　　The most important service rendered by the press and the magazines is that of educating people to approach printed matter with distrust.

750　　All progress is based upon universal innate desire on the part of every organism to live beyond its income.

Dr. John Button, Jr.
751　　We sit at breakfast, we sit on the train on the way to work, we sit at work, we sit at lunch, we sit all afternoon . . . a hodgepodge of sagging livers, sinking gall bladders, drooping stomachs, compressed intestines and squashed pelvic organs.

Red Buttons
752　　There's a great new rice diet that always works—you use one chopstick.

753　　He's a real loser. He moved into a new neighborhood and got run over by the Welcome Wagon.

Pat Buttram
754　　A folksinger is someone who sings through his nose by ear.

Richard E. Byrd
755　　A man doesn't begin to attain wisdom until he recognizes that he is no longer indispensable.

George Gordon, Lord Byron
756　　The English winter—ending in July, to recommence in August.

757　　I wish he would explain his explanation.

758　　Society is now one polished horde, form'd of two mighty tribes, the Bores and Bored.

759   Though I love my country, I do not love my countrymen.

760   Talent may in time be forgiven, but genius never!

761   To my extreme mortification, I grow wiser every day.

762   And if I laugh at any mortal thing,
'Tis that I may not weep.

763   It is awful work, this love, and prevents all a man's projects of good or glory.

764   He was the mildest-mannered man that ever scuttled ship or cut a throat.

765   Let us have wine and women, mirth and laughter,
Sermons and soda water the day after.

766   For a man to become a poet he must be in love, or miserable.

767   All who joy would win must share it—
Happiness was born a twin.

768   With just enough of learning to misquote.

James Branch Cabell
769   The optimist proclaims that we live in the best of all possible worlds; and the pessimist fears this is true.

Samuel Parkes Cadman
770   The lunatic asylum of the solar system. [The earth.]

Julius Caesar
771   I would rather be first in a small village in Gaul than second in command in Rome.

James Callaghan
772   I've never been one to say that Britain was joining a happy band of brothers. [On the European Economic Community.]

Simon Cameron
773   An honest politician is one who when he is bought will stay bought.

Roy Campanella
774   You gotta be a man to play baseball for a living but you gotta have a lot of little boy in you, too.

Thomas Campbell
775   For I fear I have nothing original in me—excepting original sin.

776   What millions died—that Caesar might be great!

Albert Camus
777   Politics and the fate of mankind are shaped by men without ideals and without greatness. Men who have greatness within them don't go in for politics.

778   Charm is a way of getting the answer yes without having asked any clear question.

Dorothy Canfield
779   One of the many things nobody ever tells you about middle age is that it's such a nice change from being young.

George Canning
780   Nothing is so fallacious as facts—except figures.

Joe Cannon
781   Sometimes in politics one must duel with skunks, but no one should be fool enough to allow the skunks to choose the weapons.

The Archbishop of Canterbury
782   I do not read advertisements—I would spend all my time wanting things.

Eddie Cantor
783   Words fascinate me. They always have. For me, browsing in a dictionary is like being turned loose in a bank.

784   We call our rich relatives the kin we love to touch.

785   It takes twenty years to make an overnight success.

Karel Čapek
786   If dogs could talk, perhaps we'd find it just as hard to get along with them as we do with people.

787   A man is something that feels happy, plays the piano, likes going for a walk and, in fact, wants to do a whole lot of things that are really unnecessary.

Mortimer Caplan
788   There is one difference between a tax collector and a taxidermist —the taxidermist leaves the hide.

Al Capone
789 My rackets are run on strictly American lines and they're going to stay that way!

Truman Capote
790 That's not writing, that's typing.

Thaddeus Caraway
791 I have long heard of the reputation for wisdom and wit of the senator from Massachusetts, but his speech today has convinced me that his mind is like the land of his native state—barren by nature and impoverished by cultivation. [On Henry Cabot Lodge.]

Jerome Cardan
792 When women cannot be revenged, they do as children do—they cry.

Thomas Carlyle
793 His mind was a kind of extinct sulphur pit. [On Napoleon III.]

794 How long will John Bull allow this absurd monkey to dance on his chest? [On Benjamin Disraeli.]

795 The greatest of faults, I should say, is to be conscious of none.

796 Make yourself an honest man and then you may be sure there is one rascal less in the world.

797 I do not hate him nearly as much as I fear I ought to.

798 I do not believe in the collective wisdom of individual ignorance.

799 History is the biography of great men.

800 History, a distillation of rumor.

801 If you are ever in doubt as to whether or not you should kiss a pretty girl, always give her the benefit of the doubt.

802 There is a great discovery still to be made in literature, that of paying literary men by the quantity they do not write.

803 The public is an old woman. Let her maunder and mumble.

804 One finds also a kind of sincerity in his [William Wordsworth's] speech. But for prolixity, thinness, endless dilution, it excels all the other speech I had heard from mortals.

805 God Almighty never created a man half as wise as he [Daniel Webster] looks.

806   Incessant scribbling is death to thought.

807   One life, a little gleam of time between two eternities.

Stokeley Carmichael
808   Politics is war without violence. War is politics with violence.

Andrew Carnegie
809   Pity the poor millionaire—for the way of the philanthropist is hard.

810   The man who dies ... rich dies disgraced.

Dale Carnegie
811   The ideas I stand for are not mine. I borrowed them from Socrates. I swiped them from Chesterfield. I stole them from Jesus. And I put them in a book. If you don't like their rules, whose would you use?

812   You can make more friends in two months by becoming interested in other people than you can in two years by trying to get other people interested in you.

Edward Carpenter
813   Money entails duties. How shall we get the money and forget the duties? Voilà the great problem!

Lewis Carroll
814   "Tut, tut, child," said the Duchess. "Everything's got a moral if only you can find it."

815   How doth the little crocodile
Improve his shining tail.
And pour the waters of the Nile
On every golden scale!

How cheerfully he seems to grin,
How neatly spreads his claws,
And welcomes little fishes in
With gently smiling jaws!

816   When I use a word, it means just what I choose it to mean—neither more nor less.

817   "The horror of that moment," the King went on, "I shall never, never forget!"
"You will, though," the Queen said, "if you don't make a memorandum of it."

818   "Take some more tea," the March Hare said to Alice very earnestly.

"I've had nothing yet," Alice replied in an offended tone, "so I can't take any more."

"You mean you can't take less," said the Hatter. "It's very easy to take more than nothing."

819   "The time has come," the Walrus said,
"To talk of many things:
Of shoes—and ships—and sealing wax—
Of cabbages—and kings—
And why the sea is boiling hot—
And whether pigs have wings."

Jack Carson
820   A fan club is a group of people who tell an actor he's not alone in the way he feels about himself.

Jimmy Carter
821   I don't claim to know all the answers.

822   We've uncovered some embarrassing ancestors in the not-too-distant past. Some horse thieves, and some people killed on Saturday nights. One of my relatives, unfortunately, was even in the newspaper business. [On seeing a copy of his family tree.]

823   Show me a good loser and I'll show you a loser.

824   We tend to dwell on measurements, but they tell us very little about the real meaning of life. For that, we must turn to things which cannot be seen or which cannot be measured—to things like honesty, integrity, the strength of conscience, the love for God, service to others, humility, wisdom. These things are invisible. They are beyond measurement, but they comprise life's true wealth.

Mary Carter
825   My husband doesn't munch words!

Enrico Caruso
826   Watermelon: a good fruit—you eat, you drink and you wash your face.

Frank Case
827   One of the charms of Hollywood is that almost nothing they do is real or true or practical or anything resembling life.

828   People grow tired of marriage, some people do, but one is never bored with a companion who sees the world through the same ridiculous distorting lenses that we look through ourselves.

829   Whenever you see a man with handkerchief, socks and tie to match, you may be sure he is wearing a present.

830   She is a woman of few words but she uses them over and over.

Johnny Cash
831   If you don't have any time for yourself, any time to hunt or to fish, that's success.

John Cassis
832   It's nice to be important, but it's more important to be nice.

Helen Castle
833   Give the neighbor's kids an inch and they'll take a yard.

Wynn Catlin
834   Diplomacy is the art of saying "Nice Doggie!" till you can find a rock.

Marcus Parcius Cato
835   I had rather men should ask why no statue has been erected in my honor, than why one has.

836   Wise men learn more from fools than fools from wise men.

Benso di Cavour
837   I have discovered the art of fooling diplomats; I speak the truth and they never believe me.

Lord David Cecil
838   The first step to knowledge is to know that we are ignorant.

Bennett Cerf
839   Middle age is when your old classmates are so grey and wrinkled and bald they don't recognize you.

Miguel de Cervantes
840   All women are good—good for nothing, or good for something.

841   Everyone is as God made him—and very often worse.

842   A proverb is a short sentence based on long experience.

843   Riding a horse makes gentlemen of some and grooms of others.

844   There are only two nations in the world: the haves and the have-nots.

Hal Chadwick
845   No one so thoroughly appreciates the value of constructive criticism as the one who's giving it.

Marc Chagall
846   When I am finishing a picture I hold some God-made object up to it—a rock, a flower, the branch of a tree or my hand—as a kind of final test. If the painting stands up beside a thing man cannot make, the painting is authentic. If there's a clash between the two, it is bad art.

Sir Austen Chamberlain
847   If people are going to drink champagne, the larger the share of taxation on that wine, the greater will be their patriotism.

848   All governments are pretty much alike, with a tendency on the part of the last to be the worst.

Robert W. Chambers
849   All the world may not love a lover but all the world watches him.

Nicholas Chamfort
850   The threat of a neglected cold is for doctors what the threat of purgatory is for priests—a gold mine.

851   Society is composed of two great classes: those who have more dinners than appetite, and those who have more appetite than dinners.

852   Bachelors' wives and old maids' children are always perfect.

853   Paris is a city of gaieties and pleasures where four-fifths of the inhabitants die of grief.

854   The public! The public! How many fools does it take to make up a public?

855   Love is a pleasing folly; ambition is a serious stupidity.

856   Change in fashion is the tax which the industry of the poor levies on the vanity of the rich.

857   There are more fools than wise men and even in the wise man himself there is more folly than wisdom.

858   "In this world," remarked someone to me, "you have three kinds of friends: the friends who love you, the friends who do not trouble their heads about you, and the friends who hate you."

859   There are well-dressed foolish ideas just as there are well-dressed fools.

860   The loves of some people are but the results of good suppers.

861   A lover is a man who endeavors to be more amiable than it is possible for him to be: this is the reason why almost all lovers are ridiculous.

862   The memoirs of statesmen and scholars, even those thought to be modest, betray their secret vanity and remind us of the story of the saint who left a hundred thousand dollars for his own canonization.

863   Philosophy, like medicine, has many drugs, few good remedies and almost no specifics.

864   A woman is like your shadow—follow her, she flies, fly from her, she follows.

865   There are two things I have always loved madly: they are women and celibacy.

William Ellery Channing
866   Every human being is intended to have a character of his own: to be what no others are, and to do what no other can do.

Arthur Chapman
867   Out where the handclasp's a little stronger,
Out where the smile dwells a little longer,
That's where the West begins.

George Chapman
868   Young men think old men are fools; but old men know young men are fools.

Harry Chapman
869   Having served on various committees, I have drawn up a list of rules. Never arrive on time; this stamps you as a beginner. Don't say anything until the meeting is half over; this stamps you as being wise. Be as vague as possible; this avoids irritating the others. When in doubt, suggest that a subcommittee be appointed. Be the first to move for adjournment: this will make you popular; it's what everyone is waiting for.

Alexander Chase

870   People, like sheep, tend to follow a leader, occasionally in the right direction.

Ilka Chase

871   He's all buttoned up in an impenetrable little coat of complacency.

872   On the whole, I haven't found men unduly loath to say, "I love you." The real trick is to get them to say, "Will you marry me?"

Salmon P. Chase

873   I would rather that the people should wonder why I wasn't President than why I am.

Stuart Chase

874   Democracy . . . is a condition where people believe that other people are as good as they are.

Paul Chatfield

875   Oratory is the power to talk people out of their sober and natural opinions.

Anton Chekhov

876   If you are afraid of loneliness, do not marry.

877   If you wish women to love you, be original; I know a man who used to wear felt boots summer and winter, and women fell in love with him.

878   The university brings out all abilities, including stupidity.

Chen Chiju

879   Do unto others as you would have others do unto you. But better not expect others to do unto you what you do unto them.

Lord Chesterfield

880   To govern mankind one must not over-rate them.

881   Most people enjoy the inferiority of their best friends.

882   The less one has to do, the less time one finds to do it in.

883   If a fool knows a secret, he tells it because he is a fool.

884   Advice is always welcome; and those who want it the most always like it the least.

885   Talk often, but never long: in that case, if you do not please, at least you are sure not to tire your hearers.

886   I look upon opera as a magic scene contrived to please the eyes and ears at the expense of the understanding.

887   The vulgar only laugh, but never smile; whereas well-bred people often smile, but seldom laugh.

888   There are but two objects in marriage, love or money. If you marry for love, you will certainly have some very happy days, and probably many very uneasy ones; if for money, you will have no happy days and probably no uneasy ones.

889   Be wiser than other people if you can, but do not tell them so.

890   You must never seem to affect the character in which you have a mind to shine. Modesty is the only sure bait when you angle for praise.

891   People hate those who make them feel their own inferiority.

892   Learn to shrink yourself to the size of the company you are in.

893   Every man seeks for truth; but God only knows who has found it.

G. K. Chesterton

894   Democracy means government by the uneducated, while aristocracy means government by the badly educated.

895   English experience indicates that when the two great political parties agree about something it is generally wrong.

896   A puritan is a person who pours righteous indignation into the wrong things.

897   The artistic temperament is a disease that afflicts amateurs.

898   Christianity has not been tried and found wanting; it has been found difficult and not tried.

899   Optimism: the noble temptation to see too much in everything.

900   Silence is the unbearable repartee.

901   Thieves respect property; they merely wish the property to become their property that they may more perfectly respect it.

902   A yawn is a silent shout.

903   The Bible tells us to love our neighbors, and also to love our enemies; probably because they are generally the same people.

904   The doctrine of human equality reposes on this: that there is no man really clever who has not found that he is stupid.

905   The golden age only comes to men when they have, if only for a moment, forgotten gold.

906   I believe in getting into hot water; it keeps you clean.

907   The men who really believe in themselves are all in lunatic asylums.

908   Merely having an open mind is nothing; the object of opening the mind, as of opening the mouth, is to shut it again on something solid.

909   The only way of catching a train I ever discovered is to miss the train before.

910   Some men never feel small, but these are the few men who are.

911   He [Charles Dickens] had the supreme character of a domestic despot—that his good temper was, if possible, more despotic than his bad temper.

912   If a thing is worth doing, it is worth doing badly.

913   Blessed is he who expecteth nothing, for he shall be gloriously surprised.

914   There is a great deal of difference between an eager man who wants to read a book and the tired man who wants a book to read.

915   Journalism largely consists in saying "Lord Jones Dead" to people who never knew Lord Jones was alive.

916   There is nothing that fails like success.

917   Tolerance is the virtue of the man without convictions.

918   I gravely doubt whether women were ever married by capture. I think they pretended to be; as they do still.

919   We make our friends; we make our enemies; but God makes our next-door neighbor.

920   The only people who seem to have nothing to do with the education of the children are the parents.

921   Most of our realists and sociologists talk about a poor man as if he were an octopus or an alligator.

922   Psychoanalysis is confession without absolution.

923   A man can no more possess a private religion than he can possess a private sun and moon.

924   Tradition does not mean that the living are dead but that the dead are live.

925   The classes that wash most are those that work least.

926   With all that we hear of American hustle and hurry, it is rather strange that Americans seem to like more than we do to linger upon long words. . . . They say elevator when we say lift, just as they say automobile when we say motor and stenographer when we say typist.

Maurice Chevalier

927   Old age isn't so bad when you consider the alternative.

928   Many a man has fallen in love with a girl in a light so dim he would not have chosen a suit by it.

Edward Cheyfitz

929   Nobody believes a rumor here in Washington until it's officially denied.

Joseph H. Choate

930   You cannot live without lawyers, and certainly you cannot die without them.

Chou En-lai

931   All diplomacy is a continuation of war by other means.

Agatha Christie

932   It is completely unimportant. That is why it is so interesting.

933   An archaeologist is the best husband any woman can have: the older she gets, the more interested he is in her.

934   The best time for planning a book is while you're doing the dishes.

935   Where large sums of money are concerned, it is advisable to trust nobody.

Christina, Queen of Sweden

936   I love men, not because they are men, but because they are not women.

Chuang-tse

937   A man who knows he is a fool is not a great fool.

Lord Randolph Churchill

938   He never believed in doing something that he could get someone else to do for him. [On Stanley Baldwin.]

Winston Churchill

939   I have a tendency against which I should, perhaps, be on my guard, to swim against the stream.

940   Socialism is the philosophy of failure, the creed of ignorance and the gospel of envy.

941   He is a sheep in sheep's clothing. [On Clement Attlee.]

942   We are all worms, but I think I am a glowworm.

943   Too often the strong silent man is silent only because he does not know what to say and is reputed strong only because he has remained silent.

944   Politics are almost as exciting as war, and quite as dangerous. In war you can only be killed once, but in politics many times.

945   He has all of the virtues I dislike and none of the vices I admire.

946   It's no use sitting on me—for I am india-rubber, and I bounce!

947   Mr. Chamberlain loves the working man—he loves to see him work. [On Joseph Chamberlain.]

948   Government of the duds, by the duds and for the duds.

949   An appeaser is one who feeds a crocodile, hoping it will eat him last.

950   I was not the lion, but it fell to me to give the lion's roar.

951   The Honourable Gentleman should not generate more indignation than he can conveniently contain. [To William Wedgwood Benn.]

952   It has been said that democracy is the worst form of government, except for all those other forms that have been tried from time to time.

953   He can best be described as one of those orators who, before they get up, do not know what they are going to say; and when they are speaking do not know what they are saying; and when they have sat down, do not know what they have said. [On Lord Charles Beresford.]

954   The ability to foretell what is going to happen tomorrow, next week, next month and next year. And to have the ability afterwards to explain why it didn't happen. [On political skill.]

955   Eating words has never given me indigestion.

956   Winston Churchill once squashed Aneurin Bevan in the Commons by replying blandly to one of his questions: "I should think it hardly possible to state the opposite of the truth with more precision."

957   Some men change their party for the sake of their principles; others their principles for the sake of their party.

958   I have always considered that the substitution of the internal combustion engine for the horse marked a very gloomy milestone in the progress of mankind.

959   There is no finer investment for any community than putting milk into babies.

960   Don't argue about the difficulties. The difficulties will argue for themselves.

961   I was what people called "a troublesome boy."

962   He could "talk a bird out of a tree." [Speaking of David Lloyd George.]

963   The inherent vice of capitalism is the unequal sharing of blessings; the inherent virtue of socialism is the equal sharing of miseries.

964   For my part, I consider that it will be found much better by all parties to leave the past to history, especially as I propose to write that history myself.

965   When I get to heaven I mean to spend a considerable portion of my first million years in painting, and so get to the bottom of the subject. But then I shall require a still gayer palette than I get here below. I expect orange and vermilion will be the darkest, dullest colours upon it, and beyond them there will be a whole range of wonderful new colours which will delight the celestial eye.

966   I cannot pretend to feel impartial about colours. I rejoice with the brilliant ones and am genuinely sorry for the poor browns.

967   A friend once asked Churchill, "Why do you paint only landscapes?"
     "Because," said Winston, "a tree doesn't complain that I haven't done it justice."

968   About the Yalta Conference among Stalin, Roosevelt, and himself, he said: "I don't see any way of realizing our hopes of World Organization in six days. Even the Almighty took seven."

969   His comment on getting appendicitis during an election campaign in Dundee in 1922, in which he came bottom of the poll: "In the twinkling of an eye I found myself without office, without a seat, without a party and without an appendix."

970   Churchill was stopped by a woman who said to him, "Doesn't it thrill you, Mr. Churchill, to know that every time you make a speech the hall is packed to overflowing?"
     "It is quite flattering," Winston replied. "But whenever I feel this way I always remember that, if instead of making a political speech, I was being hanged, the crowd would be twice as big."

971   Everybody said I was the worst Chancellor of the Exchequer that ever was. And I am now inclined to agree with them.

972   To a barber who asked him how he would like his hair cut: "A man of my limited resources cannot presume to have a hair style. Get on and cut it."

973   I am informed from many quarters that a rumour has been put about that I died this morning [February 1951]. This is quite untrue.

974   On a rather hasty wartime lunch in the desert: "No gentleman would eat a ham sandwich without mustard."

975   There, but for the grace of God, goes God. [Of Sir Stafford Cripps.]

976   It is a socialist idea that making profits is a vice. I consider that the real vice is making losses.

977   In those days he was wiser than he is now; he used frequently to take my advice.

978   It saves a lot of trouble if, instead of having to earn money and save it, you can just go and borrow it.

979   Men occasionally stumble over the truth, but most of them pick themselves up and hurry off as if nothing had happened.

980   This conference should not be overhung by a ponderous or rigid agenda or led into mazes of technical details, zealously contested by hordes of experts and officials drawn up in a vast cumbrous array.

981   They are decided only to be undecided, resolved to be irresolute, adamant for drift, all-powerful for impotence.

982   The difference between Balfour and Asquith is that Arthur is wicked and moral, Asquith is good and immoral.

983   If Hitler invaded Hell I would make at least a favorable reference to the Devil in the House of Commons.

984   The nose of the bulldog has been slanted backwards so that he can breathe without letting go.

985   A fanatic is one who can't change his mind and won't change the subject.

986   Nothing in life is so exhilarating as to be shot at without result.

987   The greatest lesson in life is to know that even fools are right sometimes.

988   Personally, I'm always ready to learn, although I do not always like being taught.

989   There are a terrible lot of lies going about the world, and the worst of it is that half of them are true.

990   I always avoid prophesying beforehand, because it is much better policy to prophesy after the event has already taken place.

991   The farther backward you can look, the farther forward you are likely to see.

992   I am biased in favor of boys learning English. I would let the clever ones learn Latin as an honor, and Greek as a treat. But the only thing I would whip them for is not knowing English. I would whip them hard for that.

993   I go by tummy-time and I want my dinner.

994   Where does the family start? It starts with a young man falling in love with a girl. No superior alternative has yet been found.

995   Churchill's valet, Norman McGowan, was surprised when he first joined the household to hear Churchill muttering in his bath. McGowan thought that he was talking to him and called out, "Do you want me?" "I wasn't talking to you, Norman," Winston replied. "I was addressing the House of Commons."

996   I am an optimist. It does not seem too much use being anything else.

997   Neither of his [Sir Stafford Cripps's] colleagues can compare with him in that acuteness or energy of mind with which he devotes himself to so many topics injurious to the strength and welfare of the State.

998   The worst that can be said about him [Sir William Joynson Hicks] is that he runs the risk of being most humorous when he wishes to be most serious.

999   The price of greatness is responsibility.

1000   When the eagles are silent the parrots begin to jabber.

1001   The English never draw a line without blurring it.

1002   When I was younger I made it a rule never to take strong drink before lunch. It is now my rule never to do so before breakfast.

1003   Mr. Attlee is a very modest man. But then he has much to be modest about.

1004   When you have got a thing where you want it, it is a good thing to leave it where it is.

1005   One does not leave a convivial party before closing time.

1006   When I was called upon to be Prime Minister, now nearly two years ago, there were not many applicants for the job. Since then perhaps the market has improved.

1007   If he trips he must be sustained; if he makes mistakes they must be covered; if he sleeps he must not be wantonly disturbed; if he is no good he must be poleaxed. [On the Prime Minister.]

1008   When one wakes up after daylight one should breakfast; five hours after that, luncheon. Six hours after luncheon, dinner. Thus one becomes dependent on the sun, which otherwise meddles too much in one's affairs and upsets the routine of work.

1009   Russia is a riddle wrapped in a mystery inside an enigma.

1010   I was happy as a child with my toys in the nursery. I have been happier every year since I became a man. But this interlude of school makes a somber gray patch upon the chart of my journey.

1011   I affected a combination of the styles of Macaulay and Gibbon, the staccato antithesis of the former, and the rolling sentences and genitival endings of the latter; and I stuck in a bit of my own from time to time.

1012   We have not journeyed all this way across the centuries, across the oceans, across the mountains, across the prairies, because we are made of sugar candy. [Speech to Canadian Senate and House of Commons, 1941.]

1013   Trying to maintain good relations with the Communists is like wooing a crocodile. You do not know whether to tickle it under the chin or beat it over the head. When it opens its mouth you cannot tell whether it is trying to smile or preparing to eat you up.

1014   When you have to kill a man it costs nothing to be polite.

1015   Short words are best and the old words when short are best of all.

1016   This is the sort of English up with which I will not put.

1017   Lady Astor: If I were your wife, I'd put poison in your coffee.
        Churchill: If I were your husband, I'd drink it.

1018   Nothing is more costly, nothing is more sterile, than vengeance.

John Ciardi

1019   Gentility is what is left over from rich ancestors after the money is gone.

1020   A university is what a college becomes when the faculty loses interest in students.

1021   Joe ... was ignorant enough to feel superior to everything.

1022   You don't have to suffer to be a poet. Adolescence is enough suffering for anyone.

Cicero
1023   There is nothing so absurd but some philosopher has said it.

1024   When you have no basis for an argument, abuse the plaintiff.

1025   A lover of himself, without any rival.

1026   There is no fortress so strong that money cannot take it.

1027   I am incredibly eager ... that the history which you are writing should give prominence to my name and praise it frequently.

1028   In nothing do men approach so nearly to the gods as doing good to men.

1029   I shall always consider the best guesser the best prophet.

John Clare
1030   If life had a second edition, how I would correct the proofs.

Frank A. Clark
1031   It's hard to detect good luck—it looks so much like something you've earned.

1032   To feel sorry for the needy is not the mark of a Christian—to help them is.

1033   A father is a man who expects his son to be as good a man as he meant to be.

1034   To enjoy a friend, I need more in common with him than hating the same people.

1035   We're all generous, but with different things, like time, money, talent—criticism.

1036   The reason there's so much ignorance is that those who have it are so eager to share it.

1037   Having problems may not be so bad. We have a special place for folks who have none—it's called a cemetery.

1038   If a fellow isn't thankful for what he's got, he isn't likely to be thankful for what he's going to get.

Roy Clark

1039   Equal rights for women is OK, but there sure are some inequalities in their favor. How come diamonds are a girl's best friend, but a man's best friend is a dog?

Tom C. Clark

1040   I am convinced that every boy, in his heart, would rather steal second base than an automobile.

James Freeman Clarke

1041   A politician thinks of the next election; a statesman, of the next generation.

John Clarke

1042   Who is more busy than he that hath least to do?

Henry Clay

1043   If there were two Henry Clays, one of them would make the other President of the United States.

Georges Clemenceau

1044   America is the only nation in history which miraculously has gone directly from barbarism to degeneration, without the usual interval of civilization.

1045   I only read articles attacking me, never those that praise. They are too dangerous.

1046   Everything I know I learned after I was thirty.

1047   War is much too important a matter to be left to the generals.

Grover Cleveland

1048   I am not concerning myself about what history will think, but contenting myself with the approval of a fellow named Cleveland whom I have generally found to be a pretty good sort of fellow.

1049   Sensible and responsible women do not want to vote.

Montgomery Clift

1050   I have enough money to get by. I'm not independently wealthy, just independently lazy, I suppose.

Nonee Coan

1051   Dad says I play the violin as if the strings were still in the cat.

Irvin Shrewsbury Cobb
1052   I've just learned about his illness; let's hope it's nothing trivial.

1053   His words were long enough to run in serials.

1054   Middle age: when you begin to exchange your emotions for symptoms.

1055   Why should a worm turn? It's probably just the same on the other side.

1056   Women now insist on having all the prerogatives of the oak and all the perquisites of the clinging vine.

1057   Epitaph: A belated advertisement for a line of goods that has been permanently discontinued.

1058   I wish my ulcers and I could get together on a mutually satisfactory diet.

1059   As I understand it, sport is hard work for which you do not get paid.

1060   Behind the billboards lies New Jersey.

1061   A good storyteller is a person who has a good memory and hopes other people haven't.

1062   Advice is what older men offer to younger men when they no longer can set them a bad example.

William Cobbett
1063   The power which money gives is that of brute force; it is the power of the bludgeon and the bayonet.

Jean Cocteau
1064   What is history after all? History is the facts which become legends in the end. Legends are lies which become history in the end.

1065   Tact consists in knowing how far we may go too far.

George M. Cohan
1066   Many a bum show has been saved by the flag.

Jean-Baptiste Colbert
1067   The art of taxation consists in so plucking the goose as to obtain the largest amount of feathers with the least amount of hissing.

Lester L. Colbert
1068   When I've had a rough day, before I go to sleep I ask myself if there's anything more I can do right now. If there isn't, I sleep sound.

Frank Moore Colby

1069   A "new thinker," when studied closely, is merely a man who does not know what other people have thought.

1070   Self-esteem is the most voluble of the emotions.

1071   Satire is a lonely and introspective occupation, for nobody can describe a fool to the life without much patient self-inspection.

1072   Every improvement in communication makes the bore more terrible.

Samuel Taylor Coleridge

1073   Common-sense in an uncommon degree is what the world calls wisdom.

1074   What is an epigram? A dwarfish whole,
Its body brevity, and wit its soul.

1075   And the Devil did grin, for his darling sin
Is pride that apes humility.

1076   To most men, experience is like the stern lights of a ship which illumine only the track it has passed.

1077   Plagiarists are always suspicious of being stolen from.

1078   And in today already walks tomorrow.

1079   How inimitably graceful children are in general—before they learn to dance.

1080   Swans sing before they die; 'twere no bad thing
Should certain persons die before they sing.

John Churton Collins

1081   To profit from good advice requires more wisdom than to give it.

1082   In prosperity our friends know us; in adversity we know our friends.

1083   Truth is the object of philosophy, but not always of philosophers.

1084   The secret of success in life is known only to those who have not succeeded.

1085   Never trust a man who speaks well of everybody.

1086   Envy is the sincerest form of flattery.

George Colman (the Elder)

1087   What a pity it is that nobody knows how to manage a wife but a bachelor.

George Colman (the Younger)

1088   Oh, London is a fine town,
    A very famous city,
Where all the streets are paved with gold,
    And all the maidens pretty.

Charles Caleb Colton

1089   Many speak the truth when they say that they despise riches, but they mean the riches possessed by other men.

1090   Men will wrangle for religion; write for it; fight for it; die for it; anything but live for it.

1091   When the million applaud, you ask yourself what harm you have done; when they censure you, what good.

1092   The follies of the fool are known to the world, but are hidden from himself; the follies of the wise are known to himself, but hidden from the world.

1093   Men are born with two eyes, but with one tongue, in order that they should see twice as much as they say.

1094   It is a common observation that any fool can get money; but they are not wise that think so.

1095   We ask advice, but we mean approbation.

Confucius

1096   The superior man is dignified, but not proud; the inferior man is proud, but not dignified.

1097   The superior man understands what is right; the inferior man understands what will sell.

1098   It is easy to be rich and not haughty; it is difficult to be poor and not grumble.

1099   By nature, men are nearly alike; by practice, they get to be wide apart.

1100   The superior man is distressed by his want of ability.

1101   Choose a job you love, and you will never have to work a day in your life.

1102   To put the world right in order, we must first put the nation in order; to put the nation in order, we must first put the family in order; to put the family in order, we must first cultivate our personal life; we must first set our hearts right.

William Congreve
1103   I am always of the opinion with the learned, if they speak first.

Cyril Connolly
1104   Literature is the art of writing something that will be read twice.

1105   Those whom the gods wish to destroy they first call promising.

1106   Imprisoned in every fat man, a thin one is wildly signalling to be let out.

Mike Connolly
1107   Coexistence: what the farmer does with the turkey—until Thanksgiving.

1108   Intellectual: Someone who knows when to quote what some bright fellow once said.

1109   Tolerance is the quality that keeps a new bride from reforming her husband right away.

Sir William Connor
1110   To say that he was not at a loss for a word is one of the great understatements of all time. He was not at a loss for 500,000 words and we heard 'em, every one.

1111   I have never seen pessimism in a Company prospectus.

Joseph Conrad
1112   Gossip is what no one claims to like—but everybody enjoys.

1113   Being a woman is a terribly difficult trade, since it consists principally of dealing with men.

1114   I remember my youth and the feeling that will never come back anymore—the feeling that I could last forever, outlast the sea, the earth, and all men.

1115   You shall judge of a man by his foes as well as by his friends.

Robert A. Cook
1116   If you find a man who always agrees with you, you have to watch him, because he is apt to lie about other things too.

1117   We dribble away our life, little by little, in small packages—we don't throw it away all at once.

1118   Always tell the truth. Then you don't have to worry about what you said last.

Charles Horton Cooley
1119   There is a function of a quasi-religious nature performed by a few experts but followed in spirit by the whole university world, serving indeed as a symbol to arouse in the students and in the alumni certain congregate and hieratic emotions. I refer, of course, to football.

Calvin Coolidge
1120   I should like to be known as a former president who tried to mind his own business.

1121   Once a guest at a White House reception remarked, "Mr. President, I'm from Boston!"
The President replied, "You'll never get over it."

1122   You have to stand every day three or four hours of visitors [to the White House]. Nine-tenths of them want something they ought not to have. If you keep dead still they will run down in three or four minutes. If you even cough or smile they will start up all over again.

1123   If you don't say anything, you won't be called upon to repeat it.

1124   Business will be either better or worse.

1125   I guess I am not naturally energetic. I like to sit around and talk.

1126   Anytime you don't want anything, you get it.

1127   The business of America is business.

1128   Nothing is easier than spending public money. It does not appear to belong to anybody. The temptation is overwhelming to bestow it on somebody.

1129   Collecting more taxes than is absolutely necessary is legalized robbery.

1130   Some people are suffering from lack of work, some from lack of water, many more from lack of wisdom.

1131   No person was ever honored for what he received. Honor has been the reward for what he gave.

1132   If you see ten troubles coming down the road, you can be sure that nine will run into the ditch before they reach you.

1133   I have never been hurt by anything I didn't say.

Pierre Corneille
1134   A good memory is needed once we have lied.

Janet Cory
1135   Yesterday we called today tomorrow.

Lloyd Cory
1136   Doing God's will may not always lead to increased popularity, sales, and profits. It didn't in Bible days.

Thomas Costain
1137   I am convinced that all writers are optimists whether they concede the point or not. . . . How otherwise could any human being sit down to a pile of blank sheets and decide to write, say two hundred thousand words on a given theme?

Senator Norris Cotton
1138   The boys are in such a mood that if someone introduced the Ten Commandments, they'd cut them down to eight. [On the U.S. Senate.]

Laurence C. Coughlin
1139   The vast wasteland of TV is not interested in producing a better mousetrap but in producing a worse mouse.

Georges Courtilines
1140   His utter incapacity and his gift for the resounding phrase assured him a splendid destiny.

Norman Cousins
1141   Government in the U.S. today is a senior partner in every business in the country.

Noel Coward
1142   Alfred Lunt has his head in the clouds and his feet in the box office.

1143   I love criticism just so long as it's unqualified praise.

1144   I've over-educated myself in all the things I shouldn't have known at all.

1145   I've sometimes thought of marrying—and then I've thought again.

1146   The American public's taste is impeccable. They like me.

Hannah Cowley
1147   What is woman? Only one of nature's agreeable blunders.

William Cowper
1148   A fool must now and then be right by chance.

1149   A life of ease is a difficult pursuit.

1150   A self-made man? Yes—and worships his creator.

1151   A noisy man is always in the right.

1152   Beware of desperate steps; the darkest day,
        Lived till tomorrow, will have passed away.

1153   How much a dunce that has been sent to roam
        Excels a dunce that has been kept at home!

1154   Our severest winter, commonly called the spring.

Mercelene Cox
1155   No man knows his true character until he has run out of gas,
        purchased something on the installment plan and raised an adolescent.

James Gould Cozzens
1156   A cynic is just a man who found out when he was about ten that
        there wasn't any Santa Claus, and he's still upset.

1157   When this world makes having money so important, so essential
        to well-being, it's hardly reasonable to blame a man for anything he may
        have done to try to get himself a supply.

George Crabbe
1158   Habit with him was all the test of truth;
        "It must be right: I've done it from my youth."

1159   Observe the prudent; they in silence sit,
        Display no learning, and affect no wit;
        They hazard nothing, nothing they assume,
        But know the useful art of acting dumb.

W. Craddle
1160   He never completed his History of Ephesus,
        But his name got mentioned in numerous prefaces.

Nathalia Crane
1161   Oh, I'm in love with the janitor's boy,
            And the janitor's boy loves me;
        He's going to hunt for a desert isle
            In our geography.

Kathryn Cravens

1162   If a man is vain, flatter. If timid, flatter. If boastful, flatter. In all history, too much flattery never lost a gentleman.

Mandell Creighton

1163   The universities are a sort of lunatic asylum for keeping young men out of mischeif.

Quentin Crew

1164   The children despise their parents until the age of forty, when they suddenly become just like them—thus preserving the system.

Croesus

1165   In peace the sons bury their fathers, but in war the fathers bury their sons.

Oliver Cromwell

1166   No one rises so high as he who knows not whither he is going.

Walter Cronkite

1167   And that's the way it is . . . and most of the time we hope it isn't.

Bing Crosby

1168   Oh, the kinda singing I do, you can't hurt your voice.

1169   There's nothing I wouldn't do for him and nothing he wouldn't do for me. So we spend our lives doing nothing for each other.

George Cross

1170   A university president says he is working hard to develop a school the football team can be proud of.

Samuel McChord Crothers

1171   A prose writer gets tired of writing prose, and wants to be a poet. So he begins every line with a capital letter, and keeps on writing prose.

Moses Crowell

1172   It is a secret worth knowing that lawyers rarely go to law.

Heloise Cruse

1173   The graveyards are full of women whose houses were so spotless you could eat off the floor. Remember the second wife always has a maid.

William T. Cummings

1174   There are no atheists in the foxholes.

Will Cuppy
1175 Just when you're beginning to think pretty well of people, you run across somebody who puts sugar on sliced tomatoes.

1176 Caesar might have married Cleopatra, but he had a wife at home. There's always something.

1177 Aristotle was famous for knowing everything. He taught that the brain exists merely to cool the blood and is not involved in the process of thinking. This is true only of certain persons.

1178 *Sartor Resartus* is simply unreadable, and for me that always sort of spoils a book.

1179 The trouble with the dictionary is that you have to know how a word is spelled before you can look it up to see how it is spelled.

1180 Etiquette means behaving yourself a little better than is absolutely essential.

1181 Printing broke out in the province of Kansu in A.D. 868. The early Chinese simply could not let well enough alone.

1182 Cheops built the Great Pyramid of Gizeh about 3050 B.C. Then he felt better.

Lord Curzon
1183 Not even a public figure. A man of no experience. And of the utmost inexperience. [Of Stanley Baldwin.]

Charlotte Cushman
1184 Goethe said there would be little left of him if he were to discard what he owed to others.

John H. Cutler
1185 She has a nice sense of rumor.

Raymond Cvikota
1186 There are more deductions in today's paycheck than in a Sherlock Holmes tale.

Richard J. Daley
1187 We shall reach greater and greater platitudes of achievement.

Salvador Dalí
1188 Compared to Velázquez I am nothing, but compared to contemporary painters, I am the most big genius of modern time . . . but modesty is not my specialty.

1189   I do not paint a portrait to look like the subject; rather does the person grow to look like his portrait.

William H. Danforth
1190   Lines of least resistance make crooked rivers and crooked men.

Gabriele D'Annunzio
1191   One should always learn to love oneself; that is the only lifelong romance.

Alvin Dark
1192   Any pitcher who throws at a batter and deliberately tries to hit him is a Communist.

Clarence Darrow
1193   I never wanted to see anybody die, but there are a few obituary notices I have read with pleasure.

1194   The first half of our lives is ruined by our parents and the second half by our children.

1195   When I was a boy I was told that anybody could become President; I'm beginning to believe it.

1196   Depressions may bring people closer to the church, but so do funerals.

1197   Whenever I hear people discussing birth control, I always remember that I was the fifth.

1198   History repeats itself; that's one of the things that's wrong with history.

1199   I am a friend of the working man, and I would rather be his friend than be one.

1200   I don't like spinach, and I'm glad I don't, because if I liked it I'd eat it, and I'd just hate it.

Donald Davidson
1201   The Vermont towns, like the Vermont landscape, were swept and garnished, as if the Day of Judgment might at any moment summon them into the presence of the celestial inspector.

Richard Harding Davis
1202   No civilized person ever goes to bed the same day he gets up.

William Davy

1203   The farther I journey toward the West, the more convinced I am that the wise men came from the East.

Clarence Day

1204   If you don't go to other men's funerals they won't go to yours.

1205   If your parents didn't have any children, there's a good chance that you won't.

Doris Day

1206   Wrinkles are hereditary. Parents get them from their children.

Eugene V. Debs

1207   Intelligent discontent is the mainspring of civilization.

Warwick Deeping

1208   I spent a year in that town, one Sunday.

Edgar Degas

1209   Painting is easy when you don't know how, but very difficult when you do.

Charles de Gaulle

1210   How can one conceive of a one-party system in a country that has over two hundred varieties of cheeses?

1211   Treaties are like roses and young girls—they last while they last.

1212   I always thought I was Joan of Arc and Bonaparte. How little one knows oneself.

1213   I myself have become a Gaullist only little by little.

1214   Since a politician never believes what he says, he is surprised when others believe him.

1215   I have come to the conclusion that politics is too serious a matter to be left to the politicians.

1216   Old man, exhausted by ordeal, detached from human deeds, feeling the approach of the eternal cold, but always watching in the shadows for the gleam of hope.

1217   Deliberation is the work of many men. Action, of one alone.

1218   The graveyards are full of indispensable men.

1219   I respect those who resist me, but I cannot tolerate them.

1220   Nothing great will ever be achieved without great men, and men are great only if they are determined to be so.

1221   I was France. I was the state, the government. I spoke in the name of France. I was the independence and sovereignty of France.

Choderlos de Laclos
1222   The conversation was dull, as is always the case when we are speaking only favorably of our fellowmen.

Casimir Delavigne
1223   Ever since Adam fools have been in the majority.

Joseph-Marie de Maistre
1224   Every nation has the government that it deserves.

Demetrius
1225   The poor man is happy; he expects no change for the worse.

Michael Denham
1226   An English summer—two fine days and a thunderstorm.

Chauncey M. Depew
1227   On April 23, Shakespeare, St. George and myself were all born, and I am the only survivor.

1228   I get my exercise acting as a pallbearer to my friends who exercise.

Diane de Poitiers
1229   The years that a woman subtracts from her age are not lost. They are added to the ages of other women.

Michel de Saint-Pierre
1230   An optimist may see a light where there is none, but why must the pessimist always run to blow it out?

Madame de Staël
1231   I'm glad I'm not a man, for if I were I'd be obliged to marry a woman.

Bernard de Voto
1232   A woman is incapable of feeling love for an automobile.

Peter de Vries
1233   A politician is a man who can be verbose in fewer words than anybody else.

1234   Every novel should have a beginning, a muddle, and an end.

1235   I love being a writer. What I can't stand is the paperwork.

1236   There are times when parenthood seems nothing but feeding the mouth that bites you.

1237   Mrs. Thicknesse and I agreed that a business of his own was probably the only solution for him because he was obviously unemployable.

Thomas Robert, Lord Dewar
1238   The one thing that hurts more than paying an income tax is not having to pay an income tax.

1239   Judge a man not by his clothes, but by his wife's clothes.

1240   Love is an ocean of emotions, entirely surrounded by expenses.

1241   A husband should tell his wife everything that he is sure she will find out, and before anyone else does.

1242   Confessions may be good for the soul but they are bad for the reputation.

1243   The road to success is filled with women pushing their husbands along.

1244   Lions of society are tigers for publicity.

John Dewey
1245   Anyone who has begun to think places some portion of the world in jeopardy.

S. H. Dewhurst
1246   This fate is the newly married sir's:
To think she's his and find he's hers.

Thomas W. Dewing
1247   Why, if you're not in New York you are camping out.

Comtesse Diane
1248   Modesty is the polite concession worth makes to inferiority.

Porfirio Díaz
1249   Poor Mexico, so far from God and so near to the United States.

Charles Dickens

1250   Father is rather vulgar, my dear. The word Papa, besides, gives a very pretty form to the lips. Papa, potatoes, poultry, prunes and prism are all very good words for the lips, especially prunes and prism.

1251   Every baby born into the world is a finer one than the last.

1252   If there were no bad people, there would be no good lawyers.

1253   The virtues of mothers shall occasionally be visited upon the children, as well as the sins of the fathers.

1254   There are only two styles of portrait painting: the serious and the smirk.

1255   Credit: A person who can't pay, gets another person who can't pay, to guarantee that he can pay.

1256   Great men are seldom over-scrupulous in the arrangement of their attire.

1257   It's over, and can't be helped, and that's one consolation, as they always say in Turkey, ven they cuts the wrong man's head off.

1258   Secret, and self-contained, and solitary as an oyster.

1259   She still aims at youth, though she shot beyond it years ago.

1260   Here's the rule for bargains: "Do other men, for they would do you." That's the true business precept.

1261   Money and goods are certainly the best of references.

1262   That's the state to live and die in! ... R-r-rich!

1263   Reflect upon your present blessings, of which every man has many; not on your past misfortunes, of which all men have some.

1264   It is strange with how little notice, good, bad or indifferent, a man may live and die in London.

Emily Dickinson

1265   The pedigree of honey
Does not concern the bee;
A clover, any time, to him
Is Aristocracy.

Franklin J. Dickman

1266   The glittering generalities of the speaker have left an impression more delightful than permanent.

Denis Diderot

1267   All children are essentially criminal.

1268   Distance is a great promoter of admiration.

Marlene Dietrich

1269   How do you know love is gone? If you said that you would be there at seven, and you get there by nine, and he or she has not called the police yet—it's gone.

Phyllis Diller

1270   When I go to the beauty parlor, I always use the emergency entrance. Sometimes I just go for an estimate.

Diogenes Laertius

1271   When the people applauded him wildly, he [Phocion] turned to one of his friends and said, "Have I said something foolish?"

1272   When Thales was asked what was difficult, he said, "To know one's self." And what was easy, "To advise another."

Benjamin Disraeli

1273   Youth is a blunder; Manhood a struggle; Old Age a regret.

1274   There is no act of treachery or meanness of which a political party is not capable; for in politics there is no honour.

1275   When I want to read a novel, I write one.

1276   There is no gambling like politics.

1277   Though I sit down now, the time will come when you will hear me.

1278   Nature has given us two ears but only one mouth, that we may hear from others twice as much as we speak.

1279   I never deny, I never contradict. I sometimes forget. [On dealing with Queen Victoria.]

1280   I will not go down to posterity talking bad grammar. [Correcting proofs of a manuscript on his deathbed.]

1281   Politics is organized opinion.

1282   An arch-mediocrity presiding over a Cabinet of mediocrities. [On Lord Liverpool.]

1283   He has not a single redeeming defect. [On William Gladstone.]

1284   A sophisticated rhetorician intoxicated with the exuberance of his own verbosity. [On William Gladstone.]

1285   The Right Honourable Gentleman is reminiscent of a poker. The only difference is that a poker gives off occasional signs of warmth. [On Sir Robert Peel.]

1286   Well, if [William] Gladstone fell into the Thames, that would be a misfortune, and if anybody pulled him out, that, I suppose, would be a calamity. [Defining the two words.]

1287   The fool wonders, the wise man asks.

1288   I have always thought that every woman should marry, and no man.

1289   I never offered an opinion till I was sixty . . . and then it was one which had been in our family for a century.

1290   In politics, nothing is contemptible.

1291   The author who speaks about his own books is almost as bad as the mother who talks about her own children.

1292   The best way to become acquainted with a subject is to write a book about it.

1293   Every man has a right to be conceited until he is successful.

1294   If you are not very clever, you should be conciliatory.

1295   It is much easier to be critical than to be correct.

1296   My idea of an agreeable person is a person who agrees with me.

1297   She is an excellent creature, but she never can remember which came first, the Greeks or the Romans.

1298   Talk to a man about himself and he will listen for hours.

1299   You know who critics are?—the men who have failed in literature and art.

1300   If every man were straightforward in his opinions, there would be no conversation.

1301   The two greatest stimulants in the world are youth and debt.

1302   Be frank and explicit. That is the right line to take, when you wish to conceal your own mind and to confuse the minds of others.

1303   A man who is not a Liberal at sixteen has no heart; a man who is not a Conservative at sixty has no head.

1304   I must follow the people. Am I not their leader?

1305   As a general rule, nobody has money who ought to have it.

1306   Plagiarists, at least, have the merit of preservation.

1307   He was one of those men who think that the world can be saved by writing a pamphlet.

1308   A practical man is a man who practices the errors of his forefathers.

1309   The praise of a fool is incense to the wisest of us.

1310   Increased means and increased leisure are the two civilizers of man.

1311   Every day when he looked into the glass, and gave the last touch to his consummate toilette, he offered his grateful thanks to Providence that his family was not unworthy of him.

1312   I make it a rule to believe only what I understand.

1313   London is a modern Babylon.

1314   Mr. Kremlin himself was distinguished for ignorance, for he had only one idea, and that was wrong.

Dorothy Dix
1315   Drying a widow's tears is one of the most dangerous occupations known to man.

George Dixon
1316   Will somebody please explain to me why public relations people are almost invariably "associates"? Whom do they associate with, and who can stand it?

J. Frank Dobie
1317   The average Ph.D. thesis is nothing but a transference of bones from one graveyard to another.

Austin Dobson
1318   You need never lack praise, if you stoop to acquire it. For folly finds always its fool to admire it.

1319   Time goes, you say? Ah, no!
        Alas, Time stays; we go.

Harold Willis Dodds
1320   A mugwump is a fellow with his mug on one side of the fence and his wump on the other.

John Donne

1321 One short sleepe past, wee wake eternally,
And death shall be no more; death, thou shalt die.

1322 No man is an Iland, intire of it selfe. . . . every man is a peece of
the Continent, a part of the maine.

Joseph Donohue

1323 What's worth doing is worth doing for money.

T. A. Dorgan

1324 Life is like eating artichokes—you've got to go through so much to
get so little.

John Dos Passos

1325 Radio: the triumph of illiteracy.

Feodor Dostoevsky

1326 I believe the best definition of man is the ungrateful biped.

1327 It seems, in fact, as though the second half of a man's life is made
up of nothing but the habits he has accumulated during the first half.

1328 I admit that twice two makes four is an excellent thing, but if we
are to give everything its due, twice two makes five is sometimes a very
charming thing, too.

Kirk Douglas

1329 Life is like a B-picture script. It is that corny. If I had my life story
offered to me to film, I'd turn it down.

Norman Douglas

1330 It takes a wise man to handle a lie; a fool had better remain
honest.

1331 A lover who reasons is no lover.

1332 Nobody can misunderstand a boy like his own mother.

1333 It seldom pays to be rude. It never pays to be only half rude.

1334 We can hardly realize now the blissful quietude of the pre-tele-
phone epoch.

1335 You can tell the ideals of a nation by its advertisements.

Sir Alec Douglas-Home

1336 There are two problems in my life. The political ones are insoluble
and the economic ones incomprehensible.

Elizabeth Drew

1337   Too often travel, instead of broadening the mind, merely lengthens the conversation.

Minou Drouet

1338   This is the great folly of grownups—wanting what lasts, wanting to last. Only two things last: shoes too small and foolishness.

Peter F. Drucker

1339   When a subject becomes totally obsolete we make it a required course.

1340   In business school classrooms they construct wonderful models of a nonworld.

1341   So much of what we call management consists in making it difficult for people to work.

1342   Whenever a man's failure can be traced to management's mistakes, he has to be kept on the payroll.

1343   Long-range planning does not deal with future decisions, but with the future of present decisions.

1344   Working with people is difficult, but not impossible.

1345   When the government talks about "raising capital" it means printing it. That's not very creative, but it's what we're going to do.

1346   Management by objectives works if you know the objectives. Ninety percent of the time you don't.

William Henry Drummond

1347   De win' can blow lak hurricane
An' s'pose she blow some more,
You can't get down on Lac St. Pierre
So long you stay on shore.

John Dryden

1348   No government has ever been, or can ever be, wherein time-savers and blockheads will not be uppermost.

1349   Beware the fury of a patient man.

1350   War seldom enters but where wealth allures.

Hansell B. Duckett

1351   What this country needs is more free speech worth listening to.

John Foster Dulles

1352   The world will never have lasting peace so long as men reserve for war the finest human qualities.

1353   The measure of success is not whether you have a tough problem to deal with, but whether it's the same problem you had last year.

1354   The United Nations was not set up to be a reformatory. It was assumed that you would be good before you got in and not that being in would make you good.

1355   It is one thing to recognize evil as a fact. It is another thing to take evil to one's breast and call it good.

1356   Our people have always been endowed with a sense of mission in the world. They have believed that it was their duty to help men everywhere to get the opportunity to be and do what God designed.

Alexandre Dumas (père)

1357   We blame in others only the faults by which we do not profit.

1358   Friendship consists in forgetting what one gives, and remembering what one receives.

1359   It is often woman who inspires us with the great things that she will prevent us from accomplishing.

1360   Oh! the good times when we were so unhappy.

Alexandre Dumas (fils)

1361   All generalizations are dangerous, even this one.

1362   A husband is always a sensible man: he never thinks of marrying.

1363   Business? It's quite simple. It's other people's money.

George Du Maurier

1364   Life ain't all beer and skittles, and more's the pity; but what's the odds, so long as you're happy?

Paul Laurence Dunbar

1365   A crust of bread and a corner to sleep in,
A minute to smile and an hour to weep in,
A pint of joy to a peck of trouble,
And never a laugh but the moans come double;
    And that is life!

Raymond Duncan

1366   A lot of parents pack up their troubles and send them off to a summer camp.

Finley Peter Dunne

1367   A woman is as old as she looks to a man that likes to look at her.

1368   The Democratic Party ain't on speaking terms with itself.

1369   If a man is wise, he gets rich, and if he gets rich, he gets foolish, or his wife does.

1370   A lie with a purpose is one of the worst kind, and the most profitable.

1371   No matter whether the Constitution follows the flag or not, the Supreme Court follows the election returns.

1372   One of the strangest things about life is that the poor, who need money the most, are the very ones that never have it.

1373   The only good husbands stay bachelors; they're too considerate to get married.

1374   The past always looks better than it was; it's only pleasant because it isn't here.

1375   Trust everybody, but cut the cards.

1376   Vice is a creature of such hideous mien that the more you see it, the better you like it.

1377   Work is work if you're paid to do it, and it's pleasure if you pay to be allowed to do it.

1378   A man never becomes an orator if he has anything to say.

1379   "The American nation in the Sixth Ward is a fine people," he says. "They love th' eagle," he says, "on the back iv a dollar."

1380   A fanatic is a man that does what he thinks the Lord would do if he knew the facts of the case.

1381   There are no friends at cards or world politics.

1382   Life would not be worth living if we didn't keep our enemies.

1383   The wise people are in New York because the foolish went there first; that's the way the wise men make a living.

1384   A prophet is a man that foresees trouble.

1385   A man that would expect to train lobsters to fly in a year is called a lunatic; but a man that thinks men can be turned into angels by an election is a reformer and remains at large.

1386   Some men's domestic troubles drive them to drink, others to labor. You read about a man becoming a millionaire and think he done it by his own exertions when it was the fear of coming home empty-handed and dislike of staying around the house all day that made him rich.

1387   Ye can lade a man up to th' university, but ye can't make him think.

1388   Most vegetarians I ever see looked enough like their food to be classed as cannibals.

1389   When we think we are making a great hit with the world, we don't know what our own wives think of us.

1390   We're a great people. We are that. And the best of it is, we know we are.

C. M. Dupuy

1391   In love, she who gives her portrait promises the original.

Will Durant

1392   To speak ill of others is a dishonest way of praising ourselves; let us be above such transparent egotism.... If you can't say good and encouraging things, say nothing. Nothing is often a good thing to do and always a clever thing to say.

1393   Sixty years ago I knew everything; now I know nothing; education is a progressive discovery of our own ignorance.

1394   He had been rejected from military service. He had weak ribs. He had poor eyes. He was flatfooted. He was a professor.

1395   Every vice was once a virtue, and may become respectable again, just as hatred becomes respectable in wartime.

1396   So I should say that civilizations begin with religion and stoicism; they end with skepticism and unbelief, and the undisciplined pursuit of individual pleasure. A civilization is born stoic and dies epicurean.

Will and Ariel Durant

1397   Education is the transmission of civilization.

1398   No man who is in a hurry is quite civilized.

1399   To say nothing, especially when speaking, is half the art of diplomacy.

1400   The family is the nucleus of civilization.

1401   History is mostly guessing; the rest is prejudice.

Jimmy Durante

1402   Be awful nice to 'em goin' up, because you're gonna meet 'em all
comin' down.

Leo Durocher

1403   Nice guys finish last. [Originally written by Jimmy Cannon.]

Sue Dytri

1404   Tact: tongue in check.

Max Eastman

1405   A liberal mind is a mind that is able to imagine itself believing
anything.

1406   Repartee is a duel fought with the points of jokes.

Abba Eban

1407   History teaches us that men and nations behave wisely once they
have exhausted all other alternatives.

1408   Propaganda is the art of persuading others of what one does not
believe oneself.

Marie von Ebner-Eschenbach

1409   Even a stopped clock is right twice every day. After some years, it
can boast of a long series of successes.

1410   The successes of the day belong to bold mediocrity.

David Eccles

1411   If a man has good manners and is not afraid of other people, he
will get by—even if he is stupid.

Arnold Edinborough

1412   Canada has never been a melting pot; more like a tossed salad.

Thomas Alva Edison

1413   I never did anything worth doing by accident; nor did any of my
inventions come by accident; they came by work.

1414   Genius is one percent inspiration and ninety-nine percent perspiration.

1415   When down in the mouth, remember Jonah: he came out all right.

1416   Everything comes to him who hustles while he waits.

1417   Show me a thoroughly satisfied man—and I will show you a failure.

1418   We do not know one millionth of one percent about anything.

1419   Results! Why, man, I have gotten a lot of results. I know several thousand things that won't work.

1420   I am long on ideas, but short on time. I expect to live to be only about a hundred.

1421   There is no expedient to which a man will not go to avoid the real labor of thinking.

1422   They say [Woodrow] Wilson has blundered. Perhaps he has but I notice he usually blunders forward.

1423   I never did a day's work in my life—it was all fun.

Bob Edwards
1424   People are always ready to admit a man's ability after he gets there.

1425   Now I know what a statesman is; he's a dead politician. We need more statesmen.

1426   A little learning is a dangerous thing, but a lot of ignorance is just as bad.

Oliver Edwards
1427   I have tried in my time to be a philosopher; but, I don't know how, cheerfulness was always breaking in.

Edward Eggleston
1428   Journalism is organized gossip.

Albert Einstein
1429   Whoever undertakes to set himself up as a judge in the field of truth and knowledge is shipwrecked by the laughter of the gods.

1430   Isn't it strange that I who have written only unpopular books should be such a popular fellow?

1431   If A equals success, then the formula is A equals X plus Y plus Z. X is work. Y is play. Z is keep your mouth shut.

1432   My life is a simple thing that would interest no one. It is a known fact that I was born and that is all that is necessary.

1433   An empty stomach is not a good political adviser.

1434   The man who regards his own life and that of his fellow creatures as meaningless is not merely unhappy but hardly fit for life.

1435   I never think of the future. It comes soon enough.

1436   Nationalism is an infantile disease. It is the measles of mankind.

1437   When a man sits with a pretty girl for an hour, it seems like a minute. But let him sit on a hot stove for a minute—and it's longer than any hour. That's relativity.

1438   Common sense is the collection of prejudices acquired by age eighteen.

1439   Great spirits have always found violent opposition from mediocrities.

1440   I assert that the cosmic religious experience is the strongest and the noblest driving force behind scientific research.

1441   The example of great and pure individuals is the only thing that can lead us to noble thoughts and deeds. Money only appeals to selfishness and irresistibly invites abuse. Can anyone imagine Moses, Jesus, or Gandhi armed with the moneybags of Carnegie?

1442   Do you know that I am the only man in Princeton who never saw a football game?

1443   I think and think for months and years. Ninety-nine times, the conclusion is false. The hundredth time I am right.

1444   Solitude is painful when one is young, but delightful when one is more mature.

1445   The important thing is not to stop questioning. Curiosity has its own reason for existing. One cannot help but be in awe when he contemplates the mysteries of eternity, of life, of the marvelous structure of reality. It is enough if one tries merely to comprehend a little of this mystery every day. Never lose a holy curiosity.

Dwight D. Eisenhower

1446   I can think of nothing more boring for the American public than to have to sit in their living rooms for a whole half hour looking at my face on their television screens.

1447   There is one thing about being president. Nobody can tell you when to sit down.

1448   There are a number of things wrong with Washington. One of them is that everyone has been too long away from home.

1449   Farming looks mighty easy when your plow is a pencil, and you're a thousand miles from the corn field.

1450   This desk of mine is one at which a man may die, but from which he cannot resign.

1451   I thought it completely absurd to mention my name in the same breath as the Presidency. [Initial reaction to suggestions that he run for presidential office.]

1452   It is only governments that are stupid, not the masses of people.

1453   As quickly as you start spending federal money in large amounts, it looks like free money.

1454   I believe it's a tradition in baseball that when a pitcher has a no-hitter going, no one reminds him of it. [On being told that his birthday, October 4, 1960, would make him the oldest President to serve in office.]

1455   Oh, that lovely title, ex-President . . .

1456   I have found out in later years we were very poor, but the glory of America is that we didn't know it then. [Speaking on his childhood.]

1457   An atheist is a man who watches a Notre Dame–Southern Methodist University football game and doesn't care who wins.

1458   An intellectual is a man who takes more words than necessary to tell more than he knows.

1459   Mrs. Eisenhower and I got a nice invitation to the Inaugural Ball saying "RSVP" and I told her to answer it and say we had another engagement.

1460   In the councils of government we must guard against the acquisition of unwarranted influence, whether sought or unsought, by the military-industrial complex. The potential for the disastrous rise of misplaced power exists and will persist.

1461   I'm saving that rocker for the day when I feel as old as I really am.

1462   Politics should be the part-time profession of every citizen.

1463   I think that people want peace so much that one of these days government had better get out of their way and let them have it.

1464   No government can inoculate its people against the fatal material-ism that plagues our age. Happily, our people, though blessed with more material goods than any people in history, have always reserved their first allegiance to the kingdom of spirit, which is the true source of that freedom we value above all material things.

1465   The world is suffering from a multiplicity of fears. . . . There is a little element of truth in each, a little element of danger in each, and that means that finally there is left a little residue that you can meet only by faith, a faith in the destiny of America.

1466   None of the questions that bother us today have an easy answer and many of them have no answer at all.

1467   From this day forward, the millions of our school children will daily proclaim in every city and town, every village and rural school house, the dedication of our nation and our people to the Almighty. [On the words "under God" in the pledge of allegiance to the flag.]

1468   For any American who had the great and priceless privilege of being raised in a small town there always remains with him nostalgic memories of those days. And the older he grows the more he senses what he owed to the simple honesty and neighborliness, the integrity that he saw all around him in those days.

1469   Morale is the greatest single factor in successful wars.

1470   When I get back to familiar sights of the farmlands, the corn and the wheat, the vast horizons, the friendly people with whom I was raised, I feel more at home than I do any other place in this world that I have been roaming for long over forty years.

1471   You do not lead by hitting people over the head—that's assault, not leadership.

1472   We have heard much of the phrase "peace and friendship." This phrase, in expressing the aspiration of America, is not complete. We should say instead, "Peace and friendship, in freedom." This, I think, is America's real message to the rest of the world.

Leon Eldred
1473   If I'd known I was going to live so long, I'd have taken better care of myself.

Paul Eldridge
1474   Man is ready to die for an idea, provided that idea is not quite clear to him.

1475   Reading the epitaphs, our only salvation lies in resurrecting the dead and burying the living.

1476   Many a necklace becomes a noose.

George Eliot

1477   I'm not denyin' women are foolish: God Almighty made 'em to match the men.

1478   Animals are such agreeable friends; they ask no questions, they pass no criticisms.

1479   Blessed is the man who, having nothing to say, abstains from giving wordy evidence of the fact.

1480   He was like a cock who thought the sun had risen to hear him crow.

1481   I've never any pity for conceited people because I think they carry their comfort about with them.

1482   She is like the rest of the women—thinks two and two'll come to make five, if she cries and bothers enough about it.

1483   There is nothing will kill a man so soon as having nobody to find fault with but himself.

1484   A prig is a fellow who is always making you a present of his opinions.

1485   Among all forms of mistake, prophecy is the most gratuitous.

1486   It always seemed to me a sort of clever stupidity only to have one sort of talent—like a carrier pigeon.

1487   It is easy finding reasons why other folks should be patient.

T. S. Eliot

1488   Most of the trouble in the world is caused by people wanting to be important.

1489   And the wind shall say "Here were decent godless people;
Their only monument the asphalt road
And a thousand lost golf balls."

1490   If you want to write poetry you must earn a living some other way.

Elizabeth I, Queen of England

1491   I know that I have the body of a weak and feeble woman, but I have the heart and stomach of a king, and of a king of England, too.

1492   All my possessions for a moment of time. [Last words.]

Ebenezer Elliot
1493   What is a communist? One who hath yearnings
        For equal division of unequal earnings.
        Idler or bungler, or both, he is willing
        To fork out his copper and pocket your shilling.

Havelock Ellis
1494   To be a leader of men one must turn one's back on men.

1495   What we call progress is the exchange of one nuisance for another
        nuisance.

1496   The place where optimism most flourishes is the lunatic asylum.

Ralph Waldo Emerson
1497   Truth is beautiful, without doubt; but so are lies.

1498   A mob is a society of bodies voluntarily bereaving themselves of
        reason. . . . A mob is man voluntarily descending to the nature of the
        beast.

1499   And what is a weed? A plant whose virtues have not been discov-
        ered.

1500   Conversation is an art in which a man has all mankind for com-
        petitors.

1501   Cunning egotism: if I cannot brag of knowing something, then I
        brag of not knowing it; at any rate, brag.

1502   Do what we can, summer will have its flies.

1503   The end of the human race will be that it will eventually die of
        civilization.

1504   Every hero becomes a bore at last.

1505   Every man is wanted, and no man is wanted much.

1506   Every Stoic was a Stoic; but in Christendom, where is the Chris-
        tian?

1507   Fame is proof that the people are gullible.

1508   A hero is no braver than an ordinary man, but he is brave five
        minutes longer.

1509   If a man owns land, the land owns him.

1510   It is easy to live for others; everybody does.

1511   Keep cool: it will be all one a hundred years hence.

1512   The louder he talked of his honor, the faster we counted our spoons.

1513   Men are conservative after dinner.

1514   Men lose their tempers in defending their taste.

1515   Men wish to be saved from the mischiefs of their vices, but not from their vices.

1516   The solar system has no anxiety about its reputation.

1517   There is this benefit in brag; that the speaker is unconsciously expressing his own ideal.

1518   We are always getting ready to live, but never living.

1519   Democracy becomes a government of bullies tempered by editors.

1520   We are students of words: we are shut up in schools, and colleges, and recitation rooms, for ten or fifteen years, and come out at last with a bag of wind, a memory of words, and do not know a thing.

1521   It is certain that more people speak English correctly in the United States than in Britain.

1522   We do not quite forgive a giver. The hand that feeds us is in some danger of being bitten.

1523   A man is a golden impossibility.

1524   Money often costs too much.

1525   If you would rule the world quietly, you must keep it amused.

1526   We boil at different degrees.

1527   Much of the wisdom of the world is not wisdom.

1528   In every work of genius we recognize our own rejected thoughts; they come back to us with a certain alienated majesty.

1529   If the stars should appear one night in a thousand years, how would men believe and adore!

1530   Once I supposed that only my manner of living was superficial; that all other men's was solid. Now I find we are all alike shallow.

1531   What age was not dull? When were not the majority wicked? or what progress was ever made by society? Society is always flat and foolish.

1532   We meet people who seem to overlook and read us with a smile, but they do not tell us what they read.

1533   When we quarrel, how we wish we had been blameless!

1534   Good manners are made up of petty sacrifices.

1535   Finish every day and be done with it. You have done what you could. Some blunders and absurdities no doubt crept in; forget them as soon as you can.

1536   In art the hand can never execute anything higher than the heart can inspire.

Epictetus
1537   Good fortune, like ripe fruit, ought to be enjoyed while it is present.

1538   Contentment comes not so much from great wealth as from few wants.

Desiderius Erasmus
1539   When I get a little money, I buy books; and if any is left, I buy food and clothes.

Chancellor Ludwig Erhard
1540   A compromise is the art of dividing a cake in such a way that everyone believes that he has got the biggest piece.

Lou Erickson
1541   Keep your chin up. It helps to keep your mouth shut.

John Erskine
1542   Most people have some sort of religion; at least they know which church they're staying away from.

1543   America is the only country left where we teach languages so that no pupil can speak them.

1544   There's a difference between beauty and charm. A beautiful woman is one I notice. A charming woman is one who notices me.

1545   Music is the only language in which you cannot say a mean or sarcastic thing.

Susan Ertz
1546   Millions long for immortality who do not know what to do with themselves on a rainy Sunday afternoon.

St. John Ervine

1547   American motion pictures are written by the half-educated for the half-witted.

Evan Esar

1548   Canada's climate is nine months winter and three months late in the fall.

1549   Walking isn't a lost art—one must, by some means, get to the garage.

1550   All work and no play makes Jack a dull boy—and Jill a wealthy widow.

Euripides

1551   A wise fellow who is also worthless always charms the rabble.

1552   Time will reveal everything. It is a babbler, and speaks even when not asked.

Anthony Euwer

1553   As a beauty I'm not a great star,
        There are others more handsome by far;
            But my face I don't mind it
            Because I'm behind it—
        'Tis the folks out in front that I jar.

Bergen Evans

1554   College professor—someone who talks in other people's sleep.

1555   Education does not mean a college education. The author of the Gettysburg Address and the Second Inaugural could hardly be called uneducated.

Edward Everett

1556   I should be glad if I could flatter myself that I came as near to the central idea of the occasion in two hours as you did in two minutes. [To Abraham Lincoln.]

Karl Ewald

1557   Our family is not yet so good as to be degenerating.

W. N. Ewer

1558   I gave my life for freedom—this I know;
        For those who bade me fight had told me so.

Arthur Fadden

1559   I was such an outcast I could have had a meeting of all my friends and supporters in a telephone booth.

Clifton Fadiman

1560   Cheese: milk's leap toward immortality.

Lord Falkland

1561   When it is not necessary to make a decision, it is necessary not to make a decision.

George Faludy

1562   Most American television stations reproduce all night long what only a Roman could have seen in the Coliseum during the reign of Nero.

George Farquhar

1563   When the blind lead the blind, they both fall into—matrimony.

Negley Farson

1564   The general creased a little in the middle to signify he was bowing.

William Faulkner

1565   The writer in America isn't part of the culture of this country. He's like a fine dog. People like him around, but he's of no use. . . . The artist is still a little like the old court jester. He's supposed to speak his vicious paradoxes with some sense in them, but he isn't part of whatever the fabric is that makes a nation. It is assumed that anyone who makes a million dollars has a unique gift, though he might have made it off some useless gadget.

1566   I believe that man will not merely endure: he will prevail. He is immortal, not because he alone among creatures has an inexhaustible voice but because he has a soul, a spirit capable of compassion and sacrifice and endurance.

1567   The Swiss who are not a people so much as a neat clean quite solvent business.

William Feather

1568   One of the indictments of civilization is that happiness and intelligence are so rarely found in the same person.

1569   The reward of energy, enterprise and thrift—is taxes.

1570   When ordering lunch, the big executives are just as indecisive as the rest of us.

1571 Women lie about their age; men lie about their income.

1572 Inability to pay decides for many of us perplexing questions that worry the well-to-do.

1573 The best sermon is preached by the minister who has a sermon to preach and not by the man who has to preach a sermon.

1574 Success makes us intolerant of failure, and failure makes us intolerant of success.

1575 An invitation to a wedding involves more trouble than a summons to a police court.

1576 The determination of life insurance salesmen to succeed has made life pretty soft for widows.

1577 Few women are dumb enough to listen to reason.

François Fénelon
1578 The more you say, the less people remember.

Homer Ferguson
1579 An egghead is one who stands firmly on both feet in mid-air on both sides of an issue.

Octave Feuillet
1580 The age at which one shares everything is generally the age when one has nothing.

Eugene Field
1581 The actor who took the role of King Lear played the king as though he expected someone to play the ace.

1582 The biggest fish he ever caught were those that got away.

1583 He is so mean, he won't let his little baby have more than one measle at a time.

1584 Any color, so long as it's red, is the color that suits me best.

1585 Herein the only royal road to fame and fortune lies;
Put not your trust in vinegar—molasses catches flies.

Henry Fielding
1586 Beauty seldom recommends one woman to another.

1587 Every physician almost hath his favorite disease.

1588   How easy it is for a man to die rich, if he will but be contented to live miserable.

1589   Money is the fruit of evil as often as the root of it.

1590   Money will say more in one moment than the most eloquent lover can in years.

1591   When children are doing nothing, they are doing mischief.

1592   The family that dines the latest
Is in our street esteemed the greatest.

Temple Fielding
1593   As a member of an escorted tour, you don't even have to know the Matterhorn isn't a tube.

W. C. Fields
1594   I never vote for anyone, I always vote against.

1595   I never met a kid I liked.

1596   On the whole I'd rather be in Philadelphia.

1597   I am free of all prejudices. I hate every one equally.

1598   A man who overindulges lives in a dream. He becomes conceited. He thinks the whole world revolves around him; and it usually does.

1599   A rich man is nothing but a poor man with money.

1600   Never mind what I told you—you do as I tell you.

1601   And remember, dearie, never give a sucker an even break.

David Maxwell Fife
1602   It is dangerous to confuse children with angels.

Shannon Fife
1603   Insomnia: a contagious disease often transmitted from babies to parents.

1604   Psychiatry is the art of teaching people how to stand on their own feet while reclining on couches.

1605   Self-restraint: feeling your oats without sowing them.

Millard Fillmore
1606   May God save the country; for it is evident that the people will not. [When James K. Polk won the presidential election.]

Martin H. Fischer

1607   Education is the process of driving a set of prejudices down your throat.

1608   We humans are the greatest of the earth's parasites.

Margaret Fishback

1609   Oh, for a man to take me out
And feed me fowl or sauerkraut
Without first asking where to dine.
If such there be, would he were mine!

Dorothy Canfield Fisher

1610   What's the use of inventing a better system as long as there just aren't enough folks with sense to go around!

Lord Fisher

1611   . . . in this free country where every man can do as he likes and if he doesn't he's made to!

Willis Fisher

1612   There are always people whom it is a privilege to dislike—a privilege one would miss by not knowing them.

1613   Men have learned to travel farther and faster, though on errands not conspicuously improved. This, I believe, is called progress.

Thomas Fitch

1614   I once heard an Irishman say, "Every man loves his native land whether he was born there or not."

Edward Fitzgerald

1615   One thing is certain and the rest is Lies;
The Flower that once has blown forever dies.

1616   When I began this letter I thought I had something to say; but I believe the truth was I had nothing to do.

F. Scott Fitzgerald

1617   "What'll we do with ourselves this afternoon?" cried Daisy, "and the day after that, and the next thirty years?"

1618   No grand idea was ever born in a conference, but a lot of foolish ideas have died there.

1619   Always willing to lend a helping hand to the one above him.

1620   Optimism is the content of small men in high places.

1621   Her unselfishness came in pretty small packages well wrapped.

Denison Flamingo
1622   A garlic sandwich is two pieces of bread traveling in bad company.

1623   It's a sure sign of summer when a Scotchman throws his Christmas tree away.

Camille Flammarion
1624   There are men who would even be afraid to commit themselves on the doctrine that castor oil is a laxative.

Gustave Flaubert
1625   Nothing is more humiliating than to see idiots succeed in enterprises we have failed in.

Peter Fleming
1626   An excitement without consequence, such as you see expressed by the chorus in an opera.

Cyril Fletcher
1627   A fool and his money are soon parted. What I want to know is how they got together in the first place.

John Florio
1628   Who sleepeth with dogs shall rise with fleas.

Robert Fontaine
1629   I let my relatives support me. I never flinched. I knew they could do it.

Bernard de Fontenelle
1630   I always think of nature as a great spectacle, somewhat resembling the opera.

1631   There are three things I have always loved, and never understood —art, music, women.

Samuel Foote
1632   He is not only dull himself but the cause of dullness in others.

Esther Forbes
1633   He was so narrow-minded he could see through a keyhole with two eyes.

Malcolm Forbes

1634   Contrary to the cliché, genuinely nice guys most often finish first, or very near it.

1635   If you say what you think, don't expect to hear only what you like.

Betty Ford

1636   I wish I'd married a plumber. At least he'd be home by five o'clock.

Corey Ford

1637   She's learned to say things with her eyes that others waste time putting into words.

Gerald Ford

1638   A bronco is something that kicks and bucks, twists and turns, and very seldom goes in one direction. We have one of those things here in Washington—it's called the Congress.

1639   I'm a Ford, not a Lincoln.

1640   A government big enough to give you everything you want is a government big enough to take from you everything you have.

1641   The American people won't buy political double-talk forever.

1642   I had pro offers from the Detroit Lions and Green Bay Packers, who were pretty hard up for linemen in those days. If I had gone into professional football the name Jerry Ford might have been a household word today.

1643   A necessary condition to a healthy economy is freedom from the petty tyranny of massive government regulation.

Glenn Ford

1644   If they try to rush me, I always say, "I've got only one other speed—and it's slower."

Henry Ford

1645   A bore is a fellow who opens his mouth and puts his feats in it.

1646   It is all one to me if a man comes from Sing Sing or Harvard. We hire a man, not his history.

1647   Capital punishment is as fundamentally wrong as a cure for crime as charity is wrong as a cure for poverty.

1648   Anyone who stops learning is old, whether at twenty or eighty. Anyone who keeps learning stays young. The greatest thing in life is to keep your mind young.

1649   If money is your hope for independence you will never have it. The only real security that a man can have in this world is a reserve of knowledge, experience and ability.

1650   The question "Who ought to be boss?" is like asking "Who ought to be the tenor in the quartet?" Obviously, the man who can sing tenor.

1651   Money is like an arm or leg—use it or lose it.

1652   Philosophers dwell in the moon.

1653   My best friend is the one who brings out the best in me.

1654   I believe that the social responsibility of the corporation today is fundamentally the same as it has always been: to earn profits for shareholders by serving consumer wants with maximum efficiency. This is not the whole of the matter, but it is the heart of the matter.

1655   Everybody wants to be someplace he ain't. As soon as he gets there he wants to go right back.

1656   It is not the employer who pays wages—he only handles the money. It is the product that pays wages.

Norman Ford
1657   Never try to tell everything you know. It may take too short a time.

Simeon Ford
1658   If the Scotch knew enough to go in when it rained, they would never get any outdoor exercise.

Robert Forsythe
1659   There is nothing on earth more depressing than an Englishman feeling inferior.

1660   Listening to Mr. Woollcott on the radio is like being hit by a cream puff; you are uninjured but rather sickened.

Harry Emerson Fosdick
1661   Hating people is like burning down your own house to get rid of a rat.

1662   God is not a cosmic bellboy for whom we can press a button to get things.

Bob Foster
1663   Don't tell me that worry doesn't do any good. I know better! The things I worry about don't happen.

Gene Fowler

1664   Writing is easy. All you do is stare at a blank sheet of paper until drops of blood form on your forehead.

John Fowles

1665   The newspapers are full of what we would like to happen to us and what we hope will never happen to us.

Anatole France

1666   He despises men with tenderness.

1667   History books which contain no lies are extremely dull.

1668   If fifty million people say a foolish thing, it is still a foolish thing.

1669   It is better to understand a little than to misunderstand a lot.

1670   It is in the ability to deceive oneself that the greatest talent is shown.

1671   Never lend books, for no one ever returns them; the only books I have in my library are books that other folk have lent me.

1672   People who have no faults are terrible; there is no way of taking advantage of them.

1673   There are very honest people who do not think that they have had a bargain unless they have cheated a merchant.

1674   We reproach people for talking about themselves; but it is the subject they treat best.

1675   The books that everybody admires are those that nobody reads.

1676   A writer is rarely so well inspired as when he talks about himself.

1677   It is human nature to think wisely and act foolishly.

1678   To die for an idea is to place a pretty high price upon conjecture.

1679   The law, in its majestic equality, forbids the rich as well as the poor to sleep under bridges, to beg in the streets and to steal bread.

1680   It is not easy to be a pretty woman without causing mischief.

1681   The sciences are beneficent: they prevent man from thinking.

1682   It is better to be stupid like everybody than clever like none.

Benjamin Franklin

1683   There is no kind of dishonesty into which otherwise good people more easily and frequently fall than that of defrauding the government.

1684   Anger is never without a reason, but seldom with a good one.

1685   Creditors have better memories than debtors.

1686   God heals, and the doctor takes the fee.

1687   Here comes the orator, with his flood of words and his drop of reason.

1688   The way to see by Faith is to shut the eye of Reason.

1689   He that teaches himself hath a fool for a master.

1690   He was so learned that he could name a horse in nine languages; so ignorant that he bought a cow to ride on.

1691   His conversation does not show the minute hand, but he strikes the hour very correctly.

1692   If a man could have half his wishes, he would double his troubles.

1693   If men are so wicked with religion, what would they be without it?

1694   If your riches are yours, why don't you take them with you to the other world?

1695   If you would keep a secret from an enemy, tell it not to a friend.

1696   If you would know the value of money, go and try to borrow some.

1697   If you would lose a troublesome visitor, lend him money.

1698   Keep your eyes wide open before marriage, and half-shut afterwards.

1699   The learned fool writes his nonsense in better language than the unlearned, but still 'tis nonsense.

1700   Love your enemies, for they tell you your faults.

1701   Many a man would have been worse if his estate had been better.

1702   Teach your child to hold his tongue; he'll learn fast enough to speak.

1703   There is no little enemy.

1704   The heart of the fool is in his mouth, but the mouth of the wise man is in his heart.

1705   A learned blockhead is a greater blockhead than an ignorant one.

1706   Fish and visitors smell in three days.

1707   The use of money is all the advantage there is in having money.

1708   Who has deceived thee so oft as thyself?

1709   If thou hast wit and learning, add to them wisdom and modesty.

1710   Historians relate, not so much what is done, as what they would have believed.

1711   Thou can'st not joke an enemy into a friend, but thou may'st a friend into an enemy.

1712   Blessed is he that expects nothing, for he shall never be disappointed.

1713   Man's tongue is soft, and bone doth lack;
Yet a stroke therewith may break a man's back.

1714   When befriended, remember it; when you befriend, forget it.

1715   The world is full of fools and faint hearts; and yet every one has courage enough to bear the misfortunes, and wisdom enough to manage the affairs of his neighbor.

1716   Experience keeps a dear school, yet fools will learn in no other.

1717   Most fools think they are only ignorant.

1718   Old boys have their playthings as well as young ones; the difference is only in the price.

1719   Little rogues easily become great ones.

1720   Laziness travels so slowly that poverty soon overtakes him.

1721   Nothing dries sooner than a tear.

1722   Silence is not always a sign of wisdom, but babbling is ever a folly.

1723   In general mankind, since the improvement of cookery, eats twice as much as nature requires.

1724   It is ill manners to silence a fool, and cruelty to let him go on.

1725   If you would not be forgotten as soon as you are dead, either write things worth reading or do things worth writing.

1726   'Tis against some men's principles to pay interest, and seems against others' interest to pay the principal.

1727   Were it offered to my choice, I should have no objection to a repetition of the same life from its beginning, only asking the advantages authors have in a second edition to correct some faults of the first.

1728   Love your neighbor—but don't pull down your hedge.

1729   Mine is better than ours.

1730   Who is wise? He that learns from everyone.
          Who is powerful? He that governs his passions.
          Who is rich? He that is content.
          Who is that? Nobody.

1731   Love and toothache have many cures, but none infallible, except
          possession and dispossession.

1732   Visit your aunt, but not every day; and call at your brother's, but
          not every night.

1733   One man may be more cunning than another, but not more cun-
          ning than everybody else.

1734   A little house well filled, a little field well tilled, and a little wife
          well willed, are great riches.

1735   He that is of opinion that Money will do every Thing may well be
          suspected of doing every Thing for Money.

1736   When the well's dry, we know the worth of water.

1737   No nation was ever ruined by trade.

1738   Lost time is never found again.

1739   An empty bag cannot stand upright.

1740   If a man empties his purse into his head, no one can take it from
          him.

1741   The proud hate pride—in others.

1742   The Body
                                      of
                           Benjamin Franklin, Printer
                          (Like the cover of an old book,
                               Its contents torn out,
                      And stript of its lettering and gilding,)
                               Lies food for worms.
                        Yet the work itself shall not be lost,
                     For it will (as he believed) appear once more,
                                    In a new
                             And more beautiful edition,
                                Corrected and amended
                                        by
                                   The Author.

1743   A long life may not be good enough, but a good life is long enough.

1744 Our Constitution is in actual operation; everything appears to promise that it will last; but in this world nothing is certain but death and taxes.

1745 Three may keep a secret if two of them are dead.

1746 To bear other people's afflictions, everyone has courage and enough to spare.

1747 To find out a girl's faults, praise her to her girl friends.

1748 What maintains one vice would bring up two children.

1749 If I wished to punish a province, I would have it governed by philosophers.

1750 He's gone, and forgot nothing but to say farewell to his creditors.

1751 Great talkers, little doers.

1752 Eat to live, and not live to eat.

1753 To lengthen thy life, lessen thy meals.

1754 He is ill clothed that is bare of virtue.

1755 Men and melons are hard to know.

Jay Franklin
1756 The times are not so bad as they seem; they couldn't be.

Frederick the Great
1757 Man is made for error; it enters his mind naturally and he discovers a few truths only with the greatest effort.

Sigmund Freud
1758 The goal of all life is death.

1759 Despite my thirty years of research into the feminine soul, I have not yet been able to answer ... the great question that has never been answered: What does a woman want?

John Freund
1760 Marketing is simply sales with a college education.

Ford Frick, baseball commissioner
1761 I'd hate this to get out but I really like opera.

Egon Friedell
1762 If the animals suddenly got the gift of laughter, they'd start by laughing themselves sick about man.

1763   There are people who are too stupid to have prejudices.

Milton Friedman
1764   I am in the fortunate position of being an irresponsible academic who can say what I want.

1765   There's no such thing as a free lunch.

1766   Hell hath no fury like a bureaucrat scorned.

Shelby Friedman
1767   Income tax time is when you test your powers of deduction.

1768   Nowadays, a penny saved is ridiculous!

1769   Woodpeckers must be very superstitious. They're always knocking on wood.

Robert Frost
1770   A liberal is a man too broadminded to take his own side in a quarrel.

1771   Never ask of money spent
Where the spender thinks it went.
Nobody was ever meant
To remember or invent
What he did with every cent.

1772   Half the world is composed of people who have something to say and can't, and the other half who have nothing to say and keep on saying it.

1773   The brain is a wonderful organ; it starts working the moment you get up in the morning, and does not stop until you get into the office.

1774   By working faithfully eight hours a day, you may eventually get to be a boss and work twelve hours a day.

1775   A diplomat is a man who always remembers a woman's birthday but never remembers her age.

1776   Home is the place where, when you have to go there, they have to take you in.

1777   A receiver is appointed by the court to take what's left.

1778   A jury consists of twelve persons chosen to decide who has the better lawyer.

1779   A man will sometimes devote all his life to the development of one part of his body—the wishbone.

1780   A mother takes twenty years to make a man of her boy, and another woman makes a fool of him in twenty minutes.

1781   The reason why worry kills more people than work is that more people worry than work.

1782   The world is full of willing people; some willing to work, the rest willing to let them.

1783   Education is the ability to listen to almost anything without losing your temper or your self-confidence.

1784   Americans are like a rich father who wishes he knew how to give his sons the hardships that made him rich.

1785   The middle of the road is where the white line is—and that's the worst place to drive.

1786   Forgive me my nonsense as I also forgive the nonsense of those who think they talk sense.

1787   You've got to love what's lovable, and hate what's hateable. It takes brains to see the difference.

1788   It's a funny thing that when a man hasn't got anything on earth to worry about, he goes off and gets married.

1789   Good fences make good neighbors.

1790   I don't call myself a poet yet. It's for the world to say whether you're a poet or not. I'm one-half teacher, one-half poet and one-half farmer; that's three halves.

1791   Writing free verse is like playing tennis with the net down.

1792   You can be a little ungrammatical if you come from the right part of the country.

1793   The difference between a man and his valet: they both smoke the same cigars, but only one pays for them.

1794   How many times it thundered before Franklin took the hint! How many apples fell on Newton's head before he took the hint! Nature is always hinting at us. It hints over and over again. And suddenly we take the hint.

1795   People have got to think. Thinking isn't to agree or disagree. That's voting.

1796   Ultimately, this is what you go before God for: You've had bad luck and good luck and all you really want in the end is mercy.

J. William Fulbright

1797　It was never intended by the Founding Fathers that the President of the United States should be a ventriloquist's dummy sitting on the lap of Congress.

Robert Fulford

1798　My generation of Canadians grew up believing that, if we were very good or very smart, or both, we would someday graduate from Canada.

Buckminster Fuller

1799　The most important fact about Spaceship Earth: an instruction book didn't come with it.

Thomas Fuller

1800　A mob has many heads, but no brains.

1801　I advise thee to visit thy relations and friends; but I advise thee not to live too near them.

1802　Birth is the beginning of death.

1803　A fox should not be of the jury at a goose's trial.

1804　A constant guest is never welcome.

1805　If you would have a hen lay, you must bear with her cackling.

1806　Tombs are the clothes of the dead; a grave is but a plain suit; a rich monument is an embroidered one.

1807　The mother-in-law remembers not that she was a daughter-in-law.

1808　Lock your door and keep your neighbor honest.

1809　Old foxes want no tutors.

1810　He was a very valiant man who first adventured on eating of oysters.

1811　Repetition: No sweetness in a cabbage twice boiled.

1812　If you sleep till noon, you have no right to complain that the days are short.

1813　The best surgeon is he that has been well hacked himself.

1814　The rich widow cries with one eye and laughs with the other.

1815　Wit helps us to play the fool with more confidence.

1816   An old wrinkle never wears out.

1817   Zeal is fit only for wise men, but is found mostly in fools.

1818   A man often repents that he has spoken, but seldom that he has held his Tongue.

1819   He that has no fools, knaves, nor beggars in his family was begot by a flash of lightning.

1820   Hopes—the only tie which keeps the heart from breaking.

1821   He that gets money before he gets wit
Will be but a short while master of it.

1822   He who findeth fault meaneth to buy.

1823   Action is the proper fruit of knowledge.

C. C. and S. M. Furnas

1824   The medical profession, because of the public attitude, is made up largely of troubleshooters and repairmen when maintenance men are what are most needed.

1825   Fish hold the honors for being brain producers, even though they haven't done as well as they might with their own organism.

1826   Poor teeth have become the badge of civilization.

Zsa Zsa Gabor

1827   I never hated a man enough to give him his diamonds back.

John Kenneth Galbraith

1828   There are times in politics when you must be on the right side and lose.

1829   Politics is not the art of the possible. It consists of choosing between the disastrous and the unpalatable.

1830   Few people at the beginning of the nineteenth century needed an adman to tell them what they wanted.

1831   It is a far, far better thing to have a firm anchor in nonsense than to put out on the troubled seas of thought.

1832   Modesty is a vastly overrated virtue.

1833   One of the greatest pieces of economic wisdom is to know what you do not know.

1834   Much of the world's work, it has been said, is done by men who do not feel quite well. Marx is a case in point.

1835   One of the best ways of avoiding necessary and even urgent tasks is to seem to be busily employed on things that are already done.

1836   Wealth is not without its advantages and the case to the contrary, although it has often been made, has never proved widely persuasive.

Galileo Galilei
1837   I have never met a man so ignorant that I couldn't learn something from him.

Paul Gallico
1838   It is no accomplishment in afterlife to be an ex-football player.

1839   College football today is one of the last great strongholds of genuine, old-fashioned American hypocrisy.

George Gallup
1840   I could prove God statistically.

John Galsworthy
1841   Idealism increases in direct proportion to one's distance from the problem.

1842   The French cook; we open tins.

1843   A man of action, forced into a state of thought, is unhappy until he can get out of it.

Francis Galton
1844   Well-washed and well-combed domestic pets grow dull; they miss the stimulus of fleas.

Gordon Gammack
1845   The psychotic says two and two are five and the neurotic knows two and two are four, and hates it.

Mahatma Gandhi
1846   Hate the sin and love the sinner.

1847   For us, patriotism is the same as the love of humanity.

1848   Capital as such is not evil; it is its wrong use that is evil.

Emile Ganest
1849   A tourist is a fellow who drives thousands of miles so he can be photographed standing in front of his car.

Joe Garagiola

1850   Nolan Ryan is pitching much better now that he has his curve ball straightened out.

Mary Garden

1851   If you have a great career, why should you want a man trailing around after you?

Dave Gardner

1852   Rock music sounds like an octopus making love to a bagpipe.

John W. Gardner

1853   We must have respect for both our plumbers and our philosophers or neither our pipes or our theories will hold water.

James Garfield

1854   The President is the last person in the world to know what the people really want and think.

1855   An Englishman who was wrecked on a strange shore and wandering along the coast came to a gallows with a victim hanging on it, and fell down on his knees and thanked God that he at last beheld a sign of civilization.

1856   I am trying to do two things—dare to be a radical, and not a fool; which, if I may judge by the exhibition around me, is a matter of no small difficulty.

John Nance Garner

1857   That log house did me more good in politics than anything I ever said in a speech.

1858   You have to do a little bragging on yourself even to your relatives —man doesn't get anywhere without advertising.

1859   Vice President: a spare tire on the automobile of government.

W.I.E. Gates

1860   He has the gall of a shoplifter returning an item for a refund.

John Gay

1861   If the heart of a man is depress'd with cares,
The mist is dispell'd when a woman appears.

1862   Life is a jest, and all things show it;
I thought so once, but now I know it.

1863   Those who in quarrels interpose,
        Must often wipe a bloody nose.

1864   Men were born to lie, and women to believe them.

1865   And what's a butterfly? At best,
        He's but a caterpillar, drest.

Felix Gear
1866   I have hunted deer on occasions, but they were not aware of it.

Sir Eric Geddes
1867   We will get everything out of her that you can squeeze out of a
        lemon and a bit more. I will squeeze her until you can hear the pips
        squeak. [On international plans for Germany.]

George III of England
1868   I desire what is good; therefore everyone who does not agree with
        me is a traitor.

Chief Dan George
1869   When the white man came we had the land and they had the
        Bibles; now they have the land and we have the Bibles.

Daniel George
1870   Sir Walter Scott, one day in spring, was walking round Abbotsford
        with Lady Scott. Passing a field where there were a number of ewes and
        frolicking lambs, Sir Walter said (so the story goes): "Ah, 'tis no wonder
        that poets, from the earliest ages, have made the lamb the emblem of
        peace and innocence."
        "Delightful animals indeed," rejoined Lady Scott, "especially with
        mint sauce."

Henry George
1871   The ideal state is not that in which each gets an equal amount of
        wealth, but in which each gets in proportion to his contribution to the
        general stock.

1872   What has destroyed every previous civilization has been the ten-
        dency to the unequal distribution of wealth and power.

Paul Geraldy
1873   Generally the woman chooses the man who will choose her.

William Gerhardi
1874   I am not an early riser. The self-respect which other men enjoy in rising early I feel due to me for waking up at all.

Julian Gerow
1875   Ours seems to be the only nation on earth that asks its teenagers what to do about world affairs, and tells its goldenagers to go out and play.

J. Paul Getty
1876   The meek shall inherit the earth, but not its mineral rights.

1877   If you can count your money, you don't have a billion dollars.

1878   I have often maintained that I possess a rare talent and strong inclination to be a beachcomber. . . . If it were not for the demands made upon me by my business, I would provide living proof that a man can live quite happily for decades without ever doing any work.

1879   I sincerely regret all my divorces, because I don't like anything to be unsuccessful.

1880   In some ways, a millionaire just can't win. If he spends too freely, he is criticized for being extravagant and ostentatious. If, on the other hand, he lives quietly and thriftily, the same people who would have criticized him for being profligate will call him a miser.

Edward Gibbon
1881   The various modes of worship which prevailed in the Roman world were all considered by the people as equally true; by the philosopher as equally false; and by the magistrate as equally useful.

1882   I never make the mistake of arguing with people for whose opinions I have no respect.

1883   In the end more than they wanted freedom, they wanted security. When the Athenians finally wanted not to give to society but for society to give to them, when the freedom they wished for was freedom from responsibility, then Athens ceased to be free.

1884   History is indeed little more than the register of the crimes, follies, and misfortunes of mankind.

Philip Gibbs
1885   It's better to give than to lend, and it costs about the same.

Wolcott Gibbs
1886   He [Alexander Woollcott] wasn't exactly hostile to facts but he was apathetic about them.

Kahlil Gibran

1887   An exaggeration is a truth that has lost its temper.

1888   It is only when you are pursued that you become swift.

André Gide

1889   Art is a collaboration between God and the artist, and the less the
artist does the better.

William Schwenck Gilbert

1890   I always voted at my party's call.
And never thought of thinking for myself at all!
I thought so little, they rewarded me
By making me the ruler of the Queen's navee!

1891   I often think it's comical,
How nature always does contrive
That every boy and every gal,
That's born into the world alive,
Is either a little Liberal,
Or else a little Conservative.

1892   You've no idea what a poor opinion I have of myself, and how little
I deserve it.

1893   Isn't your life extremely flat with nothing whatever to grumble at?

1894   It isn't so much what's on the table that matters, as what's on the
chairs.

1895   No one can have a higher opinion of him than I have—and I think
he is a dirty little beast.

1896   Things are seldom what they seem.
Skim milk masquerades as cream.

1897   Of that there is no manner of doubt—
No probable, possible shadow of doubt—
No possible doubt whatever.

1898   Though I'm anything but clever,
I could talk like that forever.

1899   Darwinian Man, though well-behaved,
At best is only a monkey shaved!

1900   Stick close to your desks and never go to sea,
And you all may be rulers of the Queen's navee.

1901   I am not fond of uttering platitudes
In stained-glass attitudes.

1902   And so do his sisters and his cousins and his aunts!
        His sisters and his cousins,
        Whom he reckons up by dozens,
        And his aunts!

1903   I love my fellow creatures—I do all the good I can—
        Yet everybody says I'm such a disagreeable man!

1904   The House of Peers through all the years
        Did nothing in particular
        And did it very well.

1905   I am an intellectual chap,
        And think of things that would astonish you.

Henry Giles
1906   If the poor man cannot always get meat, the rich man cannot
        always digest it.

Strickland Gillian
1907   [On microbes]
        Adam
        Had 'em.

Hermione Gingold
1908   I got all the schooling any actress needs. That is, I learned to write
        enough to sign contracts.

Jean Giraudoux
1909   Only the mediocre are always at their best.

1910   Countries are like fruit—the worms are always inside.

1911   I forgot they were talking about me. They sound so wonderfully
        convincing.

William Ewart Gladstone
1912   I love splendor, but I hate luxury.

Ellen Glasgow
1913   In her single person she managed to produce the effect of a
        majority.

1914   The only difference between a rut and a grave is their dimensions.

Arnold Glasow
1915   Laughter is a tranquilizer with no side effects.

1916   The key to everything is patience. You get the chicken by hatching the egg—not by smashing it.

1917   You can't take it with you. You never see a U-Haul following a hearse.

1918   There is no furniture more costly than a government bureau.

1919   Never try to make your son or daughter another you; one is enough!

1920   One of life's hardest decisions is which line to stand in at the supermarket.

Carter Glass
1921   A liberal is a man who is willing to spend somebody else's money.

Montague Glass
1922   She was a singer who had to take any note above A with her eyebrows.

Jackie Gleason
1923   If you think old soldiers just fade away, just try to get into your old uniform.

John H. Glenn, Jr.
1924   A good many of us today are content to be fat, dumb and happy. With a polyunsaturated diet, the coming thirty-five-hour week, the fly-now-pay-later vacation, and fringe benefits, many of us live in a chromium-plated world where the major enemy we face is crabgrass.

Germain G. Glidden
1925   The older I grow, the more I listen to people who don't say much.

George Gobel
1926   Don't borrow trouble. Be patient and you'll have some of your own.

Bob Goddard
1927   There must be something to acupuncture—you never see any sick porcupines.

1928   I don't know what makes him so obnoxious. But whatever it is, it works.

Arthur Godfrey
1929   I'm proud to be paying taxes in the United States. The only thing is—I could be just as proud for half the money.

Hermann Goering

1930   Naturally the common people don't want war.... Voice or no voice, the people can always be brought to the bidding of the leaders.... All you have to do is to tell them they are being attacked and denounce the pacifists for lack of patriotism.

Johann Wolfgang von Goethe

1931   When ideas fail, words come in very handy.

1932   I have studied now Philosophy
And Jurisprudence, Medicine
And even, alas, Theology
From end to end with labor keen;
And here, poor fool, with all my lore
I stand no wiser than before.

1933   Everything in the world may be endured except continual prosperity.

1934   I give presents to the mother, but I think of the daughter.

1935   If children grew up according to early indications, we should have nothing but geniuses.

1936   Never tell people how you are: they don't want to know.

1937   If youth is a fault, one soon gets rid of it.

1938   If you must tell me your opinions, tell me what you believe in. I have plenty of doubts of my own.

1939   A clever man commits no minor blunders.

1940   The desert Hindus vow to eat no fish.

1941   Treat people as if they were what they ought to be and you help them to become what they are capable of being.

1942   There is nothing more terrible than energetic ignorance.

1943   Once you have missed the first buttonhole, you'll never manage to button up.

1944   To write prose, one must have something to say; but he who has nothing to say can still make verses and rhymes, where one word suggests the other, and at last something comes out which in fact is nothing but looks as if it were something.

1945   Fools and wise men are equally harmless. It is the half-fools and half-wise that are dangerous.

1946   To measure up to all that is demanded of him, a man must over-estimate his capacities.

1947   Man errs as long as he strives.

1948   Tolerance comes with age. I see no fault committed that I myself could not have committed at some time or other.

Oliver St. John Gogarty
1949   The Irish people do not gladly suffer common sense.

Robert Goheen
1950   If you feel that you have both feet planted on level ground, then the university has failed you.

Isaac Goldberg
1951   Diplomacy is to do and say the nastiest thing in the nicest way.

1952   Grammar school never taught me anything about grammar.

1953   I do not believe today everything I believed yesterday; I wonder will I believe tomorrow everything I believe today.

1954   We spend half our lives unlearning the follies transmitted to us by our parents, and the other half transmitting our own follies to our off-spring.

Morris Goldfischer
1955   If a growing object is both fresh and spoiled at the same time, chances are it is a child.

Oliver Goldsmith
1956   And still they gaz'd, and still the wonder grew
That one small head could carry all he knew.

1957   Ask me no questions, and I'll tell you no fibs.

1958   Every absurdity has a champion to defend it.

1959   People seldom improve when they have no model but themselves to copy.

1960   I always get the better when I argue alone.

1961   There is no arguing with him, for if his pistol misses fire, he knocks you down with the butt-end of it. [Of Dr. Johnson.]

1962   If you were to make little fishes talk, they would talk like whales.

1963   I was tired of always being wise.

Barry Goldwater

1964   I'm too young to retire and too old to go back to work.

1965   Minority groups now speak much more loudly than do majority groups which I classify as the forgotten American, the man who pays his taxes, prays, behaves himself, stays out of trouble and works for his government.

1966   I understand Jacqueline Kennedy has redone the White House in eighteenth-century style. Why then, I'd fit in perfectly.

1967   Extremism in the defense of liberty is no vice. Moderation in the pursuit of justice is no virtue.

Samuel Goldwyn

1968   I don't want any yes-men around me. I want everybody to tell me the truth even if it costs them their jobs.

1969   Include me out.

1970   A verbal contract isn't worth the paper it's written on.

1971   This makes me so sore it gets my dandruff up.

1972   If I could drop dead right now, I'd be the happiest man alive!

1973   Anybody who goes to see a psychiatrist ought to have his head examined.

1974   In two words: im possible.

1975   A wide screen just makes a bad film twice as bad.

1976   Why should people go out and pay money to see bad films when they can stay at home and see bad television for nothing?

1977   I read part of it all the way through.

1978   I'll give you a definite maybe.

1979   It's more than magnificent—it's mediocre.

1980   We're overpaying him but he's worth it.

1981   I would be sticking my head in a moose.

1982   The trouble with this business is the dearth of bad pictures.

1983   I have been laid up with intentional flu.

1984   I want a film that begins with an earthquake and works up to a climax.

1985   For this part I want a lady, somebody that's couth.

1986   If you can't give me your word of honor, will you give me your promise?

1987   A secretary came to Goldwyn saying, "Our files are so crowded that I suggest destroying all correspondence more than six years old." "By all means," said Goldwyn, "but be sure to make copies."

1988   I had a terrific idea this morning, but I didn't like it.

Samuel Gompers
1989   The worst crime against working people is a company which fails to operate at a profit.

Edmond and Jules de Goncourt
1990   That which, perhaps, hears more silly remarks than anything else in the world is a picture in a museum.

1991   Commerce is the art of exploiting the need or desire someone has for something.

Lord Goodman
1992   The people of this country are not a community of boy scouts. They don't really want to rally round anyone.

Paul Goodman
1993   Few great men could pass Personnel.

Adam L. Gordon
1994   Life is mostly froth and bubble,
Two things stand like stone—
Kindness in another's trouble,
Courage in our own.

Charles Gordon
1995   I know if I was chief I would never employ myself, for I am incorrigible.

Senator Thomas P. Gore
1996   He has every attribute of a dog except loyalty.

Rémy de Gourmont
1997   The terrible thing about the quest for truth is that you find it.

1998   To know what everybody knows is to know nothing.

1999   Very simple ideas lie within the reach only of complex minds.

2000   Before undergoing a surgical operation, arrange your temporal affairs. You may live.

A. P. Gouthey

2001   No man knows of what stuff he is made until prosperity and ease try him.

2002   The most glorious thing in life is to be a Christian. The most exalted privilege in life is to have intimate daily, hourly fellowship with God.

Sir Ernest Gowers

2003   When I was young, there were children's doctors but no pediatricians, ear-nose-and-throat surgeons but no otolaryngologists, skin doctors but no dermatologists, mad doctors but no psychiatrists.

Baltasar Gracian

2004   When you cannot get a thing, then is the time to have contempt for it.

2005   The wise physician, if he has failed to cure, looks out for someone who, under the name of consultation, may help him carry out the corpse.

Lord Grade

2006   All my shows are great. Some of them are bad. But they are all great.

Benjamin Graham

2007   Financial success is never having to balance your checkbook.

Billy Graham

2008   Being a Christian is more than just an instantaneous conversion —it is a daily process whereby you grow to be more and more like Christ.

2009   May the Lord bless you real good.

2010   Most of us follow our conscience as we follow a wheelbarrow. We push it in front of us in the direction we want to go.

2011   God proved His love on the Cross. When Christ hung, and bled, and died, it was God saying to the world, "I love you."

John Graham

2012   A fellow told me the other day he is so poor his hearing aid is on a party line.

Ulysses S. Grant

2013   I voted for Buchanan because I didn't know him and voted against Fremont because I did know him.

2014   I know only two tunes; one of them is "Yankee Doodle," and the other isn't.

2015   Venice would be a fine city if it were only drained.

Harley Granville-Barker

2016   The middle-class woman of England, as of America ... think of her in bulk ... is potentially the greatest money-spending machine in the world.

Thomas Gray

2017   Each in his narrow cell for ever laid,
        The rude forefathers of the hamlet sleep.

David Grayson

2018   Long ago I made up my mind to let my friends have their peculiarities.

Horace Greeley

2019   I haven't any time to make money, and I don't want any anyhow. Money is more trouble than it's worth.

Russell Green

2020   Cynic: a man who tells you the truth about your own motives.

2021   The advantage of a classical education is that it enables you to despise the wealth which it prevents you from achieving.

2022   I never repeat anyone except myself.

2023   The climate of England has been the world's most powerful colonizing impulse.

2024   Life is an experiment in the art of living, but you die before you see the result.

Dr. George Griffith

2025   Striving to outdo one's companions on the golf course and tennis court or in the swimming pool constitutes several socially acceptable forms of suicide.

John Grigg

2026   It is no part of the State's duty to facilitate the spiritual redemption of rich men by impoverishing them in this life.

2027   Lloyd George would have a better rating in British mythology if he had shared the fate of Abraham Lincoln.

Whitney Griswold

2028   Conversation in this country has fallen upon evil days. It is drowned out in singing commercials by the world's most productive economy that has so little to say for itself it has to hum it. It is hushed and shushed in dimly lighted parlors by television audiences who used to read, argue and even play bridge, an old-fashioned card game requiring speech.

2029   Year after year these congregations hear the same exhortations, the same appeals to youth to sally forth, knight-errant, and slay the same old dragons in the same old sinful world. Yet these dragons, unlike their mortal cousins the dinosaurs, have managed to keep well ahead of the game. If Darwin himself had picked them as favorites in the cosmic sweepstakes, they could not have run a better race.

2030   The presidency of a large university is an anachronism. The public demands that the president be everywhere at all times. He is thought to be omniscient, omnipresent and Mr. Chips all rolled into one.

2031   But the day when the president can play the role of "Prexy" is gone. . . . He is like a fireman who sees six fires from the window, dashes out to extinguish one, and hopes somebody else will get the other five. This is not a complaint. It's a plain statement of fact.

Helga Bergold Gross

2032   What we usually pray to God is not that His will be done, but that He approve ours.

General Alfred Gruenther

2033   When we are wrong, make us easy to change.
         When we are right, make us easy to live with.

Philip Guedalla

2034   Biography is a region bounded on the north by history, on the south by fiction, on the east by obituary, and on the west by tedium.

2035   History repeats itself; historians repeat each other.

2036   The twentieth century is only the nineteenth speaking with a slightly American accent.

2037   I had always assumed that cliché was a suburb of Paris, until I discovered it to be a street in Oxford.

2038   An Englishman is a man who lives on an island in the North Sea governed by Scotsmen.

Louise Imogen Guiney
2039   Very few can be trusted with an education.

Arthur Guiterman
2040   The Pilgrims landed, worthy men,
         And saved from wreck on raging seas,
         They fell upon their knees, and then
         Upon the aborigines.

2041   Great Caesar's bust is on the shelf,
         And I don't feel so well myself.

2042   Until the donkey tried to clear
         The fence, he thought himself a deer.

2043   Oh, the saddest of sights in a world of sin
         Is a little lost pup with his tail tucked in!

2044   The stones that Critics hurl with Harsh Intent
         A Man may use to build a Monument.

2045   Admitting Error clears the Score
         And proves you Wiser than before.

2046   Who Knows what he is Told, must know a Lot of Things that Are Not So.

2047   Don't tell your friends about your indigestion:
         "How are you!" is a greeting, not a question.

Sacha Guitry
2048   If a playwright is funny, the English look for a serious message, and if he's serious, they look for the joke.

John Gunther
2049   All happiness depends on a leisurely breakfast.

2050   I like the story, doubtless antique, that I heard near San Antonio. A child asks a stranger where he comes from, whereupon his father rebukes him gently, "Never do that, son. If a man's from Texas, he'll tell you. If he's not, why embarrass him by asking?"

Hunter Guthrie
2051   The Christian is like the ripening corn; the riper he grows the more lowly he bends his head.

Lois Haase

2052   Travel broadens the mind, flattens the finances, and lengthens the conversation.

Philip W. Haberman, Jr.

2053   A gourmet is just a glutton with brains.

Moses Hadas

2054   Thank you for sending me a copy of your book. I'll waste no time reading it.

Howard W. Haggard

2055   Longevity, barring hanging and accidents, is largely a matter of heredity.

Lord Hailsham

2056   The best way I know to win an argument is to start by being in the right.

Richard Halliburton

2057   Contentment is, after all, simply refined indolence.

Thomas Chandler Haliburton

2058   A college education shows a man how little other people know.

2059   Every woman is wrong until she cries, and then she is right, instantly.

George Savile, Marquis of Halifax, Lord Halifax

2060   Men are not hanged for stealing horses, but that horses may not be stolen.

2061   The vanity of teaching doth oft tempt a man to forget that he is a blockhead.

2062   Education is what remains when we have forgotten all that we have been taught.

2063   In this age, when it is said of a man, he knows how to live, it may be implied he is not very honest.

2064   It is flattering some men to endure them.

2065   The court may be said to be a company of well-bred fashionable beggars.

2066   Nothing hath an uglier Look to us than Reason, when it is not of our side.

2067   Everything that doth us good is so apt to do us hurt too, that it is a strong Argument for Men to be quiet.

2068   He that leaveth nothing to chance will do few things ill, but he will do very few things.

2069   There is so much wit necessary to make a skillful hypocrite that the faculty is fallen amongst bunglers, who make it ridiculous.

Frederick G. Hall
2070   Lips that touch wine jelly
        Will never touch mine, Nellie.

Robert Hall
2071   He might be a very clever man . . . but he laid so many books upon his head that his brains could not move.

A. H. Hallock
2072   Eating slowly helps to keep one slim; in other words, haste makes waist.

Margaret Halsey
2073   He must have had a magnificent build before his stomach went in for a career of its own.

2074   His handshake ought not to be used except as a tourniquet.

John Hancock
2075   There. I guess King George will be able to read that. [First signatory of the U.S. Declaration of Independence.]

W. C. Handy
2076   Life is something like this trumpet. If you don't put anything in it, you don't get anything out. And that's the truth.

Thomas Hardy
2077   I'm Smith of Stoke, and sixty-odd,
            I've lived without a dame
        From youth-time on; and would to God
            My dad had done the same.

2078 That man's silence is wonderful to listen to.

Richard Harkness
2079 What is a committee? A group of the unwilling, picked from the unfit, to do the unnecessary.

Lucille S. Harper
2080 One nice thing about egotists: They don't talk about other people.

2081 Doctor to patient: I want you to skip your vacation this year and get a good rest.

Averell Harriman
2082 Anyone who wants to be president should have his head examined.

2083 Conferences at the top level are always courteous. Name-calling is left to the foreign ministers.

Margaret Case Harriman
2084 Money is what you'd get on beautifully without if only other people weren't so crazy about it.

Alan Harrington
2085 We are all, it seems, saving ourselves for the Senior Prom. But many of us forget that somewhere along the way we must learn to dance. [On preparation for retirement.]

Everett Harris
2086 No one ever graduates from Bible study until he meets its Author face to face.

Joel Chandler Harris
2087 The rooster makes more racket than the hen that lays the egg.

2088 Liquor talks mighty loud when it gets loose from the jug.

Representative Orin Harris
2089 Beware of the man who knows the answer before he understands the question!

Richard Harris
2090 Probably the most distinctive characteristic of the successful politician is selective cowardice.

Sydney Harris

2091   When I hear somebody sigh that "Life is hard," I am always tempted to ask, "Compared to what?"

2092   Perseverance is the most overrated of traits, if it is unaccompanied by talent; beating your head against a wall is more likely to produce a concussion in the head than a hole in the wall.

2093   You may be sure that when a man begins to call himself a realist he is preparing to do something he is secretly ashamed of doing.

2094   The only way to understand a woman is to love her—and then it isn't necessary to understand her.

2095   Nobody can be so amusingly arrogant as a young man who has just discovered an old idea and thinks it is his own.

2096   Intolerance is the most socially acceptable form of egotism, for it permits us to assume superiority without personal boasting.

2097   The time to relax is when you don't have time for it.

2098   It's a toss-up as to which are finally the most exasperating—the dull people who never talk, or the bright people who never listen.

Benjamin Harrison

2099   I do not know whether it is prejudice or not, but anyway I always have a very high opinion of a state whose chief production is corn.

2100   It has seemed to me this morning that these Vermont towns are closer together than on any other route I have traveled. Perhaps it is because your state is not very large, and you have to put your towns close together in order to get them all in.

Henry S. Haskins

2101   The time to stop talking is when the other person nods his head affirmatively but says nothing.

2102   How gaily a man wakes in the morning to watch himself keep on dying.

2103   The man who is too old to learn was probably always too old to learn.

2104   No one has yet computed how many imaginary triumphs are silently celebrated by people each year to keep up their courage.

2105   The voyage of love is all the sweeter for an outside stateroom and a seat at the captain's table.

2106   Good behavior is the last refuge of mediocrity.

2107   Much more is known about the stars than about rheumatism.

2108   The truth would become more popular if it were not always stating ugly facts.

2109   The vice we embrace seems at least a cousin to virtue.

2110   It is easier to admire hard work if you don't do it.

2111   The best thing for an argument is not words and ideas, but to stop arguing.

2112   Weariness has no pain equal to being all rested up with nothing to do.

2113   No punishment of the unrighteous has ever been too severe in the eyes of the righteous.

Sir Anthony Hope Hawkins
2114   Bourgeois ... is an epithet which the riff-raff apply to what is respectable, and the aristocracy to what is decent.

Goldie Hawn
2115   Have you noticed how no man ever tells a woman she's talking too much when she's telling him how wonderful he is?

Nathaniel Hawthorne
2116   The only sensible ends of literature are, first, the pleasurable toil of writing; second, the gratification of one's family and friends; and, lastly, the solid cash.

S. I. Hayakawa
2117   We should keep [the Panama Canal]. After all, we stole it fair and square.

Friedrich Hayek
2118   What our generation has forgotten is that the system of private property is the most important guaranty of freedom, not only for those who own property, but scarcely less for those who do not.

Helen Hayes
2119   I was at a party feeling very shy because there were a lot of celebrities around, and I was sitting in a corner alone and a very beautiful young man came up to me and offered me some salted peanuts and he said, "I wish they were emeralds" as he handed me the peanuts and that was the end of my heart. I never got it back.

E.S.P. Haynes

2120   The bureaucrat is the cancer-cell of the nation.

Arthur Garfield Hays

2121   When there's a rift in the lute, the business of the lawyer is to widen the rift and gather the loot.

William Hazlitt

2122   There is not a more mean, stupid, dastardly pitiless, selfish, spiteful, envious, ungrateful animal than the public.

2123   Actors are the only honest hypocrites.

2124   He who comes up to his own idea of greatness must always have had a very low standard of it in his mind.

2125   I like a friend the better for having faults that one can talk about.

2126   Silence is one great art of conversation.

2127   There are names written in her immortal scroll at which Fame blushes.

2128   We are not satisfied to be right, unless we can prove others to be quite wrong.

2129   Words are the only things that last forever.

2130   We talk little, if we do not talk about ourselves.

2131   Anyone who has passed through the regular gradations of a classical education, and is not made a fool by it, may consider himself as having had a very narrow escape.

2132   We grow tired of everything but turning others into ridicule, and congratulating ourselves on their defects.

2133   Man is the only animal that laughs and weeps; for he is the only animal that is struck with the difference between what things are, and what they ought to be.

2134   He who draws upon his own resources easily comes to an end of his wealth.

2135   Prejudice is never easy unless it can pass itself off for reason.

2136   If mankind had wished for what is right, they might have had it long ago.

2137   The most sensible people to be met with in society are men of business and of the world, who argue from what they see and know, instead of spinning cobweb distinctions of what things ought to be.

Edward Heath

2138   I am not a product of privilege, I am a product of opportunity.

Don Hebb

2139   What's not worth doing is not worth doing well.

Friedrich Hebbel

2140   A benefactor always has something of a creditor about him.

Fred Hechinger

2141   Professional jargon is unpleasant. Translating it into English is a
bore. I narrow-mindedly outlawed the word unique. Practically every
press release contains it. Practically nothing ever is.

Ben Hecht

2142   I'm a Hollywood writer; so I put on a sports jacket and take off my
brain.

2143   Prejudice is a raft onto which the shipwrecked mind clambers and
paddles to safety.

2144   Time is a circus always packing up and moving away.

Job E. Hedges

2145   Lots of people know a good thing the minute the other fellow sees
it first.

Georg Friedrich Hegel

2146   What experience and history teaches is this—that people and
governments have never learnt anything from history or acted on principles deduced from it.

Jascha Heifetz

2147   I occasionally play works by contemporary composers and for two
reasons. First to discourage the composer from writing any more and
secondly to remind myself how much I appreciate Beethoven.

Heinrich Heine

2148   If the Romans had been obliged to learn Latin, they would never
have found time to conquer the world.

2149   One should forgive one's enemies, but not before they are hanged.

2150   Ordinarily he was insane, but he had lucid moments when he was
merely stupid.

2151   The ancient sage who concocted the maxim "Know Thyself" might have added, "Don't Tell Anyone!"

2152   Sleep is lovely, death is better still, not to have been born is of course the miracle.

2153   When words leave off, music begins.

2154   No author is a man of genius to his publisher.

2155   The world is surprised that there once was an honest man: the situation remains vacant. [Speaking of Lafayette.]

2156   He who marries is like the doge who marries the Adriatic—he doesn't know what's in it: treasures, pearls, monsters, unknown storms.

2157   Matrimony: the high sea for which no compass has yet been invented.

2158   Money is the god of our time, and Rothschild is his prophet.

2159   The music at a wedding procession always reminds me of the music of soldiers going into battle.

2160   God will forgive me the foolish remarks I have made about Him just as I will forgive my opponents the foolish things they have written about me, even though they are spiritually as inferior to me as I to thee, O God! [On his deathbed.]

2161   Silence: a conversation with an Englishman.

Joseph Heller
2162   He was a self-made man who owed his lack of success to nobody.

2163   Even when he cheated he couldn't win, because the people he cheated against were always better at cheating too.

Lillian Hellman
2164   Cynicism is an unpleasant way of saying the truth.

Arthur Helps
2165   The worst use that can be made of success is to boast of it.

2166   The absence of humility in critics is something wonderful.

2167   The greatest luxury of riches is that they enable you to escape so much good advice.

2168   Reading is sometimes an ingenious device for avoiding thought.

2169   Wise sayings often fall on barren ground; but a kind word is never thrown away.

Ernest Hemingway
2170   Never think that war, no matter how necessary, nor how justified, is not a crime.

2171   What is moral is what you feel good after and what is immoral is what you feel bad after.

2172   Literary awards usually come late in life, when the recipient is well established. It's like throwing a lifebelt to a shipwrecked man after he has reached safety.

Graham L. Hemminger
2173   Tobacco is a dirty weed. I like it.
It satisfies no normal need. I like it.
It makes you thin, it makes you lean,
It takes the hair right off your bean.
It's the worst darn stuff I've ever seen.
I like it.

L. L. Hendren
2174   Fathers send their sons to college either because they went to college or because they didn't.

Lewis C. Henry
2175   Eat, drink and be merry, for tomorrow ye diet.

O. Henry
2176   Life is made up of sobs, sniffles, and smiles, with sniffles predominating.

2177   It brings up happy old days when I was only a farmer and not an agriculturist.

2178   It was beautiful and simple as all truly great swindles are.

Katharine Hepburn
2179   I don't care what is written about me so long as it isn't true.

Heraclitus
2180   There is nothing permanent except change.

Sir Alan Herbert
2181   A highbrow is the kind of person who looks at a sausage and thinks of Picasso.

2182   The conception of two people living together for twenty-five years without having a cross word suggests a lack of spirit only to be admired in sheep.

George Herbert

2183   A piece of a churchyard fits everybody.

2184   The offender never pardons.

2185   He that pities another remembers himself.

2186   On a good bargain think twice.

2187   No lock will hold against the power of gold.

2188   Prosperity destroys fools and endangers the wise.

Jack Herbert

2189   A chip on the shoulder indicates that there is wood higher up.

Ben Herbster

2190   The greatest waste in the world is the difference between what we
are and what we could become.

Oliver Herford

2191   My sense of sight is very keen,
            My sense of hearing weak.
        One time I saw a mountain pass,
            But could not hear its peak.

2192   Modesty: the gentle art of enhancing your charm by pretending
not to be aware of it.

2193   Cat: a pygmy lion who loves mice, hates dogs, and patronizes
human beings.

2194   Darling: the popular form of address used in speaking to a person
of the opposite sex whose name you cannot at the moment recall.

2195   Diplomacy: lying in state.

2196   Zoo: a place devised for animals to study the habits of human
beings.

2197   A hair in the head is worth two in the brush.

2198   It's a strong stomach that has no turning.

2199   Liar: one who tells an unpleasant truth.

2200   Many are called but few get up.

2201   Manuscript: something submitted in haste and returned at
leisure.

2202   My wife has a whim of iron.

2203 Nothing succeeds like—failure.

2204 Only the young die good.

2205 Perhaps it was because Nero played the fiddle, they burned Rome.

2206 A rolling stone gathers no moss, but it gains a certain polish.

2207 There are more fish taken out of a stream than ever were in it.

2208 There is no time like the pleasant.

2209 There's always room at the top—after the investigation.

2210 What is my loftiest ambition? I've always wanted to throw an egg into an electric fan.

2211 I don't recall your name, but your manners are familiar.

2212 Junk is anything that has outlived its usefulness.

2213 Song: the licensed medium for bawling in public things too silly or sacred to be uttered in ordinary speech.

2214 The crab, more than any of God's creatures, has formulated the perfect philosophy of life. Whenever he is confronted by a great moral crisis in life, he first makes up his mind what is right, and then goes sideways as fast as he can.

2215 A gentleman is one who never hurts anyone's feelings unintentionally.

Herodotus
2216 Very few things happen at the right time, and the rest do not happen at all; the conscientious historian will correct these defects.

2217 Of all men's miseries the bitterest is this, to know so much and to have control over nothing.

2218 If a man insisted always on being serious, and never allowed himself a bit of fun and relaxation, he would go mad or become unstable without knowing it.

Don Herold
2219 Work is a form of nervousness.

2220 Be kind and considerate to others, depending somewhat upon who they are.

2221 The brighter you are, the more you have to learn.

2222 Conversation is the slowest form of human communication.

2223   Doctors think a lot of patients are cured who have simply quit in disgust.

2224   Sophistication: knowing enough to keep your feet out of the crack of the theater seat in front of you.

2225   There is little use to talk about your child to anyone; other people either have one or haven't.

2226   There is more sophistication and less sense in New York than anywhere else on the globe.

2227   There is nobody so irritating as somebody with less intelligence and more sense than we have.

2228   There's one thing about baldness; it's neat.

2229   What is home without a hot-water bottle?

2230   Unhappiness is in not knowing what we want and killing ourselves to get it.

2231   When one has had to work so hard to get money, why should he impose on himself the further hardship of trying to save it?

2232   Why resist temptation—there will always be more.

2233   Work is the greatest thing in the world, so we should always save some of it for tomorrow.

2234   "The more articulate, the less said" is an old Chinese proverb which I just made up myself.

2235   Genius is an infinite capacity for giving pains.

2236   Don't ever slam a door; you might want to go back.

2237   A humorist is a man who feels bad but who feels good about it.

2238   Interruptions are the spice of life.

2239   It is but a few short years from diapers to dignity and from dignity to decomposition.

2240   I wish I were either rich enough or poor enough to do a lot of things that are impossible in my present comfortable circumstances.

2241   Marriage is a mistake of youth—which we should all make.

2242   Matrimony: a woman's hairnet tangled in a man's spectacles on top of the bedroom dresser.

2243   There is nothing distinctive about living in New York; over eight million other people are doing it.

2244   I would rather sing grand opera than listen to it.

2245   Man is the only animal that plays poker.

2246   Poverty must have many satisfactions, else there would not be so many poor people.

2247   Before the advent of the radio, there were advantages in being a shut-in.

2248   Women have a wonderful sense of right and wrong, but little sense of right and left.

2249   A lot of men think that if they smile for a second, somebody will take advantage of them, and they are right.

2250   I had, out of my sixty teachers, a scant half dozen who couldn't have been supplanted by Phonographs.

2251   It is a good thing that life is not as serious as it seems to a waiter.

2252   No woman should have enough clothes to make her ask, "What'll I wear?"

2253   Women give us solace, but if it were not for women we should never need solace.

General Lewis B. Hershey
2254   A boy becomes an adult three years before his parents think he does, and about two years after he thinks he does.

Rabbi M. M. Hershman
2255   If God had wanted us to have a permissive society, He would have given us the Ten Suggestions instead of the Ten Commandments.

Herman "Pat" Herst, Jr.
2256   The easiest way to stay awake during an after-dinner speech is to deliver it.

Abraham Joshua Heschel
2257   The course of life is unpredictable . . . no one can write his autobiography in advance.

Gilbert Highet
2258   With luck and resolution and good guidance . . . the human mind can survive not only poverty, but even wealth.

Burton Hillis
2259   Experience teaches that love of flowers and vegetables is not enough to make a man a good gardener. He must also hate weeds.

Chuck Hillis
2260   It's not the bulls and bears you need to avoid—it's the bum steers.

Sidney Hillman
2261   Politics is the science of who gets what, when and why.

Louis Hirsch
2262   Horse sense is a sterling quality, but let's skip what it did for the horse.

Adolf Hitler
2263   Knowledge is ruin to many young men.

2264   All epoch-making revolutionary events have been produced not by the written but by the spoken word.

Thomas Hobbes
2265   If I had read as much as other men, I should have known no more than other men.

Sandra Hochman
2266   I gave my life to learning how to live.
        Now that I have organized it all . . .
        It is just about over.

Luther Hodges
2267   If ignorance paid dividends, most Americans could make a fortune out of what they don't know about economics.

Jimmy Hoffa
2268   I may have my faults, but being wrong ain't one of them.

2269   I do unto others what they do unto me, only worse.

Samuel Hoffenstein
2270   Babies haven't any hair;
        Old men's heads are just as bare;—
        Between the cradle and the grave
        Lies a haircut and a shave.

Eric Hoffer
2271   Communists are frustrated Capitalists.

2272   It is easier to love humanity as a whole than to love one's neighbor.

2273   The search for happiness is one of the chief sources of unhappiness.

2274   Many of the insights of the saint stem from his experience as a sinner.

2275   Charlatanism is to some degree indispensable to effective leadership.

L. K. Hogan
2276   The secret was hushed about from place to place.

J. G. Holland
2277   God gives every bird its food, but he does not throw it into the nest.

Oliver Wendell Holmes
2278   Apologizing is a very desperate habit—one that is rarely cured. Apology is only egotism wrong side out.

2279   Science is a first-rate piece of furniture for a man's upper chamber, if he has common sense on the ground floor.

2280   Everybody likes and respects self-made men; it's a great deal better to be made that way than not to be made at all.

2281   Fate tried to conceal him by naming him Smith.

2282   Give us the luxuries of life and we will dispense with necessaries.

2283   Heredity is an omnibus in which all our ancestors ride, and every now and then one of them puts his head out and embarrasses us.

2284   Humility is the first of the virtues—for other people.

2285   Man has his will, but woman has her way.

2286   One has to dismount from an idea and get into saddle again at every parenthesis.

2287   Pretty much all the honest truthtelling there is in the world is done by children.

2288   If you are dealing with a fool, dictate, but never argue, for you will lose your labor and perhaps your temper.

2289   I should like to see any kind of a man, distinguishable from a gorilla, that some good and even pretty woman could not shape a husband out of.

2290   To be seventy years young is sometimes far more cheerful and hopeful than to be forty years old.

2291   Conceit is just as natural a thing to human minds as a center is to a circle.

2292   What I call a good patient is one who, having found a good physician, sticks to him till he dies.

2293   I have always considered my face a convenience rather than an ornament.

2294   It takes me several days, after I get back to Boston, to realize that the reference "the president" refers to the president of Harvard and not to a minor official in Washington.

2295   The world's great men have not commonly been great scholars, nor the great scholars great men.

2296   You may have genius. The contrary is, of course, probable.

2297   Every library should try to be complete on something, if it were only the history of pinheads.

2298   Put not your trust in money, but put your money in trust.

2299   Morality is simply another means of living but the saints make it an end in itself.

2300   Revolutions are not made by men in spectacles.

2301   Easy-crying widows take new husbands soonest; there's nothing like wet weather for transplanting.

2302   Taxes are what we pay for a civilized society.

2303   The only prize much cared for by the powerful is power. The prize of the general is not a bigger tent, but command.

2304   Nothing is so commonplace as to wish to be remarkable.

2305   Death tugs at my ear and says: "Live, I am coming."

2306   The riders in a race do not stop when they reach the goal. There is a little finishing canter before coming to a standstill. There is time to hear the kind voices of friends and say to oneself, "The work is done."

Oliver Wendell Holmes, Jr.

2307   The great act of faith is when a man decides that he is not God.

2308   This is a court of law, young man, not a court of justice.

Thomas Hood

2309   Ben Battle was a soldier bold,
            And used to war's alarms;
        But a cannon-ball took off his legs,
            So he laid down his arms.

2310   His death, which happen'd in his berth,
        At forty-odd befell;
    They went and told the sexton, and
        The sexton toll'd the bell.

2311   I don't set up for being a cosmopolite, which to my mind signifies being polite to every country except my own.

2312   Oh! would I were dead now,
    Or up in my bed now,
    To cover my head now
    And have a good cry!

2313   The best of friends fall out, and so
    His teeth had done some years ago.

Herbert Hoover

2314   When we get sick, we want an uncommon doctor; if we have a construction job we want an uncommon engineer; when we get into a war we dreadfully want an uncommon general and an uncommon admiral. Only when we get into politics are we satisfied with the common man.

2315   I was in favor of giving former Presidents a seat in the Senate until I passed 75 years. Since then I have less taste for sitting on hard-bottomed chairs during long addresses.

2316   There are some valuable privileges attached to being President— among them the duty and right to terminate all interviews, conferences, social parties, and receptions. Therefore, he can go to bed whenever he likes.

2317   Are you seeing everything you want while in Washington? If not, let me know. I am pretty well known around here. Perhaps I can fix it up for you. [To a group of visitors at the White House.]

2318   Thank God, she doesn't have to be confirmed by the Senate. [On the birth of a granddaughter.]

2319   The thing I enjoyed most [about being President] was visits from children. They did not want public offices.

2320   I believe in that old saying "Those who do not remember the past are condemned to relive it."

2321   Once upon a time my political opponents honored me as possessing the fabulous intellectual and economic power by which I created a worldwide depression all by myself.

2322 Fishing is the chance to wash one's soul with pure air. It brings meekness and inspiration, reduces our egotism, soothes our troubles and shames our wickedness. It is discipline in the equality of men—for all men are equal before fish.

2323 Children are our most valuable natural resource.

2324 Mothers and Dads that take their children to church never get into trouble.

2325 In my opinion, we are in danger of developing a cult of the Common Man, which means a cult of mediocrity.

2326 Blessed are the young, for they shall inherit the national debt.

2327 Old reformers never die. They get thrown out.

2328 Thirty years ago, we used to believe there were only two occasions in which the American people would respect the privacy of the President —in prayer and fishing. I now detect you have lost the second part of this. . . . That is one of the degenerations of the last thirty years.

2329 My sympathy often goes out for the humble decimal point. He has a pathetic and hectic life wandering around among regimented ciphers, trying to find some of the old places he used to know when budgets were balanced.

2330 A boy has two jobs. One is just being a boy. The other is growing up to be a man.

J. Edgar Hoover
2331 Banks are an almost irresistible attraction for that element of our society which seeks unearned money.

Anthony Hope
2332 Economy is going without something you do want, in case you should someday want something which you probably won't want.

2333 Your ignorance cramps my conversation.

Bob Hope
2334 People who throw kisses are mighty near hopelessly lazy.

2335 Middle age is when your age starts to show around your middle.

2336 You know what a fan letter is—it's just an inky raspberry.

2337 You know you're getting old when the candles cost more than the cake.

2338 If I have to lay an egg for my country, I'll do it.

2339 If you watch a game, it's fun. If you play it, it's recreation. If you work at it, it's golf.

2340 A zombie has no mind of his own and walks around without knowing where he's going or what he's doing. . . . In Hollywood they call them pedestrians.

2341 The audience was swell. They were so polite, they covered their mouths when they yawned.

2342 It's a wonderful world. It may destroy itself but you'll be able to watch it all on TV.

2343 The program is nearly over! I can feel the audience is still with me—but if I run faster I can shake them off.

Horace
2344 A stomach that is seldom empty despises common food.

2345 Once a word has been allowed to escape, it cannot be recalled.

A. A. Horn
2346 That part of a man's religion which is convenient, that he'll never drop.

Edward Everett Horton
2347 A low trick I hate to stoop to is tying and untying my shoelaces. It seems to fascinate audiences . . . probably because so many women in the audience have their shoes off, or wish they did.

Edward House
2348 We actually got down to work at half past ten and finished re-making the map of the world as we would have it at half past twelve o'clock. [At the Versailles peace talks.]

A. E. Housman
2349 A tail behind, a trunk in front,
Complete the usual elephant.
The tail in front, the trunk behind,
Is what you very seldom find.

Marion Howard
2350 Life is like a blanket too short. You pull it up and your toes rebel, you yank it down and shivers meander about your shoulder; but cheerful folks manage to draw their knees up and pass a very comfortable night.

Sidney Howard

2351   One half of knowing what you want is knowing what you must give up before you get it.

Edgar Watson Howe

2352   About the only thing on a farm that has an easy time is the dog.

2353   The average man's judgment is so poor, he runs a risk every time he uses it.

2354   Don't abuse your friends and expect them to consider it criticism.

2355   Don't take up a man's time talking about the smartness of your children; he wants to talk to you about the smartness of his children.

2356   Some people never have anything except ideals.

2357   Every time a boy shows his hands, someone suggests that he wash them.

2358   Half the world does not know how the other half lives, but is trying to find out.

2359   He belongs to so many benevolent societies that he is destitute.

2360   If the fools do not control the world, it isn't because they are not in the majority.

2361   If you think before you speak, the other fellow gets in his joke first.

2362   There are few grave legal questions involved in a poor estate.

2363   Most people put off till tomorrow that which they should have done yesterday.

2364   No man's credit is as good as his money.

2365   No man would listen to you talk if he didn't know it was his turn next.

2366   One of the difficult tasks in this world is to convince a woman that even a bargain costs money.

2367   One of the surprising things of this world is the respect a worthless man has for himself.

2368   Put cream and sugar on a fly, and it tastes very much like a black raspberry.

2369   As soon as a man acquires fairly good sense, it is said he is an old fogey.

2370   The most natural man in a play is the villain.

2371   When I say "everybody says so," it means I say so.

2372   When a man dies, and his kin are glad of it, they say, "He is better off."

2373   Most people eat as though they were fattening themselves for the market.

2374   Half of the little education people have is usually wrong.

2375   If a man dies and leaves his estate in an uncertain condition, the lawyers become his heirs.

2376   Even if a farmer intends to loaf, he gets up in time to get an early start.

2377   Financial sense is knowing that certain men will promise to do certain things, and fail.

2378   There is only one thing for a man to do who is married to a woman who enjoys spending money, and that is to enjoy earning it.

2379   No woman ever falls in love with a man unless she has a better opinion of him than he deserves.

2380   A woman who has never seen her husband fishing doesn't know what a patient man she has married.

2381   Express a mean opinion of yourself occasionally; it will show your friends that you know how to tell the truth.

2382   There is nothing so well known as that we should not expect something for nothing—but we all do and call it Hope.

2383   A modest man is usually admired—if people ever hear of him.

2384   When a man says money can do everything, that settles it; he hasn't any.

2385   A fairly decent man does not need a state or national law to keep him straight; his competitors and patrons usually attend to that.

2386   A man very careless in his own morals may have the highest ideals for the guidance of the world.

2387   I express many absurd opinions, but I am not the first man to do it; American freedom consists largely in talking nonsense.

2388   Many of the optimists in the world don't own a hundred dollars, and because of their optimism never will.

2389   Most philosophers are poor, so most of them give the poor the best of it.

2390   I think I am better than the people who are trying to reform me.

2391   What people say behind your back is your standing in the community in which you live.

2392   Many a man is saved from being a thief by finding everything locked up.

2393   A thief believes everybody steals.

2394   The way out of trouble is never as simple as the way in.

2395   A woman never loafs; she shops, entertains and visits.

2396   Philosophy is common sense. If it isn't common sense, it isn't philosophy.

2397   The government is mainly an expensive organization to regulate evildoers and tax those who behave; government does little for fairly respectable people except annoy them.

2398   A successful man cannot realize how hard an unsuccessful man finds life.

2399   Every great improvement in the world's history is due, directly or indirectly, to the munificence of some man successful in the world's affairs. Every great charitable institution is founded on the surplus earnings of active men who did good while earning the money and, having learned philanthropy, closed their lives with a burst of it. The men of great learning did not build the institutions in which they teach, although nearly all of them unjustly criticize the men who did.

2400   Half the time when men think they are talking business, they are wasting time.

Nathanael Howe
2401   The way of this world is to praise dead saints and persecute living ones.

James Howell
2402   Sweet appears sour when we pay.

2403   God help the rich; the poor can beg.

2404   Who hath once the fame to be an early riser may sleep till noon.

William Dean Howells
2405   Some people can stay longer in an hour than others can in a week.

Elbert Hubbard
2406   Charity: a thing that begins at home, and usually stays there.

2407   Do not take life too seriously; you will never get out of it alive.

2408   Don't lose faith in humanity; think of all the people in the United
States who have never played you a single nasty trick.

2409   Editor: a person employed on a newspaper, whose business it is to
separate the wheat from the chaff, and to see that the chaff is printed.

2410   Every tyrant who has lived has believed in freedom—for himself.

2411   Friend: one who knows all about you and loves you just the same.

2412   Genius may have its limitations, but stupidity is not thus handicapped.

2413   The graveyards are full of people the world could not do without.

2414   If you lose in an argument, you can still call your opponent names.

2415   The final proof of greatness lies in being able to endure contumely
without resentment.

2416   No man needs a vacation so much as the person who has just had
one.

2417   The object of teaching a child is to enable him to get along without
a teacher.

2418   The path of civilization is paved with tin cans.

2419   Repartee: any reply that is so clever that it makes the listener wish
he had said it himself.

2420   Righteous indignation: your own wrath as opposed to the shock-
ing bad temper of others.

2421   You can lead a boy to college but you cannot make him think.

2422   To avoid criticism, do nothing, say nothing, be nothing.

2423   The world is moving so fast these days that the man who says it
can't be done is generally interrupted by someone doing it.

2424   Logic: an instrument used for bolstering a prejudice.

2425   This will never be a civilized country until we expend more money
for books than we do for chewing gum.

2426   A conservative is a man who is too cowardly to fight and too fat to
run.

2427   Death: to stop sinning suddenly.

2428   If you have no enemies, you are apt to be in the same predicament
in regard to friends.

2429   We never ask God to forgive anybody except where we haven't.

2430   A school should not be a preparation for life. A school should be life.

2431   All the world loves a lover; but not while the lovemaking is going on.

2432   A retentive memory may be a good thing, but the ability to forget is the true token of greatness.

2433   An optimist is a neurotic person with gooseflesh and teeth a-chatter trying hard to be brave.

2434   Perfume: any smell that is used to drown a worse one.

2435   Many a man's reputation would not know his character if they met on the street.

2436   A woman can defend her virtue from men much more easily than she can protect her reputation from women.

2437   There are temptations that require all of one's strength to yield to.

2438   One machine can do the work of fifty ordinary men. No machine can do the work of one extraordinary man.

2439   Progress needs the brakeman, but the brakeman should not spend all his time putting on the brakes.

2440   An ounce of performance is worth more than a pound of preachment.

Frank McKinney Hubbard

2441   I'll say this for adversity: people seem to be able to stand it, and that's more than I can say for prosperity.

2442   About the only thing we have left that actually discriminates in favor of the plain people is the stork.

2443   After a fellow gets famous it doesn't take long for someone to bob up that used to sit by him at school.

2444   A bad cold wouldn't be so annoying if it weren't for the advice of our friends.

2445   A fellow who knows his business is allus reticent.

2446   A bee is never as busy as it seems; it's just that it can't buzz any slower.

2447   Boys will be boys, and so will a lot of middle-aged men.

2448   A chap ought to save a few of the long evenings he spends with his girl till after they're married.

2449   Classical music is the kind that we keep hoping will turn into a tune.

2450   Don't knock the weather; nine tenths of the people couldn't start a conversation if it didn't change once in a while.

2451   A friend that ain't in need is a friend indeed.

2452   If some people didn't tell you, you'd never know they'd been away on a vacation.

2453   If you want to get rid of somebody just tell 'em something for their own good.

2454   In order to live off a garden, you practically have to live in it.

2455   It makes no difference what it is, a woman will buy anything she thinks a store is losing money on.

2456   It seems like one of the hardest lessons to be learned in this life is where your business ends and somebody else's begins.

2457   It's no disgrace to be poor, but it might as well be.

2458   It's pretty hard to tell what does bring happiness; poverty and wealth have both failed.

2459   Lack of pep is often mistaken for patience.

2460   Lots of fellows think a home is only good to borrow money on.

2461   One good thing about having one suit of clothes—you've always got your pencil.

2462   Money never made a fool of anybody; it only shows 'em up.

2463   Nobody can be as agreeable as an uninvited guest.

2464   Nobody works as hard for his money as the man who marries it.

2465   No one can feel as helpless as the owner of a sick goldfish.

2466   The only way to entertain some folks is to listen to them.

2467   The reason the way of the transgressor is hard is because it's so crowded.

2468   The richer a relative is, the less he bothers you.

2469   Success may go to one's head but the stomach is where it gets in its worst work.

2470   A sympathizer is a fellow that's for you as long as it doesn't cost anything.

2471   There isn't much to be seen in a little town, but what you hear makes up for it.

2472   There's another advantage of being poor—a doctor will cure you faster.

2473   There seems to be an excess of everything except parking space and religion.

2474   When a fellow says, "It ain't the money but the principle of the thing," it's the money.

2475   When a woman says, "I don't wish to mention any names," it ain't necessary.

2476   Who recalls when folks got along without something if it cost too much?

2477   Why doesn't the fellow who says "I'm no speechmaker" let it go at that instead of giving a demonstration?

2478   The world gets better every day—then worse again in the evening.

2479   The worst feature of a new baby is its mother's singing.

2480   There's somebody at every dinner party who eats all the celery.

2481   The chronic grumbler is a church social compared to the fellow that agrees with everything you say.

2482   Th' feller that calls you "brother" generally wants something that don't belong to him.

2483   Don't a fellow feel good after he gets out of a store where he nearly bought something?

2484   Some fellows get credit for being conservative when they are only stupid.

2485   I haven't heard of anybody who wants to stop living on account of the cost.

2486   Some folks get credit for having horse sense that hain't ever had enough money to make fools of themselves.

2487   I don't think much of a dance step where the girl looks like she was being carried out of a burning building.

2488   Only one fellow in ten thousand understands the currency question, and we meet him every day.

2489   It's pretty hard to be efficient without being obnoxious.

2490   It's sweet to be remembered, but it's often cheaper to be forgotten.

2491   Folks that blurt out just what they think wouldn't be so bad if they thought.

2492   A real gentleman is at a big disadvantage these days.

2493   You won't skid if you stay in a rut.

2494   A diplomat is a fellow that lets you do all the talking while he gets what he wants.

2495   The reason parents no longer lead their children in the right direction is because the parents aren't going that way themselves.

2496   It seems like th' less a statesman amounts to th' more he loves th' flag.

2497   Now and then an innocent man is sent t' th' legislature.

2498   'Tain't what a man don't know that hurts him; it's what he knows that just ain't so.

2499   I think some folks are foolish to pay what it costs to live.

2500   Honesty pays, but it don't seem to pay enough to suit some people.

2501   Some folks can look so busy doing nothin' that they seem indispensable.

2502   Intelligent people are always on the unpopular side of anything.

2503   Nobody kicks on being interrupted if it's by applause.

2504   A woman would rather marry a poor provider any time than a poor listener.

2505   Next to a city the loneliest place in the world when you're broke is among relatives.

2506   It's the good loser that finally loses out.

2507   No self-made man ever did such a good job that some woman didn't want to make a few alterations.

2508   Married life ain't so bad after you get so you can eat the things your wife likes.

2509   The feller that puts off marryin' till he can support a wife ain't very much in love.

2510   It's going to be fun to watch and see how long the meek can keep the earth after they inherit it.

2511   The election isn't very far off when a candidate can recognize you across the street.

2512   Everything comes to him who waits except a loaned book.

2513   The fellow that brags about how cheap he heats his home always sees the first robin.

2514   The fellow that owns his own home is always just coming out of a hardware store.

2515   The fellow that tells a good story always has to listen to a couple of poor ones.

2516   The first thing to turn green in the spring is Christmas jewelry.

2517   Florida's all right if you can keep from catching a sailfish and going to the expense of having it mounted.

2518   Fun is like life insurance: the older you get, the more it costs.

2519   The hardest thing is writing a recommendation for someone we know.

2520   Very often the quiet fellow has said all he knows.

2521   The safest way to double your money is to fold it over once and put it in your pocket.

2522   The old-time mother who used to wonder where her boy was now has a grandson who wonders where his mother is.

2523   Where ignorance is bliss it's foolish to borrow your neighbor's newspaper.

2524   The worst sensation I know of is getting up at night and stepping on a toy train of cars.

2525   Being optimistic after you've got everything you want don't count.

2526   An optimist is always broke.

2527   An optimist is a fellow who believes what's going to be will be postponed.

2528   Peace has its victories no less than war, but it doesn't have as many monuments to unveil.

2529   It would be a swell world if everything was as pleasant as the fellow who's trying to skin you.

2530   Politics makes strange postmasters.

2531   Those who are in Albany escaped Sing Sing, and those who are in Sing Sing were on their way to Albany.

2532   There's some folks standing behind the President what ought to get around where he can watch 'em.

2533   Anybody that's got time to read half of the new books has got entirely too much time.

2534   Distant relatives are the best kind, and the further the better.

2535   The hardest thing is to disguise your feelings when you put a lot of relatives on the train for home.

2536   The worst jolt most of us ever get is when we fall back on our own resources.

2537   The rich man and his daughter are soon parted.

2538   It must be great to be rich and let the other fellow keep up appearances.

2539   We are all pretty much alike when we get out of town.

2540   Of all the substitutes, a substitute speaker is worst.

2541   Some men are born great, some achieve greatness and others just keep still.

2542   The hardest thing to stop is a temporary chairman.

2543   If at first you do succeed, don't take any more chances.

2544   Look out for the fellow who lets you do all the talking.

2545   A loafer always has the correct time.

2546   Of all the home remedies, a good wife is the best.

2547   Stew Nugent has decided to go to work till he can find something better.

2548   The fellow that says "I may be wrong, but—" does not believe there can be any such possibility.

2549   Gossip: vice enjoyed vicariously—the sweet, subtle satisfaction without the risk.

2550   Knowin' all about baseball is just about as profitable as bein' a good whittler.

2551   Lots of folks confuse bad management with destiny.

2552   Some people pay a compliment as if they expected a receipt.

Harold S. Hubert
2553   Children need love, especially when they do not deserve it.

Chief Justice Charles Evans Hughes
2554   The United States is the greatest law factory the world has ever known.

2555   There will always be a multitude who are congenitally unable to think straight.

J. B. Hughes
2556   If Moses had been a committee, the Israelites would still be in Egypt.

Rupert Hughes
2557   Love is a wonderful thing and highly desirable in marriage.

Thomas Hughes
2558   Life isn't all beer and skittles.

Victor Hugo
2559   Everything bows to success, even grammar.

2560   Melancholy is the pleasure of being sad.

2561   When a woman is speaking to you, listen to what she says with her eyes.

2562   A compliment is something like a kiss through a veil.

2563   Paris is nothing but an immense hospitality.

Cordell Hull
2564   Never insult an alligator until you've crossed the river.

Josephine Hull
2565   Playing Shakespeare is very tiring. You never get to sit down unless you're a king.

David Hume
2566   Avarice, the spur of industry.

George Humphrey
2567   It's a terribly hard job to spend a billion dollars and get your money's worth.

2568   I don't think you can spend yourself rich. [On spending during business declines.]

2569   You can't set a hen in one morning and have chicken salad for lunch.

2570   Balancing this budget is not simply a bookkeeping exercise or a businessman's fetish. It is the very keystone of financial responsibility.

Hubert Humphrey

2571   If you can't cry a little bit in politics, the only other thing you'll have is hate.

James Gibbons Huneker

2572   A critic is a man who expects miracles.

2573   Berlioz says nothing in his music, but he says it magnificently.

2574   Lawyers earn a living by the sweat of their browbeating.

2575   My corns ache, I get gouty and my prejudices swell like varicose veins.

G. W. Hunt

2576   We don't want to fight, but, by jingo, if we do,
        We've got the ships, we've got the men, we've got the money, too.

Nelson Bunker Hunt

2577   A billion dollars isn't what it used to be.

Jack Hurley

2578   Every young man should have a hobby. Learning how to handle money is the best one.

Fannie Hurst

2579   I'm not happy when I'm writing, but I'm more unhappy when I'm not.

Kenneth Hutchins

2580   He may be wrong, he probably is, but why do you have to tell him? The trouble is that men like to think they know best. Why not let him think it? It is not a very high price to pay for peace and security and good health.

Robert M. Hutchins

2581   The death of democracy is not as likely to be assassination from ambush. It will be a slow extinction from apathy, indifference and undernourishment.

2582   The college graduate is presented with a sheepskin to cover his intellectual nakedness.

2583   Whenever I feel like exercise, I lie down until the feeling passes.

2584   Whether four years of strenuous attention to football and fraternities is the best preparation for professional work has never been seriously investigated.

2585   It has been said that we have not had the three R's in America, we had the six R's: remedial readin', remedial 'ritin', and remedial 'rithmetic.

2586   The university exists only to find and to communicate the truth.

2587   The object of education is to prepare the young to educate themselves throughout their lives.

2588   My idea of education is to unsettle the minds of the young and inflame their intellects.

2589   There's no reason why the University [of Chicago] should be stuck with me at fifty-one because I was a promising young man at thirty.

2590   More free time means more time to waste. The worker who used to have only a little time in which to get drunk and beat his wife now has time to get drunk, beat his wife—and watch TV.

Robert Hutchinson

2591   Vegetarianism is harmless enough, although it is apt to fill a man with wind and self-righteousness.

Barbara Hutton

2592   Money alone can't bring you happiness, but money alone has not brought me unhappiness. I won't say my previous husbands thought only of my money, but it had a certain fascination for them.

Aldous Huxley

2593   Idealism is the noble toga that political gentlemen drape over their will to power.

2594   That men do not learn very much from the lessons of history is the most important of all the lessons that history has to teach.

2595   To his dog, every man is Napoleon; hence the constant popularity of dogs.

2596   We are all geniuses up to the age of ten.

2597   Experience is not what happens to a man; it is what a man does with what happens to him.

2598   Every man who knows how to read has it in his power to magnify himself, to multiply the ways in which he exists, to make his life full, significant and interesting.

2599   The only completely consistent people are the dead.

2600   Facts do not cease to exist because they are ignored.

2601   Like every man of sense and good feeling, I abominate work.

2602   Technological progress has merely provided us with more efficient means for going backward.

2603   The silent bear no witness against themselves.

Thomas Henry Huxley

2604   If a little knowledge is dangerous, where is the man who has so much as to be out of danger?

2605   The great end of life is not knowledge but action.

Socrates Hyacinth

2606   Texas is one great, windy lunatic.

Lee Iacocca

2607   We at Chrysler borrow money the old-fashioned way. We pay it back.

Henrik Ibsen

2608   It is inexcusable for scientists to torture animals; let them make their experiment on journalists and politicians.

2609   Oh, we all get run over—once in our lives. But one must pick oneself up again. And behave as if it was nothing.

2610   Money may be the husk of many things, but not the kernel. It brings you food, but not appetite; medicine, but not health; acquaintances, but not friends; servants, but not loyalty; days of joy, but not peace or happiness.

Harold Ickes

2611   A simple, barefoot Wall Street lawyer. [On Wendell Willkie.]

2612   Show me the man who insists that he welcomes criticism if only it is "constructive," and I will show you a man who does not want any criticism at all.

J. J. Ingalls
2613   Delaware: a state that has three counties when the tide is out, and two when it is in.

The Reverend Charles Inge
2614   A certain young gourmet of Crediton
Took some pâté de foie gras and spread it on
A chocolate biscuit,
Then murmured, "I'll risk it."
His tomb bears the date that he said it on.

William R. Inge
2615   A good government remains the greatest of human blessings and no nation has ever enjoyed it.

2616   In dealing with Englishmen you can be sure of one thing only, that the logical solution will not be adopted.

2617   It is useless for the sheep to pass resolutions in favor of vegetarianism while the wolf remains of a different opinion.

2618   Originality is undetected plagiarism.

2619   Literature flourishes best when it is half a trade and half an art.

2620   Worry is interest paid on trouble before it falls due.

2621   A man may build himself a throne of bayonets, but he cannot sit on it.

2622   There are two kinds of fools: one says, "This is old, therefore it is good"; the other says, "This is new, therefore it is better."

2623   It is becoming impossible for those who mix with their fellowmen to believe that the grace of God is distributed denominationally.

2624   Gambling: a disease of barbarians superficially civilized.

2625   History may be divided into events which do not matter and events which probably never occurred.

2626   I have never understood why it should be considered derogatory to the Creator to suppose that He has a sense of humor.

2627   To marry is to get a binocular view of life.

2628   Patriotism varies, from a noble devotion to a moral lunacy.

2629   The whole of nature is a conjugation of the verb eat, in the active and passive.

2630   It was said that Mr. Gladstone could persuade most people of most things, and himself of anything.

Robert G. Ingersoll
2631   Few rich men own their property. Their property owns them.

2632   In the republic of mediocrity, genius is dangerous.

2633   Hope is the only universal liar who never loses his reputation for veracity.

2634   A mule has neither pride of ancestry nor hope of posterity.

Washington Irving
2635   The Almighty Dollar, that great object of universal devotion throughout the land.

2636   I am always at a loss to know how much to believe of my own stories.

Christopher Isherwood
2637   Life is not so bad, if you have plenty of luck, a good physique and not too much imagination.

José Iturbi
2638   The only time you realize you have a reputation is when you're not living up to it.

Andrew Jackson
2639   There goes a man made by the Lord Almighty and not by his tailor. [On Sam Houston.]

2640   Private life would be a paradise compared to the best situation here; and if once more there, it would take a writ of habeas corpus to remove me into public life again. [On Washington, D.C.]

Holbrook Jackson
2641   As soon as an idea is accepted it is time to reject it.

2642   Be contented, when you have got all you want.

2643   Man is the only animal that can be a fool.

2644   Only the rich preach content to the poor.

2645   Suffer fools gladly; they may be right.

2646   Intuition is reason in a hurry.

2647   The poor are the only consistent altruists. They sell all that they have and give to the rich.

2648   As soon as a nation becomes civilized it dies; yet man has but one idea—to become civilized. Thus he assists nature to correct her errors.

2649   In democracies, those who lead follow; those who follow lead.

2650   Love is the most subtle form of self-interest.

M. Walthall Jackson
2651   One reassuring thing about modern art is that things can't be as bad as they are painted.

Justice Robert Jackson
2652   The price of freedom of religion or of speech or of the press is that we must put up with, and even pay for, a good deal of rubbish.

Robert H. Jackson
2653   Perhaps you have heard about the college executives who were discussing what they wanted to do after retirement age. One hoped to run a prison or school of correction so the alumni would never come back to visit. Another chose to manage an orphan asylum so he would not be plagued with advice from parents.

Henry Jacobsen
2654   Humility is the ability to see ourselves as God describes us.

Jens Peter Jacobsen
2655   It requires so infinitely much tact to handle enthusiasm.

M. W. Jacobus
2656   A Christian is like a locomotive; a fire must be kindled in the heart of the thing before it will go.

James I of Great Britain
2657   I can make a lord, but only God Almighty can make a gentleman.

Henry James
2658   Life is a predicament which precedes death.

William James

2659   Man, biologically considered, . . . is the most formidable of all the beasts of prey, and, indeed, the only one that preys systematically on its own species.

2660   A great many people think they are thinking when they are merely rearranging their prejudices.

2661   When you have to make a choice and don't make it, that is in itself a choice.

2662   The ideas gained by men before they are twenty-five are practically the only ideas they shall have in their lives.

2663   The deepest principle of Human Nature is the craving to be appreciated.

2664   First a new theory is attacked as absurd; then it is admitted to be true, but obvious and insignificant; finally it is seen to be so important that its adversaries claim that they themselves discovered it.

2665   There is only one thing that a philosopher can be relied on to do, and that is to contradict other philosophers.

2666   Publishers are demons, there's no doubt about it.

Anna Jameson

2667   What we earnestly aspire to be, that in some sense we are.

Dr. Joseph Jastrow

2668   The psychologist has been slanderously defined as a man who tells you what everybody knows in language nobody can understand.

Thomas Jefferson

2669   I do not take a single newspaper, nor read one a month, and I feel myself infinitely the happier for it.

2670   It is the trade of lawyers to question everything, yield nothing, and to talk by the hour.

2671   Advertisements contain the only truths to be relied on in a newspaper.

2672   He hunts one half of the day, is drunk the other, and signs whatever he is bid. [On a French ruler.]

2673   It will give me philosophical evenings in the winter, and rural days in summer. [On the vice-presidency.]

2674   Perhaps an editor might divide his paper into four chapters, heading the first, Truths; 2nd, Probabilities, 3d, Possibilities; 4th, Lies.

2675   Politeness is artificial good humor, and a valuable preservative of peace and tranquillity.

2676   The nest of office being too small for all of them to cuddle into at once, the contest is eternal which shall crowd the other out. For this purpose, they are divided into two parties, the Ins and the Outs.

2677   If a nation expects to be ignorant and free, in a state of civilization, it expects what never was and never will be.

2678   I sincerely believe that banking establishments are more dangerous than standing armies, and that the principle of spending money to be paid by posterity, under the name of funding, is but swindling futurity on a large scale.

2679   When he was seventy-six, Jefferson remarked that he had "organs of digestion which accept and concoct, without ever murmuring, whatever the palate chooses to consign to them."

2680   Amplification is the vice of modern oratory. It is an insult to an assembly of reasonable men, disgusting and revolting instead of persuading. Speeches measured by the hour die by the hour.

2681   The natural progress of things is for liberty to yield and government to gain ground.

2682   No man will ever bring out of the Presidency the reputation which carries him into it.

2683   Eternal vigilance is the price of liberty.

2684   Resort is had to ridicule only when reason is against us.

2685   It accorded well with two favorite ideas of mine, of leaving commerce free, and never keeping an unnecessary soldier.

2686   The merchants will manage commerce the better, the more they are left free to manage for themselves.

2687   That one hundred and fifty lawyers should do business together ought not to be expected. [On the U.S. Congress.]

2688   The most valuable of all talents is that of never using two words when one will do.

J. Jenkins

2689   To err is human, but when the eraser wears out ahead of the pencil, you're overdoing it.

Llewellyn Jenkins

2690   Banks do not raise or lower interest rates depending upon how they feel about it. A bank buys money like a grocer buys bananas—and then adds on salaries and rent and sells the product.

Keith Jennison

2691   Us country women make good wives. No matter what happens we've seen worse.

Jerome K. Jerome

2692   I like work; it fascinates me; I can sit and look at it for hours. I love to keep it by me; the idea of getting rid of it nearly breaks my heart.

2693   It is always the best policy to speak the truth, unless of course you are an exceptionally good liar.

2694   It is impossible to enjoy idling thoroughly unless one has plenty of work to do.

2695   One of the advantages of being poor is that it necessitates the cultivation of the virtues.

Douglas Jerrold

2696   He was so benevolent, so merciful a man that he would have held an umbrella over a duck in a shower of rain.

2697   In this world, truth can wait; she's used to it.

2698   Dogmatism is puppyism come to its full growth.

2699   God said, "Let us make man in our image"; and Man said, "Let us make God in our image."

2700   They say love's like the measles—all the worse when it comes late in life.

2701   Readers are of two sorts: one who carefully goes through a book, and the other who as carefully lets the book go through him.

2702   The only athletic sport I ever mastered was backgammon.

2703   Wishes are the easy pleasures of the poor.

George Jessel

2704   If you haven't struck oil in your first three minutes, stop boring!

Dr. C.E.M. Joad

2705   It has been left to our generation to discover that you can move heaven and earth to save five minutes and then not have the faintest idea what to do with them when you have saved them.

Pope John XXIII

2706   Italians come to ruin most generally in three ways—women, gambling and farming. My family chose the slowest one.

2707   When I eat alone I feel like a seminarian being punished. I tried it for one week and I was not comfortable. Then I searched through Sacred Scripture for something saying I had to eat alone. I found nothing, so I gave it up and it's much better now.

2708   Here I am at the end of the road and at the top of the heap.

2709   It often happens that I wake at night and begin to think about a serious problem and decide I must tell the Pope about it. Then I wake up completely and remember that I am the Pope.

Hiram Johnson

2710   The first casualty when war comes is truth.

General Hugh S. Johnson

2711   The nearest thing to immortality in this world is a government bureau.

Lyndon B. Johnson

2712   They ain't like the folk you were reared with. [About foreigners.]

2713   I wish I could be like an animal in the forest—go to sleep under a tree, eat when I feel like it, read a bit and after a while, do whatever I want to do.

2714   Why should I listen to all those student peaceniks marching up and down the streets? They wouldn't know a Communist if they tripped over one. They simply don't understand the world the way I do.

2715   Never trust a man whose eyes are too close to his nose.

2716   You ain't learnin' nothin' when you're talkin'.

2717   I don't have any handicap. I'm all handicap. [On golf.]

2718   The best fertilizer for a piece of land is the footprints of its owner.

2719   When you crawl out on a limb, you always have to find another one to crawl back on.

2720   The Vice Presidency is a good place for a young man who needs experience.

2721   You take the Panhandle, for instance. We get hail there the size of a basketball, and the snow piles up so deep the people have to follow the jackrabbit tunnels out when the spring comes.

2722   I seldom think of politics more than eighteen hours a day.

2723   At the card game one of the boys looked across the table and said: "Now, Reuben, play the cards fair. I know what I dealt you."

2724   A town that can't support one lawyer can always support two.

2725   In 1790, the nation which had fought a revolution against taxation without representation discovered that some of its citizens weren't much happier about taxation with representation.

2726   The Secretary of Labor is in charge of finding you a job, the Secretary of the Treasury is in charge of taking half the money you make away from you, and the Attorney General is in charge of suing you for the other half.

2727   My White House job pays more than public school systems but the tenure is less certain.

2728   An hour late and a dollar short, that's the way I've been all my life.

2729   We haven't done anything for business this week—but it is only Monday morning.

Nunnally Johnson
2730   He gradually wormed his way out of my confidence.

Philander Chase Johnson
2731   Cheer up, the worst is yet to come.

Samuel Johnson
2732   A cucumber should be well-sliced, dressed with pepper and vinegar, and then thrown out.

2733   Patriotism is the last refuge of a scoundrel.

2734   Adversity is the state in which a man most easily becomes acquainted with himself, being especially free from admirers then.

2735   A fishing rod is a stick with a hook at one end and a fool at the other.

2736   Sir, he was dull in company, dull in his closet, dull everywhere. He was dull in a new way, and that made many think him great.

2737   I hate mankind, for I think myself one of the best of them, and I know how bad I am.

2738   The Irish are a fair people; they never speak well of one another.

2739   Marriage has many pains, but celibacy has no pleasures.

2740   Admiration begins where acquaintance ceases.

2741   No man but a blockhead ever wrote except for money.

2742   Of all noises, I think music is the least disagreeable.

2743   Second marriage: the triumph of hope over experience.

2744   That fellow seems to me to possess but one idea, and that a wrong
one.

2745   Treating your adversary with respect is giving him an advantage
to which he is not entitled.

2746   We are inclined to believe those whom we do not know because
they have never deceived us.

2747   When two Englishmen meet, their first talk is of the weather.

2748   You raise your voice when you should reinforce your argument.

2749   Your manuscript is both good and original; but the part that is
good is not original, and the part that is original is not good.

2750   Man is seldom so harmlessly occupied as when he is making
money.

2751   He talks like a watch which ticks away minutes, but never strikes
the hour.

2752   Much may be made of a Scotchman, if he be caught young.

2753   I am willing to love all mankind, except an American.

2754   Whoever thinks of going to bed before twelve o'clock is a scoundrel.

2755   As peace is the end of war, so to be idle is the ultimate purpose of
the busy.

2756   If he does really think that there is no distinction between vice
and virtue, when he leaves our houses let us count our spoons.

2757   Campbell is a good man, a pious man. I am afraid he has not been
in the inside of a church for many years, but he never passes a church
without pulling off his hat. This shows that he has good principles.

2758   A man seldom thinks with more earnestness of anything than he
does of his dinner.

2759   [Thomas Sheridan] is dull, naturally dull; but it must have taken
him a great deal of pains to become what we now see him. Such excess of
stupidity, sir, is not in Nature.

SAMUEL JOHNSON

2760   A continual feast of commendation is only to be attained by merit or by wealth.

2761   No man practices so well as he writes. I have, all my life long, been lying till noon; yet I tell all young men, and tell them with great sincerity, that nobody who does not rise early will ever do any good.

2762   Nothing flatters a man as much as the happiness of his wife; he is always proud of himself as the source of it.

2763   To a lady who asked Johnson how he came to define pastern as the knee of a horse in his dictionary: "Ignorance, madam, pure ignorance."

2764   A man who has not been to Italy is always conscious of his inferiority.

2765   Surely life, if it be not long, is tedious, since we are forced to call in the assistance of so many trifles to rid us of our time.

2766   Sir, when a man is tired of London, he is tired of life; for there is in London all that life can afford.

2767   Oats: a grain, which in England is generally given to horses, but in Scotland supports the people.

2768   But man is not born for happiness.

2769   A small country town is not the place in which one would choose to quarrel.

2770   No man likes to live under the eye of perpetual disapprobation.

2771   A man may be so much of everything that he is nothing of anything.

2772   Criticism is a study by which men grow important and formidable at very small expense.

2773   Your levellers wish to level down as far as themselves, but they cannot bear levelling up to themselves.

2774   Justice is my being allowed to do whatever I like. Injustice is whatever prevents my doing so.

2775   You never find people laboring to convince you that you may live very happily upon a plentiful income.

2776   One of the disadvantages of wine is that it makes a man mistake words for thoughts.

2777   Read over your compositions and, when you meet a passage which you think is particularly fine, strike it out.

2778   People in general do not willingly read, if they can have anything else to amuse them.

2779   A wicked fellow is the most pious when he takes to it. He'll beat you all in piety.

2780   When speculation has done its worst, two and two still make four.

2781   No man will be a sailor who has contrivance enough to get himself into a jail; for being in a ship is being in a jail, with the chance of being drowned. A man in a jail has more room, better food and commonly better company.

2782   The noblest prospects which a Scotchman ever sees is the highroad that leads him to England.

2783   Towering in the confidence of twenty-one.

2784   There are, in every age, new errors to be rectified, and new prejudices to be opposed.

2785   Wine makes a man better pleased with himself; I do not say that it makes him more pleasing to others.

2786   What would you give, old gentleman, to be as young and sprightly as I am?
        Why, sir, I think I would almost be content to be as foolish.

2787   No man forgets his original trade; the rights of nations, and of kings, sink into questions of grammar, if grammarians discuss them.

2788   If the man who turnips cries,
        Cry not when his father dies,
        'Tis a proof that he had rather
        Have a turnip than his father.

2789   That observation which is called knowledge of the world will be found much more frequently to make men cunning than good.

2790   The true art of memory is the art of attention.

2791   Hope is itself a species of happiness, and, perhaps, the chief happiness which this world affords.

2792   Every man is of importance to himself.

2793   The applause of a single human being is of great consequence.

2794   What is easy is seldom excellent.

2795   It is better to live rich, than to die rich.

2796   Whatever you have, spend less.

2797   I do not say it is wrong to produce self-complacency by drinking; I only deny that it improves the mind.

2798   The writer of an epitaph should not be considered as saying nothing but what is strictly true. Allowance must be made for some degree of exaggerated praise. In lapidary inscriptions a man is not upon oath.

2799   Nothing will ever be attempted if all possible objections must be first overcome.

Eric Johnston

2800   The dinosaur's eloquent lesson is that if some bigness is good, an overabundance of bigness is not necessarily better.

2801   A statesman is a politician who is held upright by equal pressure from all directions.

Franklin P. Jones

2802   Honest criticism is hard to take, particularly from a relative, a friend, an acquaintance, or a stranger.

2803   An extravagance is anything you buy that is of no earthly use to your wife.

2804   Bargain: something you can't use at a price you can't resist.

2805   You can learn many things from children. How much patience you have, for instance.

2806   Love doesn't make the world go 'round. Love is what makes the ride worthwhile.

2807   Nothing makes you more tolerant of a neighbor's noisy party than being there.

2808   The trouble with being punctual is that nobody's there to appreciate it.

2809   Originality is the art of concealing your source.

2810   What makes resisting temptation difficult, for many people, is that they don't want to discourage it completely.

2811   Not everyone repeats gossip. Some improve it.

2812   Nothing makes a child as smart as having grandparents.

2813   And then there was the chap who meant to procrastinate someday, but kept putting it off.

2814   Don't be afraid to talk to yourself. It's the only way you can be sure somebody's listening.

2815   Conversation is the art of telling people a little less than they want to know.

Frederick Scheetz Jones

2816   Here's to the town of New Haven,
        The Home of the Truth and the Light,
        Where God talks to Jones in the very same tones
        That he uses with Hadley and Dwight. [About Yale University.]

Henry Arthur Jones

2817   If there is one beast in all the loathsome fauna of civilization I hate and despite, it is a man of the world.

Jenkin Lloyd Jones

2818   A speech is a solemn responsibility. The man who makes a bad thirty-minute speech to two hundred people wastes only a half hour of his own time. But he wastes one hundred hours of the audience's time— more than four days—which should be a hanging offense.

Leroi Jones

2819   A rich man told me recently that a liberal is a man who tells other people what to do with their money.

Dr. Thomas Jones

2820   Friends may come and go, but enemies accumulate.

T. S. Jones, Jr.

2821   Across the fields of yesterday
            He sometimes comes to me,
        A little lad just back from play—
            The lad I used to be.

Ben Jonson

2822   Talking is the disease of age.

2823   They say princes learn no art truly but the art of horsemanship. The reason is, the brave beast is no flatterer. He will throw a prince as soon as his groom.

2824   He was not of an age, but for all time!

Joseph II of Austria

2825   Russia: a colossus of brass on a pedestal of clay.

Joseph Joubert

2826   Children have more need of models than of critics.

2827   One of the bad things about our literature is that our scholars have little wit and our men of wit are not scholars.

2828   To mediocre people, the mediocre is the excellent.

2829   He who has imagination without learning has wings and no feet.

2830   Statesmanship is the art of understanding and leading the masses, or the majority. Its glory is to lead them, not where they want to go, but where they ought to go.

Benjamin Jowett

2831   Even the youngest among us is not infallible.

2832   The time he can spare from the adornment of his person he devotes to the neglect of his duties.

2833   It is most important in this world to be pushing, but it is fatal to seem so.

John A. Joyce

2834   There's No Pocket in a Shroud.

Peggy Joyce

2835   It takes all the fun out of a bracelet if you have to buy it yourself.

P. W. Joyce

2836   An Irishman, before answering a question, always asks another.

Carl Jung

2837   I could not say I believe. I know! I have had the experience of being gripped by something that is stronger than myself, something that people call God.

Juvenal

2838   We all live in a state of ambitious poverty.

Franz Kafka

2839   In the fight between you and the world, back the world.

Henry Kaiser

2840   I always view problems as opportunities in work clothes.

Harry Karrs

2841   Sooner or later, a grandparent begins to wonder why babies are entrusted to young people.

Lionel M. Kauffman

2842   Children are a great comfort in your old age—and they help you to reach it faster, too.

R. W. Kauffman

2843   Nobody enjoys a wedding but the mother of the bride; she enjoys a good cry.

George S. Kaufman

2844   Things are so bad on Broadway today an actor is lucky to be miscast.

Kenneth B. Keating

2845   Too often our Washington reflex is to discover a problem and then throw money at it, hoping it will somehow go away.

Irene Keepin

2846   A friend is a person who does his knocking before he enters instead of after he leaves.

Emery Kelen

2847   The press conference is the politician's way of being informative without actually saying anything.

Clarence Buddington Kelland

2848   The obvious duty of a toastmaster is to be so infernally dull that the succeeding speakers will appear brilliant by contrast.

Helen Keller

2849   I can see, and that is why I can be so happy, in what you call the dark, but which to me is golden. I can see a God-made world, not a man-made world.

2850   It is a moment I shall never forget. I was alone and unable to communicate with anyone. I did not know the names of anything. I did not even know things had names. Then one day, after she had tried a number of approaches, my teacher held my hand under the water pump on our farm. As the cool water ran over my hand, and arm, she spelled the word water into my other hand. She spelled it over and over, and suddenly, I knew there was a name for things and that I would never be completely alone again.

James Kelly

2851   A tale never loses in the telling.

2852   He that forecasts all difficulties that he may meet with in business, will never set about it.

Jacqueline Kennedy

2853   I felt like a moth hanging on the windowpane. [On her first night in the White House.]

2854   The shades you pull down at night—they are enormous and they have pulleys and ropes. You're like a sailor taking in a sail. I'm afraid it will always be a little impossible for the people who live there. It's an office building. [On the White House.]

John F. Kennedy

2855   Sure, it's a big job—but I don't know anyone who can do it better than I can.

2856   Kissing babies gives me asthma.

2857   Forgive your enemies, but never forget their names.

2858   I know that when things don't go well they like to blame the Presidents, and that is one of the things which Presidents are paid for.

2859   The day before my inauguration President Eisenhower told me, "You'll find that no easy problems ever come to the President of the United States. If they are easy to solve, somebody else has solved them." I found that hard to believe, but now I know it is true.

2860   I am deeply touched—not as deeply touched as you have been by coming to this dinner, but nevertheless, it is a sentimental occasion. [Raising funds.]

2861   I appreciate your welcome. As the cow said to the Maine farmer, "Thank you for a warm hand on a cold morning."

2862   It was absolutely involuntary. They sank my boat. [On why he was a war hero.]

2863   Washington is a city of Southern efficiency and Northern charm.

2864   There is no city in the United States in which I get a warmer welcome and less votes than Columbus, Ohio.

2865   I think this is the most extraordinary collection of talent, of human knowledge, that has ever been gathered together at the White House—with the possible exception of when Thomas Jefferson dined alone. [At a dinner honoring Nobel Prize winners.]

2866   Those of you who regard my profession of political life with some disdain should remember that it made it possible for me to move from being an obscure lieutenant in the United States Navy to Commander-in-Chief in fourteen years with very little technical competence.

2867   My experience in government is that when things are noncontroversial, beautifully coordinated and all the rest, it must be that there is not much going on.

2868   I do not think it altogether inappropriate to introduce myself to this audience. I am the man who accompanied Jacqueline Kennedy to Paris, and I have enjoyed it.

2869   A child miseducated is a child lost.

2870   Will Rogers once said it is not the original investment in a Congressman that counts; it is the upkeep.

2871   I understand nearby there was a farmer who planted some corn. He said to his neighbor, "I hope I break even this year. I really need the money."

2872   I have just received the following telegram from my generous Daddy. It says, "Dear Jack: Don't buy a single vote more than is necessary. I'll be damned if I'm going to pay for a landslide."

2873   I have the best of both worlds. A Harvard education and a Yale degree. [After receiving an honorary Yale degree.]

2874   You will recall what Senator Dirksen said about the rocking chair —it gives you a sense of motion without any sense of danger.

Joseph P. Kennedy

2875   Whenever you're sitting across from some important person, always picture him sitting there in a suit of long red underwear. That's the way I always operated in business.

2876   Don't get mad, get even.

Robert Kennedy

2877   I am not one of those who think that coming in second or third is winning.

2878   One fifth of the people are against everything all the time.

2879   Only those who dare to fail greatly can ever achieve greatly.

Rose Kennedy

2880   I have always believed that God never gives a cross to bear larger than we can carry. No matter what, he wants us to be happy, not sad. Birds sing after a storm. Why shouldn't we?

Joseph O. Kern II

2881   Obesity is really widespread.

F. G. Kernan

2882   Tact: ability to tell the man he's open-minded when he has a hole in his head.

Clark Kerr

2883   A university anywhere can aim no higher than to be as British as possible for the sake of the undergraduates, as German as possible for the sake of the public at large—and as confused as possible for the preservation of the whole uneasy balance.

Jean Kerr

2884   Hope is the feeling you have that the feeling you have isn't permanent.

2885   I'm tired of all this nonsense about beauty being only skin-deep. That's deep enough. What do you want—an adorable pancreas?

2886   If you can keep your head when all about you are losing theirs, it's just possible you haven't grasped the situation.

2887   You don't seem to realize that a poor person who is unhappy is in a better position than a rich person who is unhappy, because the poor person has hope. He thinks money would help.

Charles Franklin Kettering

2888   My interest is in the future because I am going to spend the rest of my life there.

2889   If you want to kill any idea in the world today, get a committee working on it.

2890   You can be sincere and still be stupid.

2891   We need to teach the highly educated person that it is not a disgrace to fail and that he must analyze every failure to find its cause. He must learn how to fail intelligently, for failing is one of the greatest arts in the world.

2892   The world hates change; yet it is the only thing that has brought progress.

John Maynard Keynes

2893   In the long run we are all dead.

2894   He had only one illusion—France—and only one disillusion—mankind. [On Georges Clemenceau.]

Ayatollah Khomeini

2895   I know that during my long life I have always been right about what I said.

Nikita Khrushchev

2896   Politicians are the same all over. They promise to build a bridge even where there is no river.

2897   If someone hits me on the left cheek, I would not turn my own. I would hit him on the right cheek, and so hard that it would knock his head off.

2898   If you live amongst wolves, you have to act like a wolf.

2899   I don't like the life here in New York. There is no greenery. It would make a stone sick.

2900   The Communist system must be based on the will of the people, and if the people should not want that system, then that people should establish a different system.

2901   Economics is a subject that does not greatly respect one's wishes.

John Kieran

2902   I am a part of all that I have read.

Sören Aabye Kierkegaard

2903   Life can only be understood backwards, but it must be lived forwards.

Ben King

2904   Nothing to do but work,
           Nothing to eat but food,
       Nothing to wear but clothes,
           To keep one from going nude.

       Nothing to breathe but air,
           Quick as a flash 'tis gone;
       Nothing to fall but off,
           Nowhere to stand but on.

Doris King

2905   Isn't Beverly Sills a suburb of Los Angeles?

Charles Kingsley

2906   It's all in the day's work, as the huntsman said when the lion ate him.

Rudyard Kipling

2907   Father, Mother and Me,
Sister and Auntie say
All the people like us are We,
And every one else is They.

2908   I've taken my fun where I've found it;
    I've rogued an' I've ranged in my time;
I've 'ad my pickin' o' sweethearts,
    An' four o' the lot was prime.

2909   I keep six honest serving men
    (They taught me all I know):
Their names are What and Why and When
And How and Where and Who.

2910   There was a small boy of Quebec
Who was buried in snow to the neck;
    When they said, "Are you friz?"
    He replied, "Yes, I is—
But we don't call this cold in Quebec."

2911   Gardens are not made by singing "Oh, how beautiful," and sitting in the shade.

2912   Youth had been a habit of hers for so long that she could not part with it.

2913   I never made a mistake in my life; at least, never one that I couldn't explain away afterwards.

2914   The silliest woman can manage a clever man, but it needs a very clever woman to manage a fool.

2915   When 'Omer smote 'is bloomin' lyre,
He'd 'eard men sing by land an' sea;
An' what he thought 'e might require,
'E went an' took—the same as me!

2916   Politicians: Little Tin Gods on wheels.

Lisa Kirk

2917   A gossip is one who talks to you about others; a bore is one who talks to you about himself; and a brilliant conversationalist is one who talks to you about yourself.

Lane Kirkland

2918   If hard work were such a wonderful thing, surely the rich would have kept it all to themselves.

Henry Kissinger

2919 The illegal we do immediately, the unconstitutional takes a little longer.

2920 I think it fair to say that my own estimate of myself may be at variance with that of some of my critics.

2921 There cannot be a crisis next week—my schedule is already full.

2922 I've always acted alone. Americans admire that enormously. Americans admire the cowboy leading the caravan alone on his horse, the cowboy entering a village or city alone on his horse.

2923 Now when I bore people at a party they think it's their fault.

2924 Seen one president, you've seen them all.

2925 Power is the ultimate aphrodisiac.

C.H.B. Kitchin

2926 One of the penalties of wealth, Sergeant, is that the older you grow, the more people there are in the world who would rather have you dead than alive.

Fletcher Knebel

2927 The Supreme Court has handed down the Eleventh Commandment: "Thou shalt not, in thy classrooms, read the first ten."

2928 No other city in the United States can divest the visitor of so much money with so little enthusiasm. In Dallas, they take it away with gusto; in New Orleans, with a bow; in San Francisco, with a wink and a grin. In New York, you're lucky if you get a grunt.

William S. Knudsen

2929 Everybody wants to go from A to B sitting down.

Paul de Kock

2930 At eighteen, one adores at once; at twenty, one loves; at thirty, one desires; at forty, one reflects.

Arthur Koestler

2931 The principal mark of genius is not perfection but originality, the opening of new frontiers.

Will Kommen

2932 If you look like your passport photo, you're too ill to travel.

Ted Koppel

2933   Consider this paradox: Almost everything that is publicly said these days is recorded. Almost nothing of what is said is worth remembering.

Alfred Korzybski

2934   God may forgive you your sins, but your nervous system won't.

Karl Kraus

2935   Diagnosis is one of the commonest diseases.

2936   Psychoanalysis is the disease it purports to cure.

Irving Kristol

2937   Wage and price controls are a military solution to an economic problem.

Ray A. Kroc

2938   It's a matter of having principles. It's easy to have principles when you're rich. The important thing is to have principles when you're poor.

2939   We work on the KISS systems. KISS is short for "Keep It Simple, Stupid."

Louis Kronenberger

2940   The trouble with our age is all signposts and no destination.

Joseph Wood Krutch

2941   Logic is the art of going wrong with confidence.

Sir Henry Labouchère

2942   I don't object to Gladstone always having the ace of trumps up his sleeve, but merely to his belief that God Almighty put it there.

Jean de La Bruyère

2943   The best way to get on in the world is to make people believe it's to their advantage to help you.

2944   The duty of a judge is to administer justice, but his practice is to delay it.

2945   It is a great misfortune neither to have enough wit to talk well nor enough judgment to be silent.

2946   There are no ugly women; there are only women who do not know how to look pretty.

2947   There are only two ways of getting on in the world: by one's own industry, or by the stupidity of others.

2948   A fool is one whom bigger fools believe to be a man of merit.

2949   Man does not live long enough to be benefited by his faults; he is committing them during the whole course of his life, and it is as much as he can do, if after many errors he dies at last improved.

2950   All men's misfortunes proceed from their aversion to being alone; hence gambling, extravagance, dissipation, wine, women, ignorance, slander, envy and forgetfulness of what we owe to God and ourselves.

Jean de La Fontaine
2951   This beast is very wicked; when it is attacked, it defends itself.

2952   What is called discretion in men is called cunning in animals.

2953   He knows the universe but not himself.

Fiorello La Guardia
2954   I invented the low blow.

2955   Statistics are like alienists—they will testify for either side.

2956   When I make a mistake it's a beaut! [Comment on an indefensible appointment.]

R. D. Laing
2957   Insanity—a perfectly rational adjustment to an insane world.

S. Lall
2958   When you live on the banks of the River Pudma, you must make friends with the crocodile.

Thomas Lamance
2959   Many of us don't know what poor losers we are until we try dieting.

Hedy Lamarr
2960   Any girl can be glamorous. All you have to do is stand still and look stupid.

Charles Lamb
2961   Borrowers of books—those mutilators of collections, spoilers of the symmetry of shelves, and creators of odd volumes.

2962   He is no lawyer who cannot take two sides.

2963   The human species is composed of two distinct races; the men who borrow, and the men who lend.

2964   Satire does not look pretty upon a tombstone.

2965   New Year's Day is every man's birthday.

2966   Charles Lamb, when a little boy, walking in a churchyard with his sister and reading the epitaphs, said to her, "Mary, where are all the naughty people buried?"

2967   There is nothing so nice as doing good by stealth and being found out by accident.

2968   My theory is to enjoy life, but the practice is against it.

2969   Nothing puzzles me more than time and space, and yet nothing puzzles me less, for I never think about them.

2970   We read to say that we have read.

2971   I have been trying all my life to like Scotchmen, and am obliged to desist from the experiment in despair.

2972   In everything that relates to science, I am a whole encyclopedia behind the rest of the world.

2973   The vices of some men are magnificent.

Edwin H. Land
2974   The bottom line is in heaven.

Melville D. Landon
2975   A bore is a man who spends so much time talking about himself that you can't talk about yourself.

2976   Levity is the soul of wit.

Walter Savage Landor
2977   Ambition is but avarice on stilts and masked.

2978   But when we play the fool, how wide the theater expands.

2979   I never did a single wise thing in the whole course of my existence, although I have written many which have been thought so.

Andrew Lang
2980   He missed an invaluable opportunity to hold his tongue.

2981   He uses statistics as a drunken man uses lampposts—for support rather than for illumination.

George T. Lanigan

2982   A squeak's heard in the orchestra
          As the leader draws across
        The intestines of the agile cat
          The tail of the noble hoss.

Lao-tzu

2983   The farther one pursues knowledge, the less one knows.

Ring Lardner

2984   I've known what it is to be hungry, but I always went right to a restaurant.

2985   She had two complexions, A.M. and P.M.

2986   Shut up, he explained.

2987   He gave her a look that you could have poured on a waffle.

2988   He looked at me as if I was a side dish he hadn't ordered.

2989   They gave each other a smile with a future in it.

2990   Mr. [Irvin] Cobb took me into his library and showed me his books, of which he has a complete set.

2991   How can you write if you can't cry?

2992   This story is slightly immoral, but so, I guess, are all stories based on truth.

François de La Rochefoucauld

2993   Conceit causes more conversation than wit.

2994   Gratitude is merely a secret hope of greater favors.

2995   Greater qualities are necessary to bear good fortune than bad.

2996   If we had no faults of our own, we should take less pleasure in noticing the faults of others.

2997   In the misfortune of our best friends we find something which is not displeasing to us.

2998   A man who is always satisfied with himself is seldom satisfied with others.

2999   The reason lovers are never weary of each other is because they are always talking about themselves.

3000   To refuse praise is to seek praise twice.

3001   Sometimes there are accidents in our life the skillful extraction from which demands a little folly.

3002   We always like those who admire us but we do not always like those whom we admire.

3003   Wit sometimes enables us to act rudely with impunity.

3004   We are never made as ridiculous through the qualities we have as through those we pretend to.

3005   We confess little faults in order to suggest that we have no big ones.

3006   We give ourselves credit for the opposite faults of those we have: when we are weak, we boast of being obstinate.

3007   We often forgive those who bore us, but we cannot forgive those whom we bore.

3008   We seldom find people ungrateful so long as we are in a condition to render them service.

3009   We should have very little pleasure were we never to flatter ourselves.

3010   We think very few people sensible except those who agree with us.

3011   We would often be ashamed of our best actions if the world only knew the motives behind them.

3012   What is called liberality is often merely the vanity of giving.

3013   What makes us so bitter against people who outwit us is that they think themselves cleverer than we are.

3014   You are never so easily fooled as when you are trying to fool someone else.

3015   An old man gives good advice in order to console himself for no longer being in condition to set a bad example.

3016   In jealousy there is more self-love than love.

3017   Our enemies come nearer the truth in their opinions of us than we do in our opinion of ourselves.

3018   We are always bored by those whom we bore.

3019   One of the reasons that we find so few persons rational and agreeable in conversation is that there is hardly a person who does not think more of what he wants to say than of his answer to what is said.

3020   A clever man reaps some benefits from the worst catastrophe, and a fool can turn even good luck to his disadvantage.

3021   There are no fools so troublesome as those who have wit.

3022   Gallantry consists in saying empty things in an agreeable manner.

3023   Our repentance is not so much regret for the evil we have done, as fear of its consequences.

3024   The hunger for applause is the source of all conscious literature and heroism.

3025   The love of justice is, in most men, nothing more than the fear of suffering injustice.

3026   Moderation has been called a virtue wherewith to curb the ambition of the great, and to console men of moderate means for their small fortunes and insignificant merits.

3027   To establish oneself in the world, one does all one can to seem established there.

3028   In whatever terms people may praise us, they never teach us anything new.

3029   Why can we remember the tiniest detail that has happened to us, and not remember how many times we have told it to the same persons?

3030   Solemnity is a trick of the body to hide the faults of the mind.

3031   What makes the vanity of other people intolerable is that it wounds our own.

3032   There are people whose only merit consists in saying and doing stupid things at the right time, and who ruin all if they change their manners.

3033   Vanity is the greatest of all flatterers.

3034   When our vices leave us, we flatter ourselves with the idea that we have left them.

3035   Virtue would not go far if vanity did not keep it company.

3036   Some wicked people would be less dangerous had they no redeeming qualities.

3037   In everyday existence we please others more by our faults than by our merits.

3038   Though rarely bold enough to assert that we have no faults, and that our enemies have no virtues, we are not far from believing it.

3039   It is easier to preach virtue than to practice it.

3040   Everyone complains of his memory, and no one complains of his judgment.

3041   It takes great skill to know how to conceal one's skill.

3042   Nothing prevents us from being natural so much as the desire to appear so.

Doug Larson
3043   The only nice thing about being imperfect is the joy it brings to others.

A. A. Latimer
3044   Budget: a mathematical confirmation of your suspicions.

Johann Kaspar Lavater
3045   If you wish to appear agreeable in society you must consent to be taught many things which you already know.

3046   Never say you know a man until you have divided an inheritance with him.

Gian Vincenzo Lavina
3047   A person who deprives you of solitude without providing you with company. [A bore.]

Andrew Bonar Law
3048   If I am a great man, then a good many of the great men of history are frauds.

3049   A man with the vision of an eagle but with a blind spot in his eye. [On Lord Birkenhead.]

D. H. Lawrence
3050   Nearly all people in England are of the superior sort, superiority being an English ailment.

3051   When I wish I was rich, then I know I am ill.

3052   I am very fond of Sussex—it is so full of sky and wind and weather.

Jerome Lawrence
3053   A neurotic is a man who builds a castle in the air. A psychotic is the man who lives in it. A psychiatrist is the man who collects the rent.

Stephen Leacock

3054   The general idea, of course, in any first-class laundry is to see that no shirt or collar ever comes back twice.

3055   It's called political economy because it has nothing to do with either politics or economy.

3056   Many a man in love with a dimple makes the mistake of marrying the whole girl.

3057   Men are able to trust one another, knowing the exact degree of dishonesty they are entitled to expect.

3058   The parent who could see his boy as he really is would shake his head and say, "Willie is no good; I'll sell him."

3059   Angling: The name given to fishing by people who can't fish.

3060   Lord Ronald said nothing; he flung himself from the room, flung himself upon his horse and rode madly off in all directions.

3061   Advertising may be described as the science of arresting the human intelligence long enough to get money from it.

3062   To borrow money, big money, you have to wear your clothes in a certain way, walk in a certain way, and have about you an air of solemnity and majesty—something like the atmosphere of a Gothic cathedral.

3063   It was Einstein who made the real trouble. He announced in 1905 that there was no such thing as absolute rest. After that there never was.

3064   There is an old motto that runs, "If at first you don't succeed, try, try again." This is nonsense. It ought to read, "If at first you don't succeed, quit, quit at once."

Frank Leahy

3065   Egotism is the anesthetic that dulls the pain of stupidity.

Edward Lear

3066   The Owl and the Pussy-Cat went to sea
          In a beautiful pea-green boat

       .   .   .   .
       They dined on mince with slices of quince,
          Which they ate with a runcible spoon,
       And hand in hand, on the edge of the sand,
          They danced by the light of the moon.

3067   The Pobble who has no toes
          Had once as many as we;
       When they said, "Some day you may lose them all,"

He replied, "Fish fiddle-de-de!"
And his Aunt Jobiska made him drink
    Lavender water tinged with pink,
For she said, "The World in general knows
    There's nothing so good for a Pobble's toes!"

3068   There was an Old Man with a beard,
Who said, "It is just as I feared!
    Two Owls and a Hen
    Four Larks and a Wren,
Have all built their nests in my beard!"

F. R. Leavis
3069   He doesn't know what he means, and he doesn't know he doesn't know.

Stanislaus J. Lec
3070   Is it progress if a cannibal uses knife and fork?

Alexandre Ledru-Rollin
3071   There go my people. I must find out where they are going so I can lead them.

Robert E. Lee
3072   Abandon your animosities and make your sons Americans!

Richard Le Gallienne
3073   A critic is a man created to praise greater men than himself, but he is never able to find them.

Sir Frederick Leith-Ross
3074   Inflation is like sin; every government denounces it and every government practices it.

Ruth Lemezis
3075   Tree: an object that will stand in one place for years, then jump in front of a lady driver.

Jack Lemmon
3076   The way my wife finds fault with me, you'd think there was a reward.

V. I. Lenin
3077   No amount of political freedom will satisfy the hungry masses.

3078   The way to crush the bourgeoisie is to grind them between the millstones of taxation and inflation.

3079   It is true that liberty is precious—so precious that it must be rationed.

3080   Whenever the cause of the people is entrusted to professors, it is lost.

Pope Leo XIII
3081   No one is so rich that he does not need another's help, no one so poor as not to be useful in some way to his fellow man; and the disposition to ask assistance from others with confidence and to grant it with kindness is part of our very nature.

John Leonard
3082   The rich are different from you and me because they have more credit.

Leonardo Da Vinci
3083   I have offended God and mankind because my work didn't reach the quality it should have.

Max Lerner
3084   Either men will learn to live like brothers or they will die like beasts.

Stanislaus Leszcynski
3085   Misers are very good people; they amass wealth for those who wish their death.

David Letterman
3086   Fall is my favorite season in Los Angeles, watching the birds change color and fall from the trees.

Oscar Levant
3087   Underneath this flabby exterior is an enormous lack of character.

3088   So little time and so little to do.

3089   Tell me, George [Gershwin], if you had it to do all over, would you fall in love with yourself again?

3090   An epigram is only a wisecrack that's played Carnegie Hall.

3091   I've given up reading books; I find it takes my mind off myself.

3092   The first thing I do in the morning is brush my teeth and sharpen my tongue.

3093   A pun is the lowest form of humor—when you don't think of it first.

3094   In my last movie I played an unsympathetic character—myself.

3095   This is Oscar Levant speaking. It's an identification that I have to make because I suffer from amnesia.

3096   I'm a study of a man in chaos in search of frenzy.

3097   Behind the phony tinsel of Hollywood lies the real tinsel.

3098   I once said cynically of a politician, "He'll doublecross that bridge when he comes to it."

3099   A smattering of ignorance.

Sam Levenson
3100   Remember when your mother used to say, "Go to your room"? This was a terrible penalty. Now when a mother says the same thing, a kid goes to his room. There he's got an air conditioner, a TV set, an intercom, a shortwave radio—he's better off than he was in the first place.

3101   Insanity is hereditary; you can get it from your children.

3102   Never lend money to a friend. It's dangerous—it could damage his memory.

3103   One of the virtues of being very young is that you don't let the facts get in the way of your imagination.

Dick Levin
3104   Buy low, sell high, collect early, and pay late.

Joseph E. Levine
3105   You can fool all the people all of the time if the advertising is right and the budget is big enough.

Leonard Louis Levinson
3106   History is the short trudge from Adam to atom.

3107   He is a fine friend. He stabs you in the front.

3108   Beverly Hills—a pool's paradise.

3109   Statistics—figures used as arguments.

Clive Staples Lewis

3110   The future is something which everyone reaches at the rate of sixty minutes an hour, whatever he does, whoever he is.

Jerry Lewis

3111   When I was a kid I said to my father one afternoon, "Daddy, will you take me to the zoo?" He answered, "If the zoo wants you let them come and get you."

Joe E. Lewis

3112   It doesn't matter if you're rich or poor, as long as you've got money.

John L. Lewis

3113   A labour-baiting, poker-playing, whiskey-drinking evil old man. [On John N. Garner.]

Sinclair Lewis

3114   Our American professors like their literature clear, cold, pure, and very dead.

3115   People will buy anything that's one to a customer.

3116   When audiences come to see us authors lecture, it is largely in the hope that we'll be funnier to look at than to read.

3117   "The trouble with this country is," observed Herndon, "that there are too many people going about saying 'The trouble with this country is—.'"

Liberace

3118   My great virtue is that I have no vanity. People criticize me, but when they meet me nobody can help liking me.

3119   An unnerving squeal went up, like forty thousand Persian cats having their tails trodden on simultaneously. [*Manchester Guardian* on Liberace's appearance.]

Georg Christoph Lichtenberg

3120   What a blessing it would be if we could open and shut our ears as easily as we do our eyes.

3121   What astonished him was that cats should have two holes cut in their skins at exactly the same places where their eyes were.

3122   Nothing contributes more to peace of mind than to have no opinions whatever.

3123   This book has had the effect which good books usually have: it has made the fools more foolish, the intelligent more intelligent, and left the majority as they were.

3124   Among the greatest discoveries on which human intelligence has lighted in recent times, there ought, in my opinion, to be reckoned the art of criticizing books without having read them.

3125   It is a sure sign of an improved character, if you like paying debts as much as getting money.

3126   To err is human—the animals never err, except for the smartest among them.

3127   Everyone is a genius at least once a year; a real genius has his original ideas closer together.

3128   Sometimes men come by the name of genius in the same way that certain insects come by the name of centipede, not because they have a hundred feet, but because most people can't count above fourteen.

3129   One of the main conveniences of marriage is that if you can't stand a visitor you can pass him along to your wife.

3130   Language originated before philosophy, and that's what is the matter with philosophy.

3131   Some people read only because they are too lazy to think.

3132   I look upon reviews as a sort of infant disease to which newborn books are subject.

3133   How is it that animals do not squint? Is this another prerogative of the human species?

3134   Autumn repays the earth the leaves which summer lent it.

3135   Queerer things than books, surely, it would be hard to find in the world. Printed by people who do not understand them; sold by people who do not understand them; bound, reviewed, and read by people who do not understand them; and nowadays even written by people who do not understand them.

Beatrice Lillie
3136   Bohemians are people who sit on the floor and drink black coffee when all the while there are chairs and cream in the room.

Abraham Lincoln
3137   Am I not destroying my enemies when I make friends of them?

3138   For people who like that kind of a book, that is the kind of a book they will like.

3139   God must have loved the plain people; he made so many of them.

3140   He can compress the most words into the smallest ideas of any man I ever met.

3141   I don't know who my grandfather was; I am much more concerned to know what his grandson will be.

3142   If this is coffee, please bring me some tea; but if this is tea, please bring me some coffee.

3143   It has been my experience that folks who have no vices have very few virtues.

3144   No man has a good enough memory to make a successful liar.

3145   I was not accustomed to flattery; I was like the Hoosier who loved gingerbread better than any man and got less of it.

3146   When you have got an elephant by the hind legs and he is trying to run away, it's best to let him run.

3147   My early life is characterized in a single line of Gray's "Elegy": "The short and simple annals of the poor."

3148   With educated people, I suppose, punctuation is a matter of rule; with me it is a matter of feeling. But I must say I have a great respect for the semicolon; it's a useful little chap.

3149   I don't think much of a man who is not wiser today than he was yesterday.

3150   I have now come to the conclusion never again to think of marrying, and for this reason—I can never be satisfied with anyone who would be blockhead enough to have me.

3151   But if the good people, in their wisdom, shall see fit to keep me in the background, I have been too familiar with disappointments to be very much chagrined.

3152   If I were to try to read, much less answer, all the attacks made on me, this shop might as well be closed for any other business. I do the very best I know how—the very best I can; and I mean to keep doing so until the end. If the end brings me out all right, what is said against me won't amount to anything. If the end brings me out wrong, ten thousand angels swearing I was right would make no difference.

3153   Nobody has ever expected me to be President. In my poor, lean lank face, nobody has ever seen that any cabbages were sprouting.

3154 If you once forfeit the confidence of your fellow citizens, you can never regain their respect and esteem. It is true that you may fool all the people some of the time; you can even fool some of the people all the time; but you can't fool all the people all the time.

3155 The lady bearer of this says she has two sons who want to work. Set them at it if possible. Wanting to work is so rare a want that it should be encouraged.

3156 I can make a brigadier-general in five minutes, but it is not easy to replace a hundred and ten horses.

3157 "A drop of honey catches more flies than a gallon of gall." So with men. If you would win a man to your cause, first convince him that you are his sincere friend. Therein is a drop of honey which catches his heart, which, say what he will, is the highroad to his reason.

3158 War does not admit of holidays.

3159 A jury too often has at least one member more ready to hang the panel than to hang the traitor.

3160 His [man's] first discovery was the fact that he was naked; and his first invention was the fig-leaf apron. This simple article, the apron made of leaves, seems to have been the origin of clothing—the one thing for which nearly half of the toil and care of the human race has ever since been expended.

3161 It is better only sometimes to be right, than at all times to be wrong.

3162 God selects his own instruments, and sometimes they are queer ones; for instance, He chose me to steer the ship through a great crisis.

3163 Bad promises are better broken than kept.

3164 Military glory—that attractive rainbow that rises in showers of blood, that serpent's eye that charms to destroy.

3165 A nation may be said to consist of its territory, its people and its laws. The territory is the only part which is of certain durability.

3166 Your note, requesting my "signature with a sentiment," was received, and should have been answered long since, but that it was mislaid. I am not a very sentimental man; and the best sentiment I can think of is, that if you collect the signatures of all persons who are no less distinguished than I, you will have a very undistinguishing mass of names.

3167   It is said an Eastern monarch once charged his wise men to invent an aphorism to be ever in view, and which should be true and appropriate in all times and situations. They presented him the words, "And this, too, shall pass away."

3168   Few can be induced to labor exclusively for posterity; and none will do it enthusiastically. Posterity has done nothing for us.

3169   As for being President, I feel like the man who was tarred and feathered and ridden out of town on a rail. To the man who asked him how he liked it, he said, "If it wasn't for the honor of the thing, I'd rather walk."

3170   An honest laborer digs coal at about seventy cents a day, while the President digs abstractions at about seventy dollars a day. The coal is clearly worth more than the abstractions, and yet what a monstrous inequality in the prices.

3171   I leave it to my audience—if I had another face to wear, do you think I would wear this one? [Lincoln had been called a "two-faced" man by Stephen Douglas.]

3172   Books serve to show a man that those original thoughts of his aren't very new, after all.

3173   Consciences differ in different individuals.

3174   He reminds me of the man who murdered both his parents, and then when sentence was about to be pronounced, pleaded for mercy on the grounds that he was an orphan.

3175   I hold that if the Almighty had ever made a set of men that should do all the eating and none of the work, He would have made them with mouths only and no hands; and if He had ever made another class that He intended should do all the work and no eating, He would have made them with hands only and no mouths.

3176   I happen, temporarily, to occupy the White House. I am a living witness that any one of your children may look to come here as my father's child has.

3177   Back in the days when I performed my part as a keelboatman, I made the acquaintance of a trifling little steamboat which used to bustle and puff and wheeze about the Sangamon River. It had a five-foot boiler and seven-foot whistle, and every time it whistled, it stopped.

3178   I will not say that he willfully misquotes, but he does fail to quote accurately.

3179   Lincoln said that Stephen Douglas's debate argument was "as thin as the homeopathic soup that was made by boiling the shadow of a pigeon that had been starved to death."

3180   First of all, he has a wife and a baby; together they ought to be worth $500,000 to any man. Secondly, he has an office in which there is a table worth $1.50 and three chairs worth, say, $1. Last of all, there is in one corner a large rat hole, which will bear looking into. [Credit information on a friend.]

3181   Somewhat like the boy in Kentucky who stubbed his toe while running to see his sweetheart. The boy said he was too big to cry, and far too badly hurt to laugh. [On how he felt after a political setback in 1862.]

3182   When Lincoln was carrying two of his sons, Willie and Tad, and both were yelling, he was asked what was wrong.
        "Just what's the matter with the whole world. I've got three walnuts and each wants two."

3183   What kills a skunk is the publicity it gives itself.

3184   I choose always to make my statute of limitations a short one. [Commenting on his desire to forgive an old opponent.]

3185   A woman is the only thing I am afraid of that I know will not hurt me.

3186   I should think a man's legs ought to be long enough to reach from his body to the ground.

3187   Tact: the ability to describe others as they see themselves.

3188   The shepherd drives the wolf from the sheep's throat, for which the sheep thanks the shepherd as his liberator, while the wolf denounces him for the same act as the destroyer of liberty.

3189   Surely God would not have created such a being as man ... to exist only for a day! No, no, man was made for immortality.

3190   The best thing about the future is that it comes only one day at a time.

3191   With malice toward none, with charity for all ... let us finish the work we are in, to bind up the nation's wounds.

3192   My politics are short and sweet, like the old woman's dance.

3193   I believe I shall never be old enough to speak without embarrassment when I have nothing to talk about.

3194   Honest statesmanship is the wise employment of individual meanness for the public good.

3195   Nearly all men can stand adversity, but if you want to test a man's character, give him power.

3196   My father taught me to work, but not to love it. I never did like to work, and I don't deny it. I'd rather read, tell stories, crack jokes, talk, laugh—anything but work.

3197   You cannot strengthen the weak by weakening the strong. You cannot help the wage-earner by pulling down the wage-payer. You cannot help the poor by destroying the rich. You cannot help men permanently by doing for them what they could and should do for themselves.

3198   What is conservatism? Is it not adherence to the old and tried, against the new and untried?

3199   To sin by silence when they should protest makes cowards out of men.

John A. Lincoln

3200   A committee is a cul de sac to which ideas are lured and then quietly strangled.

3201   Fastidiousness is the ability to resist a temptation in the hope that a better one will come along.

3202   The Devil is a gentleman who never goes where he is not welcome.

3203   Opinion surveys: people who don't matter reporting on opinions that do matter.

3204   A dilemma is a politician trying to save both his faces at once.

Anne Morrow Lindbergh

3205   The most exhausting thing in life, I have discovered, is being insincere. That is why so much social life is exhausting; one is wearing a mask.

Charles A. Lindbergh, Jr.

3206   But I have seen the science I worshipped and the aircraft I loved destroying the civilization I expected them to serve.

3207   It was not the outer grandeur of the Roman but the inner simplicity of the Christian that lived on through the ages.

Henry G. Link

3208   If you wish to make a man your enemy, tell him simply, "You are wrong." This method works every time.

Walter Lippmann

3209   In order to avoid the embarrassment of calling a spade a spade, newspapermen have agreed to talk about the credibility gap. This is a polite euphemism for deception. [On the Lyndon Johnson administration.]

3210   I simply can't stand Washington. It's impossible to think or breathe in the place.

3211   Mr. Coolidge's genius for inactivity is developed to a very high point. [On Calvin Coolidge.]

3212   We must remember that in time of war what is said on the enemy's side of the front is always propaganda and what is said on our side of the front is truth and righteousness, the cause of humanity and a crusade for peace. Is it necessary for us at the height of our power to stoop to such self-deceiving nonsense?

3213   Unless the reformer can invent something which substitutes attractive virtues for attractive vices, he will fail.

3214   I hope Mr. [Dean] Acheson will write a book explaining how he persuaded himself to believe that a government could be conducted without the support of the people.

3215   Where all think alike, no one thinks very much.

Mary Wilson Little

3216   He who devotes sixteen hours a day to hard study may become as wise at sixty as he thought himself at twenty.

3217   It is difficult to see why lace should be so expensive; it is mostly holes.

3218   The penalty of success is to be bored by the attentions of people who formerly snubbed you.

3219   Politeness is one half good nature and the other half good lying.

3220   If man is only a little lower than the angels, the angels should reform.

3221   The tombstone is about the only thing that can stand upright and lie on its face at the same time.

3222   A youth with his first cigar makes himself sick; a youth with his first girl makes other people sick.

Livy

3223   Nothing stings more deeply than the loss of money.

Li Liweng

3224   To teach rich men to enjoy life would mean to ask them to give money away, which is difficult, to say the least.

David Lloyd George

3225   A politician is a person with whose politics you don't agree. If you agree with him he is a statesman.

3226   What is our task? To make Britain a fit country for heroes to live in.

3227   He has sufficient conscience to bother him, but not enough to keep him straight. [On Ramsay MacDonald.]

3228   It is easy to settle the world upon a soap box.

3229   A pygmy posturing before the footlights in the robes of a giant. [On Lord Gladstone, son of the former prime minister.]

3230   Poincaré knows everything and understands nothing—Briand understands everything and knows nothing.

3231   With me a change of trouble is as good as a vacation.

3232   Liberty has restraints but no frontiers.

3233   The finest eloquence is that which gets things done.

3234   Don't be afraid to take a big step if one is indicated. You can't cross a chasm in two small jumps.

Thomas Lode

3235   Her neck was like a stately tower.

Vince Lombardi

3236   Winning isn't everything. It's the only thing. [John Wayne may have said this first in a movie.]

Earl Long

3237   I have the experience to be Governor. I know how to play craps. I know how to play poker. I know how to get in and out of the Baptist Church and ride horses. I know the oil and gas business. I know both sides of the streets.

Huey P. Long

3238   In a political fight, when you've got nothing in favor of your side, start a row in the opposition camp.

Henry Wadsworth Longfellow

3239   And so we plough along, as the fly said to the ox.

3240   Joy and Temperance and Repose
        Slam the door on the doctor's nose.

3241   And our hearts ... like muffled
        Drums, are beating funeral marches to the grave.

3242   Life is real! Life is earnest!
        And the grave is not its goal;
        Dust thou art, to dust returneth,
        Was not spoken of the soul.

3243   Could we read the secret history of our enemies, we should find in
        each man's life sorrow and suffering enough to disarm all hostility.

3244   Perseverance is a great element of success. If you only knock long
        enough and loud enough at the gate, you are sure to wake up somebody.

3245   And the night shall be filled with music,
            And the cares, that infest the day,
        Shall fold their tents, like the Arabs,
            And as silently steal away.

Alice Roosevelt Longworth

3246   If you haven't got anything nice to say about anybody, come sit
        next to me.

3247   He [Calvin Coolidge] looks as if he had been weaned on a pickle.

P. L. Lord

3248   The old woman triumphantly announced that she had borrowed
        money enough to pay all her debts.

Louis XIV of France

3249   Every time I fill a vacant office, I make ten malcontents and one
        ingrate.

Joe Louis

3250   I don't like money actually, but it quiets my nerves.

Abbott Lawrence Lowell

3251   Universities are full of knowledge; the freshmen bring a little in
        and the seniors take none away, and knowledge accumulates.

James Russell Lowell

3252   My gran'ther's rule was safer'n 'tis to crow:
        Don't never prophesy—onless ye know.

3253   Three fifths of him genius and two fifths sheer fudge.

3254   Blessed are they who have nothing to say, and who cannot be persuaded to say it.

3255   The foolish and the dead alone never change their opinions.

3256   Granting our wish is one of Fate's saddest jokes.

3257   Let us be of good cheer, remembering that the misfortunes hardest to bear are those which never come.

3258   There is no good in arguing with the inevitable; the only argument available with an east wind is to put on your overcoat.

3259   Whatever you may be sure of, be sure of this: that you are dreadfully like other people.

3260   What men prize most is a privilege, even if it be that of chief mourner at a funeral.

3261   He mastered whatever was not worth the knowing.

3262   A great man is made up of qualities that meet or make great occasions.

3263   His [Alexander Pope's] more ambitious works may be defined as careless thinking carefully versified.

3264   The pressure of public opinion is like the pressure of the atmosphere; you can't see it—but, all the same, it is sixteen pounds to the square inch.

3265   A ginooine statesman should be on his guard,
Ef he must hev beliefs, not to b'lieve 'em tu hard.

3266   The question of common-sense is always "What is it good for?"
—a question which would abolish the rose and be answered triumphantly by the cabbage.

J. W. Lowther
3267   There are three golden rules for parliamentary speakers: stand up, speak up, and shut up.

Sir John Lubbock
3268   A room without books is a body without a soul.

3269   Long meals make short lives.

Edward Verrall Lucas
3270   I am a believer in punctuality though it makes me very lonely.

3271   People who are late are often so much jollier than the people who have to wait for them.

3272   How many years some of us have to spend in this world before we realize that we are not the center of observation!

3273   Few women and fewer men have enough character to be idle.

3274   The older I grow, the more respect I have for the wise people who cannot read or write.

3275   Every saint has a bee in his halo.

Clare Booth Luce
3276   No good deed goes unpunished.

3277   Much of what Mr. [George] Wallace calls his global thinking is, no matter how you slice it, still globaloney.

3278   The politicians were talking themselves red, white, and blue in the face.

3279   The opiate of the intellectuals . . . but no cure except as a guillotine might be called a cure for a case of dandruff. [On Communism.]

Henry Luce
3280   The profit motive is not a noble motive. It is not a gallant motive. It is not artistic. It is not dignified. And yet it seems useful.

Charles Luckman
3281   Success is the old ABC—ability, breaks and courage.

Marshall Lumsden
3282   There's only one thing that can keep growing without nourishment: the human ego.

Martin Luther
3283   Christian life consists of faith and charity.

John Lyly
3284   Children and fools speak true.

Robert Lynd
3285   Life, it seems to me, is worth living, but only if we avoid the amusements of grown-up people.

3286   There is nothing that makes us feel so good as the idea that someone else is an evildoer.

3287   Every man of genius is considerably helped by being dead.

3288   When an Englishman is totally incapable of doing any work whatsoever, he describes himself in the income-tax form as a "gentleman."

3289   A woman in a London police court once said, "My husband is no gentleman: he puts on his trousers before his socks."

3290   There is more pleasure in being shocked by the sin of one's neighbor or one's neighbor's wife than in eating cream buns.

3291   The rich never feel so good as when they are speaking of their possessions as responsibilities.

3292   Nothing can happen but the suspicious man believes that somebody did it on purpose.

3293   The telephone is the greatest nuisance among conveniences, the greatest convenience among nuisances.

Russell Lynes
3294   The only gracious way to accept an insult is to ignore it; if you can't ignore it, top it; if you can't top it, laugh at it; if you can't laugh at it, it's probably deserved.

3295   A lady is a woman who makes a man behave like a gentleman.

3296   Religious snobs talk about God as though nobody had ever heard of Him before.

Leverett Lyon
3297   Those who work out our federal budget
Have a policy—really a honey—
We shall live on our national income,
Even if we must borrow the money!

3298   The "coffee break," up in our tower,
Were better called the "coffee hour"!

3299   Each of June's new graduates
Has left his college hall.
The world is now his oyster,
The future is his thrall.
He thinks he knows a great, great deal
More than his parents do—
And, speaking of that state of mind,
The chances are it's true!

3300   I know just how to cure the world
       And make it safe and stable;
       But I haven't time to do it,
       And those that have, aren't able.

3301   Of all my Merry Christmas cards,
       This was the cutest quip:
       "Merry Christmas" from an editor
       On a rejection slip!

3302   On New Year's Day, some years ago,
       I swore off alcohol;
       And, one year later, I eschewed
       Pipes, cigarettes, et al.
       The next, I quit profanity
       As something not too nice.
       And then abandoned slot machines,
       Card games, roulette and dice.
       Thus curing faults each year, I reached
       A state of such perfection
       That I have not a single flaw
       Now calling for correction.
       But New Year's Day is now for me
       A ruined Institution;
       For what is New Year's Day without
       A New Year's resolution?

3303   We thank Thee, Lord, for giving us
       Thy gift of bread and meat.
       We thank Thee, too—a little more—
       That we are here to eat!

Edward George Bulwer-Lytton, Lord Lytton

3304   There is no man so friendless but that he can find a friend sincere
       enough to tell him disagreeable truths.

3305   If you wish to be loved, show more of your faults than your virtues.

3306   It is difficult to say who do you the most mischief: enemies with
       the worst intentions or friends with the best.

3307   We may live without friends; we may live without books;
       But civilized man cannot live without cooks.

3308   Every man loves and admires his own country because it produced
       him.

3309   Give, and you may keep your friend if you lose your money; lend,
       and the chances are that you lose your friend if ever you get back your
       money.

3310   Revolutions are not made with rose water.

3311   Men who make money rarely saunter; men who save money rarely swagger.

General Douglas MacArthur

3312   By profession I am a soldier and take pride in that fact. But I am prouder—infinitely prouder—to be a father. A soldier destroys in order to build; the father only builds, never destroys. The one has the potentiality of death; the other embodies creation and life. And while the hordes of death are mighty, the battalions of life are mightier still. It is my hope that my son, when I am gone, will remember me not from the battle but in the home repeating with him our simple daily prayer, "Our Father Who Art in Heaven."

3313   Today the guns are silent. A great tragedy has ended. A great victory has been won. The skies no longer rain death—the seas bear only commerce—men everywhere walk upright in the sunlight. The entire world is quietly at peace. The holy mission has been completed. And in reporting this to you, the people, I speak for the thousands of silent lips, forever stilled among the jungles and the beaches and in the deep waters of the Pacific which marked the way. I speak for the unnamed brave millions homeward bound to take up the challenge of that future which they did so much to salvage from the brink of disaster.

3314   There is no security on this earth; there is only opportunity.

3315   Build me a son, O Lord, who will be strong enough to know when he is weak, and brave enough to face himself when he is afraid, one who will be proud and unbending in honest defeat, and humble and gentle in victory.

Build me a son whose wishes will not take the place of deeds; a son who will know Thee—and that to know himself is the foundation stone of knowledge.

Lead him, I pray, not in the path of ease and comfort, but under the stress and spur of difficulties and challenge. Here let him learn to stand up in the storm; here let him learn compassion for those who fail.

Build me a son whose heart will be clear, whose goal will be high; a son who will master himself before he seeks to master other men; one who will reach into the future, yet never forget the past.

And after all these things are his, add, I pray, enough of a sense of humor, so that he may always be serious, yet never take himself too seriously. Give him humility, so that he may always remember the simplicity of true greatness, the open mind of true wisdom, and the meekness of true strength.

Then, I, his father, will dare to whisper, "I have not lived in vain."

3316   I am closing my fifty-two years of military service. When I joined
the Army, even before the turn of the century, it was the fulfillment of all
my boyish hopes and dreams. The world has turned over many times
since I took the oath on the Plain at West Point, and the hopes and
dreams have all since vanished, but I still remember the refrain of one of
the most popular barracks ballads of that day, which proclaimed most
proudly that old soldiers never die; they just fade away. And like the old
soldier of that ballad, I now close my military career and just fade away,
an old soldier who tried to do his duty as God gave him the light to see
that duty. Good-by.

Rose Macaulay

3317   It was a book to kill time for those who like it better dead.

3318   It is scarcely necessary to say that, in this hot competition of
bigots and slaves, the University of Oxford had the unquested preemi-
nence. The glory of being further behind the age than any other portion
of the British people is one which that learned body acquired early, and
has never lost.

Thomas Babington Macaulay

3319   The object of oratory alone is not the truth, but persuasion.

3320   I am far from insensible to the pleasure of having fame, rank and
this opulence which has come so late.

3321   The Puritan hated bear-baiting, not because it gave pain to the
bear, but because it gave pleasure to the spectators.

3322   Perhaps no person can be a poet, or even enjoy poetry, without a
certain unsoundness of mind.

3323   We know no spectacle so ridiculous as the British public in one of
its periodical fits of morality.

3324   It really deserves the praise, whatever that praise may be worth, of
being the best book ever written by any man on the wrong side of the
question of which he was profoundly ignorant.

3325   The measure of a man's real character is what he would do if he
knew he never would be found out.

Desmond MacCarthy

3326   The authorities were at their wits' end, nor had it taken them long
to get there.

Dwight Macdonald

3327   Conversation means being able to disagree and still continue the
conversation.

Ronald Mackenzie

3328   My education was so sound that I know hardly anything.

Don MacLean

3329   Washington has a large assortment of peace monuments. We build one after every war.

Seumas MacManus

3330   He is as good as his word—and his word is no good.

Harold Macmillan

3331   One newspaper, I am told, has perpetually in type the headline "Mac At Bay." I suggest they also keep in type "Mac Bounces Back."

3332   People are so much nicer to you in other countries than they are at home. At home, you always have to be a politician; when you're abroad, you almost feel yourself a statesman.

3333   I'd like that translated, if I may. [Watching Khrushchev pound his shoe.]

3334   Jaw-jaw is better than war-war. [Echoing Churchill's 1954 dictum "Talking jaw to jaw is better than going to war."]

3335   He is forever poised between a cliché and an indiscretion.

3336   I have never found, in a long experience of politics, that criticism is ever inhibited by ignorance.

3337   It is, of course, a trite observation to say that we live "in a period of transition." Many people have said this at many times. Adam may well have made the remark to Eve on leaving the Garden of Eden.

Salvadore de Madariaga

3338   The Anglo-Saxon conscience does not prevent the Anglo-Saxon from sinning; it merely prevents him from enjoying his sin.

3339   Puns should be punished unless they be pungent.

James Madison

3340   If men were angels, no government would be necessary.

Maurice Maeterlinck

3341   All our knowledge merely helps us to die a more painful death than the animals that know nothing.

3342   The living are the dead on holiday.

Bishop William Connor Magee

3343   The man who makes no mistakes does not usually make anything.

Robert F. Mager

3344   If you're not sure where you are going, you're liable to end up someplace else.

Sir John Pentland Mahaffy

3345   Ireland is a country in which the probable never happens and the impossible always does.

Norman Mailer

3346   The function of socialism is to raise suffering to a higher level.

3347   The indispensable requirement for a good newspaper—as eager to tell a lie as the truth.

Douglas Malloch

3348   The biggest liar in the world is They Say.

George Leigh Mallory

3349   Because it's there. [On why he wanted to climb Mount Everest.]

3350   Hollywood is the place where inferior people have a way of making superior people feel inferior.

Mae Maloo

3351   There's one thing to be said for inviting trouble: it generally accepts.

André Malraux

3352   The truth about a man lies first and foremost in what he hides.

Lord Mancroft

3353   Cricket is a game which the English, not being a spiritual people, have invented to give themselves some conception of eternity.

3354   Happy is the man with a wife to tell him what to do and a secretary to do it.

Horace Mann

3355   We go by the major vote, and if the majority are insane, the sane must go to the hospital.

Earl of Mansfield

3356   Give your decisions, never your reasons; your decisions may be right, your reasons are sure to be wrong.

Katherine Mansfield

3357   Regret is an appalling waste of energy; you can't build on it; it's only good for wallowing in.

Mao Tse-tung

3358   I am a lone monk walking the world with a leaky umbrella.

3359   Politics is war without bloodshed, while war is politics with bloodshed.

3360   There is a serious tendency towards capitalism among the well-to-do peasants.

E. M. Marais

3361   Man does not transmit a single acquired memory to his progeny. The son of the greatest mathematician does not inherit even the multiplication table.

John Phillips Marquand

3362   I know a fellow who's as broke as the Ten Commandments.

Don Marquis

3363   Fishing is a delusion entirely surrounded by liars in old clothes.

3364   He is so unlucky that he runs into accidents which started out to happen to somebody else.

3365   Hope is all right and so is Faith, but what I would like to see is a little Charity.

3366   An idea isn't responsible for the people who believe in it.

3367   If you make people think they're thinking, they'll love you; but if you really make them think, they'll hate you.

3368   The more conscious a philosopher is of the weak spots of his theory, the more certain he is to speak with an air of final authority.

3369   Most of the people living in New York have come here from the farm to try to make enough money to go back to the farm.

3370   Procrastination is the art of keeping up with yesterday.

3371   Publishing a volume of verse is like dropping a rose petal down the Grand Canyon and waiting for the echo.

3372   The successful people are the ones who can think up things for the rest of the world to keep busy at.

3373   There is always a comforting thought in time of trouble when it is not our trouble.

3374   Young man, if she asks you if you like her hair that way, beware; the woman has already committed matrimony in her heart.

3375   Middle age is the time when a man is always thinking that in a week or two he will feel as good as ever.

3376   I don't think anything is ever quite the same to us after we are dead.

3377   When a man tells you that he got rich through hard work, ask him whose.

3378   Every cloud has its silver lining, but it is sometimes a little difficult to get it to the mint.

3379   An optimist is a guy who has never had much experience.

3380   That stern and rockbound coast felt like an amateur when it saw how grim the Puritans that landed on it were.

3381   Stroke a platitude until it purrs like an epigram.

3382   If you are president the trouble happens to you,
        But if you are a tyrant you can arrange things so
        That most of the trouble happens to other people.

3383   If you want to get rich from writing, write the sort of thing that's read by persons who move their lips when they're reading to themselves.

Harry Marsh
3384   A baby-sitter is a teenager who comes in to act like an adult while the adults go out and act like teenagers.

Ngaio Marsh
3385   Longevity is one of the more dubious rewards of virtue.

Sir Richard Marsh
3386   As far as socialism means anything, it must be about the wider distribution of smoked salmon and caviar.

John Marshall, U.S. Supreme Court
3387   The power to tax involves the power to destroy.

Thomas R. Marshall
3388   I come from Indiana, the home of more first-rate second-class men than any state in the Union.

3389   The Vice President of the United States is like a man in a cataleptic state; he cannot speak, he cannot move; he suffers no pain; and yet
he is perfectly conscious of everything that is going on about him.

3390   Once there were two brothers. One ran away to sea, the other was
elected Vice President, and nothing was ever heard of either of them
again.

Boris Marshalov
3391   Congress is so strange. A man gets up to speak and says nothing.
Nobody listens—and then everybody disagrees.

Martial
3392   He does not write at all whose poems no man reads.

3393   If fame is to come only after death, I am in no hurry for it.

3394   Lawyers are men who hire out their words and anger.

3395   You often ask me, Priscus, what sort of man I should be, if all of a
sudden I became rich and powerful. Do you think that anybody can tell
you what his future character will be? Tell me, if you became a lion, what
sort of lion would you be?

3396   You are not in debt, Sextus. I assure you, Sextus, you are not in
debt, for a man is in debt, Sextus, only if he can pay.

3397   I have bought a property in the country for a good round sum,
Caecilianus, and ask you to lend me a thousand. Won't you give me an
answer? I fancy from your silence you are saying, "You won't pay it
back." That is just why I am asking for it, Caecilianus.

3398   I don't know whether Phoebus fled from the dinner table of
Thyestes: at any rate, Ligurinus, we fell from yours. Splendid, indeed, it
is, and magnificently supplied with good things, but when you recite you
spoil it all. I don't want you to set before me a turbot or a two-pound
mullet: I don't want your mushrooms or your oysters. I want you to keep
your mouth shut!

3399   You ask why I won't marry a rich wife? Because I don't want to
pass as my wife's husband. The wife should be inferior to the husband,
Priscus. That is the only way to ensure equality between the two.

3400   Conceal a flaw, and the world will imagine the worst.

3401   Tomorrow's life is too late. Live today.

Dean Martin
3402   If you drink, don't drive. Don't even putt.

Nadine Martin

3403   If that skunk ever bites you, you'll get claustrophobia.

Harriet Martineau

3404   The men who pass most comfortably through the world are those
who possess good digestion and hard hearts.

H. E. Martz

3405   He who builds a better mousetrap these days runs into material
shortages, patent-infringement suits, work stoppages, collusive bidding,
discount discrimination—and taxes.

Andrew Marvell

3406   But at my back I always hear
Time's winged chariot hurrying near.

Groucho Marx

3407   I don't have a photograph, but you can have my footprints.
They're upstairs in my socks.

3408   Go, and never darken my towels again.

3409   Either this man is dead or my watch has stopped.

3410   My mother loved children—she would have given anything if I
had been one.

3411   From the moment I picked your book up until I laid it down I was
convulsed with laughter. Someday I intend reading it.

3412   I was so long writing my review that I never got around to reading
the book.

3413   There's one way to find out if a man is honest—ask him. If he says
"Yes," you know he is a crook.

3414   I find television very educating. Every time somebody turns on the
set I go into the other room and read a book.

3415   She got her good looks from her father—he's a plastic surgeon.

3416   Military intelligence is a contradiction in terms.

3417   I didn't like the play, but then I saw it under adverse conditions—
the curtain was up.

3418   I'm leaving because the weather is too good. I hate London when
it's not raining.

3419   I always enjoy myself. It's the other people I have trouble enjoying.

3420   No man goes before his time—unless the boss leaves early.

Harpo Marx

3421   He [Alexander Woollcott] is just a big dreamer with a good sense of double-entry bookkeeping.

Karl Marx

3422   The arch-philistine Jeremy Bentham was the insipid, pedantic, leather-tongued oracle of the bourgeois intelligence of the nineteenth century.

3423   The oppressed are allowed once every few years to decide which particular representatives of the oppressing class are to represent and repress them.

3424   The philosophers have only interpreted the world; the thing, however, is to change it.

3425   The wealthy man is the man who is much, not the one who has much.

Jan Masaryk

3426   Dictators always look good until the last ten minutes.

John Masefield

3427   His face was filled with broken commandments.

3428   To get the whole world out of bed
And washed and dressed and warmed and fed,
To work, and back to bed again,
Believe me, Saul, costs worlds of pain.

Thomas L. Masson

3429   The best way to study human nature is when nobody else is present.

3430   "Be yourself!" is about the worst advice you can give to some people.

3431   To feel themselves in the presence of true greatness many men find it necessary only to be alone.

3432   It must be a hard life to be the child of a psychologist.

3433   Reputation: what others are not thinking about you.

3434   A senior always feels like the university is going to the kids.

3435   There are seventy million books in American libraries, but the one you want to read is always out.

3436   Think of what would happen to us in America if there were no humorists; life would be one long *Congressional Record.*

3437   When billing and cooing results in matrimony, the billing always comes after the cooing.

3438   You can always get someone to love you—even if you have to do it yourself.

Shailer Mathews

3439   An epigram is a half-truth so stated as to irritate the person who believes the other half.

3440   If it is more blessed to give than to receive, then most of us are content to let the other fellow have the greater blessing.

William Mathews

3441   Proverbs, it has well been said, should be sold in pairs, a single one being but a half-truth.

Brander Matthews

3442   A highbrow is a person educated beyond his intelligence.

3443   During a discussion, Professor Brander Matthews was explaining to Nicholas Murray Butler the main points of an article he had written on the subject of plagiarism. "In the case of the first man to use an anecdote there is originality; in the case of the second, there is plagiarism; with the third, it is lack of originality, and with the fourth it is drawing from a common stock."
    "Yes," interjected Butler, "and in the case of the fifth, it is research."

Reginald Maudling

3444   We're a Conservative country that votes Labour from time to time. [On England.]

Somerset Maugham

3445   It was such a lovely day I thought it was a pity to get up.

3446   I've always been interested in people, but I've never liked them.

3447   American women expect to find in their husbands a perfection that English women only hope to find in their butlers.

3448   It is a funny thing about life; if you refuse to accept anything but the best you very often get it.

3449 To do each day two things one dislikes is a precept I have followed scrupulously: every day I have got up and I have gone to bed.

3450 Self-complacency is the death of the artist.

3451 Tolerance: another word for indifference.

3452 At a dinner party one should eat wisely but not too well, and talk well but not too wisely.

3453 It is good to be on your guard against an Englishman who speaks French perfectly; he is very likely to be a cardsharper or an attaché in the diplomatic service.

3454 People ask you for criticism but they only want praise.

3455 People will sometimes forgive you the good you have done them, but seldom the harm they have done you.

3456 The great change in manners today is the relaxation of what is proper. It makes relations among the young so much easier and more friendly. You can be companions. When I was a boy, you were expected to protect young girls. For instance, if you were playing lawn tennis, you would be considered a cad if you didn't lob her a high ball so she could return it easily. That made for curious relations and bad tennis.

3457 Marriage is a very good thing, but I think it's a mistake to make a habit of it.

3458 I have always been convinced that if a woman once made up her mind to marry a man, nothing but instant flight could save him.

3459 She plunged into a sea of platitudes, and with the powerful breast stroke of a channel swimmer made her confident way toward the white cliffs of the obvious.

3460 I should like to have been present when the lady, on being reproached for burning the candle at both ends, said, "Why, I thought that was the very way to make both ends meet."

3461 In heaven when the blessed use the telephone they will say what they have to say and not a word besides.

3462 There is no need for the writer to eat a whole sheep to be able to tell what mutton tastes like. It is enough if he eats a cutlet. But he should do that.

3463 Money is like a sixth sense without which you cannot make a complete use of the other five.

3464 If you are a writer, live a long time. I have found that longevity counts more than talent.

3465   Only a mediocre person is always at his best.

David W. Maurer
3466   You can't cheat an honest man.

André Maurois
3467   The only thing experience teaches us is that experience teaches us nothing.

3468   To have the license number of one's automobile as low as possible is a social advantage in America.

3469   When you become used to never being alone, you may consider yourself Americanized.

3470   Growing old is no more than a bad habit, which a busy man has no time to form.

3471   He who wants to do everything will never do anything.

3472   We owe to the Middle Ages the two worst inventions of humanity —romantic love and gunpowder.

3473   The average value of conversations could be enormously improved by the constant use of four simple words: "I do not know," or of Louis XIV's favorite remark: "I shall see."

3474   To be witty is not enough. One must possess sufficient wit to avoid having too much of it.

3475   Politeness: not speaking evil of people with whom you have just dined until you are at least a hundred yards from their house.

Maury Maverick
3476   Democracy is liberty plus economic security. We Americans want to pray, think as we please—and eat regular.

Elsa Maxwell
3477   We live in a cocktail culture whose unlovely symbol is the ring on the best mahogany.

3478   The best parties are given by people who can't afford them.

3479   Protocol may be defined as the code of etiquette which protects royalty from the competition of intellectual and social superiors.

Louis B. Mayer
3480   The number one book of the ages was written by a committee, and it was called the Bible. [Said to writers who complained about changes made in their work.]

Milton Mayer
3481   I have never been able to understand why it is that just because I am unintelligible nobody understands me.

William G. McAdoo
3482   It is impossible to defeat an ignorant man in argument.

Mary Margaret McBride
3483   When a Missourian stops calling it Mizzoura, he's getting upstage.

John L. McCaffrey
3484   The mechanics of running a business are really not very complicated when you get down to essentials. You have to make some stuff and sell it to somebody for more than it cost you. That's about all there is to it, except for a few million details.

L. S. McCandles
3485   The best thing about getting old is that all those things you couldn't have when you were young you no longer want.

J. E. McCann
3486   "'Tis better to have loved and lost,"
         Than to marry and be bossed.

Eugene McCarthy
3487   Being in politics is like being a football coach. You have to be smart enough to understand the game and dumb enough to think it's important.

3488   The only thing that saves us from the bureaucracy is its inefficiency.

3489   It is dangerous for a national candidate to say things that people might remember.

Claude McDonald
3490   Sometimes a majority simply means that all the fools are on the same side.

Neil McElroy
3491   In the space age, man will be able to go around the world in two hours—one hour for flying, and the other to get to the airport.

J. P. McEvoy
3492   The Japanese have a word for it. It's judo—the art of conquering by yielding. The Western equivalent of judo is "Yes, dear."

"Fibber" McGee (Jim Jordan)
3493   A farm is a hunk of land on which, if you get up early enough mornings and work late enough nights, you'll make a fortune—if you strike oil on it.

Danny McGoorty
3494   I have never liked working. To me a job is an invasion of privacy.

Laurence McKinney
3495   This backward Man, this view obstructor
Is known to us as the Conductor.

Migon McLaughlin
3496   No one really listens to anyone else, and if you try it for a while you'll see why.

3497   Most of us become parents long before we have stopped being children.

3498   We're all born brave, trusting and greedy, and most of us remain greedy.

3499   There are a handful of people whom money won't spoil, and we count ourselves among them.

Marshall McLuhan
3500   Canada is the only country in the world that knows how to live without an identity.

Luke McLuke
3501   Do right and fear no man; don't write and fear no woman.

Robert N. McMurry
3502   As one retiring chief executive said to his successor, "Yesterday was the last day you heard the truth from your subordinates."

Steve McQueen
3503   I'd rather wake up in the middle of nowhere than in any city on earth.

Merle L. Meacham
3504   Xerox: a trademark for a photocopying device that can make rapid reproductions of human error, perfectly.

Margaret Mead
3505   Women want mediocre men, and men are working hard to be as mediocre as possible.

3506 Everybody is overworked. Now the main occupation of the educated man is not his job, but helping his wife at home.

George Meany
3507 Anybody who has any doubt about the ingenuity or the resourcefulness of a plumber never got a bill from one.

Hughes Mearns
3508 As I was going up the stair
I met a man who wasn't there!
He wasn't there again today!
I wish, I wish he'd stay away!

Alexander Meiklejohn
3509 Democracy is the art of thinking independently together.

Golda Meir
3510 Don't be humble. You're not that great.

3511 Whether women are better than men I cannot say—but I can say they are certainly no worse.

Lord Melbourne
3512 Nobody learns anything from experience; everybody does the same thing over and over again.

3513 Nobody ever did anything very foolish except from some strong principle.

3514 Raphael was employed to decorate the Vatican not because he was a great painter but because his uncle was architect to the Pope.

3515 Things are coming to a pretty pass when religion is allowed to invade private life.

Menander
3516 In many ways the saying "Know thyself" is lacking. Better to know other people.

3517 It is hard to find the relatives of a poor man.

H. L. Mencken
3518 Under democracy one party always devotes its chief energies to trying to prove that the other party is unfit to rule—and both commonly succeed, and are right.

3519 It is impossible to imagine Goethe or Beethoven being good at billiards or golf.

3520   It is inaccurate to say I hate everything. I am strongly in favor of common sense, common honesty, and common decency. This makes me forever ineligible for any public office.

3521   Why authors write I do not know. As well ask why a hen lays an egg or a cow stands patiently while a farmer burglarizes her.

3522   I know of no existing nation that deserves to live, and I know of very few individuals.

3523   A good politician is quite as unthinkable as an honest burglar.

3524   When I hear a man applauded by the mob I always feel a pang of pity for him. All he has to do to be hissed is to live long enough.

3525   The learned are seldom pretty fellows, and in many cases their appearance tends to discourage a love of study in the young.

3526   Democracy is the theory that the common people know what they want, and deserve to get it good and hard.

3527   Conscience: the inner voice which warns us that someone may be looking.

3528   The difference between a moral man and a man of honor is that the latter regrets a discreditable act even when it has worked.

3529   A gentleman is one who never strikes a woman without provocation.

3530   Honeymoon: the time during which the bride believes the bridegroom's word of honor.

3531   I go on working for the same reason that a hen goes on laying eggs.

3532   Injustice is relatively easy to bear; what stings is justice.

3533   It is a sin to believe evil of others, but it is seldom a mistake.

3534   It is hard to believe that a man is telling the truth when you know that you would lie if you were in his place.

3535   A judge is a law student who marks his own examination papers.

3536   Love is like war: easy to begin but very hard to stop.

3537   Love is the triumph of imagination over intelligence.

3538   Man is always looking for someone to boast to; woman is always looking for a shoulder to put her head on.

3539   The objection to Puritans is not that they try to make us think as they do, but that they try to make us do as they think.

3540   The older I grow, the more I distrust the familiar doctrine that age brings wisdom.

3541   Opera in English is, in the main, just about as sensible as baseball in Italian.

3542   Say what you will about the Ten Commandments, you must always come back to the pleasant fact that there are only ten of them.

3543   There is no record in human history of a happy philosopher; they exist only in romantic legends.

3544   'Tis more blessed to give than to receive; for example, wedding presents.

3545   The truth that survives is simply the lie that is pleasantest to believe.

3546   When women kiss, it always reminds me of prize fighters shaking hands.

3547   Don't overestimate the decency of the human race.

3548   The first Rotarian was the first man to call John the Baptist Jack.

3549   In the main there are two sorts of books: those that no one reads and those that no one ought to read.

3550   A celebrity is one who is known to many persons he is glad he doesn't know.

3551   A cynic is a man who, when he smells flowers, looks around for a coffin.

3552   The demagogue is one who preaches doctrines he knows to be untrue to men he knows to be idiots.

3553   What men, in their egoism, constantly mistake for a deficiency of intelligence in woman is merely an incapacity for mastering that mass of small intellectual tricks, that complex of petty knowledge, that collection of cerebral rubber stamps, which constitute the chief mental equipment of the average male.

3554   Historian: an unsuccessful novelist.

3555   What men value in this world is not rights but privileges.

3556   Man weeps to think that he will die so soon; woman, that she was born so long ago.

3557   Politician: any citizen with influence enough to get his old mother a job as charwoman in the City Hall.

3558 An idealist is one who, on noticing that a rose smells better than a cabbage, concludes that it will also make better soup.

3559 The men the American people admire most extravagantly are the most daring liars; the men they detest most violently are those who try to tell them the truth.

3560 A man may be a fool and not know it, but not if he is married.

3561 My guess is that well over eighty percent of the human race goes through life without having a single original thought.

3562 There's always an easy solution to every human problem—neat, plausible and wrong.

3563 Hope: a pathological belief in the occurrence of the impossible.

3564 Lawyer: one who protects us against robbery by taking away the temptation.

3565 Man makes love by braggadocio. Woman makes love by listening —once a woman passes a certain point in intelligence, she finds it almost impossible to get a husband; she simply cannot go on listening without snickering.

3566 Love is the delusion that one woman differs from another.

3567 To be in love is merely to be in a state of perpetual anesthesia.

3568 If, after I depart this vale, you ever remember me and have thought to please my ghost, forgive some sinner and wink your eye at some homely girl.

3569 Metaphysics is almost always an attempt to prove the incredible by an appeal to the unintelligible.

3570 The chief value of money lies in the fact that one lives in a world in which it is overestimated.

3571 Morality is the theory that every human act must either be right or wrong and that ninety-nine percent of them are wrong.

3572 Optimist: the sort of man who marries his sister's best friend.

3573 Pensioner: a kept patriot.

3574 Philosophy consists largely of one philosopher arguing that all others are jackasses. He usually proves it, and I should add that he also usually proves that he is one himself.

3575 Popularity: the capacity for listening sympathetically when men boast of their wives and women complain of their husbands.

3576 A prohibitionist is the sort of man one wouldn't care to drink with—even if he drank.

3577 Puritanism: the haunting fear that someone, somewhere, may be happy.

3578 God must love the poor, said Lincoln, or he wouldn't have made so many of them. He must love the rich or he wouldn't divide so much mazuma among so few of them.

3579 This bombastic style has marked all English official utterance for many years. . . . Some of its masterpieces are famous—for example, the sign reading "These basins are for casual ablutions only." [Formerly hanging in the men's washroom of the British Museum.]

3580 We take pride in the fact that we are thinking animals, and like to believe that our thoughts are free, but the truth is that nine-tenths of them are rigidly conditioned by the babbling that goes on around us from birth, and that the business of considering this babbling objectively, separating the truth in it from the false, is an intellectual feat of such stupendous difficulty, few men are ever able to achieve it.

3581 The man who boasts that he habitually tells the truth is simply a man with no respect for it. It is not a thing to be thrown about loosely like small change; it is something to be cherished and hoarded, and disbursed only when absolutely necessary.

3582 Wealth: any income that is at least $100 more a year than the income of one's wife's sister's husband.

3583 Wife: one who is sorry she did it, but would undoubtedly do it again.

3584 Wife: a former sweetheart.

3585 A woman usually respects her father, but her view of her husband is mingled with contempt, for she is of course privy to the transparent devices by which she snared him.

3586 Women hate revolutions and revolutionists. They like men who are docile and well regarded at the bank and never late at meals.

3587 Immorality: the morality of those who are having a better time.

3588 The easiest job I have ever tackled in this world is that of making money. It is, in fact, almost as easy as losing it. Almost, but not quite.

3589 I am an amused spectator of the world.

Aubrey Menen

3590   I admire the saints because they are such uncompromisingly difficult people to get on with. My brother always says that it's a happy bishop who hasn't got a saint in his diocese.

3591   The essence of success is that it is never necessary to think of a new idea oneself. It is far better to wait until somebody else does it, and then to copy him in every detail, except his mistakes.

Sir Robert Menzies

3592   I never feel comfortable in the presence of policemen, unless they're sitting beside me at a function.

George Meredith

3593   Kissing don't last; cookery do!

3594   She poured a little social sewage into his ears.

3595   Cynicism is intellectual dandyism.

3596   Heiresses are never jilted.

3597   "Poetry," said Emilia, "seems like talking on tiptoe."

3598   She had the mouth that smiles in repose.

3599   Woman will be the last thing civilized by man.

3600   Women are such expensive things.

Jules Michelet

3601   How beautifully everything is arranged by Nature; as soon as a child enters the world, it finds a mother ready to take care of it.

3602   Metaphysics: the art of bewildering oneself methodically.

George Mikes

3603   On the Continent people have good food, in England people have good table manners.

John Stuart Mill

3604   His eminence was due to the flatness of the surrounding landscape.

Edna St. Vincent Millay

3605   And if I loved you Wednesday,
      Well, what is that to you?
   I do not love you Thursday—
      So much is true.

3606   The rain has such a friendly sound
        To one who's six feet underground.

Arthur Miller

3607   A good newspaper is a nation talking to itself.

3608   Radio: death in the afternoon and into the night.

3609   Nobody dast blame this man. You don't understand: Wil was a
        salesman. And for a salesman, there is no rock bottom to the life. He
        don't put a bolt to a nut, he don't tell you the law or give you medicine.
        He's a man way out there in the blue, riding on a smile and a shoeshine.
        And when they start not smiling back—that's an earthquake. And then
        you get yourself a couple of spots on your hat, and you're finished.
        Nobody dast blame this man. A salesman is got to dream, boy. It comes
        with the territory.

John Miller

3610   People who take time to be alone usually have depth, originality,
        and quiet reserve.

Olin Miller

3611   It's far easier to forgive an enemy after you've got even with him.

3612   Writing is the hardest way of earning a living, with the possible
        exception of wrestling alligators.

3613   A man who won't lie to a woman has very little consideration for
        her feelings.

3614   You probably wouldn't worry about what people think of you if
        you could know how seldom they do.

Former Senator Eugene Millikin

3615   If the distinguished Senator will allow me, I will try to extricate
        him from his thoughts.

Chuck Mills

3616   I give the same halftime speech over and over. It works best when
        my players are better than the other coach's players.

A. A. Milne

3617   Bores can be divided into two classes; those who have their own
        particular subject, and those who do not need a subject.

3618   No doubt Jack the Ripper excused himself on the grounds that it
        was human nature.

3619   Sydney Smith, or Napoleon or Marcus Aurelius (somebody about that time) said that after ten days any letter would answer itself. You see what he meant.

Newton Minow

3620   Children will watch anything, and when a broadcaster uses crime and violence and other shoddy devices to monopolize a child's attention it's worse than taking candy from a baby. It is taking precious time from the process of growing up.

Mistinguette

3621   A kiss can be a comma, a question mark or an exclamation point. That's basic spelling that every woman ought to know.

Henry Mitchell

3622   All anybody needs to know about prizes is that Mozart never won one.

Addison Mizner

3623   The poor ye have with ye always—but they are not invited.

3624   Some people's genius lies in giving infinite pains.

3625   Don't talk about yourself; it will be done when you leave.

3626   Where there's a will, there's a lawsuit.

3627   It's a strong stomach that has no turning.

3628   A lie in time saves nine.

3629   Never call a man a fool; borrow from him.

3630   Never drink from your finger bowl—it contains only water.

3631   A woman on time is one in nine.

3632   Misery loves company, but company does not reciprocate.

Wilson Mizner

3633   The cuckoo who is on to himself is halfway out of the clock.

3634   A drama critic is a person who surprises the playwright by informing him what he meant.

3635   A fellow who is always declaring he's no fool usually has his suspicions.

3636   The gent who wakes up and finds himself a success hasn't been asleep.

3637   A good listener is not only popular everywhere, but after a while he knows something.

3638   I know of no sentence that can induce such immediate and brazen lying as the one that begins, "Have you read—."

3639   I respect faith, but doubt is what gets you an education.

3640   The man who won't loan money isn't going to have many friends —or need them.

3641   Money is the only substance which can keep a cold world from nicknaming a citizen "Hey, you!"

3642   Most hard-boiled people are half-baked.

3643   The most effective water power in the world—women's tears.

3644   The only bird that gives the poor a real tumble is the stork.

3645   The only sure thing about luck is that it will change.

3646   Some of the greatest love affairs I've known have involved one actor—unassisted.

3647   When a woman tells you her age, it's all right to look surprised, but don't scowl.

3648   When you take stuff from one writer, it's plagiarism; but when you take it from many writers, it's research.

3649   Women can instantly see through each other, and it's surprising how little they observe that's pleasant.

3650   Gambling: the sure way of getting nothing for something.

3651   Life's a tough proposition, and the first hundred years are the hardest.

3652   I hate careless flattery, the kind that exhausts you in your effort to believe it.

3653   The worst-tempered people I've ever met were people who knew they were wrong.

3654   Hollywood is a sewer with service from the Ritz Carlton.

3655   I've had ample contact with lawyers, and I'm convinced that the only fortune they ever leave is their own.

3656   I've known countless people who were reservoirs of learning yet never had a thought.

3657   In the battle of existence, talent is the punch; tact is the clever footwork.

3658   There's nothing so comfortable as a small bankroll. A big one is always in danger.

3659   I've had several years in Hollywood and I still think the movie heroes are in the audience.

3660   Popularity is exhausting. The life of the party almost always winds up in a corner with an overcoat over him.

R. M. Moberly
3661   I maintain Christianity is a life much more than a religion.

Amedeo Modigliani
3662   A beefsteak is more important than a drawing. I can easily make a drawing, but I cannot make a beefsteak.

Allan Mogensen and Lillian Gilbreth
3663   Work smarter, not harder.

Raymond Moley
3664   Real equality is not to be decreed by law. It cannot be given and it cannot be forced.

3665   He walks as if balancing the family tree on his nose.

3666   A political war is one in which everyone shoots from the lip.

Molière
3667   That must be wonderful; I don't understand it at all.

3668   For more than forty years I have been speaking prose without knowing it.

3669   A lover even tries to stand well with the house dog.

3670   The world, dear Agnes, is a strange affair.

Marilyn Monroe
3671   When they said Canada, I thought it would be up in the mountains somewhere.

3672   I don't mind living in a man's world as long as I can be a woman in it.

Vaughn Monroe
3673   It now costs more to amuse a child than it once did to educate his father.

Mary Wortley Montagu
3674   I despise the pleasure of pleasing people whom I despise.

3675   I sometimes give myself admirable advice, but I am incapable of taking it.

Charles Edward Montague
3676   War hath no fury like a noncombatant.

Michel-Eyquem de Montaigne
3677   A good marriage would be between a blind wife and a deaf husband.

3678   Eloquence flourished most in Rome when public affairs were in the worst condition.

3679   May God defend me from myself.

3680   No one is exempt from talking nonsense; the mistake is to do it solemnly.

3681   A doctor gets no pleasure out of the health of his friends.

3682   When I play with my cat, who knows but that she regards me more of a plaything than I do her?

3683   We believe nothing so firmly as what we least know.

3684   Seeing she could not make fools wise, fortune has made them lucky.

3685   I prefer the company of peasants because they have not been educated sufficiently to reason incorrectly.

3686   He who is not very strong in memory should not meddle with lying.

3687   Pythagoras used to say life resembles the Olympic Games; a few men strain their muscles to carry off a prize; others bring trinkets to sell to the crowd for a profit; and some there are (and not the worst) who seek no further advantage than to look at the show and see how and why everything is done. They are spectators of other men's lives in order better to judge and manage their own.

3688   I tell the truth, not as much as I would but as much as I dare—and I dare more and more as I grow older.

3689   The heart is a triumphant and mighty emperor that ends as the breakfast of a silly little worm.

3690   Men are most apt to believe what they least understand.

3691   Stability itself is nothing else than a more sluggish motion.

Baron de Montesquieu

3692   I have always observed that to succeed in the world one should seem a fool, but be wise.

3693   What orators lack in depth they give you in length.

3694   We should weep for men at their birth, not at their death.

Charles L. Montesquieu

3695   Politeness is a desire to so contrive it, by word and manner, that others will be pleased with us and with themselves.

3696   Republics are brought to their ends by luxury; monarchies, by poverty.

Maria Montessori

3697   The first idea that the child must acquire, in order to be actively disciplined, is that of the difference between good and evil; and the task of the educator lies in seeing that the child does not confound good with immobility, and evil with activity.

Count Montroud

3698   If anything lucky happens to you, don't fail to go and tell it to your friends in order to annoy them.

Dwight L. Moody

3699   Character: what you are in the dark.

Stan Mooneyham

3700   It is a lot easier emotionally to handle the fact that millions of people are starving if we don't see them as individuals.

George Moore

3701   Taking something from one man and making it worse is plagiarism.

3702   There is nothing so consoling as to find that one's neighbor's troubles are at least as great as one's own.

3703   To be able to distinguish between a badly and well-written book is not enough; a professor of literature can do that occasionally.

3704   There is always a right and a wrong way, and the wrong way always seems the more reasonable.

3705   The incomparable stupidity of life teaches us to love our parents; divine philosophy teaches us to forgive them.

Mary Tyler Moore
3706   There's one beneficial effect of going to Moscow. You come home waving the American flag with all your might!

Henry Morgan
3707   A kleptomaniac is a person who helps himself because he can't help himself.

3708   Any man with ambition, integrity—and $10,000,000—can start a daily newspaper.

J. Pierpont Morgan
3709   Anybody has a right to evade taxes if he can get away with it. No citizen has a moral obligation to assist in maintaining the government.

3710   A man has two reasons for doing anything—a good reason and the real reason.

3711   I am not in Wall Street for my health.

3712   That is not what I asked you. I asked you to tell me how it could be done legally. Come back tomorrow or the next day and tell me how it can be done.

3713   I don't know as I want a lawyer to tell me what I cannot do. I hire him to tell me how to do what I want to do.

3714   If you have to ask how much it costs, you can't afford it.

Lewis Henry Morgan
3715   The time will come when human intelligence will rise to the mastery of property.

Christopher Morley
3716   Genius, cried the commuter,
        As he ran for the 8:13,
        Consists of an infinite capacity
        For catching trains.

3717   By the time the youngest children have learned to keep the place tidy, the oldest grandchildren are on hand to tear it to pieces again.

3718   Dancing is wonderful training for girls; it's the first way you learn to guess what a man is going to do before he does it.

3719   I hate to see men overdressed; a man ought to look like he's put together by accident, not added up on purpose.

3720   Life is a foreign language: all men mispronounce it.

3721   No man is lonely while eating spaghetti—it requires so much attention.

3722   There is only one rule for being a good talker: learn to listen.

3723   All cities are mad, but the madness is gallant. All cities are beautiful, but the beauty is grim.

3724   The trouble with wedlock is, there's not enough wed and too much lock.

3725   Lots of times you have to pretend to join a parade in which you're not really interested in order to get where you're going.

3726   Pop used to say about the Presbyterians, it don't prevent them committing all the sins there are but it keeps them from getting any fun out of it.

3727   Only the sinner has a right to preach.

3728   This is the most unselfish of eras because hardly anyone is egotist enough to wish to do his own thinking. There are always so many ready and eager to do it for us.

John Morley, Viscount Morley of Blackburn
3729   Letter-writing: that most delightful way of wasting time.

3730   Three things matter in a speech: who says it, how he says it, and what he says—and, of the three, the last matters the least.

3731   You have not converted a man because you have silenced him.

3732   In politics the choice is constantly between two evils.

3733   Theodore Roosevelt: a combination of St. Paul and St. Vitus.

3734   The great business of life is to be, to do, to do without, and to depart.

3735   Every man of us has all the centuries in him.

Colin Morris
3736   Your theology is what you are when the talking stops and the action starts.

Desmond Morris
3737   Clearly, then, the city is not a concrete jungle, it is a human zoo.

Dwight W. Morrow

3738   Any party which takes credit for the rain must not be surprised if its opponents blame it for the drought.

Charles W. Morton

3739   Among a husband's other uses, most wives find him a handy thing with which to impress other women.

3740   The smallest piece of silver which can qualify as a wedding gift is a marmalade spoon.

Grandma Moses (Anna Mary Moses)

3741   I found it [painting] was a lot easier than embroidering.

Bill Moyers

3742   There are honest journalists like there are honest politicians— they stay bought.

Daniel Patrick Moynihan

3743   The great corporations of this country were not founded by ordinary people. They were founded by people with extraordinary energy, intelligence, ambition, aggressiveness. All those factors go into the primordial capitalist urge.

Robert K. Mueller

3744   Those who think they know it all are very annoying to those of us who do.

Malcolm Muggeridge

3745   Never forget that only dead fish swim with the stream.

Ethel Watts Mumford

3746   Think of your ancestors and your posterity, and you will never marry.

3747   In the midst of life we are in debt.

3748   When folly is bliss, 'tis ignorance to be otherwise.

3749   Knowledge is power, if you know it about the right person.

3750   A man of courage never needs weapons, but he may need bail.

3751   Oh wad some power the giftie gie us to see some people before they see us.

Lewis Mumford

3752   Our national flower is the concrete cloverleaf.

Saki (Hector Hugh Munro)

3753 Bernard Shaw had discovered himself and gave ungrudgingly of his discovery to the world.

3754 He is one of those people who would be enormously improved by death.

3755 He's simply got the instinct for being unhappy highly developed.

3756 I'm living so far beyond my income that we may almost be said to be living apart.

3757 Children are given to us to discourage our better emotions.

3758 That woman's art-jargon tires me ... she's so fond of talking of certain pictures as "growing on one," as though they were a sort of fungus.

3759 The sacrifices of friendship were beautiful in her eyes as long as she was not asked to make them.

3760 All decent people live beyond their incomes nowadays, and those who aren't respectable live beyond other people's. A few gifted individuals manage to do both.

3761 "No one has ever said it," observed Lady Caroline, "but how painfully true it is that the poor have us always with them!"

3762 Scandal is merely the compassionate allowance which the gay make to the humdrum. Think how many blameless lives are brightened by the blazing indiscretions of other people.

3763 The young man turned to him with a disarming candor which instantly put him on his guard.

Rupert Murdoch

3764 The buck stops with the guy who signs the checks.

3765 Money in itself doesn't interest me. But you must make money to go on building the business.

Thomas A. Murphy

3766 General Motors is not in the business of making cars. General Motors is in the business of making money.

Edward R. Murrow

3767 When the politicians complain that TV turns their proceedings into a circus, it should be made clear that the circus was already there, and that TV has merely demonstrated that not all performers are well trained.

Abraham Myerson

3768   The environmentalists seem to believe that if cats gave birth to kittens in a stove, the offspring would be biscuits.

Joe Namath

3769   When you win, nothing hurts.

Dub Nance

3770   There's one thing for which you can be thankful—only you and God have all the facts about yourself.

Napoléon Bonaparte

3771   If I were not Napoléon I would be Alexander.

3772   The English have no exalted sentiments. They can all be bought.

3773   It is cowardly to commit suicide. The English often kill themselves. It is a malady caused by the humid climate.

3774   The surest way to remain poor is to be an honest man.

3775   All empires die of indigestion.

3776   Rascality has limits; stupidity has not.

3777   Soldiers win battles and generals get the credit.

3778   Doctors will have more lives to answer for in the next world than even we generals.

3779   All celebrated people lose dignity on a close view.

3780   Men take only their needs into consideration—never their abilities.

3781   We must laugh at man to avoid crying for him.

3782   In love, victory goes to the man who runs away.

3783   A man occupied with public or other important business cannot, and need not, attend to spelling.

3784   There is no greater misfortune for a man than to be governed by his wife; in such a case he is neither himself nor his wife, he is a perfect nonentity.

3785   Circumstances! I make circumstances!

Ogden Nash

3786   Progress might have been all right once but it has gone on too long.

3787   Parents were invented to make children happy by giving them something to ignore.

3788   Why did the Lord give us so much quickness of movement unless it was to avoid responsibility?

3789   Marriage is the alliance of two people, one of whom never remembers birthdays and the other never forgets them.

3790   Marriage is the only known example of the happy meeting of the immovable object and the irresistible force.

3791   A family is a unit composed not only of children but of men, women, an occasional animal and the common cold.

3792   Middle age is when you're sitting at home on Saturday night and the telephone rings and you hope it isn't for you.

3793   Democrats are to the manna born.

3794   I think that I shall never see
        A billboard lovely as a tree,
        Perhaps, unless the billboards fall,
        I'll never see a tree at all.

3795   People who work sitting down get paid more than people who work standing up.

3796   I would live all my life in nonchalance and insouciance
        Were it not for making a living, which is rather a nouciance.

3797   To keep your marriage brimming
        With love in the loving cup,
        Whenever you're wrong, admit it,
        Whenever you're right, shut up.

Gamal Abdel Nasser
3798   Abdel Nasser is no more than a transient phenomenon that will run its course and leave.

George Jean Nathan
3799   Politics is the diversion of trivial men who, when they succeed at it, become important in the eyes of more trivial men.

3800   Patriotism is often a veneration of real estate above principles.

3801   Bad officials are elected by good citizens who do not vote.

3802   He writes his plays for the ages—the ages between five and twelve.

3803   Opening night: the night before the play is ready to open.

3804   An optimist is a fellow who believes a housefly is looking for a way to get out.

3805   A happy man may be a successful bishop, dogcatcher, movie actor or sausage-monger, but no happy man ever produced a first-rate piece of painting, sculpture, music or literature.

3806   The test of a real comedian is whether you laugh at him before he opens his mouth.

3807   He has ever been the tin can on his own tail.

3808   Hollywood impresses me as being ten million dollars' worth of intricate and highly ingenious machinery functioning elaborately to put skin on baloney.

3809   I drink to make other people interesting.

3810   In the theater, a hero is one who believes that all women are ladies, a villain one who believes that all ladies are women.

3811   Too much youth, in short, is a bore, since youth lacks variety and has little to fall back upon but animal spirits, which are an even greater bore.

Jacklyn Nation
3812   Would you say a man who has had a hair transplant has a "re-seeded hairline"?

Shri Jawaharlal Nehru
3813   Democracy is good. I say this because other systems are worse.

3814   You don't change the course of history by turning the faces of portraits to the wall.

3815   All my major works have been written in prison. I would recommend prison not only to aspiring writers but to aspiring politicians, too.

3816   Apart from my dislike of their cutting off other people's heads, the tribesmen are fine men.

John Kirk Nelson
3817   More and more these days I find myself pondering on how to reconcile my net income with my gross habits.

Johann Nestroy
3818   If you don't lose your mind over certain things, you haven't got a mind to lose.

3819   Spring is a fine thing: you get the enjoyment of a thief and still remain an honest man.

Dorothy Nevill

3820 The real art of conversation is not only to say the right thing in the right place but to leave unsaid the wrong thing at the tempting moment.

Edwin Newman

3821 He does not speak as much as exhale, and he exhales polysyllabically. [On William F. Buckley, Jr.]

Douglas Newton

3822 The worldwide fraternity of children is the greatest of savage tribes, and the only one which shows no sign of dying out.

Howard W. Newton

3823 Tact is the art of making a point without making an enemy.

3824 The thoughtless are rarely wordless.

Nicholas I of Russia

3825 I do not rule Russia; ten thousand clerks do.

Beverley Nichols

3826 Marriage is a book of which the first chapter is written in poetry and the remaining chapters in prose.

3827 The worst thing you can possibly do to a woman is to deprive her of a grievance.

Ben Nicholson

3828 My tutor does watercolors; they are like the work of a girl of fourteen when she was twelve.

Sir Godfrey Nicholson

3829 A platitude is a truth we are tired of hearing.

Meredith Nicholson

3830 A man who can be a hero to his wife's relations may face the rest of the world fearlessly.

Sir Seymour Nicks

3831 It is no excuse when you are neglecting your wife to say it doesn't matter because she is only a relation by marriage.

Harold Nicolson

3832 The Irish do not want anyone to wish them well; they want everyone to wish their enemies ill.

3833   The great secret of successful marriage is to treat all disasters as incidents and none of the incidents as disasters.

Reinhold Niebuhr
3834   Man's capacity for justice makes democracy possible, but man's inclination to injustice makes democracy necessary.

Friedrich Wilhelm Nietzsche
3835   Plato is a bore.

3836   Blessed are the forgetful, for they get the better even of their blunders.

3837   He who cannot lie doesn't know what truth is.

3838   I do not give alms; I am not poor enough for that.

3839   The last Christian died on the cross.

3840   A married philosopher is necessarily comic.

3841   Neighbors praise unselfishness because they profit by it.

3842   No small art is it to sleep; it is necessary to keep awake all day for that purpose.

3843   A high civilization is a pyramid: it can stand only on a broad base; its primary prerequisite is a strong and soundly consolidated mediocrity.

3844   In every real man a child is hidden that wants to play.

3845   The advantage of a bad memory is that one enjoys several times the same good things for the first time.

3846   At bottom every man knows well enough that he is a unique being, only once on this earth; and by no extraordinary chance will such a marvelously picturesque piece of diversity in unity as he is ever be put together a second time.

3847   Better know nothing than half-know many things.

3848   The future influences the present just as much as the past.

3849   Love is the state in which man sees things most decidedly as they are not.

3850   In individuals, insanity is rare, but in groups, parties, nations and epochs it is the rule.

3851   The earth has a skin and that skin has diseases; one of its diseases is called man.

3852   "I have done this," says memory; "I can't have done this," says pride. In the end, memory yields.

3853   That roguish and cheerful vice, politeness.

3854   A man who is very busy seldom changes his opinions.

H. K. Nixon

3855   Everyone has ancestors and it is only a question of going back far enough to find a good one.

Richard M. Nixon

3856   There is one thing solid and fundamental in politics—the law of change. What's up today is down tomorrow.

3857   I would have made a good pope.

3858   Always remember others may hate you but those who hate you don't win unless you hate them. And then you destroy yourself.

3859   I wanted to be a sports writer, but it took me too long to turn out my stuff. I found I could become Vice President faster than I could become a newspaperman.

Louis Nizer

3860   Most lawyers who win a case advise their clients that "We have won," and when justice has frowned upon their cause that "You have lost."

Montagu Norman

3861   There is no problem about money, except who has it.

Kathleen Norris

3862   Life is easier to take than you'd think; all that is necessary is to accept the impossible, do without the indispensable, and bear the intolerable.

3863   From birth to age eighteen, a girl needs good parents. From eighteen to thirty-five, she needs good looks. From thirty-five to fifty-five, a woman needs personality. And from fifty-five on, the old lady needs cash.

Lord Northcliffe

3864   Journalism—a profession whose business it is to explain to others what it personally does not understand.

Edgar Wilson "Bill" Nye

3865   At a Fourth of July celebration, it is wonderful how many great men there are and how they swarm on the speaker's platform.

3866   Be virtuous and you will be happy; but you will be lonesome, sometimes.

3867   I do not believe that it will always be popular to wear mourning for our friends, unless we feel a little doubtful about where they went.

3868   I rise from bed the first thing in the morning not because I am dissatisfied with it, but because I cannot carry it with me during the day.

3869   Kind words will never die—neither will they buy groceries.

3870   Let every man who pants for fame select his own style of pant and go ahead.

3871   Many public speakers are good extemporaneous listeners.

3872   Self-made men are very apt to usurp the prerogative of the Almighty and overwork themselves.

3873   We are both great men, but I have succeeded better in keeping it a profound secret than he has.

3874   There must be at least 500,000,000 rats in the United States; of course, I am speaking only from memory.

3875   Winter lingered so long in the lap of Spring that it occasioned a great deal of talk.

Johnson O'Connor

3876   Three characteristics of top executives are: slow speech, impressive appearance, and a complete lack of sense of humor.

Clifford Odets

3877   There are two kinds of marriages—where the husband quotes the wife, or where the wife quotes the husband.

Al Okin

3878   My grandson recites the Gettysburg Address and he's only nine. Lincoln didn't say it until he was fifty.

Lane Olinghouse

3879   The average barber now makes more money per word than the average writer.

Vic Oliver

3880   If a man runs after money, he's money-mad; if he keeps it, he's a capitalist; if he spends it, he's a playboy; if he doesn't get it, he's a ne'er-do-well; if he doesn't try to get it, he lacks ambition. If he gets it without working for it, he's a parasite; and if he accumulates it after a lifetime of hard work, people call him a fool who never got anything out of life.

Austin O'Malley

3881   All things come to him who waits—even justice.

3882   The best blood will at some time get into a fool or a mosquito.

3883   The best throw of the dice is to throw them away.

3884   Better a bald head than none at all.

3885   Circumstantial evidence is like a blackberry, which when red or white is really green.

3886   An Englishman thinks seated; a Frenchman, standing; an American, pacing; an Irishman, afterward.

3887   A gentleman never heard the story before.

3888   God shows his contempt for wealth by the kind of person he selects to receive it.

3889   A hole is nothing at all, but you can break your neck in it.

3890   If you keep your mouth shut you will never put your foot in it.

3891   It is a foolish man that hears all he hears.

3892   In levying taxes and in shearing sheep it is well to stop when you get down to the skin.

3893   It is as easy to give advice to yourself as to others, and as useless.

3894   Marriage is a meal where the soup is better than the dessert.

3895   Music is another lady that talks charmingly and says nothing.

3896   No man can have a reasonable opinion of women until he has long lost interest in hair restorers.

3897   The person that always says just what he thinks at last gets just what he deserves.

3898   Practical prayer is harder on the soles of your shoes than on the knees of your trousers.

3899   Revenge is often like biting a dog because the dog bit you.

3900 The smaller the head, the bigger the dream.

3901 Some men can live up to their loftiest ideals without ever going higher than a basement.

3902 The statesman shears the sheep, the politician skins them.

3903 There are ten church members by inheritance for one by conviction.

3904 There should be more in American liberty than the privilege we enjoy in insulting the President with impunity.

3905 Those that think it permissible to tell white lies soon grow color-blind.

3906 Ugliness is a point of view: an ulcer is wonderful to a pathologist.

3907 We smile at the women who are eagerly following the fashions in dress whilst we are as eagerly following the fashions in thought.

3908 Exclusiveness is a characteristic of recent riches, high society and the skunk.

3909 God is good to the Irish, but no one else is: not even the Irish.

3910 The three most important events of human life are equally devoid of reason: birth, marriage and death.

3911 Show me a genuine case of platonic friendship, and I shall show you two old or homely faces.

3912 A politician is like quicksilver; if you try to put your finger on him, you will find nothing under it.

3913 Surgery: by far the worst snob among the handicrafts.

3914 It is a mad thief, or a successful author, that plunders the dead.

3915 When there is no will, there is no way for the lawyers.

Aristotle Onassis
3916 After a certain point money is meaningless. It ceases to be the goal. The game is what counts.

Eugene O'Neill
3917 None of us can help the things life has done to us. They're done before you realize it, and once they're done they make you do other things until at last everything comes between you and what you'd like to be, and you have lost your true self forever.

3918 For de little stealin' dey gits you in jail soon or late. For de big stealin' dey makes you emperor and puts you in de Hall o' Fame when you croaks.

Tip O'Neill

3919   I'm against any deal I'm not in on.

Robert Orben

3920   Do you ever get the feeling that the only reason we have elections is to find out if the polls were right?

3921   The detective series on TV always end at precisely the right moment—after the criminal is arrested and before the court turns him loose.

3922   If someone calls me fat, I don't get angry. I just turn the other chin.

3923   Answering a harasser: Sir, I'd like to give you a going-away present, but you've got to do your part.

3924   Whoever said nothing is impossible never tried to slam a revolving door.

3925   Sometimes I get the feeling that the two biggest problems in America today are making ends meet—and making meetings end.

3926   Middle age is when everything starts to click—your elbows, knees, and neck.

3927   More than ever before, Americans are suffering from back problems—back taxes, back rent, back auto payments.

3928   And so, in conclusion, may the Bluebird of Happiness fly over your shopping cart and stamp everything with last year's prices.

3929   Most new homes are being bought on the layaway plan. You pay for them until they lay you away.

3930   One of the most perplexing questions of our time: Where do all the solutions go after a candidate gets elected?

3931   Sometimes I get the feeling that the whole world is against me—but deep down I know that's not true. Some of the smaller countries are neutral.

3932   A specialist is someone who has focused all of his ignorance on to one subject.

3933   Yesterday I was at a wedding where the minister looked at the couple and solemnly pronounced them person and person.

3934   I've been working all my life, but somehow it seems longer.

3935   For a real quick energy boost, nothing beats having the boss walk in.

3936   What is happening to our drive, to our spirit, to our initiative? This morning I saw two robins standing in line for worm stamps.

Lord Boyd Orr
3937   If people have to choose between freedom and sandwiches, they will take sandwiches.

José Ortega y Gasset
3938   To learn English, you must begin by thrusting the jaw forward, almost clenching the teeth, and practically immobilizing the lips. In this way the English produce the series of unpleasant little mews of which their language consists.

William A. Orton
3939   If you keep your mind sufficiently open, people will throw a lot of rubbish into it.

George Orwell
3940   The typical socialist ... a prim little man with a white-collar job, usually a secret teetotaller and often with vegetarian leanings.

3941   A man receiving charity practically always hates his benefactor— it is a fixed characteristic of human nature.

Sir William Osler
3942   The desire to take medicine is perhaps the greatest feature which distinguishes man from animals.

3943   There are only two sorts of doctors: those who practice with their brains, and those who practice with their tongues.

3944   With half an hour's reading in bed every night as a steady practice, the busiest man can get a fair education before the plasma sets in the periganglionic spaces of his gray cortex.

3945   One of the first duties of the physician is to educate the masses not to take medicine.

3946   A physician who treats himself has a fool for a patient.

3947   Taking a lady's hand gives her confidence in her physician.

3948   Avoid wine and women—choose a freckle-faced girl for a wife; they are invariably more amiable.

Martha Ostenso
3949   Edith was a little country bounded on the north, south, east, and west by Edith.

Sir Thomas Overbury

3950   The man who has not anything to boast of but his illustrious ancestors is like a potato—the only good belonging to him is underground.

Ovid

3951   Let the man who does not wish to be idle fall in love.

3952   A woman is always buying something.

David Owen

3953   A consultant is someone who will take your watch off your wrist and tell you what time it is.

Robert Owen

3954   All the world is queer save thee and me, and even thou art a little queer.

Kate M. Owney

3955   An old-timer is one who remembers when we counted our blessings instead of our calories.

Earl of Oxford and Asquith

3956   You should read it, though there is much that is skipworthy.

3957   A Balliol education gives a man a tranquil sense of effortless superiority.

Satchel Paige

3958   Don't look back. Something may be gaining on you.

Barry Pain

3959   Don't answer back if you're out to make money, but do if you're out for enjoyment.

Val Palmer

3960   Aren't women's magazines funny? Half the pages list fattening recipes, the other half diets.

Lord Palmerston

3961   Die, my dear doctor, that's the last thing I shall ever do.

3962   Dirt is not dirt, but only matter in the wrong place.

Ivan N. Panin

3963   The husband needs to be blind at times; the wife, deaf; both need much of the time to be dumb.

3964   My neighbor tells me there is no God; I give him his dinner; this much I owe him. I keep my eye on my spoons: this much I owe to myself.

Paul Parfait

3965   Of all men, Adam was the happiest; he had no mother-in-law.

Dorothy Parker

3966   Some men break your heart in two,
Some men fawn and flatter,
Some men never look at you;
And that cleans up the matter.

3967   The affair between Margot Asquith and Margot Asquith will live as one of the prettiest love stories in all literature.

3968   And where does she find them? [On hearing that Clare Booth Luce was always kind to her social inferiors.]

3969   A girl's best friend is her mutter.

3970   Men seldom make passes at girls who wear glasses.

3971   She ran the whole gamut of the emotions from A to B.

3972   The best way to keep children home is to make the home atmosphere pleasant—and let the air out of the tires.

3973   The two most beautiful words in the English language are: "Check enclosed."

3974   By the time you swear you're his,
Shivering and sighing,
And he vows his passion is
Infinite, undying—
Lady, make a note of this:
One of you is lying.

3975   The only ism Hollywood believes in is plagiarism.

3976   Wit has truth in it; wisecracking is simply calisthenics with words.

Suzy Parker

3977   I do everything for a reason. Most of the time the reason is money.

Charles H. Parkhurst

3978   The wicked flee when no man pursueth, but they make better time when someone is after them.

3979   The man who lives by himself and for himself is apt to be corrupted by the company he keeps.

C. Northcote Parkinson

3980   Work expands so as to fill the time available for its completion. The thing to be done swells in importance and complexity in a direct ratio with the time to be spent.

3981   Expenditure rises to meet income. Individual expenditure not only rises to meet income but tends to surpass it . . . [and] what is true of individuals is also true of governments.

Vernon L. Parrington

3982   Very little happens to a teacher after he has achieved his professorship.

Blaise Pascal

3983   If all men knew what each said of the other, there would not be four friends in the world.

3984   Had Cleopatra's nose been shorter, the whole face of the world would have been different.

3985   I have made this a rather long letter because I haven't had time to make it shorter.

3986   To be a real philosopher one must be able to laugh at philosophy.

3987   Continued eloquence wearies.

3988   The heart has its reasons which reason does not understand.

3989   Since we cannot know all that is to be known of everything, we ought to know a little about everything.

3990   Vanity is so secure in the heart of man that everyone wants to be admired: even I who write this, and you who read this.

3991   Those we call the ancients were really new in everything.

3992   Men despise religion; they hate, and fear it is true.

3993   There are only two kinds of men: the righteous, who believe themselves sinners; the rest, sinners, who believe themselves righteous.

3994   Man is but a reed, the weakest in nature, but he is a thinking reed.

Victoria Pasternak

3995   You'll find in no park or city
        A monument to a committee.

Louis Pasteur

3996   When I approach a child, he inspires in me two sentiments: tenderness for what he is, and respect for what he may become.

William Penn Patrick
3997   Those who condemn wealth are those who have none and see no chance of getting it.

Bruce Patterson
3998   Psychologist: a man who, when a beautiful girl enters the room, watches everybody else.

Thomas Love Peacock
3999   I never failed to convince an audience that the best thing they could do was to go away.

Norman Vincent Peale
4000   Americans are so tense and keyed up that it is impossible even to put them to sleep with a sermon.

4001   The trouble with most of us is that we would rather be ruined by praise than saved by criticism.

Hesketh Pearson
4002   There is no stronger craving in the world than that of the rich for titles, except that of the titled for riches.

Lester Pearson
4003   Not only did he not suffer fools gladly, he did not suffer them at all. [On Dean Acheson.]

4004   The grim fact is that we prepare for war like precocious giants and for peace like retarded pygmies.

4005   The situation is one something like living with your wife. Sometimes it is difficult and even irritating to live with her but it is always impossible to live without her.

Westbrook Pegler
4006   Golf was, I should say offhand, the most useless outdoor game ever devised to waste the time and try the spirit of man.

4007   I am a member of the rabble in good standing.

Mario Pei
4008   If you scoff at language study ... how, save in terms of language, will you scoff?

Claiborne Pell
4009   People only leave by way of the box—ballot or coffin. [On life in Washington.]

Mary L. Pendered

4010   Nobody knows why men marry, so it's best to make the most of any chance you happen to get.

William Penn

4011   To be like Christ is to be a Christian.

4012   I expect to pass through life but once. If therefore, there be any kindness I can show, or any good thing I can do to any fellow being, let me do it now, and not defer or neglect it, as I shall not pass this way again.

Boise Penrose

4013   Public office is the last refuge of a scoundrel.

Samuel Pepys

4014   My wife, poor wretch, is troubled with her lonely life.

4015   Strange to say what delight we married people have to see these poor fools decoyed into our condition.

4016   Coming home tonight I did go to examine my wife's accounts, and finding things that seemed somewhat doubtful I was angry, though she did make it pretty plain; but confessed that when she do miss a sum she do add something to other things to make it, and upon my being very angry she do protest she will here lay up something for herself and buy her a necklace with, which madded me and so still trouble me, for I fear she will forget by degrees the way of living cheap and under sense of want.

4017   Most men that do thrive in the world do forget to take pleasure during the time that they are getting their estate, but reserve that till they have got one, and then it is too late for them to enjoy it.

S. J. Perelman

4018   I don't know much about medicine, but I know what I like.

Shimon Peres

4019   Iran is rich enough to support revolution as industry.

Pericles

4020   Master, I marvel how the fishes live in the sea.
        Why, as men do a-land: the great ones eat up the little ones.

Evita Perón

4021   Without fanaticism one cannot accomplish anything.

Juan Perón

4022   If I had not been born Perón, I should have liked to be Perón.

Marshal Pétain

4023   To write one's memoirs is to speak ill of everyone except oneself.

Laurence J. Peter

4024   America is the land of opportunity if you're a businessman in Japan.

4025   Only a mediocre person is always at his best.

4026   The modern child will answer you back before you've said anything.

4027   Work is achieved by those employees who have not yet reached their level of incompetence.

4028   There are two kinds of egotists: those who admit it, and the rest of us.

4029   Don't worry about middle age: you'll outgrow it.

4030   A pessimist is a man who looks both ways before crossing a one-way street.

4031   An economist is an expert who will know tomorrow why the things he predicted yesterday didn't happen today.

4032   There are some men who, in a fifty-fifty proposition, insist on getting the hyphen too.

Laurence J. Peter and Raymond Hull

4033   If you don't know where you are going, you will probably end up somewhere else.

Petronius

4034   We trained hard ... but every time we were beginning to form up into teams, we would be reorganized. I was to learn later in life that we tend to meet any new situation by reorganizing ... and a wonderful method it can be for creating the illusion of progress while producing inefficiency and demoralization.

Arthur L. Phelps

4035   A Canadian is a fellow who has become a North American without becoming an American.

Kaye Phelps

4036   Let not the atom bomb
        Be the final sequel—
        In which all men—
        Are cremated equal.

William Lyon Phelps

4037   At a certain age some people's minds close up; they live on their intellectual fat.

4038   A cold is both positive and negative; sometimes the Eyes have it and sometimes the Nose.

4039   If I were running the world I would have it rain only between 2 and 5 A.M.—anyone who was out then ought to get wet.

4040   This is the final test of a gentleman: his respect for those who can be of no possible service to him.

4041   Nature makes boys and girls lovely to look upon so they can be tolerated until they acquire some sense.

4042   If happiness truly consisted in physical ease and freedom from care, then the happiest individual would not be either a man or a woman; it would be, I think, an American cow.

4043   Know thyself. A Yale undergraduate left on his door a placard for the janitor on which was written, "Call me at 7 o'clock; it is absolutely necessary that I get up at seven. Make no mistake. Keep knocking until I answer." Under this he had written: "Try again at ten."

Prince Philip of England

4044   I am convinced that the greatest contribution Britain has made to the national life of Uruguay was teaching the people football.

4045   It's no good shutting your eyes and saying "Britain is Best" three times a day after meals, and expect it to be so. [Opening the Design Centre for British Industries.]

4046   The trouble with senior management to an outsider is that there are too many one-ulcer men holding down two-ulcer jobs.

4047   On his opening of the Melbourne Olympic Games, 1956: I made, if I may say so, the best speech of my life. It consisted of exactly twelve words.

4048   It is my invariable custom to say something flattering to begin with so that I shall be excused if by any chance I put my foot in it later on.

4049   In the normal way, I am not noticeably reticent about talking of things about which I know nothing.

4050   Dontopedalogy—the art of opening your mouth and putting your foot in it.

4051   British food is something like a small child. When it's good, it's very, very good; when it's bad, it's absolutely awful.

4052   After many years' experience, I have come to learn that the present moment, whatever it may be, is never a good one for raising money.

4053   It is not a bad idea to remind the people who live in towns and get their milk in tins or bottles and butter in packets, that it all starts with the cow.

4054   We all know that dinners are occupational hazards for Lord Mayors.

4055   I am referred to in that splendid language [Urdu] as "Fella belong Mrs. Queen."

4056   Privilege is privilege—whether it is due to money or intellect or whether you have six toes.

4057   The only active sport which I follow is polo—and most of the work's done by the pony!

4058   All money nowadays seems to be produced with a natural homing instinct for the Treasury.

H. I. Phillips
4059   Oratory: the art of making deep noises from the chest sound like important messages from the brain.

Wendell Phillips
4060   You can always get the truth from an American statesman after he has turned seventy or given up hope of the Presidency.

4061   The Puritan's idea of Hell is a place where everybody has to mind his own business.

Eden Phillpots
4062   We always think every other man's job is easier than our own. And the better he does it, the easier it looks.

Pablo Picasso

4063   When I was a child my mother said to me, "If you become a soldier you'll be a general. If you become a monk you'll end up as the pope." Instead I became a painter and wound up as Picasso.

4064   I have been called a charlatan and a genius. It's possible both statements may be true.

4065   I'd like to live like a poor man with lots of money.

4066   Work is a necessity for man. Man invented the alarm clock.

Franklin Pierce

4067   In a body where there are more than one hundred talking lawyers, you can make no calculation upon the termination of any debate and frequently, the more trifling the subject, the more animated and protracted the discussion. [On the U.S. Congress.]

Arthur Wing Pinero

4068   A financier is a pawnbroker with imagination.

4069   How many "coming men" has one known! Where on earth do they all go to?

4070   If there were many more like her, the stock of halos would give out.

4071   A married woman's as old as her husband makes her feel.

William Pitt

4072   It was a saying of Lord Chatham that the parks were the lungs of London.

4073   Don't tell me of a man's being able to talk sense; everyone can talk sense—can he talk nonsense?

Plato

4074   Of all the animals, the boy is the most unmanageable.

4075   Democracy ... is a charming form of government, full of variety and disorder, and dispensing a sort of equality to equals and unequals alike.

4076   The Athenians do not mind a man being clever, as long as he keeps it to himself.

4077   Man is a two-legged animal without feathers.

4078   Poets utter great and wise things which they do not themselves understand.

4079   Wise men talk because they have something to say; fools, because they have to say something.

4080   There is far greater peril in buying knowledge than in buying meat and drink.

4081   Love: a grave mental disease.

4082   The rich have many consolations.

J. R. Platt
4083   It's just as sure a recipe for failure to have the right idea fifty years too soon as five years too late.

Plautus
4084   I much prefer a compliment, insincere or not, to sincere criticism.

4085   A mouse never trusts his life to one hole only.

4086   The more might, the more right.

Gary Player
4087   The harder you work the luckier you get.

Willis Player
4088   A liberal is a person whose interests aren't at stake at the moment.

Pliny the Elder
4089   There is no book so bad but something valuable may be derived from it.

Pliny the Younger
4090   You say there is nothing to write about. Then write to me that there is nothing to write about.

4091   Prosperity tries the fortunate, adversity the great.

John J. Plomp
4092   You know children are growing up when they start asking questions that have answers.

George W. Plunkitt
4093   If my worst enemy was given the job of writing my epitaph when I'm gone, he couldn't do more than write: "George W. Plunkitt. He seen his opportunities and he took 'em."

4094   The politician who steals is worse than a thief. He is a fool. With the grand opportunities all around for a man with political pull, there's no excuse for stealin' a cent.

Plutarch
4095   A prating barber asked Archelaus how he would be trimmed. He answered, "In silence."

4096   It is indeed desirable to be well descended, but the glory belongs to our ancestors.

Edgar Allan Poe
4097   I have great faith in fools; self-confidence my friends call it.

4098   The people have nothing to do with the laws but to obey them.

4099   Of puns it has been said that they who most dislike them are least able to utter them.

Karl Otto Pöhl
4100   Nothing is more permanent than a temporary government budget deficit.

John Garland Pollard
4101   Executive ability is deciding quickly and getting somebody else to do the work.

4102   Genealogy: tracing yourself back to people better than you are.

Channing Pollock
4103   A critic is a legless man who teaches running.

4104   He admits that there are two sides to every question—his own and the wrong side.

4105   No man in the world has more courage than the man who can stop after eating one peanut.

4106   Marriage: a great institution, and no family should be without it.

Robert Pollock
4107   With one hand he put
A penny in the urn of poverty
And with the other took a shilling out.

Georges Pompidou
4108   A statesman is a politician who places himself at the service of the nation. A politician is a statesman who places the nation at his service.

Mary Pettibone Poole

4109   Culture is what your butcher would have if he were a surgeon.

4110   He who laughs, lasts.

Alexander Pope

4111   Damn with faint praise, assent with civil leer,
        And, without sneering, teach the rest to sneer.

4112   A family is but too often a commonwealth of malignants.

4113   Histories are more full of examples of the fidelity of dogs than of
        friends.

4114   I am dying, sir, of a hundred good symptoms.

4115   Amusement is the happiness of those that cannot think.

4116   A little learning is a dangerous thing;
        Drink deep, or taste not the Pierian spring.

4117   Sir, I admit your general rule,
        That every poet is a fool;
        But you yourself may serve to show it,
        That every fool is not a poet.

4118   He that would pun would pick a pocket.

4119   The difference between what is commonly called ordinary com-
        pany and good company is only hearing the same things said in a little
        room or in a large salon, at small tables or at great tables, before two
        candles or twenty sconces.

4120   I am his Highness' dog at Kew.
        Pray tell me, sir, whose dog are you?

4121   To be angry is to revenge the fault of others upon ourselves.

4122   Teach me to feel another's woe, to hide the fault I see; that mercy I
        to others show, that mercy show to me.

4123   Blessed is he who expects nothing, for he shall never be disap-
        pointed.

4124   An honest man's the noblest work of God.

Dan Post

4125   An egotist is a man who thinks that if he hadn't been born, people
        would have wondered why.

Enoch Powell

4126   I was born a Tory. I am a Tory and I shall die a Tory!

Gil Pratt

4127   When we were in Florence we visited the Pizza Palace.

George D. Prentice

4128   A bare assertion is not necessarily the naked truth.

4129   Be gentle in old age; peevishness is worse in second childhood than in first.

4130   A dentist at work in his vocation always looks down in the mouth.

4131   The difference between us and our neighbor is that we don't tell half of what we know while he doesn't know half of what he tells.

4132   The Great Author of All made everything out of nothing, but many a human author makes nothing out of everything.

4133   In these days the greater part of whitewashing is done with ink.

4134   Many a writer seems to think he is never profound except when he can't understand his own meaning.

4135   A pin has as much head as some authors, and a good deal more point.

4136   Some members of Congress would best promote the country's peace by holding their own.

4137   Some people use one half their ingenuity to get into debt, and the other half to avoid paying it.

4138   There are two periods when Congress does no business: one is before the holidays, and the other after.

4139   When a young man complains that a young lady has no heart, it is a pretty certain sign that she has his.

4140   What man wants: all he can get; what woman wants: all she can't get.

4141   If a woman could talk out of the two sides of her mouth at the same time, a great deal would be said on both sides.

Keith Preston

4142   We wanted Li Wing
But we winged Willie Wong,
A sad but excusable
Slip of the Tong.

4143   A modernist married a fundamentalist wife,
And she led him a catechism and dogma life.

4144   The great god Ra whose shrine once covered acres
Is filler now for crossword-puzzle makers.

4145   I am the captain of my soul;
I rule it with stern joy;
And yet I think I had more fun
When I was cabin boy.

4146   Two things make woman slow, we find,
In going any place;
For first she must make up her mind
And then her face.

John Boynton Priestley

4147   We should behave toward our country as women behave toward the men they love. A loving wife will do anything for her husband except stop criticizing and trying to improve him. We should cast the same affectionate but sharp glance at our country.

4148   We cannot get grace from gadgets. In the Bakelite house of the future, the dishes may not break, but the heart can. Even a man with ten shower baths may find life flat, stale and unprofitable.

4149   His wife might not be a clever woman, but she was a cosy woman, and there was a lot to be said for cosiness in this very uncosy world.

Matthew Prior

4150   They talk most who have the least to say.

Herbert V. Prochnow, Sr.

4151   A plagiarist is someone who improves upon something that was poorly written.

4152   The quickest way to become convinced that spanking is unnecessary is to become a grandparent.

4153   If you don't think there is a perfect person in the world, you haven't heard a political campaign speech.

4154   In high-priced restaurants they ought to have one table at which you could starve at reasonable prices.

4155   Old gardeners never die. They just spade away and then throw in the trowel.

4156   Pocket calculators don't do a whole lot for the brain, but they provide wonderful training for the fellow who plans to make a living by working only his forefinger.

4157   The real reason you can't take it with you is that it goes before you do.

4158   To err is human—but usually a much better excuse is demanded.

4159   A person proud of his knowledge is ignorant.

4160   Before credit cards, we always knew exactly how much we were broke.

4161   In controversial matters, my perception's rather fine; I always see both points of view—the one that's wrong, and mine.

4162   You can get about everything on credit now except some good easy money.

4163   Let's face it, there's only one perfect child in the world—and every mother has it.

4164   Procrastination is the greatest labor-saving invention of all time.

4165   A piece of furniture with a wood top is almost human.

4166   A smart wife has the steaks on when her husband returns from his fishing trip.

4167   Some people won't take it with them because they didn't save any to take.

4168   We like the person in a heated discussion who says nothing in a calm voice and without emotion.

4169   Enough is just a little more than the neighbors have.

4170   Some people not only keep you from being lonely but make you wish you were.

4171   If you don't like worms, what's the sense of being the early bird?

4172   We have no time for the person who keeps talking about himself. We like the brilliant fellow who talks about us.

4173   An optimist is a person who drops a dollar in the collection plate and expects a twenty dollar sermon.

4174   Most folks would learn more by listening than talking but it isn't as much fun.

4175   Wealth doesn't buy happiness, but it buys some interesting substitutes.

4176   It's remarkable how easy it is to read the traffic signs if a motor-cycle cop is just back of you.

4177   For each dollar the United States spends it takes in about 90 cents. It is only the large number of dollars we spend which makes this work.

4178   Many a man who doesn't play golf can't give it up.

4179   The nicest thing about not going away on a vacation is that you don't have to come home to rest up from it.

4180   A child who knows the value of a dollar must be pretty discouraged.

4181   The only good thing about an egotist is that he doesn't talk about other people.

4182   The ranch-type house did away with the unsightly clutter in the attic and basement. Now it's in the garage.

4183   The trouble with political jokes is that they sometimes get elected.

4184   He is the kind of a friend you can depend on—always around when he needs you.

4185   It used to be that a fool and his money were soon parted, but now it happens to everybody.

4186   "It's me" is called poor English, but we really think it ain't so bad.

4187   Never put off until tomorrow what you can do today, because by that time there will be a tax on it.

4188   It isn't easy to love your neighbor as your pelf.

4189   You can say what you want to around home because no one pays any attention to you.

4190   When there is nothing to be said, some person prepares a speech on it.

4191   The man who never makes a mistake must get tired of doing nothing.

4192   It has taken three generations to go from farm to garden to can opener.

4193   After the first hour a large cocktail party sounds like a zoo at feeding time.

4194   A husband looked at his house, his car and his furniture and said it was wonderful so many people made a living on what he had not paid for.

4195   It's not hard to be an executive. Things change so fast you can't be wrong all the time.

4196   This country might have fewer problems today if the Indians had adopted more stringent immigration laws.

4197   The trouble with the world is that there are too many clowns who aren't in the circus.

4198   If you think no one cares if you're alive, try missing a few installment payments.

4199   Just when you think the human race is becoming more intelligent, another song of that kind makes the hit parade.

4200   You can fool all the people some of the time, but you can fool yourself all the time.

4201   Have you ever been at a party when you were too tired to listen and too courteous to leave?

4202   One half the world knows how the other half lives, but they don't know how many installments they are behind.

4203   Some men are born great, some achieve greatness, and some just grate on you.

4204   An honest man is never a successful fisherman.

4205   We suppose the reason some youngsters run away from home is that they don't like to stay there alone.

4206   There is no fool like an old fool—you just can't beat experience.

4207   An empty head almost always goes with a stuffed shirt.

4208   A sign says "Drive slow—you may meet a fool." Better say, "Drive slow—two fools may meet."

4209   A good thing about the world is that conditions never get so bad they couldn't get worse.

4210   Many of us know how to say nothing—few of us know when.

4211   Whenever you feel depressed with what life has done to you, take a look at the family album.

4212   It pays to smile, but if you want to enjoy a good laugh look in the mirror.

4213   Nowadays, kids just have to go to college. How else are they going to get a good high school education?

4214   If you have the determination to keep everlastingly at it, you will attain success as well as a nervous breakdown.

4215 Don't you hate to take advice from somebody who needs it himself?

4216 If you are stupid you don't get lonesome because of a lack of company.

4217 The most common investment problem seems to be the lack of money.

4218 Enough money means more money than you now have.

4219 Most wives probably wonder how their husbands know so much about money and have so little of it.

4220 An ounce of keeping your mouth closed is worth a pound of explanation.

4221 He who hesitates is lost—except a bachelor.

4222 The best way to drive a nail without mashing your fingers is to hold the hammer with both hands.

4223 If one person can do a job in one hour, four persons can do it in four hours.

4224 Money doesn't make fools of persons, but it does tend to show them up.

4225 Nature abhors a vacuum and she sometimes fills an empty head with conceit.

4226 Half the world consists of people who have something to say and don't, and the other half who have nothing to say and keep on saying it.

4227 What the world needs is a tabloid Bible.

4228 Holding a political candidate to the facts is impossible. It's like asking Beethoven where he got the statistics for his Fifth Symphony.

4229 The fellow who argues that all religions should unite probably doesn't speak to his brother-in-law.

4230 A pedagog works against ignorance, but a demagog gets a profit out of it.

4231 When we hear some popular songs, we are sure the illiteracy rate is still pretty high.

4232 There may be songs that never die, but it isn't the fault of TV or radio.

4233 Not only are the sins of the fathers visited upon the children but now-a-days the sins of the children are visited upon the fathers.

4234   Many politicians are for and against an issue and they don't care who knows it.

4235   Always borrow from a pessimist. He never expects to be repaid.

4236   Is a lame duck a politician whose goose has been cooked?

4237   There is still one born every minute, but the Internal Revenue Service gets to him first.

4238   In the old days men blazed trails. Now they burn up the roads.

4239   Our international troubles must be serious because it takes hundreds of luncheon speakers every week to solve them.

4240   A doctor says singing increases blood pressure. Well, we've listened to some that did.

4241   The dove brings peace, and the stork brings tax exemptions.

4242   Only one animal—man—can be skinned and live.

4243   Two can live as cheap as one, but nowadays it takes both of them to earn enough to do it.

4244   The line is often busy when your conscience tries to speak.

4245   He who laughs last may laugh best, but he soon gets a reputation for being dumb.

4246   If at first you don't succeed, you're like most other people.

4247   A politician advocates rigid economy with free spending.

4248   One thing we ought to keep as sound as a dollar is the dollar.

4249   Nations that live by the sword perish by the pensions.

4250   When both the speaker and the audience are confused, the speech is "profound."

4251   A fool and his money are soon invited places.

4252   If you were to list the ten smartest people in town, who would be the other nine?

4253   Those who say you can't take it with you never saw a car packed for a vacation trip.

4254   Experience is a wonderful thing, for it enables you to recognize a mistake when you make it again.

4255   The easiest way to tell the difference between young plants and weeds is to pull up everything. If they come up again, they're weeds.

4256   Being bald has its good points. If you have no hair at all on your head, there is no temptation to part it in the middle.

4257   Too often it is the love of the other fellow's money which is the root of all evil.

4258   The difficult part about making good is that you have to repeat it every day.

4259   A diplomat leads a difficult life. When he isn't straddling an issue, he is dodging one.

4260   In every election some good candidate receives the solid backing of all the good people who don't vote.

4261   Etiquette is knowing how to yawn with your mouth closed.

4262   An executive is one who hires others to do what he is hired to do.

4263   If men had no faith in each other, they would have to live within their incomes.

4264   If a fisherman fibs to us,
        Is his fib amphibious?

4265   Football makes a nation hardy. You build up a lot of strong resistance sitting on a cold concrete seat.

4266   With each friend you buy you get an enemy free.

4267   A banker is a person who is willing to make a loan if you present sufficient evidence to show you don't need it.

4268   A thing of beauty is a great expense.

4269   All you have to do in business is to stand and watch the world go by, and it certainly will.

4270   When children run away from home, it is possible they may be looking for their mothers.

4271   First you have to teach a child to talk; then you have to teach it to keep quiet.

4272   A visitor from Mars could easily pick out the civilized nations. They have the best implements of war.

4273   Nothing helps a person's complexion like putting it to bed before 2 A.M.

4274   A conservative is a person who thinks a rich man should have a square deal.

4275   A conservative says that a radical may sometimes be right, but when he is, he is right for the wrong reasons.

4276   The fellow who never makes a mistake takes his orders from one who does.

4277   Some are bent with toil, and some get crooked trying to avoid it.

4278   The minority is always wrong—at the beginning.

4279   The Germans live to work whereas other people work to live. [Ascribed to a Zurich banker by Herbert V. Prochnow.]

4280   Sometimes a nation abolishes God, but fortunately God is more tolerant.

4281   The greatest misfortune in government is that those out of office always know the answers to the nation's problems.

4282   To err may be human, but to admit it isn't.

4283   Nothing dies faster than a new idea in a committee meeting.

4284   It's remarkable how large a part ignorance plays in making a man satisfied with himself.

4285   Ignorance is a voluntary condition.

4286   Imagination is what makes a politician think he is a statesman.

4287   As an inducement to hard work and economy nothing beats a big family.

4288   No man ever realizes how wonderful it is to be poor until he gets over it.

4289   A radical is a person who feels he might get a little more if he howled a little louder.

4290   One thing we have never been able to save for a rainy day is an umbrella.

4291   "Company policy" means "there is no understandable reason for this action."

4292   Sometimes you can tell by watching a person what kind of past he is going to have.

4293   How far a little scandal throws its beams.

4294   Sleep is the rest we need to keep from getting fed up with ourselves.

4295   For most of us, ice skating is a sedentary sport.

4296   The best thing you can do for spring fever is absolutely nothing.

4297   Straddling an issue is like straddling the middle of the road. You are liable to be hit from both sides.

4298   A landlord is a person who pays for a house once and then quits.

4299   Ignorance of the law is no excuse. Neither is the ignorance of the lawmaker.

4300   A luxury becomes a necessity if you can make the down payment on it.

4301   We long for the good old days when a special delivery letter arrived ahead of the regular mail.

4302   The difference between psychoneurosis and nervousness is about $150.

4303   When money talks, there are few interruptions.

4304   An opinion is a minimum of facts combined with prejudice and emotion.

4305   The trouble with opportunity is that it always comes disguised as hard work.

4306   In golf the ball usually lies poorly, but the player well.

4307   Few persons despair of the human race after looking in the mirror.

4308   The only successful substitute for brains is silence.

4309   Tolerance is the patience shown by a wise man when he listens to an ignoramus.

4310   There is never any traffic congestion on the straight and narrow path.

4311   When you define a living wage, it depends on whether you are giving or getting it.

4312   If a man can't do simple arithmetic, he can always become a waiter in a nightclub.

4313   Circus: an entertaining performance in competition with the human race.

4314   A monopolist is a fellow who manages to get an elbow on each arm of his theater chair.

4315   If you could sell your experience for what it cost you, you would have a fortune.

4316   With which finger should a person stir his coffee?

4317   Even the Government is finding out that the "get" is the most difficult part of any budget.

4318   A business consultant is a man who tells you what is going to happen and is willing to bet your money on it.

4319   The modern patriot: the fellow who is sincerely sorry he has but one income to give to his country.

4320   If a man has personality and ability, he soon gets to the point where he is overpaid.

4321   Times are good when everyone has more money than he can use to buy the things he doesn't need.

4322   Nearly every man is a firm believer in heredity until his son makes a fool of himself.

4323   Poverty is no disgrace, but it's difficult to think of anything else in its favor.

4324   Inexperienced stenographer: "Is water-works all one word, or do you spell it with a hydrant in the middle?"

4325   One primary difference between an animal and a man is that an animal doesn't keep on grabbing for more when it has had enough.

4326   The *Congressional Record* is one of the few publications that does not carry advertising—that is, paid advertising.

4327   Confidence is the feeling you sometimes have before you fully understand the situation.

Herbert V. Prochnow, Jr.

4328   The person who never worries may not be smart enough to know what's going on.

4329   Flattery is telling the other person what he thinks of himself.

4330   It's strange how you can hear a rattle in your car easier than one in your head.

4331   Today a dollar earned is a nickel saved.

4332   Somehow we couldn't help but like the boy who said he climbed the tree to put back an apple that had fallen down.

4333   Nothing is more powerful than hope. One little nibble will keep a person fishing all day.

4334   There are 5,280 feet in a mile, except when you detour there are 10,560.

4335   First men fight for freedom, and then they make laws gradually to take it away.

4336   A conviction is what a vice president has when he knows what the president thinks.

4337   No fisherman who tells the truth is very interesting.

4338   If I understand what the economists are saying, the situation is hopeless—but improving.

4339   Very few of us take advantage of opportunities to keep quiet.

4340   Why does a man say he has been fishing when he didn't catch anything?

4341   The way to stay poor is to pretend to be rich.

4342   It's hard to suffer in silence, because that takes all the pleasure out of the suffering.

4343   One person you have to watch if you are going to save money is yourself.

4344   A punctual person is patient, because he gets that way waiting for those who are not punctual.

4345   Most of us would prefer to be miserably rich than happily poor.

4346   No one knows how to save money as well as the person who hasn't any.

4347   It isn't easy for an idea to squeeze into a head filled with prejudices.

4348   In the old days a delinquent was a youngster who owed a few cents on an overdue library book.

4349   We nominate for the Hall of Fame the scientist who said dead leaves help a lawn in the fall.

4350   Don't worry what people are thinking about you. They aren't thinking about you, but about themselves.

4351   An optimist is a person who saves the pictures in the seed catalog to compare them with the flowers and vegetables he grows.

4352   We like the fellow who comes right out and says he agrees with us.

4353   It is very difficult to like a person with whom you can't find any fault.

4354   You can lead high school graduates to college, but you cannot make them think.

4355   No person is humble who thinks he is.

4356   Most people can't save because their neighbors are always doing something they can't afford.

4357   Things never seem so bad if you know your neighbor is having a worse time.

4358   Most families don't mind paying the piper if they can do it on the instalment plan.

4359   Enthusiasm without intelligence is disaster.

4360   A precocious child doesn't take a second piece of cake when he goes visiting. He takes two the first time.

4361   It's all right for children to have original ideas, but not in mathematics.

4362   If an infant can't think, why does it yell as soon as it sees the kind of world it's in.

4363   Teachers are never fully appreciated by parents until it rains all day Saturday.

4364   The hardest task for a child is to learn good manners without seeing any.

4365   One of the greatest assets to any neighborhood is a man who owns a good stepladder and will let the neighbors use it.

4366   The way most fishermen catch fish is by the tale.

4367   An unusual child is one that asks the sort of questions his parents can answer.

4368   Patience may merely mean a person is not smart enough to know what to do next.

4369   We all admire the wisdom of people who ask us for advice.

4370   The time when the fish bite is just before you get there and right after you leave.

4371   Maybe drive-in banking was invented so the new cars could see their real owners.

4372   Poise: the ability to be ill at ease naturally.

4373   Nothing's so apt to make you feel lonesome as being punctual.

4374   Nothing makes you as sure of yourself as ignorance.

4375   Confidence is the feeling you have before you know what you are talking about.

4376   If you know you don't know much, you're smarter than most people.

4377   The way college tuition fees are going up it costs almost as much to be smart as to be ignorant.

4378   Historians tell us about the past and economists about the future. Thus only the present is confusing.

Marcel Proust
4379   People who are not in love fail to understand how an intelligent man can suffer because of a very ordinary woman. This is like being surprised that anyone should be stricken with cholera because of a creature so insignificant as the comma bacillus.

Joseph Pulitzer
4380   What is everybody's business is nobody's business—except the journalist's.

Nathan Pusey
4381   The true business of liberal education is greatness.

Snell Putney
4382   If the people of a democracy are allowed to do so, they will vote away the freedoms which are essential to that democracy.

Pytheas
4383   His impromptus smell of the lamp. [Describing Demosthenes' orations.]

Francis Quarles
4384   Physicians of all men are most happy; what good success they have, the world proclaimeth, and what faults they commit, the earth covereth.

Matt Quay
4385   If you have a weak candidate and a weak platform, wrap yourself up in the American flag and talk about the Constitution.

Robert Quillen
4386   Another good reducing exercise consists in placing both hands against the table edge and pushing back.

4387   Character is made by what you stand for; reputation, by what you fall for.

4388   A hick town is one where there is no place to go where you shouldn't be.

4389   There is some co-operation between wild creatures; the stork and the wolf usually work the same neighborhood.

4390   Discussion is an exchange of knowledge; argument an exchange of ignorance.

4391   Violent exercise is like a cold bath. You think it does you good because you feel better when you stop it.

François Rabelais
4392   He was subject to a kind of disease which at that time they called lack of money.

4393   If you wish to avoid seeing a fool you must first break your mirror.

4394   I owe much; I have nothing; the rest I leave to the poor.

Arthur William Radford
4395   A decision is the action an executive must take when he has information so incomplete that the answer does not suggest itself.

Sir Walter Raleigh
4396   The difference between a rich man and a poor man, is this—the former eats when he pleases, and the latter when he can get it.

Paul Ramadier
4397   A minister of finance is a legally authorized pickpocket.

Stanley J. Randall
4398   The closest to perfection a person ever comes is when he fills out a job application form.

W. B. Rands
4399   Never do today what you can
          Put off till tomorrow.

Lieutenant Colonel William H. Rankin
4400   Someday I would like to stand on the moon, look down through a quarter of a million miles of space and say, "There certainly is a beautiful earth out tonight."

John W. Raper
4401   There is no pleasure in having nothing to do; the fun is having lots to do and not doing it.

Burton Rascoe

4402   In national affairs a million is only a drop in the budget.

4403   What no wife of a writer can ever understand is that a writer is working when he's staring out the window.

John Raudonis

4404   Part of today's problem is that our paychecks are minus tax and our bills are plus.

Clayton Rawson

4405   Can't a critic give his opinion of an omelette without being asked to lay an egg?

John Ray

4406   A fat housekeeper makes lean executors.

4407   A woman's mind and the winter wind change oft.

Charles Reade

4408   We go on fancying that each man is thinking of us, but he is not; he is like us: he is thinking of himself.

4409   Make 'em laugh; make 'em cry; make 'em wait.

Ronald Reagan

4410   The thought of being president frightens me and I do not think I want the job.

4411   The taxpayer, that's someone who works for the Federal government but doesn't have to take a civil service examination.

4412   I am very proud to be called a pig. It stands for pride, integrity and guts.

4413   Governments tend not to solve problems, only to rearrange them.

4414   Some 25 years ago, you could make a long-distance call on a privately owned telephone system from San Francisco to New York for $28. For that same amount of money, you could send 1,376 letters. Today, you could make the same telephone call for two dollars and a half and for that amount you can only send 41 letters. So the government is investigating the Bell System! [When governor of California.]

4415   We've been creeping closer to socialism, a system that someone once said works only in heaven, where it isn't needed, and in hell, where they've already got it.

Thomas Brackett Reed

4416   A statesman is a successful politician who is dead.

4417   They never open their mouths without subtracting from the sum of human knowledge.

4418   Let a man proclaim a new principle. Public sentiment will surely be on the other side.

4419   Theodore [Roosevelt], if there is one thing more than another for which I admire you, it is your original discovery of the Ten Commandments.

J. Tudor Rees

4420   Some people have such open minds that nothing stays in them long.

4421   Before our highways became choked with motor vehicles, it was good to be alive; today it is a surprise.

Joseph Ernest Renan

4422   The ignorance of French society gives me a rough sense of the infinite.

4423   All history is incomprehensible without Christ.

Jules Rénard

4424   A cold in the head causes less suffering than an idea.

4425   Writing is the only profession where no one considers you ridiculous if you earn no money.

4426   Literature is an occupation in which you have to keep proving your talent to people who have none.

4427   You can recover from the writing malady only by falling mortally ill and dying.

Auguste Renoir

4428   She even makes mistakes in spelling, and in my opinion that's essential in a woman.

Agnes Repplier

4429   Conversation between Adam and Eve must have been difficult at times because they had nobody to talk about.

James Reston

4430   A government is the only known vessel that leaks from the top.

4431   The professional politician is one of the mysteries of American life, a bundle of paradoxes, shrewd as a fox, naive as a schoolboy. He has great respect for the people yet treats them like boobs, and is constitutionally unable to keep his mouth shut.

4432   People are always dying in the *New York Times* who don't seem to die in other papers, and they die at greater length and maybe even with a little more grace.

4433   Age seventeen is the point in the journey when the parents retire to the observation car; it is the time when you stop being critical of your eldest son and he starts being critical of you. [Sally and James Reston.]

4434   A dollar saved today is seventy-five cents earned tomorrow.

4435   Helping your eldest son pick a college is one of the great educational experiences of life—for the parents. Next to trying to pick his bride, it's the best way to learn that your authority, if not entirely gone, is slipping fast.

Charles Revson
4436   In the factory we make cosmetics; in the drugstore we sell hope.

4437   I don't meet competition, I crush it.

Sir Joshua Reynolds
4438   There is no expedient to which a man will not resort to avoid the real labor of thinking.

4439   He who resolves never to ransack any mind but his own will be soon reduced, from mere barrenness, to the poorest of all imitations: he will be obliged to imitate himself.

Paul Richard
4440   The vagabond, when rich, is called a tourist.

E. H. Richards
4441   A wise old owl sat on an oak,
The more he sat the less he spoke;
The less he spoke the more he heard;
Why aren't we like that wise old bird?

Rebecca Richards
4442   Oh, to be only half as wonderful as my child thought I was when he was small, and only half as stupid as my teenager now thinks I am.

Sir Alfred Richardson

4443 The French look exactly like French, the faces of Dutchmen are Dutch. Danes look like Danes and Egyptians look very Canalish. Americans have a sad countenance. They probably look like this because they developed catarrh when they landed on Plymouth Rock.

Jean-Paul Richter

4444 Spring makes everything young again except man.

4445 A variety of nothing is better than a monotony of something.

4446 Every year sees a man less easy to save. At sixty all missionary effort is hopeless; it takes burning at the stake.

4447 Women cure all their sorrows by talking.

Hyman G. Rickover

4448 Trying to make things work in government is sometimes like trying to sew a button on a custard pie.

S. J. Ridley

4449 A bachelor is one who thinks one can live as cheap as two.

Philip Rieff

4450 Scholarship is polite argument.

Mary Roberts Rinehart

4451 He soft-soaped her until she couldn't see for the suds.

Cyril Ritchard

4452 Matinee audience: two thousand dear ladies. All very careful and diplomatic with one another. Ever so sweet and catty, you know. I can hear that sweet-and-catty sound through the curtain while the house lights are still on. They all applaud with their gloves on, never too hard or too much. They're busier watching each other than the show.

Comte de Rivarol

4453 Friendship among women is only a suspension of hostilities.

4454 It is an immense advantage to have done nothing, but one should not abuse it.

4455 The personal pronoun "I" should be the coat of arms of some individuals.

Chalmers Roberts

4456   The trouble with daily journalism is that you get so involved with "Who hit John?" that you never really know why John had his chin out in the first place.

James Jeffrey Roche

4457   Pay as you go, but not if you intend going for good.

4458   Some men borrow books; some men steal books; and others beg presentation copies from the authors.

4459   I'd rather be handsome than homely;
I'd rather be youthful than old;
If I can't have a bushel of silver
I'll do with a barrel of gold.

4460   Be not concerned if thou findest thyself in possession of unexpected wealth; Allah will provide an unexpected use for it.

John Wilmot, Lord Rochester

4461   Before I got married I had six theories about bringing up children; now I have six children, and no theories.

4462   He never says a foolish thing nor ever does a wise one.

John D. Rockefeller, Sr.

4463   It was a friendship founded on business, which is a good deal better than a business founded on friendship.

John D. Rockefeller, Jr.

4464   I was born into it and there was nothing I could do about it. It was there, like air or food or any other element.... The only question with wealth is what you do with it.

John D. Rockefeller III

4465   Well, yes. You could say we have independent means.

Lucy Rockefeller

4466   When it's raining porridge, you'll always find John's bowl right side up.

Nelson Rockefeller

4467   Thanks a thousand.

Francis Rodman

4468   Matrimony is a process by which a grocer acquired an account the florist had.

James L. Rogers

4469   There is very little to admire in bureaucracy, but you have got to hand it to the Internal Revenue Service.

Will Rogers

4470   I don't make jokes. I just watch the government and report the facts.

4471   I tell you, all politics is apple sauce.

4472   We can't all be heroes because somebody has to sit on the curb and clap as they go by.

4473   He is the first president to discover that what the American people want is to be left alone. [On Calvin Coolidge.]

4474   Any nation is heathen that ain't strong enough to punch you in the jaw.

4475   The more you read and observe about this politics thing, the more you've got to admit that each party's worse than the other. The one that's out always looks the best.

4476   He can take a batch of words and scramble them together and leaven them properly with a hunk of oratory and knock the White House door-knob right out of a candidate's hand. [On William Jennings Bryan.]

4477   What the country needs is dirtier fingernails and cleaner minds.

4478   Everybody is ignorant, only on different subjects.

4479   Everything is funny, as long as it is happening to somebody else.

4480   Gentlemen, you have just been listening to that Chinese sage, On Too Long.

4481   The good old horse-and-buggy days: then you lived until you died and not until you were just run over.

4482   A holding company is a thing where you hand an accomplice the goods while the policeman searches you.

4483   In Hollywood the woods are full of people that learned to write but evidently can't read; if they could read their stuff, they'd stop writing.

4484   My folks didn't come over on the *Mayflower,* but they were there to meet the boat.

4485   No party is as bad as its leaders.

4486   Our foreign dealings are an open book—generally a checkbook.

4487   The United States never lost a war or won a conference.

4488   Let advertisers spend the same amount of money improving their product that they do on advertising and they wouldn't have to advertise it.

4489   The business of government is to keep the government out of business—that is, unless business needs government aid.

4490   In a real estate man's eye, the most exclusive part of the city is wherever he has a house to sell.

4491   You can't say that civilization don't advance, for in every war they kill you a new way.

4492   I would rather be the man who bought the Brooklyn Bridge than the man who sold it.

4493   Politics has got so expensive that it takes a lot of money even to get beat with.

4494   This country has come to feel the same when Congress is in session as when the baby gets hold of a hammer.

4495   The short memories of American voters is what keeps our politicians in office.

4496   We are all here for a spell, get all the good laughs you can.

4497   Maybe ain't ain't so correct, but I notice that lots of folks who ain't using ain't ain't eating.

4498   There is no more independence in politics than there is in jail.

4499   Ukulele: a so-called musical instrument which, when listened to, you cannot tell whether one is playing on it or just monkeying with it.

4500   With Congress, every time they make a joke it's a law; and every time they make a law it's a joke.

4501   Wrigley was the first man to discover that American jaws must wag; so why not give them something to wag against.

4502   America is a nation that conceives many odd inventions for getting somewhere but can think of nothing to do when it gets there.

4503   I never lack material for my humor column when Congress is in session.

4504   The income tax has made more liars out of the American people than golf has. Even when you make a tax form out on the level, you don't know when it's through if you are a crook or a martyr.

4505   I can remember way back when a liberal was one who was generous with his own money.

4506   The only time people dislike gossip is when you gossip about them.

4507   There's no trick to being a humorist when you have the whole government working for you.

4508   There ain't nothing that breaks up homes, country and nations like somebody publishing their memoirs.

4509   There is only one thing that can kill the movies, and that is education. . . . Some say, what is the salvation of the movies? I say, run 'em backward. It can't hurt 'em and it's worth a trial.

4510   Our constitution protects aliens, drunks and U.S. Senators. There ought to be one day (just one) when there is an open season on Senators.

4511   One-third of the people in the United States promote, while the other two-thirds provide.

4512   If you can build a business up big enough, it's respectable.

4513   One way to solve the traffic problem would be to keep all cars that aren't paid for off the streets.

4514   Just be glad you're not getting all the government you're paying for.

Eleanor Roosevelt
4515   Always be on time. Do as little talking as humanly possible. Remember to lean back in the parade car so everybody can see the President. Be sure not to get too fat, because you'll have to sit three in the back seat.

Franklin D. Roosevelt
4516   I ask you to judge me by the enemies I have made.

4517   A reactionary is a somnambulist walking backwards.

4518   A Liberal is a man who uses his legs and his hands at the behest of his head.

4519   I am busy as a one-armed paper hanger with the itch!

4520   The ablest man I ever met is the man you think you are.

4521   It got to a point where I had to get a haircut or a violin.

4522   A conservative is a man with two perfectly good legs who has never learned to walk.

4523   A radical is a man with both feet firmly planted in the air.

4524   It is Easter day—pouring and raw. I suppose you are out sleighing in a samovar! Pin a rose on Lenin when you attend the May first celebration. He is a great man because dead. [A letter to the U.S. ambassador to Russia.]

4525   Bill supports me for three and a half years out of every four. [About William Allen White.]

4526   When you feel that British accent creeping up on you and your trousers riding up to the knee, take the first steamer home for a couple of weeks holiday. [A letter to the U.S. ambassador to Great Britain.]

4527   Be sincere; be brief; be seated. [On speech-making.]

4528   We have always held to the hope, the belief, the conviction that there is a better life, a better world, beyond the horizon.

4529   The test of our progress is not whether we add more to the abundance of those who have much; it is whether we provide enough for those who have too little.

4530   Philosophy? Philosophy. I am a Christian and a Democrat—that's all.

4531   Let me assert my firm belief that the only thing we have to fear is fear itself.

Theodore Roosevelt

4532   The reactionary is always willing to take a progressive attitude on any issue that is dead.

4533   McKinley shows all the backbone of a chocolate eclair.

4534   No president has ever enjoyed himself as much as I.

4535   I think there is only one quality worse than hardness of heart and that is softness of head.

4536   A man who has never gone to school may steal from a freight car; but if he has a university education, he may steal the whole railroad.

4537   The most successful politician is he who says what everybody is thinking most often and in the loudest voice.

4538   You don't live there [the White House]. You are only Exhibit A to the country.

4539   It may be that the voice of the people is the voice of God in fifty-one cases out of a hundred; but in the remaining forty-nine it is quite as likely to be the voice of the devil, or, what is still worse, the voice of a fool.

4540   When they call the roll in the Senate, the senators do not know whether to answer "present" or "not guilty."

4541   The various admirable movements in which I have been engaged have always developed among their members a large lunatic fringe.

4542   We demand that big business give the people a square deal; in return we must insist that when anyone engaged in big business honestly endeavors to do right he shall himself be given a square deal.

4543   The best executive is the one who has sense enough to pick good men to do what he wants done, and self-restraint enough to keep from meddling with them while they do it.

John W. Roper
4544   To say the right thing at the right time, keep still most of the time.

Billy Rose
4545   Never invest your money in anything that eats or needs repairing.

Dante Gabriel Rossetti
4546   The worst moment for the atheist is when he is really thankful and has nobody to thank.

Gioacchino Antonio Rossini
4547   Give me a laundry list and I'll set it to music.

4548   How wonderful opera would be if there were no singers.

4549   Wagner has beautiful moments but awful quarter hours.

Winton G. Rossiter
4550   If it ain't broke, don't fix it—unless you are a consultant.

Edmond Rostand
4551   To offend is my pleasure; I love to be hated.

4552   One has always been less unhappy than one thinks—just as one has always slept better.

Jules Rostand
4553   Everybody wants to live longer but nobody wants to grow old.

Leo Rosten
4554   Any man who hates dogs and babies can't be all bad.

Sir Nathan Meyer Rothschild
4555   I've got to keep breathing. It'll be my worst business mistake if I don't.

Jean-Jacques Rousseau

4556   There is a period of life when we go backwards as we advance.

4557   To write a love letter we must begin without knowing what we intend to say, and end without knowing what we have written.

4558   As soon as any man says of the affairs of state, What does it matter to me? the state may be given up as lost.

4559   I love idleness. I love to busy myself about trifles, to begin a hundred things and not finish one of them, to come and go as my fancy bids me, to change my plan every moment, to follow a fly in all its circlings, to try and uproot a rock to see what is underneath, eagerly to begin on a ten years' task and to give it up after ten minutes: in short to fritter away the whole day inconsequentially and incoherently, and to follow nothing but the whim of the moment.

4560   Insults are the arguments employed by those who are in the wrong.

Joseph Roux

4561   God often visits us, but most of the time we are not at home.

Carl Rowan

4562   My advice to any diplomat who wants to have a good press is to have two or three kids and a dog.

Helen Rowland

4563   A bachelor never quite gets over the idea that he is a thing of beauty and a boy forever.

4564   A Bachelor of Arts is one who makes love to a lot of women, and yet has the art to remain a bachelor.

4565   Before marriage, a man will lie awake all night thinking about something you said; after marriage, he'll fall asleep before you finish saying it.

4566   Every man wants a woman to appeal to his better side, his nobler instincts and his higher nature—and another woman to help him forget them.

4567   A fool and her money are soon courted.

4568   The hardest task of a girl's life is to prove to a man that his intentions are serious.

4569   The honeymoon is not over until we cease to stifle our sighs and begin to stifle our yawns.

4570   In the spring a young man's fancy lightly turns—and turns—and turns.

4571   Love is woman's eternal spring and man's eternal fall.

4572   It takes one woman twenty years to make a man of her son, and another woman twenty minutes to make a fool of him.

4573   A man loses his illusions first, his teeth second, and his follies last.

4574   Marriage is the miracle that transforms a kiss from a pleasure into a duty, and a life from a luxury into a necessity.

4575   Nobody is as sophisticated as a boy of nineteen who is just recovering from a baby-grand passion.

4576   The softer a man's head, the louder his socks.

4577   Some men feel that the only thing they owe the woman who marries them is a grudge.

4578   Wedding: the point at which a man stops toasting a woman and begins roasting her.

4579   When you see a married couple coming down the street, the one who is two or three steps ahead is the one that's mad.

4580   Failing to be there when a man wants her is a woman's greatest sin, except to be there when he doesn't want her.

4581   A husband is what is left of a man after the nerve is extracted.

4582   When it comes to making love, a girl can always listen so much faster than a man can talk.

4583   After a few years of marriage, a man can look right at a woman without seeing her—and a woman can see right through a man without looking at him.

4584   Love, the quest; marriage, the conquest; divorce, the inquest.

4585   After you have been married five years, there should always be someone to dinner.

4586   Some men think that being married to a woman means merely seeing her in the mornings instead of in the evenings.

4587   When a girl marries, she exchanges the attentions of many men for the inattention of one.

4588   When a man makes a woman his wife, it's the highest compliment he can pay her, and it's usually the last.

4589   From the day on which she weighs 140, the chief excitement of a woman's life consists in spotting women who are fatter than she is.

4590   Marriage is like twirling a baton, turning handsprings, or eating with chopsticks. It looks so easy till you try it.

Robert Ruark
4591   A man can build a staunch reputation for honesty by admitting he was in error, especially when he gets caught at it.

Arthur Rubinstein
4592   What good are vitamins? Eat four lobsters, eat a pound of caviar —live! If you are in love with a beautiful blonde with an empty face and no brain at all, don't be afraid, marry her—live!

4593   When I was young I used to go into the practice room and lock the door behind me. I'd put a beautiful novel in with my sheet music and a box of cherries on the right-hand side of the piano and a box of chocolates on the left and play runs with my left hand and eat cherries with my right and all the time be reading my book.

Dagobert Runes
4594   You have laughed God out of your schools, out of your books, and out of your life, but you cannot laugh Him out of your death.

Damon Runyon
4595   The race may not be to the swift nor the victory to the strong, but that's how you bet.

4596   Much as he is opposed to lawbreaking, he is not bigoted about it.

Dean Rusk
4597   One of the best ways to persuade others is with your ears—by listening to them.

John Ruskin
4598   An artist should be fit for the best society and keep out of it.

4599   There is hardly anything in the world that some man cannot make a little worse and sell a little cheaper.

4600   When a man is wrapped up in himself he makes a pretty small package.

4601   You knock a man into the ditch, and then you tell him to remain content in the position in which Providence has placed him.

4602   The first of all English games is making money.

4603   The public is just a great baby.

4604   The first test of a truly great man is his humility. Really great men have a curious feeling that the greatness is not in them but through them. And they see something divine in every other man and are endlessly, incredibly merciful.

4605   There is really no such thing as bad weather, only different kinds of good weather.

Bertrand Russell

4606   Patriotism is the willingness to kill and be killed for trivial reasons.

4607   I can only say that, while my own opinions as to ethics do not satisfy me, other people's satisfy me even less.

4608   One should respect public opinion in so far as is necessary to avoid starvation and keep out of prison, but anything that goes beyond this is voluntary submission to an unnecessary tyranny.

4609   Few people can be happy unless they hate some other person, nation, or creed.

4610   One of the symptoms of an approaching nervous breakdown is the belief that one's work is terribly important.

4611   The place of the father in the modern suburban family is a very small one, particularly if he plays golf.

4612   I am persuaded that there is absolutely no limit to the absurdities that can, by government action, come to be generally believed.

4613   Christian humility is preached by the clergy, but practiced only by the lower classes.

4614   Even when the experts all agree, they may well be mistaken.

4615   The fundamental defect of fathers is that they want their children to be a credit to them.

4616   Most people would die sooner than think; in fact, they do so.

4617   The trouble with the world is that the stupid are cocksure and the intelligent full of doubt.

4618   We have two kinds of morality side by side: one which we preach but do not practice, and another which we practice but seldom preach.

4619   The degree of one's emotion varies inversely with one's knowledge of the facts—the less you know the hotter you get.

4620   Undoubtedly the desire for food has been, and still is, one of the main causes of great political events.

4621   Men who are unhappy, like men who sleep badly, are always proud of the fact.

4622   To be able to fill leisure intelligently is the last product of civilization.

Richard Russell
4623   If we have to start over again with another Adam and Eve, I want them to be Americans, not Russians.

Michael Sadler
4624   Education is the established church of the United States. It is one of the religions that Americans believe in. It has its own orthodoxy, its pontiffs and its noble buildings.

L. A. Safian
4625   Egotism is nature's compensation for mediocrity.

Françoise Sagan
4626   Men have more problems than women. In the first place, they have to put up with women.

4627   I like men to behave like men—strong and childish.

Charles-Augustin Sainte-Beuve
4628   A critic is a fellow whose watch is five minutes ahead of other people's.

4629   It is rare that, after having given the key of her heart, a woman does not change the lock the day after.

Augustus Saint-Gaudens
4630   What garlic is to salad, insanity is to art.

Joseph Salak
4631   Today women often push carts through supermarkets at speeds over $65 an hour.

Sir Marcus Samuel
4632   The price of an article is exactly what it will fetch.

4633   There are men of so much courage and independence that they would rather be in a minority and wrong than right with the majority.

4634   A little learning is a dangerous thing, but none at all is fatal.

4635   Where there are two Ph.D.s in a developing country, one is Head of State and the other is in exile.

Paul Samuelson
4636   Man does not live by GNP alone.

Carl Sandburg
4637   I won't take my religion from any man who never works except with his mouth.

4638   Slang is language that takes off its coat, spits on its hands, and goes to work.

4639   Life is like an onion; you peel it off one layer at a time, and sometimes you weep.

4640   I am an idealist. I don't know where I'm going but I'm on my way.

4641   In these times you have to be an optimist to open your eyes when you awake in the morning.

4642   Valor is a gift. Those having it never know for sure whether they have it till the test comes. And those having it in one test never know for sure if they will have it when the next test comes.

Colonel Harland Sanders
4643   I was sixty-six years old. I still had to make a living. I looked at my social security check of 105 dollars and decided to use that to try to franchise my chicken recipe. Folks had always liked my chicken.

George Santayana
4644   Fanaticism consists in redoubling your effort when you have forgotten your aim.

4645   Life is not a spectacle or a feast; it is a predicament.

4646   An artist may visit a museum, but only a pedant can live there.

4647   Broad-mindedness is the result of flattening high-mindedness out.

4648   The Difficult is that which can be done immediately; the Impossible that which takes a little longer.

4649   It is a great advantage for a system of philosophy to be substantially true.

4650   There is no cure for birth or death save to enjoy the interval.

4651   Those who cannot remember the past are condemned to repeat it.

4652   To be brief is almost a condition of being inspired.

4653   Music is essentially useless, as life is.

4654   Intolerance itself is a form of egoism, and to condemn egoism intolerantly is to share it.

4655   For an idea ever to be fashionable is ominous, since it must afterward be always old-fashioned.

4656   Boston is a moral and intellectual nursery always busy applying first principles to trifles.

4657   History is always written wrong, and so always needs to be rewritten.

4658   Mankind is a tribe of animals, living by habits and thinking in symbols; and it can never be anything else.

4659   A musical education is necessary for musical judgment. What most people relish is hardly music; it is rather a drowsy reverie relieved by nervous thrills.

4660   By nature's kindly disposition, most questions which it is beyond a man's power to answer do not occur to him at all.

4661   Few revolutionists would be such if they were heirs to a baronetcy.

4662   We all carry on pleasantly our temporal affairs, although we know that tomorrow we die.

4663   Why should not things be largely absurd, futile and transitory? They are so, and we are so, and they and we go very well together.

4664   The highest form of vanity is love of fame. It is a passion easy to deride but hard to understand, and in men who live at all by imagination almost impossible to eradicate.

4665   Perhaps the only true dignity of man is his capacity to despise himself.

4666   The family is one of nature's masterpieces.

John Singer Sargent
4667   Every time I paint a portrait I lose a friend.

William Saroyan
4668   The greatest happiness you can have is knowing that you do not necessarily require happiness.

4669   You write a hit play the same way you write a flop.

4670   Everybody has got to die, but I have always believed an exception would be made in my case. Now what?

Jean-Paul Sartre
4671   Three o'clock is always too late or too early for anything you want to do.

Vidal Sassoon
4672   The only place where success comes before work is in a dictionary.

John Godfrey Saxe
4673   He says a thousand pleasant things—but never says "Adieu."

4674   The worm was punished for early rising.

Francis Scarfe
4675   Language is simplified gesture, and poetry is simplified language. . . .
Poetry is a sort of dancing with the voice.

Mary Schafer
4676   They went at it hammer and tongues.

Erwin H. Schell
4677   Remember that when an employee enters your office he is in a strange land.

August Wilhelm von Schlegel
4678   The historian is a prophet looking backwards.

Arthur Schnabel
4679   The notes I handle no better than many pianists. But the pauses between the notes—ah, that is where the art resides!

Arthur Schopenhauer
4680   Reading is thinking with someone else's head instead of one's own.

4681   The first forty years of life give us the text; the next thirty supply the commentary.

4682   It is difficult to keep quiet if you have nothing to do.

4683   Politeness is like an air cushion: there is nothing inside, but it softens the shocks of life.

4684 The doctor sees all the weakness of mankind, the lawyer all the wickedness, the priest all the stupidity.

4685 Rudeness is better than any argument; it totally eclipses intellect.

4686 Politeness is a tacit agreement that people's miserable defects, whether moral or intellectual, shall on either side be ignored and not be made the subject of reproach.

Charles M. Schulz

4687 My life has no purpose, no direction, no aim, no meaning, and yet I'm happy. I can't figure it out. What am I doing right?

Robert Schumann

4688 In order to compose, all you need to do is remember a tune that nobody else has thought of.

4689 When I was a young man I vowed never to marry until I found the ideal woman. Well, I found her—but, alas, she was waiting for the ideal man.

Albert Schwabacher, Jr.

4690 Most women would be better off if they paid less attention to their investments, not more. . . . And the women could continue to do what they do best—be women.

Albert Schweitzer

4691 Example is not the main thing in influencing others. It is the only thing.

Cyril Scott

4692 Women who are not vain about their clothes are often vain about not being vain about their clothes.

Sir Walter Scott

4693 It requires no small talents to be a decided bore.

4694 Many of our cares are but a morbid way of looking at our privileges.

4695 The most effectual way of conferring a favor is condescending to accept one.

4696 When a man hasn't a good reason for doing a thing, he has a good reason for letting it alone.

4697 If a gentleman chooses to walk about with a couple of pounds of gunpowder in his pocket, if I give him the shelter of my roof, I may at least be permitted to exclude him from the seat next the fire.

4698   Oh what a tangled web we weave
        When first we practise to deceive!

Sir Charles Sedley

4699   She deceiving, I believing;
        What need lovers wish for more?

Lee Segall

4700   It's possible to own too much. A man with one watch knows what
        time it is; a man with two watches is never quite sure.

Seneca

4701   Not he who has little, but he who wishes more, is poor.

4702   A great fortune is a great slavery.

4703   He who receives a benefit with gratitude repays the first install-
        ment on his debt.

4704   A man who has taken your time recognizes no debt; yet it is the
        one he can never repay.

4705   What difference does it make how much you have? What you do
        not have amounts to much more.

Eric Sevareid

4706   Consultant: any ordinary guy more than fifty miles from home.

Marquise de Sévigné

4707   Fortune is always on the side of the biggest battalions.

4708   Religious people spend so much time with their confessors be-
        cause they like to talk about themselves.

4709   He lacked only a few vices to be perfect.

Anthony Ashley Cooper, Third Earl of Shaftesbury

4710   Everyone thinks himself well-bred.

William Shakespeare

4711   When my love swears that she is made of truth,
        I do believe her, though I know she lies.

4712   Better a witty fool than a foolish wit.

4713   Everyone can master a grief but he that has it.

4714   God made him, and therefore let him pass for a man.

4715   Gratiano speaks an infinite deal of nothing, more than any man in all Venice.

4716   He draweth out the thread of his verbosity finer than the staple of his argument.

4717   I can easier teach twenty what were good to be done than be one of the twenty to follow mine own teaching.

4718   I have no other but a woman's reason; I think him so because I think him so.

4719   I had rather have a fool to make me merry than experience to make me sad.

4720   I will praise any man that will praise me.

4721   I thank God I am as honest as any man living that is an old man and no honester than I.

4722   A miser grows rich by seeming poor; an extravagant man grows poor by seeming rich.

4723   There was never yet philosopher that could endure the toothache patiently.

4724   Unbidden guests are often welcomest when they are gone.

4725   Vanity keeps persons in favor with themselves who are out of favor with all others.

4726   When I tell him he hates flatterers, he says he does, being then the most flattered.

4727   A young man married is a man that's marred.

4728   Men at some time are masters of their fates:
The fault, dear Brutus, is not in our stars,
But in ourselves that we are underlings.

4729   Be not afraid of greatness: some are born great, some achieve greatness and some have greatness thrust upon 'em.

4730   I love to hear him lie.

4731   Maids want nothing but husbands, and when they have them, they want everything.

4732   "So-so" is good, very good, very excellent maxim; and yet it is not; it is but so-so.

4733   One pain is lessened by another's anguish.

4734   One may smile, and smile, and be a villain.

4735   Yon Cassius has a lean and hungry look;
He thinks too much: such men are dangerous.

4736   He is winding the watch of his wit; by and by it will strike.

4737   Do you not know I am a woman? When I think, I must speak.

4738   The world is a stage, but the play is badly cast.

4739   What a piece of work is a man! How noble in reason! How infinite in faculty! In form, in moving, how express and admirable! In action how like an angel! In apprehension how like a god! The beauty of the world! The paragon of animals! And yet, to me, what is this quintessence of dust?

4740   Poor and content is rich—and rich enough.

4741   This fellow's wise enough to play the fool.

4742   All the world's a stage,
And all the men and women merely players:
They have their exits and their entrances;
And one man in his time plays many parts.

William V. Shannon

4743   Experience suggests that the first rule of politics is never to say never. The ingenious human capacity for manoeuvre and compromise may make acceptable tomorrow what seems outrageous or impossible today.

Artie Shaw

4744   The Good Old Days are neither better nor worse than the ones we're living through right now.

George Bernard Shaw

4745   Democracy substitutes election by the incompetent many for appointment by the corrupt few.

4746   It is dangerous to be sincere unless you are also stupid.

4747   A government which robs Peter to pay Paul can always depend on the support of Paul.

4748   Englishmen will never be slaves. They are free to do whatever the government and public opinion allow them to do.

4749   When a man wants to murder a tiger he calls it sport; when a tiger wants to murder him he calls it ferocity.

4750   Assassination is the extreme form of censorship.

4751   An asylum for the sane would be empty in America.

4752   Baseball has the great advantage over cricket of being sooner ended.

4753   Beauty is all very well at sight, but who can look at it when it has been in the house three days?

4754   The best reformers the world has ever seen are those who commence on themselves.

4755   The British churchgoer prefers a severe preacher because he thinks a few home truths will do his neighbors no harm.

4756   Censorship ends in logical completeness when nobody is allowed to read any books except the books nobody can read.

4757   The chief objection to playing wind instruments is that it prolongs the life of the player.

4758   Common people do not pray; they only beg.

4759   The devil can quote Shakespeare for his own purpose.

4760   England and America are two countries separated by the same language.

4761   An Englishman does everything on principle: he fights you on patriotic principles; he robs you on business principles; he enslaves you on imperial principles.

4762   All my life, affection has been showered upon me, and every forward step I have made has been in spite of it.

4763   An Englishman thinks he is moral when he is only uncomfortable.

4764   A gentleman is a gentleman the world over; loafers differ.

4765   Everything happens to everybody sooner or later if there is time enough.

4766   Few people think more than two or three times a year; I have made an international reputation for myself by thinking once or twice a week.

4767   Gambling promises the poor what property performs for the rich —something for nothing.

4768   Greek scholars are privileged men; few of them know Greek, and most of them know nothing else.

4769   Hamlet's experiences simply could not have happened to a plumber.

4770   He is a man of great common sense and good taste—meaning thereby a man without originality or moral courage.

4771   He who can, does; he who cannot, teaches.

4772   Human beings are the only animals of which I am thoroughly and cravenly afraid.

4773   I enjoy convalescence; it is the part that makes the illness worth while.

4774   I dislike feeling at home when I'm abroad.

4775   If all economists were laid end to end, they would not reach a conclusion.

4776   If history repeats itself, and the unexpected always happens, how incapable must man be of learning from experience.

4777   If you are a bore, strive to be a rascal also so that you may not discredit virtue.

4778   I have never thought much of the courage of a lion-tamer; inside the cage he is, at least, safe from other men.

4779   I often quote myself; it adds spice to my conversation.

4780   I strive automatically to bring the world into harmony with my own nature.

4781   It is a woman's business to get married as soon as possible, and a man's to keep unmarried as long as he can.

4782   Kings are not born; they are made by universal hallucination.

4783   Leave it to the coward to make a religion of his cowardice by preaching humility.

4784   Lack of money is the root of all evil.

4785   A learned man is an idler who kills time by study.

4786   The liar's punishment is not in the least that he is not believed, but that he cannot believe anyone else.

4787   Martyrdom is the only way in which a man can become famous without ability.

4788   Men have to do some awfully mean things to keep up their respectability.

4789   The more things a man is ashamed of, the more respectable he is.

4790   The most anxious man in a prison is the warden.

4791   My specialty is being right when other people are wrong.

4792   My way of joking is to tell the truth; it's the funniest joke in the world.

4793   Nothing soothes me more after a long and maddening course of pianoforte recitals than to sit and have my teeth drilled.

4794   The 100 percent American is 99 percent an idiot.

4795   Obscenity can be found in every book except the telephone directory.

4796   The only way a woman can provide for herself decently is to be good to some man that can afford to be good to her.

4797   The other evening, feeling rather in want of a headache, I bethought me that I had not been to a music hall for a long time.

4798   Patriotism is your conviction that this country is superior to all other countries because you were born in it.

4799   The pessimist thinks everybody as nasty as himself, and hates them for it.

4800   Science is always wrong: it never solves a problem without creating ten more.

4801   The secret of being miserable is to have leisure to bother about whether you are happy or not.

4802   Self-denial is not a virtue; it is only the effect of prudence on rascality.

4803   Success covers a multitude of blunders.

4804   There are fools everywhere, even in asylums.

4805   Take care to get what you like, or you will end by liking what you get.

4806   There are not competent people enough in the world to go round; somebody must get the incompetent lawyers and doctors.

4807   There are only two classes in good society in England: the equestrian classes and the neurotic classes.

4808   Old men are dangerous: it doesn't matter to them what is going to happen to the world.

4809   There is no love sincerer than the love of food.

4810   There is no satisfaction in hanging a man who does not object to it.

4811   There is not much harm in a lion; he has no ideals, no religion, no politics, no chivalry, no gentility.

4812   There is only one religion, though there are a hundred versions of it.

4813   There may be some doubt as to who are the best people to have charge of children, but there can be no doubt that parents are the worst.

4814   The truth is the one thing that nobody will believe.

4815   The things most people want to know about are usually none of their business.

4816   Virtue is insufficient temptation.

4817   We are told that when Jehovah created the world he saw that it was good; what would he say now?

4818   What is the matter with the poor is poverty; what is the matter with the rich is uselessness.

4819   What man is capable of the insane self-conceit of believing that an eternity of himself would be tolerable even to himself.

4820   What really flatters a man is that you think him worth flattering.

4821   When a stupid man is doing something he is ashamed of, he always declares that it is his duty.

4822   When you read a biography remember that the truth is never fit for publication.

4823   Why was I born with such contemporaries?

4824   The worst cliques are those which consist of one man.

4825   With the exception of capitalism, there is nothing so revolting as revolution.

4826   You don't expect me to know what to say about a play when I don't know who the author is, do you?

4827   You must not suppose, because I am a man of letters, that I never tried to earn an honest living.

4828   The test of a man or woman's breeding is how they behave in a quarrel.

4829   A man never tells you anything until you contradict him.

4830   Capable persons are never liked.

4831   If parents would only realize how they bore their children.

4832   Love is a gross exaggeration of the difference between one person and everybody else.

4833   A drama critic is a man who leaves no turn unstoned.

4834   I must have been an insufferable child; all children are.

4835   What we want is to see the child in pursuit of knowledge, and not knowledge in pursuit of the child.

4836   People always get tired of one another. I grow tired of myself whenever I am left alone for ten minutes, and I am certain that I am fonder of myself than anyone can be of another person.

4837   The ordinary Britisher imagines God is an Englishman.

4838   You see things; and you say "Why?" But I dream things that never were; and I say "Why not?"

4839   We don't bother much about dress and manners in England, because as a nation we don't dress well and we've no manners.

4840   When a man teaches something he does not know to somebody else who has no aptitude for it, and gives him a certificate of proficiency, the latter has undergone the education of a gentleman.

4841   We learn from experience that men never learn anything from experience.

4842   When a thing is funny, search it for a hidden truth.

4843   We were not fairly beaten, my lord. No Englishman is ever fairly beaten.

4844   Liberty means responsibility. That is why most men dread it.

4845   He knows nothing; he thinks he knows everything—that clearly points to a political career.

4846   Beware of false knowledge; it is more dangerous than ignorance.

4847   I cannot learn languages; men of ordinary capacity can learn Sanskrit in less time than it takes me to buy a German dictionary.

4848   Martyrdom is the only way in which a man can become famous without ability.

4849 To the person with a toothache, even if the world is tottering, there is nothing more important than a visit to a dentist.

4850 Does any man seriously believe that a modern Prime Minister is a more enlightened ruler than Julius Caesar because he drives a motorcar, writes his dispatches by electric light and instructs his stockbroker through a telephone?

4851 First love is only a little foolishness and a lot of curiosity.

4852 He practiced the utmost economy in order to keep the most expensive habits.

4853 The relation of superior to inferior excludes good manners.

4854 He's a devout believer in the department of witchcraft called medical science.

4855 Make money; and the whole nation will conspire to call you a gentleman.

4856 All great art and literature is propaganda.

4857 You can draw a line and make other chaps toe it. That's what I call morality.

4858 You'll never have a quiet world till you knock the patriotism out of the human race.

4859 Reading made Don Quixote a gentleman, but believing what he read made him mad.

4860 Men have to do some awfully mean things to keep up their respectability.

4861 We live in an atmosphere of shame. We are ashamed of everything that is real about us. Ashamed of ourselves, our relations, of our incomes, of our accents, of our opinions, of our experience. The more things a man is ashamed of, the more respectable he is.

4862 Of all the damnable waste of human life that ever was invented, clerking is the very worst.

4863 People who are hard, grasping ... and always ready to take advantage of their neighbors, become very rich.

4864 Man is the only animal which esteems itself rich in proportion to the number and voracity of its parasites.

4865 A foolish expedient for making idle people believe they are doing something very clever, when they are only wasting their time. [On chess.]

4866 Books are always the better for not being read. Look at our classics.

4867   You know very well that after a certain age a man has only one speech.

4868   The utmost I can bear for myself in my best days is that I was one of the hundred best playwrights in the world, which is hardly a supreme distinction.

4869   I derived my education from the uneducated.

4870   You are right in your impression that a number of persons are urging me to come to the United States. But why on earth do you call them my friends?

4871   It is nearly fifty years since I was assured by a conclave of doctors that if I did not eat meat I should die of starvation.

4872   The ideal wife is one who does everything that the ideal husband likes, and nothing else.

4873   All men are comic, especially deans, bishops and drum majors, who dress their parts.

4874   To a young woman who said "What a wonderful thing is youth," Shaw said, "Yes—and what a crime to waste it on children."

4875   I am a Millionaire. That is my religion.

4876   The reasonable man adapts himself to the world; the unreasonable one persists in trying to adapt the world to himself. Therefore all progress depends on the unreasonable man.

4877   Vulgarity in a king flatters the majority of the nation.

4878   A man who has had his dinner is never a revolutionist: his politics are all talk.

4879   Nothing offends children more than to play down to them. All the great children's books—the *Pilgrim's Progress, Robinson Crusoe, Grimm's Fairy Tales* and *Gulliver's Travels*—were written for adults.

R. E. Shay
4880   Depend on the rabbit's foot if you will, but remember it didn't work for the rabbit!

Bishop Fulton J. Sheen
4881   An atheist is a man who has no invisible means of support.

4882   Baloney is the unvarnished lie laid on so thick you hate it. Blarney is flattery laid on so thin you love it.

4883   Every child should have an occasional pat on the back as long as it is applied low enough and hard enough.

4884   I feel it is time that I also pay tribute to my four writers, Matthew, Mark, Luke and John.

Edward B. Sheldon

4885   A voice like a slate pencil.

Odell Shepard

4886   Quite literally, a man's memory is what he forgets with.

Philip Henry Sheridan

4887   If I owned Hell and Texas, I'd rent out Texas and live in Hell.

Richard Brinsley Sheridan

4888   The Right Honourable Gentleman is indebted to his memory for his jests and to his imagination for his facts. [On Henry Dundas.]

4889   It contained a great deal both of what was new and what was true, but unfortunately what was new was not true and what was true was not new.

4890   I think the interpreter is the hardest to be understood of the two.

4891   A wise woman will always let her husband have her way.

4892   Tom, my dear, tip your hat. Don't you know enough to decapitate when you meet a lady? [Mrs. Malaprop]

R. C. Sheriff

4893   When a man retires and time is no longer a matter of urgent importance, his colleagues generally present him with a clock.

Senator Sherman

4894   The constitution provides for every accidental contingency in the Executive, except of a vacancy in the mind of the president.

William Tecumseh Sherman

4895   Vox populi, vox humbug.

4896   If forced to choose between the penitentiary and the White House for four years, I would say the penitentiary, thank you.

4897   Grant stood by me when I was crazy, and I stood by him when he was drunk, and now we stand by each other.

Louis Sherwin
4898   Hollywood: they know only one word of more than one syllable here, and that is fillum.

Robert E. Sherwood
4899   She is on the verge of tears, her favorite perch.

Robert Shnayerson
4900   National Pride is a modern form of tribalism.

Edgar A. Shoaff
4901   A cynic is a person searching for an honest man, with a stolen lantern.

4902   Old age is when you first realize other people's faults are no worse than your own.

Jean Sibelius
4903   Pay no attention to what the critics say; there has never been set up a statue in honor of a critic.

Henryk Sienkiewicz
4904   The greater the philosopher, the harder it is for him to answer the questions of the average man.

Sigismund, Emperor of the Holy Roman Empire
4905   I am the King of Rome, and above grammar.

William Simon
4906   We have a love-hate relationship with inflation. We hate inflation, but we love everything that causes it.

4907   Unfortunately good economics is not always perceived to be good politics.

Frank H. Simonds
4908   There is but one way for a newspaperman to look at a politician, and that is down.

Lee Simonson
4909   Any event, once it has occurred, can be made to appear inevitable by a competent historian.

Upton Sinclair
4910   It is difficult to get a man to understand something when his salary depends upon his not understanding it.

Osbert Sitwell

4911   I am most fond of talking and thinking; that is to say, talking first and thinking afterward.

4912   I have always said that if I were a rich man, I would employ a professional praiser.

B. F. Skinner

4913   The real problem is not whether machines think but whether men do.

Cornelia Otis Skinner

4914   Mosquitoes were using my ankles for filling stations.

4915   One learns in life to keep silent and draw one's own confusions.

John Sloan

4916   Since we have to speak well of the dead, let's knock them while they're alive.

Adam Smith

4917   Man is an animal that makes bargains; no other animal does this—no dog exchanges bones with another.

4918   Oxford: a sanctuary in which exploded systems and obsolete prejudices find shelter and protection after they have been hunted out of every corner of the world.

4919   Wherever there is great property, there is great inequality . . . for one very rich man, there must be at least five hundred poor.

4920   What can be added to the happiness of a man who is in health, out of debt, and has a clear conscience?

4921   The propensity to truck, barter, and exchange . . . is common to all men, and to be found in no other race of animals.

4922   The object of the game is to make money, hopefully a lot of it.

"Adam Smith"

4923   The market will not go up unless it goes up, nor will it go down unless it goes down, and it will stay the same unless it does either.

Alexander Smith

4924   To sit for one's portrait is like being present at one's own creation.

Alfred E. Smith

4925   Nobody shoots at Santa Claus.

4926   No matter how thin you slice it, it's still baloney.

Harold Smith
4927   Psychiatrists say it's not good for a man to keep too much to himself. The Internal Revenue Service says the same thing.

Logan Pearsall Smith
4928   All reformers, however strict their conscience, live in houses just as big as they can pay for.

4929   If you want to be thought a liar always tell the truth.

4930   It is almost always worthwhile to be cheated; people's little frauds have an interest which amply repays what they cost us.

4931   We grow with years more fragile in body, but morally stouter, and can throw off the chill of a bad conscience almost at once.

4932   I cannot forgive my friends for dying; I do not find these vanishing acts of theirs at all amusing.

4933   A best seller is the gilded tomb of a mediocre talent.

4934   To suppose as we all suppose, that we could be rich and not behave as the rich behave, is like supposing that we could drink all day and stay sober.

4935   There are two things to aim at in life; first, to get what you want; and, after that, to enjoy it. Only the wisest of mankind achieve the second.

4936   Those who set out to serve God and Mammon soon discover that there is no God.

4937   The spread of atheism among the young is something awful; I give no credit, however, to the report that some of them do not believe in Mammon.

4938   I love money; just to be in the room with a millionaire makes me less forlorn.

4939   It is the wretchedness of being rich that you have to live with rich people.

4940   It's an odd thing about this universe that though we all disagree with each other, we are all of us always in the right.

4941   Thank heavens! The sun has gone in, and I don't have to go out and enjoy it.

4942   When we say we are certain so-and-so can't possibly have done it, what we mean is that we think he very likely did.

4943   How awful to reflect that what people say of us is true!

4944   What is more enchanting than the voices of young people, when you can't hear what they say?

4945   The denunciation of the young is a necessary part of the hygiene of older people, and greatly assists the circulation of their blood.

4946   When people come and talk to you of their aspirations, before they leave you had better count your spoons.

4947   There are few sorrows, however poignant, in which a good income is of no avail.

4948   When they come downstairs from their ivory towers, idealists are apt to walk straight into the gutter.

Sydney Smith

4949   He struck me much like a steam engine in trousers. [On Daniel Webster.]

4950   He not only overflowed with learning, he stood in the slop. [On Macaulay.]

4951   I am convinced digestion is the great secret of life.

4952   Benevolence is a natural instinct of the human mind; when A sees B in distress, his conscience always urges him to entreat C to help him.

4953   The best way of answering a bad argument is to let it go on.

4954   The first receipt to farm well is to be rich.

4955   He has returned from Italy a greater bore than ever; he bores on architecture, painting, statuary, and music.

4956   He is remarkably well, considering that he has been remarkably well for so many years.

4957   I have been looking for a person who disliked gravy all my life; let us swear eternal friendship.

4958   I have the most perfect confidence in your indiscretion.

4959   I have gout, asthma, and seven other maladies, but am otherwise very well.

4960   I have no relish for the country; it is a kind of healthy grave.

4961   I heard him speak disrespectfully of the equator.

4962   I like him and his wife; he is so ladylike, and she's such a perfect gentleman.

4963   In composing, as a general rule, run your pen through every other word you have written; you have no idea what vigor it will give your style.

4964   I never read a book before reviewing it; it prejudices one so.

4965   It was so hot here that I found there was nothing left for it but to take off my flesh and sit in my bones.

4966   It would be an entertaining change in human affairs to determine everything by minorities; they are almost always in the right.

4967   Macaulay has occasional flashes of silence that make his conversation perfectly delightful.

4968   Marriage resembles a pair of shears, so joined that they cannot be separated; often moving in opposite directions, yet always punishing anyone who comes between them.

4969   No furniture is so charming as books, even if you never open them or read a single word.

4970   Poverty is no disgrace to a man, but it is confoundedly inconvenient.

4971   The preterpluperfect tense has always occasioned him much uneasiness though he has appeared to the world cheerful and serene.

4972   What a mystery is the folly and stupidity of the good.

4973   When I hear any man talk of an unalterable law, I am convinced that he is an unalterable fool.

4974   When I take a gun in hand, the safest place for a pheasant is just opposite the muzzle.

4975   You and I are exceptions to the laws of nature; you have risen by your gravity, and I have sunk by my levity.

4976   I think breakfast so pleasant because no one is conceited before one o'clock.

4977   My handwriting looks as if a swarm of ants, escaping from an ink bottle, had walked over a sheet of paper without wiping their legs.

4978   Children are horribly insecure. The life of a parent is the life of a gambler.

4979   He has spent all his life in letting down empty buckets into empty wells; and he is frittering away his age in trying to draw them up again.

4980   Correspondences are like small clothes before the invention of suspenders; it is impossible to keep them up.

4981   It is always considered a piece of impertinence in England if a man
of less than two or three thousand a year has any opinion at all upon
important subjects.

4982   The clergy are allowed about twenty-six hours every year for the
instruction of their fellow creatures.

4983   When advised by his doctor to take a walk on an empty stomach,
Sydney Smith inquired: "Whose?"

4984   I look upon Switzerland as an inferior sort of Scotland.

4985   Take short views, hope for the best, and trust in God.

4986   The observances of the church concerning feasts and fasts are
tolerably well kept since the rich keep the feasts and the poor keep the
fasts.

4987   I have asked several men what passes in their minds when they
are thinking; and I never could find any man who could think for two
minutes together.

4988   The further he went west, the more convinced he felt that the wise
men came from the east.

Tobias George Smollett
4989   Some folks are wise and some are otherwise.

Sam Snead
4990   The only reason I ever played golf in the first place was so I could
afford to hunt and fish.

Socrates
4991   As to marriage or celibacy, let a man take which course he will, he
will be sure to repent.

4992   By all means marry; if you get a good wife, you'll become happy; if
you get a bad one, you'll become a philosopher.

4993   Once made equal to man, woman becomes his superior.

4994   See one promontory, one mountain, one sea, one river, and see all.

4995   As for me, all I know is that I know nothing.

George E. Sokolsky
4996   The first duty of the parents is to make the child realize from
infancy that there is nothing extraordinary about him.

Anastasio Somoza

4997   Democracy down here is like a baby—and nobody gives a baby everything to eat right away. I'm giving 'em liberty, but in my style.

John Philip Sousa

4998   Jazz will endure just as long as people hear it through their feet instead of their brains.

Robert Southey

4999   What are little girls made of . . . ?
Sugar and spice and all things nice,
And such are little girls made of.

5000   The vanquished have no friends.

General Carl Spaatz

5001   He thinks things through very clearly before going off half-cocked.

Francis Joseph, Cardinal Spellman

5002   You've heard of the three ages of man: youth, middle age, and "you're looking wonderful!"

Herbert Spencer

5003   A jury is a group of twelve people of average ignorance.

5004   Marriage: a ceremony in which rings are put on the finger of the lady and through the nose of the gentleman.

5005   To play billiards well is a sign of an ill-spent youth.

5006   The ultimate result of shielding men from the effects of folly is to fill the world with fools.

Baruch Spinoza

5007   If you want the present to be different from the past, study the past.

Charles Haddon Spurgeon

5008   Feel for others—in your pocket.

5009   Train your child in the way you now know you should have gone yourself.

5010   Nobody ever outgrows Scripture; the book widens and deepens with our years.

5011   By perseverance the snail reached the ark.

Joseph Stalin
5012   A single death is a tragedy, a million deaths is a statistic.

Laurence Stallings
5013   Hollywood—a place where the inmates are in charge of the asylum.

Frank L. Stanton
5014   'Taint no use to sit and whine
         'Cause the fish ain't on your line;
         Bait your hook an' keep on tryin'
             Keep a-goin'!

Freya Stark
5015   A good many men still like to think of their wives as they do of their religion, neglected but always there.

E. M. Statler, "Statler Hotel Service Code"
5016   A man may wear a red necktie, a green vest and tan shoes, and still be a gentleman.

Christina Stead
5017   A self-made man is one who believes in luck and sends his sons to Oxford.

Richard Steele
5018   Ceremony is the invention of wise men to keep fools at a distance.

5019   Good breeding is an expedient to make fools and wise men equals.

5020   A woman seldom writes her mind but in her postscript.

5021   What's the first excellence in a lawyer? Tautology. What the second? Tautology. What the third? Tautology.

Lincoln Steffens
5022   A child awakened out of a deep sleep expressed all the crying babies and all the weeping idealists in the world. "Oh, dear," he said, "I have lost my place in my dream."

5023   We have on the radio every Sunday a stroke of culture, a symphony concert from New York or somewhere with a toothwash. That's the culture part, the toothwash.

5024   Dumb and cheerful. That's a combination often seen, so often that one suspects a connection. As close as cause and effect, apparently.

Gertrude Stein

5025   In the United States there is more space where nobody is than where anybody is. This is what makes America what it is.

5026   Money is always there but the pockets change; it is not in the same pockets after a change, and that is all there is to say about money.

5027   Knowledge is the thing you know and how can you know more than you do know.

5028   Hemingway's remarks are not literature.

5029   And if it is less like anything does it make any difference and if it is more like anything does it make any difference and yet if it is not like anything at all it is an oil painting.

5030   A rose is a rose is a rose is a rose.

John Steinbeck

5031   Coney Island: where the surf is one third water and two thirds people.

5032   Hard-covered books break up friendships. You loan a hard-covered book to a friend and when he doesn't return it you get mad at him. It makes you mean and petty. But twenty-five cent books are different.

Mark Steinbeck

5033   Ask not what you can do for your country, for they are liable to tell you.

Stendhal

5034   Life is too short, and the time we waste in yawning never can be regained.

5035   The shepherd always tries to persuade the sheep that their interests and his own are the same.

5036   Rich people have no passions, except that of hurt vanity.

Casey Stengel

5037   They say you can't do it, but sometimes it doesn't always work.

5038   Ability is the art of getting credit for all the home runs somebody else hits.

5039   The Mets has come along slow, but fast!

5040   The British are very consistent. They were just as calm about my arrival tonight as they were back in 1924.

5041   I'll never make the mistake of bein' seventy again!

Sir James Fitzjames Stephen

5042   So we may put him [John Dalton] down as a liberal-conservative, which perhaps may be defined as a man who thinks things ought to progress, but would rather they remained as they are.

James Stephens

5043   Sleep is an excellent way of listening to an opera.

5044   Women are wiser than men because they know less and understand more.

5045   Finality is death. Perfection is finality. Nothing is perfect. There are lumps in it.

Gil Stern

5046   Man is a complex being; he makes deserts bloom—and lakes die.

Laurence Sterne

5047   Men tire themselves in pursuit of rest.

5048   'Tis known by the name of perseverance in a good cause, and obstinacy in a bad one.

5049   My father picked up an opinion as a man in the state of nature picks up an apple—it becomes his own—and if he is a man of spirit, he would lose his life rather than give it up.

Albert Sterner

5050   There is no such thing as modern art. There is art—and there is advertising.

Roger Stevens

5051   Whenever I think, I make a mistake.

Adlai Stevenson

5052   An independent is the guy who wants to take politics out of politics.

5053   A lie is an abomination unto the Lord and a very present help in time of trouble.

5054   I believe in the forgiveness of sin and the redemption of ignorance.

5055   Someone asked me ... how I felt and I was reminded of a story that a fellow townsman of ours used to tell—Abraham Lincoln. They asked him how he felt once after an unsuccessful election. He said he felt like a little boy who has stubbed his toe in the dark. He said that he was too old to cry, but it hurt too much to laugh. [Commenting on election defeat.]

5056   He who slings mud generally loses ground.

5057   The idea that you can merchandise candidates for high office like breakfast cereal—that you can gather votes like box tops—is, I think, the ultimate indignity to the democratic process.

5058   Asked if as a boy he had ever thought of the possibility he would grow up to be President:
"Yes, but I just dismissed it as a normal risk that any red-blooded American boy has to take."

5059   They used to say that if you worked in wartime Washington you would get one of three things: galloping frustration, ulcers, or a sense of humor. I guess I got them all.

5060   After one hard day of handshaking in the 1952 campaign he told a friend: "Perhaps the saddest part of all this is that a candidate must reach into a sea of hands, grasp one, not knowing whose it is, and say, 'I'm glad to meet you,' realizing that he hasn't and probably never will meet that man."

5061   If you would make a speech or write one
Or get an artist to indite one
Think not because 'tis understood
By men of sense, 'tis therefore good,
Make it so clear and simply planned
No blockhead can misunderstand.

5062   When I was a boy I never had much sympathy for a holiday speaker. He was just a kind of interruption between the hot dogs, a fly in the lemonade.

5063   Man does not live by words alone, despite the fact that sometimes he has to eat them.

5064   Eggheads of the world unite; you have nothing to lose but your yolks.

5065   Once [women] read Baudelaire. Now it is the *Consumers' Guide.* Once they wrote poetry. Now it's the laundry list.

5066   I remember my father telling me the story of the preacher delivering an exhortation to his flock, and as he reached the climax of his exhortation, a man in the front row got up and said, "O Lord, use me. Use me, O Lord—in an advisory capacity!"

5067   To the victor belong the toils.

5068   That which seems the height of absurdity in one generation often becomes the height of wisdom in another.

5069   A hungry man is not a free man.

5070   A free society is one where it is safe to be unpopular.

5071   I'm not an old, experienced hand at politics. But I am now seasoned enough to have learned that the hardest thing about any political campaign is how to win without proving that you are unworthy of winning.

5072   I sometimes marvel at the extraordinary docility with which Americans submit to speeches.

5073   I recall the story of a man in my home town of Bloomington who was interviewed by a newspaper reporter on his one hundredth anniversary. After congratulating the old gentleman on his anniversary, the reporter asked him a few questions: "To what do you attribute your longevity?"
    The centenarian thought for a moment and, holding up his hand and ticking off the items on his fingers, began: "I never smoked, I never drank liquor, and I never overate; and I always rise at six in the morning."
    To that the reporter remarked: "I had an uncle who acted the same way but he only lived to be eighty. How do you account for that?"
    "He didn't keep it up long enough," came the reply.

5074   Moderate Progressivism: don't just do something—stand there.

5075   Flattery is all right—if you don't inhale.

5076   When you leave here, don't forget why you came. [To a Princeton University class]

5077   While I am not in favor of maladjustment, I view this cultivation of neutrality, this breeding of mental neuters, this hostility to eccentricity and controversy with grave misgiving. One looks back with dismay at the possibility of a Shakespeare perfectly adjusted to bourgeois life in Stratford, a Wesley contentedly administering a country parish, George Washington going to London to receive a barony from George III, or Abraham Lincoln prospering in Springfield with nary a concern for the preservation of the crumbling Union.

5078   A politician is a statesman who approaches every question with an open mouth.

Robert Louis Stevenson
5079   Politics is perhaps the only profession for which no preparation is thought necessary.

5080   Every man has a sane spot somewhere.

5081   Everyone lives by selling something.

5082   Give me the young man who has brains enough to make a fool of himself.

5083   If your morals make you dreary, depend on it they are wrong.

5084   I've a grand memory for forgetting.

5085   Marriage is one long conversation, chequered by disputes.

5086   Life's awful like a lot of monkeys scramblin' for empty seats.

5087   There is nothing more certain than that age and youth are right, except perhaps that both are wrong.

5088   The child that is not clean and neat
With lots of toys and things to eat,
He is a naughty child, I'm sure—
Or else his dear papa is poor.

5089   A child should always say what's true
And speak when he is spoken to,
And behave mannerly at table;
At least as far as he is able.

5090   All natural talk is a festival of ostentation; and by the laws of the game each accepts and fans the vanity of the other.

5091   He sows hurry and reaps indigestion.

5092   Vanity dies hard; in some obstinate cases it outlives the man.

5093   I never weary of great churches. It is my favorite kind of mountain scenery. Mankind was never so happily inspired as when it made a cathedral.

George Craig Stewart
5094   The Church after all is not a club of saints; it is a hospital for sinners.

Max Stirner
5095   If it be right to me, it is right.

Johannes Stobaeus

5096   Farming is a most senseless pursuit, a mere laboring in a circle. You sow that you may reap, and then you reap that you may sow. Nothing ever comes of it.

Sir Edmund Stockdale

5097   Money isn't everything—but it's a long way ahead of what comes next.

Donald J. Stocking

5098   You don't buy a stock because it has real value. You buy it because you feel there is always a greater fool down the street ready to pay more than you paid.

Benjamin Stolberg

5099   An expert is a person who avoids the small errors as he sweeps on to the grand fallacy.

Christopher Stone

5100   I hate horses—they're uncomfortable in the middle and dangerous at both ends.

Irving Stone

5101   His mind was like a soup dish, wide and shallow, it could hold a small amount of nearly anything, but the slightest jarring spilled the soup into somebody's lap. [On William Jennings Bryan.]

Rex Stout

5102   Nothing is more admirable than the fortitude with which millionaires tolerate the disadvantages of their wealth.

5103   There are two kinds of statistics, the kind you look up and the kind you make up.

Lionel Strachey

5104   A brilliant epigram is a solemn platitude gone to a masquerade ball.

5105   Statistics are mendacious truths.

5106   When humor is meant to be taken seriously, it's no joke.

5107   To be patriotic, hate all nations but your own; to be religious, all sects but your own; to be moral, all pretenses but your own.

Igor Stravinsky

5108   A good composer does not imitate, he steals.

Barbra Streisand

5109   Why does a woman work ten years to change a man's habits and then complain that he's not the man she married?

August Strindberg

5110   Literature is printed nonsense.

5111   Society is a madhouse whose wardens are the officials and police.

Simeon Strunsky

5112   If you want to understand democracy, spend less time in the library with Plato, and more time in the busses with people.

Bishop William Stubbs

5113   I have only three rules of life: never do anything underhand, never get your feet wet, go to bed at ten.

Frank Sullivan

5114   Two can live as cheap as one, but it costs them twice as much.

William Graham Sumner

5115   If you ever live in a country run by a committee, be on the committee.

5116   We throw all our attention on the utterly idle question whether A has done as well as B, when the only question is whether A has done as well as he could.

Billy Sunday

5117   Try praising your wife, even if it does frighten her at first.

Alfred Sutro

5118   Modesty is one of the seven deadly virtues.

Willie Sutton

5119   That's where the money is.

Gloria Swanson

5120   If I look like this, I need the trip. [On her passport photo.]

Jonathan Swift

5121   'Tis an old maxim in the schools,
        That flattery's the food of fools,
        Yet now and then your men of wit
        Will condescend to take a bit.

5122   She wears her clothes as if they were thrown on with a pitchfork.

5123   Argument is the worst sort of conversation.

5124   Every man desires to live long, but no man would be old.

5125   Faith, that's as well said as if I had said it myself.

5126   Fine words! I wonder where you stole 'em.

5127   Happiness is the perpetual possession of being well deceived.

5128   It is a miserable thing to live in suspense; it is the life of a spider.

5129   I never knew any man in my life who could not bear another's misfortune perfectly like a Christian.

5130   May you live all the days of your life.

5131   Thou hast a head, and so has a pin.

5132   No man will take counsel, but every man will take money; therefore, money is better than counsel.

5133   Punning is a talent which no man affects to despise but he that is without it.

5134   There are few wild beasts more to be dreaded than a talking man having nothing to say.

5135   We are so fond of one another because our ailments are the same.

5136   When you have done a fault, be always pert and insolent, and behave yourself as if you were the injured person.

5137   Censure is the tax a man pays to the public for being eminent.

5138   The latter part of a wise man's life is taken up in curing the follies, prejudices, and false opinions he had contracted in the former.

5139   A very little wit is valued in a woman, as we are pleased with a few words spoken plain by a parrot.

5140   What religion is he of? Why, he is an Anythingarian.

5141   We have just enough religion to make us hate but not enough to make us love one another.

5142   When a true genius appears in the world you may know him by this sign, that the dunces are all in confederacy against him.

5143   My stomach serves me instead of a clock.

5144   Satire is a sort of glass wherein beholders do generally discover everybody's face but their own.

5145   It is remarkable with what Christian fortitude and resignation we can bear the suffering of other folks.

5146   He was an ingenious man that first found out about eating and drinking.

5147   Words are but wind; learning is nothing but words; ergo, learning is nothing but wind.

5148   As universal a practice as lying is, and as easy a one as it seems, I do not remember to have heard three good lies in all my conversation, even from those who were most celebrated in that faculty.

5149   Elephants are always drawn smaller in life, but a flea always larger.

5150   What they do in heaven we are ignorant of; but what they do not do we are told expressly, that they neither marry nor are given in marriage.

5151   So, naturalists observe, a flea
        Hath smaller fleas that on him prey;
        And these have smaller still to bite 'em;
        And so proceed ad infinitum.

5152   Taverns are places where madness is sold by the bottle.

5153   The greatest advantage I know of being thought a wit by the world is that it gives one the greater freedom of playing the fool.

5154   I must complain the cards are ill-shuffled, till I have a good hand.

5155   No wise man ever wished to be younger.

5156   He was a bold man that first eat an oyster.

5157   It is useless for us to attempt to reason a man out of a thing he has never been reasoned into.

Algernon Charles Swinburne

5158   One, whom we see not, is; and one, who is not, we see;
        Fiddle, we know, is diddle; and diddle, we take it, is dee.

Arthur D. Sylvester

5159   It's the inherent right of the government to lie to save itself.

Joshua Sylvester

5160   Who readeth much, and never meditates,
           Is like the greedy eater of much food,
        Who so surcloys his stomach with his cates,
           That commonly they do him little good.

Publilius Syrus

5161   A small debt produces a debtor; a large one an enemy.

5162   That sick man does badly who makes his physician his heir.

5163   It is a very hard undertaking to seek to please everybody.

5164   No man is happy who does not think himself happy.

5165   No one knows what he can do till he tries.

5166   Better be ignorant of a matter than half know it.

Tacitus

5167   Necessity reforms the poor, and satiety the rich.

Robert A. Taft

5168   Of course sometimes it is not possible to prepare an address fully, but it is much better to do so even if you intend to speak extemporaneously.

William Howard Taft

5169   Politics, when I am in it, makes me sick.

5170   I feel certain that he would not recognize a generous impulse if he met it in the street. [On Woodrow Wilson.]

5171   When Taft was campaigning, someone threw a cabbage at him. It rolled to Taft's feet. "I see," was his comment, "that one of my adversaries has lost his head."

5172   I have come to the conclusion that the major part of the President is to increase the gate receipts of expositions and fairs and bring tourists into the town.

5173   Some men are graduated from college cum laude, some are graduated summa cum laude, and some are graduated mirabile dictu.

Charles M. de Talleyrand-Perigord

5174   He only thinks he is deaf because he can no longer hear anyone talking about him. [About a political opponent.]

5175   Don't trust first impulses—they are always good.

5176   If you wish to appear agreeable in society, you must consent to be taught many things which you know already.

5177   Never speak ill of yourself; your friends will always say enough on that subject.

5178   She is intolerable, but that is her only fault.

5179   The art of putting the right men in the right places is first in the science of government; but that of finding places for the discontented is the most difficult.

5180   An important art of politicians is to find new names for institutions which under old names have become odious to the public.

Booth Tarkington
5181   The only good in pretending is the fun we get out of fooling ourselves that we fool somebody.

A.J.P. Taylor
5182   He objected to ideas only when others had them. [On Ernest Bevin.]

Baylard Taylor
5183   Shelved around me lie the mummied authors.

Deems Taylor
5184   God help us if the younger generation ever stops being the despair of its grandparents.

Harold Taylor
5185   A student is not a professional athlete. . . . He is not a little politician or junior senator looking for angles . . . an amateur promoter, a gladhander, embryo Rotarian, café-society leader, quiz kid, or man about town. A student is a person who is learning to fulfill his powers and to find ways of using them in the service of mankind.

Sir Henry Taylor
5186   Conscience is, in most men, an anticipation of the opinion of others.

5187   I have heard it remarked by a statesman of high reputation, that most great men have died of overeating themselves.

Sir William Temple
5188   When all is done, human life is, at the greatest and best, but like a froward child, that must be played with and humored a little to keep it quiet, till it falls asleep, and then the care is over.

Alfred, Lord Tennyson
5189   Charm us, orator, till the lion looks no larger than the cat.

Terence

5190   Nothing is said that has not been said before.

5191   There is nothing that can't be made worse by telling.

5192   There is a demand nowadays for men who can make wrong appear right.

5193   She never was really charming till she died.

Tertullian

5194   Nothing that is God's is obtainable by money.

William Makepeace Thackeray

5195   A clever, ugly man every now and then is successful with the ladies, but a handsome fool is irresistible.

5196   He that hath ears to hear, let him stuff them with cotton.

5197   If a man's character is to be abused, there's nobody like a relative to do the business.

5198   To love and win is the best thing; to love and lose, the next best.

5199   When I walk with you I feel as if I had a flower in my buttonhole.

5200   Even when I am reading my lectures I often think to myself, "What a humbug you are," and I wonder the people don't find it out.

5201   As an occupation in declining years, I declare I think saving is useful, amusing and not unbecoming. It must be a perpetual amusement. It is a game that can be played by day, by night, at home and abroad, and at which you must win in the long run. . . . What an interest it imparts to life!

5202   How hard it is to make an Englishman acknowledge that he is happy.

Margaret Thatcher

5203   Ladies and gentlemen, I stand before you tonight in my green chiffon evening gown, my face softly made up, my hair softly waved. . . . The Iron Lady of the Western World? Me? A cold warrior? Well, yes—if that is how they wish to interpret my defence of the values and freedom fundamental to our way of life. [Referring to the Soviet magazine *Red Star*, which had called her the "Iron Lady."]

5204   You don't tell deliberate lies, but sometimes you have to be evasive.

5205   I don't mind how much my ministers talk—as long as they do what I say.

5206   I usually make up my mind about a man in ten seconds, and I very rarely change it.

5207   I've got a woman's ability to stick to a job and get on with it when everyone else walks off and leaves it.

Ernest L. Thayer
5208   There was ease in Casey's manner as he stepped into his place,
There was pride in Casey's bearing and a smile on Casey's face;
And when responding to the cheers he lightly doffed his hat,
No stranger in the crowd could doubt 'twas Casey at the bat.

Angela Thirkell
5209   He began to realize the deep truth that no one, broadly speaking, ever wishes to hear what you have been doing.

5210   If one cannot invent a really convincing lie, it is often better to stick to the truth.

A.E.W. Thomas
5211   ... like the type of civil servant who has a difficulty for every solution.

Dylan Thomas
5212   Somebody's boring me. . . . I think it's me.

Gwyn Thomas
5213   I remember those happy days and often wish I could speak into the ears of the dead the gratitude which was due to them in life and so ill-returned.

Norman Thomas
5214   I would rather be right than president, but I am perfectly willing to be both.

Robert Bailey Thomas
5215   If you want the time to pass quickly, just give your note for ninety days.

Harold Thompson
5216   A ring on the finger is worth two on the phone.

Harry Thompson

5217 Be kind. Remember everyone you meet is fighting a hard battle.

Roy Thompson

5218 It is part of the social mission of every great newspaper to provide a refuge and a home for the largest possible number of salaried eccentrics.

W. H. Thompson

5219 We are none of us infallible—not even the youngest of us.

Henry David Thoreau

5220 It is an interesting question how far men would retain their relative rank if they were divested of their clothes.

5221 Be not simply good; be good for something.

5222 City life: millions of people being lonesome together.

5223 Every generation laughs at the old fashions, but follows religiously the new.

5224 I have three chairs in my house: one for solitude, two for friendship, three for company.

5225 It is not worth while to go round the world to count the cats in Zanzibar.

5226 A man is rich in proportion to the number of things which he can afford to let alone.

5227 The mass of men lead lives of quiet desperation.

5228 My dwelling was small, and I could hardly entertain an echo in it.

5229 Not that the story need be long, but it will take a long while to make it short.

5230 The rarest quality in an epitaph is truth.

5231 I cannot easily buy a blankbook to write thoughts in; they are commonly ruled for dollars and cents.

5232 I have received no more than one or two letters in my life that were worth the postage.

5233 There are nowadays professors of philosophy, but not philosophers.

5234 What is commonly called friendship is only a little more honor among rogues.

5235   Spring—an experience in immortality.

5236   A kitten is so flexible that she is almost double; the hind parts are equivalent to another kitten with which the forepart plays. She does not discover that her tail belongs to her until you tread upon it.

5237   The youth gets together materials for a bridge to the moon, and at length the middle-aged man decides to make a woodshed with them.

5238   If words were invented to conceal thought, newspapers are a great improvement on a bad invention.

5239   When I read some of the rules for speaking and writing the English language correctly—as that a sentence must never end with a participle—and perceive how implicitly even the learned obey it, I think
Any fool can make a rule
And every fool will mind it.

Jeremy Thorpe

5240   Greater love hath no man than this, that he lay down his friends for his life.

5241   I am a bit of a showman, and I don't mind admitting it.

James Thurber

5242   Early to rise and early to bed makes a male healthy, wealthy and dead.

5243   He fell down a great deal during his boyhood because of a trick he had of walking into himself.

5244   Well, if I called the wrong number, why did you answer the phone?

5245   While he was not dumber than an ox he was not any smarter.

5246   With sixty staring me in the face, I have developed inflammation of the sentence structure and a definite hardening of the paragraphs.

5247   The dog has seldom been successful in pulling man up to its level of sagacity, but man has frequently dragged the dog down to his.

5248   I'm sixty-five and I guess that puts me in with the geriatrics, but if there were fifteen months in every year, I'd only be forty-eight.

5249   Word has somehow got around that the split infinitive is always wrong. That is of a piece with the outworn notion that it is always wrong to strike a lady.

5250   It is better to have loafed and lost than never to have loafed at all.

5251   A lady of forty-seven who has been married twenty-six years and has six children knows what love really is and once described it for me like this: "Love is what you've been through with somebody."

5252   Love is the strange bewilderment which overtakes one person on account of another person.

5253   A man is a golden impossibility.

5254   A pinch of probably is worth a pound of perhaps.

5255   It is better to ask some of the questions than to know all the answers.

5256   Man wants a great deal here below, and woman even more.

5257   You can fool too many of the people too much of the time.

Fritz Thyssen
5258   When I rest I rust.

Lewis Timberlake
5259   There are no dollar signs on tombstones.

Charles W. Tobey
5260   The things that are wrong with the country today are the sum total of all the things that are wrong with us as individuals.

Ernst Toller
5261   All history is the propaganda of the victorious.

Leo Tolstoy
5262   History would be an excellent thing if only it were true.

5263   History is nothing but a collection of fables and useless trifles, cluttered up with a mass of unnecessary figures and proper names.

5264   All happy families are alike, but each unhappy family is unhappy in its own way.

5265   He never chooses on opinion; he just wears whatever happens to be in style.

5266   He will do almost anything for the poor, except get off their backs.

5267   If I had children now, I should send them to the ballet. At any rate it is better than the university. Their feet alone might be spoiled in the ballet, but at the university it is their heads.

5268   He who has money has in his pocket those who have none.

5269   Repay evil with good and you deprive the evildoer of all the pleasure of his wickedness.

Lily Tomlin

5270   Ninety-eight percent of the adults in this country are decent, hard-working, honest Americans. It's the other lousy two percent that get all the publicity. But then—we elected them.

Giovanni Torriano

5271   Think much, speak little and write less.

Arturo Toscanini

5272   I kissed my first woman and smoked my first cigarette on the same day; I have never had time for tobacco since.

A. Tournier

5273   After the rogues, what honest people dread most of all is a court of law.

Arnold Toynbee

5274   America is a large, friendly dog in a very small room. Every time it wags its tail it knocks over a chair.

5275   To be able to fill leisure intelligently is the last product of civilization.

5276   Man has mastered nature but, in doing that, he has enslaved himself to the new man-made environment that he has conjured up all around him. Man has condemned himself now to live in cities and to make his living by working in factories and offices.

Herbert Beerbohm Tree

5277   A man never knows what a fool he is until he hears himself imitated by one.

5278   I don't like her. But don't misunderstand me: my dislike is purely platonic.

George Macaulay Trevelyan

5279   Once in every man's youth there comes the hour when he must learn, what no one ever yet believed save on the authority of his own experience, that the world was not created to make him happy.

Claire Trevor

5280   What a holler would ensue, if people had to pay the minister as much to marry them as they have to pay a lawyer to get them a divorce.

Anthony Trollope

5281   Success is a poison that should only be taken late in life and then only in small doses.

5282 Success is the necessary misfortune of life, but it is only to the very unfortunate that it comes early.

Leon Trotsky
5283 No one who has wealth to distribute ever omits himself.

Herb True
5284 We're overlooking one of the biggest sources of natural gas in the country—politicians.

Harry S. Truman
5285 I was about as popular as a skunk in the parlor.

5286 I learned that a great leader is a man who has the ability to get other people to do what they don't want to do and like it.

5287 A politician is a man who understands government and it takes a politician to run a government. A statesman is a politician who's been dead for fifteen years.

5288 Pierce didn't know what was going on and even if he had, he wouldn't have known what to do about it. [On Franklin Pierce.]

5289 The White House is the finest jail in the world.

5290 If you can't convince them confuse them.

5291 I always considered statesmen to be more expendable than soldiers.

5292 Any man who has had the job I've had and didn't have a sense of humor wouldn't still be here.

5293 Whenever a fellow tells me he's bipartisan, I know he's going to vote against me.

5294 If they want to ask me some impudent questions, I'll try to give them some impudent answers.

5295 I'm not going to demagogue until I have something to demagogue about.

5296 Some of the Presidents were great and some of them weren't. I can say that, because I wasn't one of the great Presidents, but I had a good time trying to be one, I can tell you that.

5297 My father was not a failure. After all, he was the father of a President of the United States.

5298 Where politics goes in the front door, statesmanship flies out the transom.

5299   Don't talk about rope in the house of somebody who has been hanged.

5300   If I felt any better, I couldn't stand it.

5301   Well, the speech seems to have made a hit according to all the papers. Shows you never can tell. I thought it was rotten.

5302   These men who live in the past remind me of a toy I'm sure all of you have seen. The toy is a small wooden bird called the Floogie Bird. Around the Floogie Bird's neck is a label reading: "I fly backwards. I don't care where I'm going. I just want to see where I've been."

5303   I have found the best way to give advice to your children is to find out what they want and then advise them to do it.

5304   The buck stops here.

5305   What I want to know is how to break out of politics.

5306   I rather think there is an immense shortage of Christian charity among so-called Christians.

5307   Democracy is based on the conviction that man has the moral and intellectual capacity, as well as the inalienable right, to govern himself with reason and justice.

5308   I studied the lives of great men and famous women, and I found that the men and women who got to the top were those who did the jobs they had in hand, with everything they had of energy and enthusiasm and hard work.

5309   In my Sunday School class there was a beautiful little girl with golden curls. I was smitten at once and still am.

5310   You don't set a fox to watching the chickens just because he has a lot of experience in the hen house.

5311   When you become forty, you should take it a little slower, work a little harder, take a little more time to think, and you will be all right. . . . I guess the best assurance of a long life is to get yourself a set of long-living parents like I did.

Sophie Tucker
5312   I've been rich and I've been poor; rich is better.

E. Horsfall Turner
5313   It is an inflexible rule of mine not to make impromptu speeches without good warning. . . . As Lord Goddard said, they are not worth the paper they are written on.

Mark Twain

5314   The universal brotherhood of man is our most precious possession—what there is of it.

5315   Talking of patriotism, what humbug it is; it is a word which always commemorates a robbery. There isn't a foot of land in the world which doesn't represent the ousting and reousting of a long line of successive owners.

5316   Fleas can be taught nearly everything a Congressman can.

5317   Be careful about reading health books. You may die of a misprint.

5318   Suppose you were an idiot and suppose you were a member of Congress. But I repeat myself.

5319   I admire him, I freely confess it. And when his time comes I shall buy a piece of the rope for a keepsake. [On Cecil Rhodes.]

5320   I was seldom able to see an opportunity until it had ceased to be one.

5321   I never could tell a lie that anybody would doubt, nor a truth that anybody would believe.

5322   Adam and Eve had many advantages, but the principal one was that they escaped teething.

5323   The difference between the right word and the almost right word is the difference between lightning and the lightning bug.

5324   Has any boyhood dream ever been fulfilled? I must doubt it. Look at Brander Matthews. He wanted to be a cowboy. What is he today? Nothing but a professor in a university. Will he ever be a cowboy? It is hardly conceivable.

5325   By trying, we can easily learn to endure adversity. Another man's, I mean.

5326   Whoever has lived long enough to find out what life is knows how deep a debt of gratitude we owe to Adam, the first great benefactor of our race. He brought death into the world.

5327   Classic: A book which people praise and don't read.

5328   There are people who can do all fine and heroic things but one: keep from telling their happiness to the unhappy.

5329   His ignorance covered the whole earth like a blanket and there was hardly a hole in it anywhere.

5330   Man is the only animal that blushes. Or needs to.

5331   Happiness ain't a thing in itself—it's only a contrast with something that ain't pleasant.

5332   I could have become a soldier myself if I had waited. I had got part of it learned; I knew more about retreating than the man that invented retreating.

5333   Nothing so needs reforming as other people's habits.

5334   Thunder is good, thunder is impressive; but it is lightning that does the work.

5335   Good breeding consists in concealing how much we think of ourselves and how little we think of the other person.

5336   Don't part with your illusions. When they are gone you may still exist but you have ceased to live.

5337   There are two times in a man's life when he should not speculate: when he can't afford it, and when he can.

5338   April 1. This is the day upon which we are reminded of what we are on the other three hundred and sixty-four.

5339   It is better to keep your mouth shut and appear stupid than to open it and remove all doubt.

5340   When red-headed people are above a certain social grade their hair is auburn.

5341   We have a criminal jury system which is superior to any in the world and its efficiency is only marred by the difficulty of finding twelve men every day who don't know anything and can't read.

5342   He had had much experience of physicians, and said, "The only way to keep your health is to eat what you don't want, drink what you don't like, and do what you'd druther not."

5343   The principal difference between a cat and a lie is that a cat has only nine lives.

5344   We haven't all had the good fortune to be ladies; we haven't all been generals, or poets, or statesmen; but when the toast works down to the babies, we stand on common ground.

5345   I am no lazier now than I was forty years ago, but that is because I reached the limit forty years ago. You can't go beyond possibility.

5346   The habits of all peoples are determined by their circumstances. The Bermudians lean upon barrels because of the scarcity of lamp-posts.

5347   He died two years ago of over-cerebration. He was a poor sort of a creature and by nature and training a fraud. As a liar he was well enough and had some success but no distinction.

5348   It takes some little time to accept and realize the fact that while you have been growing old, your friends have not been standing still.

5349   Mules and donkeys and camels have appetites that anything will relieve temporarily, but nothing satisfy.

5350   He could foretell wars and famines, though that was not so hard, for there was always a war and generally a famine somewhere.

5351   There are several good protections against temptation: but the surest is cowardice.

5352   In Paris they just simply opened their eyes and stared when we spoke to them in French! We never did succeed in making those idiots understand their own language.

5353   Training is everything. The peach was once a bitter almond; cauliflower is nothing but cabbage with a college education.

5354   I have noticed my conscience for many years, and I know it is more trouble and bother to me than anything else I started with.

5355   Work consists of whatever a body is obliged to do, and Play consists of whatever a body is not obliged to do.

5356   Carlyle said "a lie cannot live." It shows that he did not know how to tell them.

5357   There comes a time in every rightly-constructed boy's life when he has a raging desire to go somewhere and dig for hidden treasure.

5358   Grief can take care of itself; but to get the full value of joy, you must have somebody to share it with.

5359   The man who is born stingy can be taught to give liberally—with his hands; but not with his heart.

5360   There is an old-time toast which is golden for its beauty: "When you ascend the hill of prosperity may you not meet a friend."

5361   He had no principles and was delightful company.

5362   My mother had a great deal of trouble with me but I think she enjoyed it.

5363   All say, "How hard it is that we have to die"—a strange complaint to come from the mouths of people who have had to live.

5364   Truth is the most valuable thing we have. Let us economize it.

5365   Let us be thankful for the fools. But for them the rest of us could not succeed.

5366   Few things are harder to put up with than the annoyance of a good example.

5367   Let us not be too particular. It is better to have old second-hand diamonds than none at all.

5368   It could probably be shown by facts and figures that there is no distinctly native American criminal class except Congress.

5369   Forget and forgive. This is not difficult, when properly understood. It means that you are to forget inconvenient duties, and forgive yourself for forgetting. In time, by rigid practice and stern determination, it comes easy.

5370   He imagined that he was in love with her, wheras I think she did the imagining for him.

5371   The proverb says that Providence protects children and idiots. This is really true. I know it because I have tested it.

5372   If you pick up a starving dog and make him prosperous, he will not bite you. This is the principal difference between a dog and a man.

5373   They spell it Vinci and pronounce it Vinchy; foreigners always spell better than they pronounce.

5374   I was gratified to be able to answer promptly, and I did. I said I didn't know.

5375   There are times when one would like to hang the whole human race and finish the farce.

5376   The man with a new idea is a crank, until the idea succeeds.

5377   She was not quite what you would call refined, she was not quite what you would call unrefined. She was the kind of person that keeps a parrot.

5378   Every one is a moon, and has a dark side which he never shows to anybody.

5379   Noise proves nothing. Often a hen who has merely laid an egg cackles as if she has laid an asteroid.

5380   October. This is one of the peculiarly dangerous months to speculate in stocks. The others are July, January, September, April, November, May, March, June, December, August and February.

5381   Modesty died when clothes were born.

5382   Few of us can stand prosperity. Another man's, I mean.

5383   Always do right. This will gratify some people, and astonish the rest.

5384   We should be careful to get out of an experience only the wisdom that is in it—and stay there, lest we be like the cat that sits down on a hot stove-lid. She will never sit down on a hot stove-lid again—and that is well; but also she will never sit down on a cold one anymore.

5385   We ought never to do wrong when people are looking.

5386   The reports of my death are greatly exaggerated.

5387   Wagner's music is better than it sounds.

5388   I like criticism, but it must be my way.

5389   Adam was human; he didn't want the apple for the apple's sake; he wanted it because it was forbidden.

5390   All I care to know is that a man is a human being—that is enough for me; he can't be any worse.

5391   Be good and you will be lonesome.

5392   All you need in this life is ignorance and confidence, and then success is sure.

5393   Animals talk to each other; I never knew but one man who could understand them—I knew he could because he told me so himself.

5394   A banker is a fellow who lends you his umbrella when the sun is shining and wants it back the minute it begins to rain.

5395   Barring the natural expression of villainy which we all have, the man looked honest enough.

5396   The emperor sent his troops to the field with immense enthusiasm; he will lead them in person—when they return.

5397   Get your facts first, and then you can distort them as much as you please.

5398   A good memory and a tongue tied in the middle is a combination which gives immortality to conversation.

5399   Hain't we got all the fools in town on our side, and ain't that a big enough majority in any town?

5400   Have a place for everything and keep the thing somewhere else; this is not advice, it is merely custom.

5401 Never run after your own hat—others will be delighted to do it; why spoil their fun.

5402 The older we grow the greater becomes our wonder at how much ignorance one can contain without bursting one's clothes.

5403 Only presidents, editors, and people with tapeworms have the right to use the editorial "we."

5404 "On with the dance, let joy be unconfined" is my motto, whether there's any dance to dance or any joy to unconfine.

5405 Principles have no real force except when one is well fed.

5406 Put all your eggs in one basket, and—watch the basket.

5407 Repartee is something we think of twenty-four hours too late.

5408 Soap and education are not as sudden as a massacre, but they are more deadly in the long run.

5409 Some of the commonest English words are not in use with us— such as 'ousemaid, 'ospital, 'otel, 'istorian.

5410 There are no people who are quite so vulgar as the overrefined ones.

5411 He liked to like people, therefore people liked him.

5412 He was a very inferior farmer when he first began, and he is now rising from affluence to poverty.

5413 His money is twice tainted: 'taint yours and 'taint mine.

5414 I am an old man and have known a great many troubles, but most of them never happened.

5415 I can live for two months on a good compliment.

5416 If you don't like the weather in New England, just wait a few minutes.

5417 If you tell the truth, you don't have to remember anything.

5418 I have never let my schooling interfere with my education.

5419 In our country we have those three unspeakably precious things: freedom of speech, freedom of conscience, and the prudence never to practice either.

5420 In the first place God made idiots; this was for practice; then he made school boards.

5421 It is a difference of opinion that makes horse races.

5422   It is a mistake that there is no bath that will cure people's manners, but drowning would help.

5423   It is inferior for coffee, but it is pretty fair tea.

5424   It is more trouble to make a maxim than it is to do right.

5425   It is not best that we use our morals weekdays; it gets them out of repair for Sundays.

5426   It seems such a pity that Noah and his party did not miss the boat.

5427   It used to be a good hotel, but that proves nothing—I used to be a good boy.

5428   It usually takes me more than three weeks to prepare a good impromptu speech.

5429   It was wonderful to find America, but it would have been more wonderful to miss it.

5430   I've never heard a blue jay use bad grammar, but very seldom; and when they do, they are as ashamed as a human.

5431   The man who is a pessimist before forty-eight knows too much; the man who is an optimist after forty-eight knows too little.

5432   There is no use in your walking five miles to fish when you can depend on being just as unsuccessful near home.

5433   There isn't a Parellel of Latitude but thinks it would have been the Equator if it had had its rights.

5434   There's always something about your success that displeases even your best friends.

5435   Thrusting my nose firmly between his teeth, I threw him heavily to the ground on top of me.

5436   To be good is noble, but to teach others how to be good is nobler —and less trouble.

5437   To cease smoking is the easiest thing I ever did; I ought to know because I've done it a thousand times.

5438   To eat is human; to digest, divine.

5439   Truth is stranger than fiction; fiction is obliged to stick to the possibilities, truth isn't.

5440   Truth is stranger than fiction—to some people.

5441   Virtue has never been as respectable as money.

5442 Wrinkles should merely indicate where smiles have been.

5443 Part of the secret of success in life is to eat what you like and let the food fight it out inside.

5444 The first half of life consists of the capacity to enjoy without the chance; the last half consists of the chance without the capacity.

5445 He had only one vanity; he thought he could give advice better than any other person.

5446 I was young and foolish then; now I am old and foolisher.

5447 I was sorry to have my name mentioned as one of the great authors, because they have a sad habit of dying off. Chaucer is dead, Spenser is dead, so is Milton, so is Shakespeare, and I am not feeling very well myself.

5448 Most people are bothered by those passages of Scripture they do not understand . . . the passages that bother me are those I do understand.

5449 The burnt child shuns the fire until the next day.

5450 Civilization is a limitless multiplication of unnecessary necessaries.

5451 Water, taken in moderation, cannot hurt anybody.

5452 We do not deal much in facts when we are contemplating ourselves.

5453 What a good thing Adam had—when he said a good thing, he knew nobody had said it before.

5454 Whatever a man's age, he can reduce it several years by putting a bright-colored flower in his buttonhole.

5455 What is the difference between a taxidermist and a tax collector? The taxidermist takes only your skin.

5456 When in doubt, tell the truth.

5457 When I speak my native tongue in its utmost purity in England, an Englishman can't understand me at all.

5458 When some men discharge an obligation you can hear the report for miles around.

5459 When you cannot get a compliment in any other way, pay yourself one.

5460   A wise man does not waste so good a commodity as lying for naught.

5461   Compliments always embarrass a man. You do not know anything to say. It does not inspire you with words. There is nothing you can say in answer to a compliment. I have been complimented myself a great many times, and they always embarrass me—I always feel that they have not said enough.

5462   In his private heart no man much respects himself.

5463   I asked Tom if countries always apologized when they had done wrong, and he says, "Yes; the little one does."

5464   As for me, I hope to be cremated. I made that remark to my pastor once, who said, with what he seemed to think was an impressive manner: "I wouldn't worry about that, if I had your chances."

5465   Console yourself with the reflection that you are giving the doctor pleasure, and that he is getting paid for it. [Giving advice for a proper frame of mind for undergoing a surgical operation.]

5466   When a man's dog turns against him, it is time for a wife to pack her trunk and go home to mamma.

5467   Never learn to do anything. If you don't learn you'll always find someone else to do it for you. [Mark Twain's mother.]

5468   Duties are not performed for duty's sake, but because their neglect would make the man uncomfortable. A man performs but one duty—the duty of contenting his spirit, the duty of making himself agreeable to himself.

5469   Well enough for old folks to rise early, because they have done so many mean things all their lives they can't sleep anyhow.

5470   Be virtuous and you will be eccentric.

5471   Why do you sit there looking like an envelope without any address on it?

5472   Fame is a vapor; popularity an accident; the only earthly certainty is oblivion.

5473   He [Rudyard Kipling] is a stranger to me, but he is a most remarkable man—and I am the other one. Between us, we cover all knowledge; he knows all that can be known, and I know the rest.

5474   When I was a boy of fourteen, my father was so ignorant I could hardly stand to have the old man around. But when I got to be twenty-one, I was astonished at how much he had learned in seven years.

5475 Nothing is made in vain, but the fly came near it.

5476 It takes your enemy and your friend, working together, to hurt you to the heart; the one to slander you and the other to get the news to you.

5477 The proper office of a friend is to side with you when you are in the wrong. Nearly anybody will side with you when you are in the right.

5478 All the modern inconveniences. [Gadgets.]

5479 The man who does not read good books has no advantage over the man who can't read them.

5480 I am different from Washington; I have a higher, grander standard of principle. Washington could not lie. I can lie, but I won't.

5481 In all matters of opinion, our adversaries are insane.

5482 Good friends, good books and a sleepy conscience: this is the ideal life.

5483 I would rather have my ignorance than another man's knowledge, because I have got so much more of it.

5484 Life would be infinitely happier if we could only be born at the age of eighty and gradually approach eighteen.

5485 A lie can travel half way around the world while the truth is putting on its shoes.

5486 George Washington, as a boy, was ignorant of the commonest accomplishments of youth. He could not even lie.

5487 Names are not always what they seem. The common Welsh name Bzjxxllwcp is pronounced Jackson.

5488 In a museum in Havana there are two skulls of Christopher Columbus, "one when he was a boy and one when he was a man."

5489 There is no sadder sight than a young pessimist, except an old optimist.

5490 I never write metropolis for seven cents because I can get the same price for city. I never write policeman because I can get the same money for cop.

5491 My philological studies have satisfied me that a gifted person ought to learn English (barring spelling and pronouncing) in thirty hours, French in thirty days, and German in thirty years.

5492 The very ink with which history is written is merely fluid prejudice.

5493 Every man is wholly honest to himself and to God, but not to anyone else.

5494 Etiquette requires us to admire the human race.

5495 Many a small thing has been made large by the right kind of advertising.

5496 Information seems to stew out of me naturally, like the precious otter of roses out of an otter.

5497 To me, Poe's prose is unreadable—like Jane Austen's. No, there is a difference. I would read his prose on a salary, but not Jane's.

5498 You may have noticed that the less I know about a subject, the more confidence I have, and the more new light I throw on it.

5499 I told [the Frenchman] in French. . . . He said he could not understand me. I repeated. Still, he did not understand. He appeared to be very ignorant of French.

5500 I am going to write you . . . but not now, for I haven't anything to do and I can't write letters except when I am rushed.

5501 Whenever you find that you are on the side of the majority, it is time to reform (or pause and reflect).

5502 I used to worship the mighty genius of Michael Angelo—that man who was great in poetry, painting, sculpture, architecture—great in everything he undertook. But I do not want Michael Angelo for breakfast —for luncheon—for dinner—for tea—for supper—for between meals. I like a change, occasionally. In Genoa, he designed everything; in Milan, he or his pupils designed everything, nearly, and what he did not design he used to sit on a favorite stone and look at, and they showed us the stone. In Pisa, he designed everything but the old shot tower and they would have attributed that to him if it had not been so awfully out of the perpendicular. . . . He designed St. Peter's; he designed the Pope; he designed the Pantheon, the uniform of the Pope's soldiers, the Tiber, the Vatican, the Colosseum, the Capitol. . . . The eternal bore designed the Eternal City, and unless all men and books do lie, he painted everything in it! Dan said the other day to the guide, "Enough, enough, enough! Say no more! Lump the whole thing! Say that the Creator made Italy from designs by Michael Angelo!" I never felt so fervently thankful, so soothed, so tranquil, so filled with a blessed peace, as I did yesterday when I learned that Michael Angelo was dead.

5503 He would come in and say he had changed his mind—which was a gilded figure of speech, because he hadn't any.

5504 I was born modest; not all over, but in spots.

5505   It isn't so astonishing, the number of things that I can remember, as the number of things I can remember that aren't so.

5506   When I was younger I could remember anything, whether it happened or not; but I am getting old, and soon I shall remember only the latter.

5507   I'm opposed to millionaires, but it would be dangerous to offer me the position.

5508   Modesty antedates clothes and will be resumed when clothes are no more.

5509   I was born modest, but it didn't last.

5510   It is at our mother's knee that we acquire our noblest and truest and highest ideals, but there is seldom any money in them.

5511   In an age when we would rather have money than health, and would rather have another man's money than our own, he lived and died unsordid.

5512   The Moral Sense teaches us what is right, and how to avoid it when unpopular.

5513   It's my opinion that everyone I know has morals, though I wouldn't like to ask. I know I have. But I'd rather teach them than practice them any day. "Give them to others"—that's my motto.

5514   We often feel sad in the presence of music without words; and often more than that in the presence of music without music.

5515   We called him Barney for short. We couldn't use his real name, there wasn't time.

5516   Necessity is the mother of "taking chances."

5517   There was things which he stretched, but mainly he told the truth.

5518   He was as shy as a newspaper is when referring to its own merits.

5519   Obscurity and a competence—that is the life that is best worth living.

5520   The pause—that impressive silence, that eloquent silence, that geometrically progressive silence which often achieves a desired effect where no combination of words howsoever felicitous could accomplish it.

5521   There are three kinds of people—commonplace men, remarkable men and lunatics.

5522   When we were finishing our house, we found we had a little cash left over, on account of the plumber not knowing it.

5523   I refused to attend his funeral. But I wrote a very nice letter explaining that I approved of it.

5524   I think I can say, and say with pride, that we have legislatures that bring higher prices than any in the world.

5525   He will remember me, because I was the person who did not ask for an office.

5526   Honest poverty is a gem that even a king might be proud to call his own, but I wish to sell out.

5527   Although [my father] left us a sumptuous legacy of pride in his fine Virginian stock and its national distinction, I presently found that I could not live on that alone without occasional bread to wash it down with.

5528   Prosperity is the best protector of principle.

5529   Do not put off till tomorrow what can be put off till day-after-tomorrow just as well.

5530   Public servants: persons chosen by the people to distribute the graft.

5531   It is a gratification to me to know that I am ignorant of art.

5532   The radical in one century is the conservative of the next. The radical invents the views. When he has worn them out, the conservative adopts them.

5533   The rain is famous for falling on the just and unjust alike, but if I had the management of such affairs I would rain softly and sweetly on the just, but if I caught a sample of the unjust outdoors I would drown him.

5534   I've seen this river so wide that it had only one bank.

5535   The river Nile is lower than it has been for 150 years. This news will be chiefly interesting to parties who remember the former occasion.

5536   It used to take me all vacation to grow a new hide in place of the one they flogged off me during school term.

5537   There ain't no way to find out why a snorer can't hear himself snore.

5538   It is my custom to keep on talking until I get the audience cowed.

5539   He could charm an audience an hour on a stretch without ever getting rid of an idea.

5540   The first time I ever saw St. Louis, I could have bought it for six million dollars, and it was the mistake of my life that I did not do it.

5541   My time is taken up answering letters of strangers. . . . What does possess strangers to write so many letters? I never could find that out. However, I suppose I did it myself when I was a stranger.

5542   English afternoon tea is an affront to luncheon and an insult to dinner.

5543   His voice was like the distressing noise which a nail makes when you screech it across a windowpane.

5544   Travel is no longer any charm for me. I have seen all the foreign countries I want to see except heaven and hell, and I have only a vague curiosity as concerns one of those.

5545   One of the worst things about civilization is that anybody that gits a letter with trouble in it comes and tells you all about it and makes you feel bad, and the newspapers fetches you the troubles of everybody all over the world, and keeps you downhearted and dismal most of the time, and it's such a heavy load for a person.

5546   Forty years ago I was not so good-looking. A looking glass then lasted me three months. Now I can wear it out in two days.

5547   Now look here, old friend, I know the human race; and I know that when a man comes to Washington, I don't care if it's from Heaven, it's because he wants something.

5548   I met [an old man] out in Iowa who had come up from Arkansas. I asked him whether he had experienced much cold during the preceding winter, and he exclaimed, "Cold! If the thermometer had been an inch longer we'd all have frozen to death!"

5549   Wit is the sudden marriage of ideas which before their marriage were not perceived to have any relation.

5550   I love work. Why, sir, when I have a piece of work to perform, I go away to myself, sit down in the shade, and muse over the coming enjoyment. Sometimes I am so industrious that I muse too long.

5551   I do not like work even when another person does it.

5552   Write without pay until somebody offers pay. If nobody offers within three years, the candidate may look upon this circumstance with the most implicit confidence as the sign that sawing wood is what he was intended for.

5553   As to the Adjective: when in doubt, strike it out.

5554   Its name is Public Opinion. It is held in reverence. It settles everything. Some think it is the voice of God.

William M. Tweed

5555   As long as I count the votes, what are you going to do about it?

John Tyler

5556   Here lies the body of my good horse, "The General." For twenty years he bore me around the circuit of my practice, and in all that time he never made a blunder. Would that his master could say the same! John Tyler [Inscription over the grave of his horse.]

Sigrid Undset

5557   He was not made for climbing the tree of knowledge.

Justice Vaisey

5558   A gentleman's agreement is an arrangement which is not an agreement, between two persons, neither of whom is a gentleman, with each expecting the other to be strictly bound while he himself has no intention of being bound at all.

Paul Valéry

5559   The trouble with our times is that the future is not what it used to be.

5560   Politics is the art of preventing people from busying themselves with what is their own business.

5561   Science is a collection of successful recipes.

5562   As to the presidency, the two happiest days of my life were those of my entry upon the office and those of my surrender of it.

S. W. Vandegrift

5563   My father often boasted that when he left medical school he knew a little anatomy, less physiology and one drug, ipecac.

Cornelius Vanderbilt

5564   What do I care about the law? Hain't I got the power!

5565   You have undertaken to cheat me. I will not sue you, for the law takes too long. I will ruin you.

Frank Vanderlip

5566   A conservative is a man who does not think that anything should be done for the first time.

5567   Anyone who tries to understand the money question goes crazy.

Frederick F. Van de Water

5568   Haymaking has merit as a spectacle, if you sit in the shade at the edge of the mowing and watch the jolly farmer at his toil.

5569   I have decided, after three years, that I am extremely tired of farming. I am also extremely tired.

Willard D. Vandiver

5570   I come from a state that raises corn and cotton and cockleburs and Democrats, and frothy eloquence neither convinces nor satisfies me. I am from Missouri. You have got to show me.

Henry Van Dyke

5571   Remember that what you possess in the world will be found at the day of your death to belong to another, but what you are will be yours forever.

5572   There is a loftier ambition than merely to stand high in the world. It is to stoop down and lift mankind a little higher.

5573   No man's credit is as good as his money.

5574   He that planteth a tree is the servant of God;
He provideth a kindness for many generations,
And faces that he hath not seen shall bless him.

Lord Vansittart

5575   The beauty of being young is that so many things have, delusively, a personal reference to you; only to age is it plain that things matter and you don't.

5576   The lives of great men rarely remind us of anything sublime.

Bill Vaughn

5577   My father asserted that there was no better place to bring up a family than in a rural environment. . . . There's something about getting up at 5 A.M., feeding the stock and chickens, and milking a couple of cows before breakfast that gives you a lifelong respect for the price of butter and eggs.

5578   America is a land where a citizen will cross the ocean to fight for democracy—and won't cross the street to vote in a national election.

5579   We hope that, when the insects take over the world, they will remember with gratitude how we took them along on all our picnics.

5580   A three-year-old child is a being who gets almost as much fun out of a fifty-six dollar set of swings as it does out of finding a small green worm.

5581   Economists report that a college education adds many thousands of dollars to a man's lifetime income—which he then spends sending his son to college.

5582   A statesman is any politician it's considered safe to name a school after.

5583   Money won't buy happiness, but it will pay the salaries of a large research staff to study the problem.

5584   A real patriot is the fellow who gets a parking ticket and rejoices that the system works.

5585   It's hard for the modern generation to understand Thoreau, who lived beside a pond but didn't own water skis or a snorkel.

Thorstein Veblen
5586   Socialism is a dead horse.

Lupe Velez
5587   First time you buy a house you see how pretty the paint is and buy it. The second time you look to see if the basement has termites. It's the same with men.

Louis Vermeil
5588   The prime purpose of eloquence is to keep other people from speaking.

Victoria, Queen of Great Britain
5589   He speaks to me as if I were a public meeting. [On William Gladstone.]

Gore Vidal
5590   There is no human problem which could not be solved if people would simply do as I advise.

5591   The more money an American accumulates, the less interesting he becomes.

5592   Whenever a friend succeeds, a little something in me dies.

Marshal de Villars
5593   God save me from my friends, I can protect myself from my enemies.

Voltaire
5594   In general, the art of government consists in taking as much money as possible from one class of citizens to give to the other.

5595   When it is a question of money, everybody is of the same religion.

5596   The art of medicine consists of amusing the patient while nature cures the disease.

5597   Common sense is not so common.

5598   The fate of a nation has often depended upon the good or bad digestion of a prime minister.

5599   Ideas are like beards: men do not have them until they grow up.

5600   I know I am among civilized men because they are fighting so savagely.

5601   Illusion is the first of all pleasures.

5602   The infinitely little have pride infinitely great.

5603   The multitude of books is making us ignorant.

5604   In the great game of human life one begins by being a dupe and ends by being a rogue.

5605   Originality is nothing but judicious imitation.

5606   Satire lies about literary men while they live, and eulogy lies about them when they die.

5607   The secret of being a bore is to tell everything.

5608   To forgive our enemies their virtues—that is a greater miracle.

5609   We use ideas merely to justify our evil, and speech merely to conceal our ideas.

5610   When he who hears doesn't know what he who speaks means, and when he who speaks doesn't know what he himself means—that is philosophy.

5611   A woman can keep one secret—the secret of her age.

5612   The punishment of criminals should be of use: when a man is hanged he is good for nothing.

5613   A long dispute means that both parties are wrong.

5614   My life's dream has been a perpetual nightmare.

5615   My prayer to God is a very short one: "O Lord, make my enemies ridiculous!" God has granted it.

5616   Enthusiasm is not always the companion of total ignorance; it is often that of erroneous information.

5617   Prejudice is an opinion without judgment.

5618   Prejudice is the reason of fools.

5619   A good imitation is the most perfect originality.

5620   He who is only wise lives a sad life.

5621   The superfluous is very necessary.

5622   Talking about a mutual acquaintance, a friend said to Voltaire, "It is good of you to say such pleasant things of him when he says such spiteful ones of you."
"Perhaps," replied Voltaire, "we are both mistaken."

5623   God is always on the side of the heaviest battalions.

5624   Work spares us from three great evils: boredom, vice and want.

Wernher von Braun
5625   We can lick gravity, but sometimes the paperwork is overwhelming. [Speaking of space engineering.]

Dayton Voorhees
5626   There was an old man of Nantucket
Who kept all his cash in a bucket;
But his daughter named Nan
Ran away with a man—
And as for the bucket—Nantucket.

Mary Heaton Vorse
5627   The art of writing is the art of applying the seat of the pants to the seat of the chair.

Harry V. Wade
5628   Youth today must be strong, unafraid, and a better taxpayer than its father.

5629   Aziz Esset, a gentleman of importance in Egypt, says his name can be pronounced by opening a soda bottle slowly.

5630   Though General Sherman lived on into the peace, he never said what he thought of it.

5631   The ideal voice for radio may be defined as having no substance, no sex, no owner, and a message of importance to every housewife.

Phil Walden
5632   If you can make money and have fun and power—that's what it's all about.

Charles Walgreen

5633   Mrs. Walgreen portrayed her husband as possessing a canny modesty: "He used to come home and remark, 'Well, today I hired another man who is smarter than I am.' " I would comment that nobody in the drug business was smarter than he was. But Charles would say, 'The only really smart thing about me is that I know enough to hire men who are smarter than I am.' "

James J. Walker

5634   A reformer is a guy who rides through a sewer in a glass-bottomed boat.

5635   If you're there before it's over, you're on time.

Stanley Walker

5636   He was an author whose works were so little known as to be almost confidential.

Edgar Wallace

5637   He had so much money that he could afford to look poor.

Ira Wallach

5638   Statistics indicate that, a a result of overwork, modern executives are dropping like flies on the nation's golf courses.

Graham Wallas

5639   The little girl had the making of a poet in her who, being told to be sure of her meaning before she spoke, said: "How can I know what I think till I see what I say?"

Madena R. Wallingford

5640   What is intended as a little white lie often ends up as a double feature in Technicolor.

Horace Walpole

5641   I never knew but one woman who would not take gold—and she took diamonds.

5642   I never understand anything until I have written about it.

5643   Spring has set in with its usual severity.

5644   The wisest prophets make sure of the event first.

5645   There are playthings for all ages; the playthings of old people is to talk of the playthings of their youth.

5646   In my youth I thought of writing a satire on mankind, but now in my age I think I should write an apology for them.

Frank Walsh
5647   The three basic needs of the average American are food, clothing, and tax shelter.

Izaak Walton
5648   That which is everybody's business is nobody's business.

5649   I have laid aside business, and gone a-fishing.

James P. Warburg
5650   No man can be a conservative until he has something to lose.

William Warburton
5651   Orthodoxy is my doxy; heterodoxy is another man's doxy.

5652   Enthusiasm is that temper of the mind in which the imagination has got the better of the judgment.

Artemus Ward
5653   I'm not a politician and my other habits are good.

5654   By a sudden and adroit movement I placed my left eye against his fist.

5655   Did you ever have the measles, and if so, how many?

5656   The ground flew up and hit me in the head.

5657   I am saddest when I sing; so are those who hear me; they are sadder even than I am.

5658   I now bid you a welcome adieu.

5659   Let us all be happy and live within our means, even if we have to borrow the money to do it with.

5660   There's a good deal of human nature in man.

5661   It is a pity that Chawcer, who had geneyus, was so unedicated; he's the wuss speller I know of.

5662   Gentlemen, I give you Upper Canada; because I don't want it myself.

5663   He is dreadfully married. He's the most married man I ever saw in my life.

5664   I have already given two cousins to the war, and I stand reddy to sacrifiss my wife's brother ruther'n not see the rebelyin krusht.

5665   Shakespeare endorses polygamy: he speaks of the Merry Wives of Windsor; how many wives did Mr. Windsor have?

5666   "Thrice is he armed that hath his quarrel just"—
And four times he who get his fist in fust.

5667   For those who like this kind of war, it is just such a war as they like.

E. F. Ware
5668   The lightning-bug is brilliant, but he hasn't any mind;
He stumbles through existence with his head-light on behind.

Charles Dudley Warner
5669   Blessed be agriculture—if one does not have too much of it.

5670   Everybody talks about the weather but nobody does anything about it.

5671   One of the best things in the world to be is a boy; it requires no experience, but needs some practice to be a good one.

5672   The thing generally raised on city land is taxes.

5673   What a man needs in gardening is a cast-iron back, with a hinge in it.

5674   There is but one pleasure in life equal to that of being called on to make an after-dinner speech, and that is not being called on to make one.

5675   I know that unremitting attention to business is the price of success, but I don't know what success is.

Robert Penn Warren
5676   Poets, we know, are terribly sensitive people, and in my observation, one of the things they are most sensitive about is cash.

George Washburn
5677   Retail merchants who are sharing in five billions of Christmas business will tell you emphatically that there is a Santa Claus.

George Washington
5678   There being no Episcopal Minister present in the place, I went to hear morning service performed in the Dutch Reformed Church—which, being in that language not a word of which I understood, I was in no danger of becoming a proselyte to its religion by the eloquence of the preacher.

5679   I die hard. But I am not afraid to go.

Thomas J. Watson

5680   Business is a game, the greatest game in the world if you know how to play it.

5681   All the problems of the world could be settled easily if men were only willing to think. The trouble is that men very often resort to all sorts of devices in order not to think, because thinking is such hard work.

Isaac Watts

5682   The tulip and the butterfly
Appear in gayer coats than I:
Let me be dressed fine as I will,
Flies, worms, and flowers exceed me still.

Lord Wavell

5683   Winston is always expecting rabbits to come out of empty hats.
[On Churchill's conduct of World War II.]

Mary Webb

5684   We are tomorrow's past.

Daniel Webster

5685   Daniel Webster, when asked what was the greatest thought that had ever entered his mind, replied: "My accountability to Almighty God."

5686   The world is governed more by appearance than by realities, so that it is fully as necessary to seem to know something as it is to know it.

5687   I was born an American, I will live an American, I will die an American and I intend to perform the duties incumbent upon me in that character to the end of my career! No man can suffer too much, and no man can fall too soon, if he suffers or if he falls in the defense of the liberties and constitution of his country.

Chaim Weizmann

5688   Miracles sometimes occur, but one has to work terribly hard for them.

Orson Welles

5689   I don't say we all ought to misbehave, but we ought to look as if we could.

5690   Now we sit through Shakespeare in order to recognize the quotations.

5691   When you're down and out, something always turns up—and it's usually the noses of your friends.

5692   I hate television. I hate it as much as peanuts. But I can't stop eating peanuts.

5693   I started at the top and worked my way down.

5694   Every actor in his heart believes everything bad that's printed about him.

Duke of Wellington
5695   Why, she not only filled the chair, she filled the room. [On his first audience with the young Queen Victoria.]

Carolyn Wells
5696   Actions lie louder than words.

5697   Charity uncovers a multitude of sins.

5698   Circumstances alter faces.

5699   Epigrams cover a multitude of sins.

5700   A guilty conscience is the mother of invention.

5701   He who loves and runs away may live to love another day.

5702   It's a wise child that owes his own father.

5703   The wages of sin is alimony.

5704   We should live and learn; but by the time we've learned, it's too late to live.

5705   A critic is a necessary evil, and criticism is an evil necessity.

5706   Dead men tell no tales.

5707   One man's fish is another man's poisson.

5708   A tutor who tooted a flute,
        Tried to teach two young tooters to toot.
            Said the two to the tutor
            "Is it harder to toot, or
        To tutor two tooters to toot?"

Gilbert Wells
5709   The man who has no secrets from his wife either has no secrets or no wife.

Herbert George Wells
5710   His studies were pursued but never effectually overtaken.

5711   What on earth would a man do with himself if something did not stand in his way?

5712   Moral indignation is jealousy with a halo.

Joan Welsh

5713   In making out your income tax return, remember it's better to give than to deceive.

Mae West

5714   He's the kind of man who picks his friends—to pieces.

5715   I never loved another person the way I loved myself.

5716   Marriage is a great institution, but I'm not ready for an institution, yet.

Rebecca West

5717   He is every other inch a gentleman.

Edward Noyes Westcott

5718   A reasonable amount of fleas is good for a dog; it keeps him from brooding over being a dog.

5719   The only man who can change his mind is a man that's got one.

Paul Westhead

5720   If Shakespeare had been in pro basketball he never would have had time to write his soliloquies. He would always have been on a plane between Phoenix and Kansas City.

Mildred Weston

5721   Two stubborn beaks
Of equal strength
Can stretch a worm
To any length.

Ruth Weston

5722   A fox is a wolf who sends flowers.

Richard Whately

5723   Honesty is the best policy, but he who is governed by that maxim is not an honest man.

5724   It is a folly to expect men to do all that they may reasonably be expected to do.

5725   Happiness is no laughing matter.

5726   Never argue at the dinner table, for the one who is not hungry always gets the best of the argument.

Edwin Percy Whipple
5727   Wit: the unexpected explosion of thought.

James Abbott McNeill Whistler
5728   I'm lonesome. They are all dying. I have hardly a warm personal enemy left.

5729   I am not arguing with you—I am telling you.

5730   "I wish I'd said that," said Oscar Wilde to Whistler, who had just made some epigrammatic remark.
"Never mind, Oscar, you will, you will" was the reply.

5731   If other people are going to talk, conversation becomes impossible.

E. B. White
5732   Democracy is the recurrent suspicion that more than half of the people are right more than half of the time.

5733   Thurber did not write the way a surgeon operates, he wrote the way a child skips rope, the way a mouse waltzes.

5734   Home was quite a place when people stayed there.

5735   Many a New Yorker spends a lifetime within the confines of an area smaller than a country village. Let him walk two blocks from his corner and he is in a strange land and will feel uneasy till he gets back.

5736   Commuter—one who spends his life
In riding to and from his wife;
A man who shaves and takes a train
And then rides back to shave again.

J. Gustav White
5737   Our language is funny—a fat chance and a slim chance are the same thing.

John White
5738   There are three kinds of people in the world: those who can't stand Picasso, those who can't stand Raphael, and those who've never heard of either of them.

T. De Vere White

5739   He discloses the workings of a mind to which incoherence lends an illusion of profundity.

Theodore H. White

5740   History is always best written generations after the event, when clouded fact and memory have all fused into what can be accepted as truth, whether it be so or not.

William Allen White

5741   A little learning is not a dangerous thing to one who does not mistake it for a great deal.

5742   Kansas is a state of the Union, but it is also a state of mind, a neurotic condition, a psychological phase, a symptom, indeed, something undreamed of in your philosophy, an inferiority complex against the tricks and manners of plutocracy—social, political and economic.

Alfred North Whitehead

5743   If America is to be civilized, it must be done [at least for the present] by the business class.

Gough Whitlam

5744   There is a great amount of talent in the Parliamentary Labour Party, but I believe that I have the greatest amount of talent at the present time.

Robert E. Whitten

5745   The child had every toy his father wanted.

Charlotte Whitton

5746   Whatever women do they must do twice as well as men to be thought half as good. Luckily, this is not difficult.

George Wickersham

5747   The modern idea of home has been well expressed as the place one goes from the garage.

Oscar Wilde

5748   Henry James writes fiction as if it were a painful duty.

5749   I choose my friends for their good looks, my acquaintances for their good characters, and my enemies for their good intellects. A man cannot be too careful in the choice of his enemies.

5750   I have the simplest tastes. I am always satisfied with the best.

5751   Democracy means simply the bludgeoning of the people, by the people, for the people.

5752   The crude commercialism of America, its materialistic spirit. . . . are entirely due to the country having adopted for its national hero a man who was incapable of telling a lie.

5753   After a good dinner, one can forgive anybody, even one's own relatives.

5754   Children begin by loving their parents; as they grow older they judge them; sometimes they forgive them.

5755   When I was young I used to think that money was the most important thing in life; now that I am old, I know it is.

5756   To love oneself is the beginning of a life-long romance.

5757   George Moore wrote brilliant English until he discovered grammar.

5758   Alas, I am dying beyond my means.

5759   All charming people are spoiled; it is the secret of their attraction.

5760   All women become like their mothers—that is their tragedy; no man does—that's his.

5761   Ambition is the last refuge of the failure.

5762   Anybody can make history; only a great man can write it.

5763   Anyone can sympathize with the sufferings of a friend, but it requires a very fine nature to sympathize with a friend's success.

5764   Arguments are extremely vulgar, for everybody in good society holds exactly the same opinions.

5765   Arguments are to be avoided; they are always vulgar and often convincing.

5766   As long as a woman can look ten years younger than her own daughter, she is perfectly satisfied.

5767   As soon as people are old enough to know better, they don't know anything at all.

5768   Bad manners make a journalist.

5769   Being natural is simply a pose, and the most irritating pose I know.

5770   Bernard Shaw is an excellent man; he has not an enemy in the world, and none of his friends like him.

5771   By persistently remaining single, a man converts himself into a permanent public temptation.

5772   Caricature is the tribute that mediocrity pays to genius.

5773   Conscience makes egotists of us all.

5774   Consistency is the last refuge of the unimaginative.

5775   A cynic is a man who knows the price of everything and the value of nothing.

5776   The difference between literature and journalism is that journalism is unreadable and literature is unread.

5777   Don't be misled into the path of virtue.

5778   Duty is what one expects from others.

5779   The English country gentleman galloping after a fox—the unspeakable in full pursuit of the uneatable.

5780   Everybody who is incapable of learning has taken to teaching.

5781   Everyone should keep someone else's diary.

5782   Experience is simply the name we give our mistakes.

5783   Fashion is a form of ugliness so intolerable that we have to alter it every six months.

5784   Fashion is that by which the fantastic becomes for a moment universal.

5785   Fashion is what one wears oneself: what is unfashionable is what other people wear.

5786   Fathers should be neither seen nor heard; that is the only proper basis for family life.

5787   Few parents nowadays pay any regard to what their children say to them; the old-fashioned respect for the young is fast dying out.

5788   Genius is born, not paid.

5789   The first duty in life is to be as artificial as possible; what the second duty is, no one has yet discovered.

5790   A gentleman is one who never hurts anyone's feelings unintentionally.

5791   He was always late on principle, his principle being that punctuality is the thief of time.

5792   The good end happily, the bad unhappily—that is what fiction means.

5793   He doesn't act on the stage—he behaves.

5794   He had the sort of face that, once seen, is never remembered.

5795   He hasn't a single redeeming vice.

5796   He is old enough to know worse.

5797   He knew the precise psychological moment when to say nothing.

5798   I beg your pardon, I didn't recognize you—I've changed a lot.

5799   I can believe anything—provided it is incredible.

5800   I can resist everything except temptation.

5801   I do not approve of anything which tampers with natural ignorance.

5802   If one hears bad music it is one's duty to drown it in conversation.

5803   If one tells the truth, one is sure sooner or later to be found out.

5804   I like Wagner's music better than anybody's; it is so loud, one can talk the whole time without other people hearing what one says.

5805   I must decline your invitation owing to a subsequent engagement.

5806   In America, the President reigns for four years, and journalism governs forever and ever.

5807   In America, the young are always ready to give to those who are older than themselves the full benefits of their inexperience.

5808   Bigamy is having one wife too many. Monogamy is the same.

5809   In examinations the foolish ask questions that the wise cannot answer.

5810   In love, one always begins by deceiving oneself, and one always ends by deceiving others; that is what the world calls a romance.

5811   Insincerity is merely a method by which we can multiply our personalities.

5812   In this world there are only two tragedies: one is not getting what one wants, and the other is getting it.

5813   It is always a silly thing to give advice, but to give good advice is absolutely fatal.

5814   It is a terrible thing for a man to find out suddenly that all his life he has been speaking nothing but the truth.

5815   It is dangerous to be sincere unless you are also stupid.

5816   It is only an auctioneer who should admire all schools of art.

5817   It is only by not paying one's bills that one can hope to live in the memory of the commercial classes.

5818   It is perfectly monstrous the way people go about nowadays saying things against one, behind one's back, that are absolutely and entirely true.

5819   Laughter is not a bad beginning for a friendship, and it is the best ending for one.

5820   Life is far too important a thing ever to talk seriously about.

5821   The longer I live the more keenly I feel that whatever was good enough for our fathers is not good enough for us.

5822   Man is a rational animal who always loses his temper when he is called upon to act in accordance with the dictates of reason.

5823   Bore: a man who is never unintentionally rude.

5824   Marriage is the one subject on which all women agree and all men disagree.

5825   Memory is the diary that we all carry about with us.

5826   Men become old but they never become good.

5827   Misfortunes one can endure, they come from the outside; but to suffer for one's faults—ah! there is the sting of life.

5828   Murder is always a mistake; one should never do anything that one cannot talk about after dinner.

5829   My own business always bores me to death; I prefer other people's.

5830   Never buy a thing you don't want merely because it is dear.

5831   No man should have a secret from his wife; she invariably finds it out.

5832   Nothing succeeds like excess.

5833   Of course, America had often been discovered before Columbus, but it had always been hushed up.

5834   The old believe everything, the middle-aged suspect everything, the young know everything.

5835   One can survive everything nowadays except death, and live down everything except a good reputation.

5836   One should always play fairly when one has the winning cards.

5837   One should never trust a woman who tells one her real age; a woman who would tell one that would tell one anything.

5838   A well-tied tie is the first serious step in life.

5839   We have everything in common with America nowadays except, of course, language.

5840   We live in an age when unnecessary things are our only necessities.

5841   We think we are generous because we credit our neighbor with the possession of those virtues that are likely to benefit us.

5842   Whenever a man does a thoroughly stupid thing, it is always from the noblest motives.

5843   Whenever one has anything unpleasant to say, one should always be quite candid.

5844   When people agree with me I always feel that I must be wrong.

5845   With an evening coat and a white tie, anybody, even a stockbroker, can gain a reputation for being civilized.

5846   Women have a wonderful instinct about things; they can discover anything except the obvious.

5847   Women love us for our defects; if we have enough of them they will forgive us everything, even our superior intellects.

5848   The world is divided into two classes: those who believe the incredible, and those who do the improbable.

5849   The youth of America is their oldest tradition; it has been going on now for three hundred years.

5850   The fatality of good resolutions is that they are always too late.

5851   If one could only teach the English how to talk and the Irish how to listen, society would be quite civilized.

5852   The reason we are so pleased to find out other people's secrets is that it distracts public attention from our own.

5853   The public have an insatiable curiosity to know everything— except what is worth knowing.

5854   One must be serious about something if one wants to have any amusement in life.

5855   One's duty as a gentleman should never interfere with one's pleasure in the slightest degree.

5856   Style depends largely on the way the chin is worn. They are worn very high at present.

5857   Memory is the diary that chronicles things that never have happened and couldn't possibly have happened.

5858   Long engagements give people the opportunity of finding out each other's character before marriage, which is never advisable.

5859   No woman should ever be quite accurate about her age. It looks so calculating.

5860   It is important not to keep a business engagement if one wants to retain any sense of the beauty of life.

5861   It is very vulgar to talk about one's own business. Only people like stock-brokers do that, and then merely at dinner parties.

5862   A heart doesn't go with modern dress. It makes one look old.

5863   The world has grown suspicious of anything that looks like a happy married life.

5864   It is most dangerous nowadays for a husband to pay any attention to his wife in public. It always makes people think that he beats her when they are alone.

5865   One can always recognize women who trust their husbands, they look so thoroughly unhappy.

5866   Good people do a great deal of harm in the world. Certainly the greatest harm they do is that they make badness of such extraordinary importance. It is absurd to divide people into good and bad. People are either charming or tedious.

5867   Thirty-five is a very attractive age; London society is full of women who have of their own free choice remained thirty-five for years.

5868   Actions are the first tragedies in life, words are the second. Words are perhaps the worst. Words are merciless.

5869   Nothing is so dangerous as being too modern; one is apt to grow old-fashioned quite suddenly.

5870   Vulgarity is simply the conduct of other people, just as falsehoods are the truth of other people.

5871   Being educated puts one almost on a level with the commercial classes.

5872   London society is entirely composed of beautiful idiots and brilliant lunatics.

5873   Only dull people are brilliant at breakfast.

5874   In modern life nothing produces such an effect as a good platitude. It makes the whole world kin.

5875   No woman, plain or pretty, has any common-sense at all. Common-sense is the privilege of our sex and we men are so self-sacrificing that we never use it.

5876   An acquaintance that begins with a compliment is sure to develop into a real friendship.

5877   Pleasure is the only thing to live for. Nothing ages like happiness.

5878   Philanthropy is the refuge of people who wish to annoy their fellow-creatures.

5879   Self-sacrifice is a thing that should be put down by law. It is so demoralizing to the people for whom one sacrifices oneself.

5880   Questions are never indiscreet, answers sometimes are.

5881   Woman's first duty in life is to her dressmaker. What the second duty is no one has yet discovered.

5882   It is always nice to be expected and not to arrive.

5883   Women are never disarmed by compliments, men always are.

5884   Modern women understand everything except their husbands.

5885   To have the reputation of possessing the most perfect social tact, talk to every woman as if you loved her, and to every man as if he bored you.

5886   Discontent is the first step in the progress of a man or a nation.

5887   Women have become so highly educated that nothing should surprise them except happy marriages.

5888   Women are pictures, men are problems: if you want to know what a woman really means, look at her, don't listen to her.

5889   Clever people never listen and stupid people never talk.

5890   It is safer to believe evil of everyone until people are found out to be good, but that requires a great deal of investigation nowadays.

5891   To get into the best society nowadays, one has either to feed people, amuse people, or shock people.

5892   Men always want to be a woman's first love—women like to be a man's last romance.

5893   We are born in an age when only the dull are treated seriously.

5894   To give an accurate description of what has never occurred is the inalienable privilege and proper occupation of the historian.

5895   All men are married women's property; that is the only true definition of what married women's property really is.

5896   All Americans dress well—they get their clothes in Paris.

5897   When good Americans die they go to Paris; when bad Americans die they go to America.

5898   If a man is a gentleman he knows quite enough, and if he is not a gentleman whatever he knows is bad for him.

5899   One should never take sides in anything—taking sides is the beginning of sincerity, and earnestness follows shortly after, and the human being becomes a bore.

5900   When a man says he has exhausted life one always knows life has exhausted him.

5901   Men know life too early, women know life too late.

5902   All thought is immoral. Its very essence is destruction. If you think of anything you kill it. Nothing survives being thought of.

5903   Men are horribly tedious when they are good husbands, and abominably conceited when they are not.

5904   A really grande passion is comparatively rare nowadays. It is the privilege of people who have nothing to do. That is the only use of the idle classes in the country.

5905   More marriages are ruined nowadays by the common sense of the husband than by anything else. How can a woman be expected to be happy with a man who insists on treating her as if she were a perfectly rational being?

5906   When a man is old enough to do wrong he should be old enough to do right also.

5907   The world has always laughed at its own tragedies, that being the only way in which it has been able to bear them; consequently, whatever the world has treated seriously belongs to the comedy side of things.

5908   When one has never heard a man's name in the course of one's life it speaks volumes for him; he must be quite respectable.

5909   One can always be kind to people one cares nothing about.

5910   Men marry because they are tired, women because they are curious; both are disappointed.

5911   It is only the intellectually lost who ever argue.

5912   One should never make one's debut with a scandal; one should reserve that to give interest to one's old age.

5913   Genius lasts longer than Beauty. That accounts for the fact that we all take such pains to over-educate ourselves.

5914   Civilized society feels that manners are of more importance than morals, and the highest respectability is of less value than the possession of a good chef. Even the cardinal virtues cannot atone for cold entrees, nor an irreproachable private life for a bad dinner and poor wines.

5915   A bad man is the sort of man who admires innocence, and a bad woman is the sort of woman a man never gets tired of.

5916   I can't help detesting my relations. I suppose it comes from the fact that we can't stand other people having the same faults as ourselves.

5917   There are only two kinds of people who are really fascinating: people who know everything, and people who know nothing.

5918   There is luxury in self-reproach. When we blame ourselves we feel no one else has a right to blame us.

5919   It is personalities not principles that move the age.

5920   Good resolutions are a useless attempt to interfere with scientific laws; their origin pure vanity, their results absolutely nil.

5921   The charm of the past is that it is past, but women never know when the curtain has fallen. They always want a sixth act.

5922   Death and vulgarity are the only two facts in the nineteenth century that one cannot explain away.

5923   Tea is the only simple pleasure left to us.

5924   Wickedness is a myth invented by good people to account for the curious attractiveness of others.

5925   Nothing that actually occurs is of the smallest importance.

5926   Dullness is the coming of age of seriousness.

5927   A truth ceases to be true when more than one person believes in it.

5928   Ambition is the last refuge of the failure.

5929   It is only the superficial qualities that last. Man's deeper nature is soon found out.

5930   Industry is the root of all ugliness.

5931   Modern morality consists in accepting the standard of one's age.

5932   A woman will flirt with anybody in the world as long as other people are looking on.

5933   Evening clothes on a London merchant remind one of a morocco binding on a cook book or a doily on a stove lid.

5934   To get back one's youth one has merely to repeat one's follies.

5935   Nowadays most people die of a sort of creeping common sense, and discover, when it is too late, that the only things one never regrets are one's mistakes.

5936   Pleasure is nature's test, her sign of approval. When we are happy we are always good; but when we are good we are not always happy.

5937   A Radical is merely a man who has never dined, and a Tory simply a gentleman who has never thought.

5938   The world has been made by fools that wise men may live in it.

5939   The aim of the liar is simply to charm, to delight, to give pleasure. He is the very basis of civilized society.

5940   I have nothing to declare except my genius. [Responding to a customs official.]

5941   Every great man nowadays has his disciples, and it is always Judas who writes the biography.

5942   We live in the age of the over-worked, and the under-educated; the age in which people are so industrious that they become absolutely stupid.

5943   The basis of action is lack of imagination. It is the last resource of those who know not how to dream.

5944   Those who try to lead the people can only do so by following the mob.

5945   When you convert someone to an idea . . . you lose your faith in it.

5946   A true artist takes no notice whatever of the public.

5947   If you don't get everything you want, think of the things you don't get that you don't want.

5948   The best way to make children is to make them happy.

5949   The books that the world calls immoral are books that show the world its own shame.

5950   Education is an admirable thing, but it is well to remember from time to time that nothing that is worth knowing can be taught.

5951   Women are meant to be loved, not to be understood.

5952   The world is a stage, but the play is badly cast.

5953   No great artist ever sees things as they really are. If he did he would cease to be an artist.

5954   On an occasion of this kind it becomes more than a moral duty to speak one's mind. It becomes a pleasure.

5955   Caution: what we call cowardice in others.

5956   Unless one is wealthy there is no use in being a charming fellow.

5957   Mr. James Payn is an adept in the art of concealing what is not worth finding.

5958   Conscience and cowardice are really the same things. Conscience is the trade name of the firm.

5959   Only the shallow know themselves.

5960   Nowadays all the married men live like bachelors, and all the bachelors live like married men.

5961   To disagree with three-fourths of the British public on all points is one of the first elements of sanity, one of the deepest consolations in all moments of spiritual doubt.

5962   Other people are quite dreadful. The only possible society is one's self.

5963   To elope is cowardly; it is running away from danger; and danger has become so rare in modern life.

5964   The advantage of the emotions is that they lead us astray.

5965   I may have said the same thing before. . . . But my explanation, I am sure, will always be different.

5966   I am afraid I play no outdoor games at all, except dominoes. I have sometimes played dominoes outside French cafés.

5967   People are very fond of giving away what they most need themselves. It is what I call the depth of generosity.

5968   I hope you have not been leading a double life, pretending to be wicked, and being really good all the time. That would be hypocrisy.

5969   The only form of lying that is absolutely beyond reproach is lying for its own sake.

5970   Pessimist: one who, when he has the choice of two evils, chooses both.

5971   Work is the refuge of people who have nothing better to do.

5972   Some cause happiness wherever they go; others whenever they go.

5973   The one duty we owe to history is to rewrite it.

5974   History is merely gossip.

5975   To do nothing at all is the most difficult thing in the world, the most difficult and the most intellectual.

5976   The only beautiful things are the things that do not concern us.

5977   It is always with the best intentions that the worst work is done.

5978   Religion is the fashionable substitute for belief.

5979   Intuition: the strange instinct that tells a woman she is right, whether she is or not.

5980   Plain women are always jealous of their husbands, beautiful women never are; they have no time, they are always occupied in being jealous of other people's husbands.

5981   There is much to be said in favor of modern journalism. By giving us the opinions of the uneducated, it keeps us in touch with the ignorance of the community.

5982   I am the only person in the world I should like to know thoroughly, but I don't see any chance of it just at present.

5983   Indiscretion is the better part of valor.

5984   The sure way of knowing nothing about life is to try to make oneself useful.

5985   The people who love only once in their lives are really the shallow people. What they call their loyalty and fidelity, I call either the lethargy of custom or their lack of imagination.

5986   Twenty years of romance makes a woman look like a ruin, but twenty years of marriage make her something like a public building.

5987   One should not be too severe on English novels; they are the only relaxation of the intellectually unemployed.

5988   It is better to be beautiful than to be good, but it is better to be good than to be ugly.

5989   The only thing to do with good advice is to pass it on; it is never of any use to oneself.

5990   The only way to get rid of a temptation is to yield to it.

5991   The public is wonderfully tolerant—it forgives everything except genius.

5992   The real tragedy of the poor is that they can afford nothing but self-denial.

5993   She is a peacock in everything but beauty.

5994   Society produces rogues, and education makes one rogue cleverer than another.

5995   There is only one class in the community that thinks more about money than the rich, and that is the poor. The poor can think of nothing else. That is the misery of being poor.

5996   There is only one thing in the world worse than being talked about, and that is not being talked about.

5997   Marriage is hardly a thing one can do now and then—except in America.

5998   A man who desires to get married should know either everything or nothing.

5999   A really well-made buttonhole is the only link between art and nature.

6000   The happiness of a married man depends on the people he has not married.

6001   I dislike modern memoirs. They are generally written by people who have either entirely lost their memories, or have never done anything worth remembering; which, however, is, no doubt, the true explanation of their popularity, as the English public always feels perfectly at its ease when a mediocrity is talking to it.

6002   No woman should have a memory. Memory in a woman is the beginning of dowdiness.

6003   A misanthrope I can understand—a womanthrope never.

6004   Wicked women bother one, good women bore one. That is the only difference between them.

6005   It is an awfully dangerous thing to come across a woman who thoroughly understands one. They always end by marrying one.

6006   Modern journalism justifies its own existence by the great Darwinian principle of the survival of the vulgarest.

6007   Nothing ages women so rapidly as having married the general rule.

6008   I like persons better than principles and I like persons with no principles better than anything else in the world.

6009   The only really humanizing influence in prison is the influence of the prisoners.

6010   England has done one thing; it has invented and established public opinion, which is an attempt to organize the ignorance of the community, and to elevate it to the dignity of physical force.

6011   Young men want to be faithful and are not; old men want to be faithless and cannot.

6012   Pluck is not so common nowadays as genius.

6013   I hate vulgar realism in literature. The man who could call a spade a spade should be compelled to use one. It is the only thing he is fit for.

6014   Among the more elderly inhabitants of the South I found a melancholy tendency to date every event of importance on the late War. "How beautiful the moon is tonight," I once remarked to a gentleman standing near me.
        "Yes," was his reply, "but you should have seen it before the War."

6015   Murderer: one who is presumed to be innocent until he is proved insane.

6016   Please do not shoot the pianist. He is doing his best.

6017   Niagara Falls is simply a vast unnecessary amount of water going the wrong way and then falling over unnecessary rocks.

6018   It is only shallow people who do not judge by appearances.

6019   No civilized man ever regrets a pleasure, and no uncivilized man ever knows what a pleasure is.

6020   [James Abbott McNeill] Whistler, with all his faults, was never guilty of writing a line of poetry.

6021   I don't like principles. I prefer prejudices.

6022   I never approve or disapprove of anything now. It is an absurd attitude to take toward life. We are not sent into the world to air our moral prejudices.

6023   I can stand brute force but brute reason is quite unbearable. There is something unfair about its use. It is like hitting below the intellect.

6024   It is a dangerous thing to reform anyone.

6025   The only way a woman can ever reform a man is by boring him so completely that he loses all possible interest in life.

6026   Relations are simply a tedious pack of people who haven't got the remotest knowledge of how to live, nor the smallest instinct about when to die.

6027   Romance lives by repetition, and repetition converts an appetite into an art.

6028   Good resolutions are simply checks that men draw on a bank where they have no account.

6029   The fatality of good resolutions is that they are always too late.

6030   Any preoccupation with ideas of what is right or wrong in conduct shows an arrested intellectual development.

6031   The English public takes no interest in a work of art until it is told the work in question is immoral.

6032   The worst of having a romance is that it leaves you so unromantic.

6033   There is no such thing as romance in our day, women have become too brilliant; nothing spoils a romance so much as a sense of humor in the woman.

6034   The only difference between a saint and a sinner is that every saint has a past, and every sinner has a future.

6035   Scandal is gossip made tedious by morality.

6036   I love scandals about other people, but scandals about myself don't interest me, they have not got the charm of novelty.

6037   A little sincerity is a dangerous thing, and a great deal of it is absolutely fatal.

6038   Society has gone to the dogs: a lot of nobodies talking about nothing.

6039   When man acts he is a puppet. When he describes he is a poet.

6040   The only thing that ever consoles a man for the stupid things he does is the praise he always gives himself for doing them.

6041   Women's styles may change but their designs remain the same.

6042   His style is chaos illumined by flashes of lightning. As a writer, he has mastered everything except language.

6043   Nobody of any real culture ever talks nowadays about the beauty of the sunset. Sunsets are quite old-fashioned.

6044   Fastidiousness is the ability to resist a temptation in the hope that a better one will come along.

6045   The history of woman is the history of the worst form of tyranny the world has ever known: the tyranny of the weak over the strong. It is the only tyranny that lasts.

6046   A map of the world that does not include Utopia is not worth glancing at.

6047   Each class preaches the importance of those virtues it need not exercise. The rich harp on the value of thrift, the idle grow eloquent over the dignity of labor.

6048   As long as war is looked upon as wicked, it will always have its fascination. When it is looked upon as vulgar, it will cease to be popular.

6049   To have been well brought up is a great drawback nowadays. It shuts one out from so much.

6050   There is hardly a person in the House of Commons worth painting, though many of them would be better for a little whitewashing.

6051   Cheap editions of great books may be delightful, but cheap editions of great men are absolutely detestable.

6052   Mr. Hall Caine, it is true, aims at the grandiose, but then he writes at the top of his voice. He is so loud that one cannot hear what he says.

6053   If a man is sufficiently unimaginative to produce evidence in support of a lie, he might just as well speak the truth at once.

6054   There are moments when art attains almost the dignity of manual labor.

6055   When Oscar Wilde was being told one of his own stories, he remarked that it was a case of the tale dogging the wag.

6056   This suspense is terrible. I hope it will last.

Thornton Wilder

6057   I rose by sheer military ability to the rank of Corporal.

6058   Literature is the orchestration of platitudes.

6059   Good-by world . . . good-by to clocks ticking . . . and Mama's sunflowers. And food and coffee. And new-ironed dresses and hot baths . . . and sleeping and waking up. Oh, earth, you're too wonderful for anybody to realize you.

6060   I would love to be the poet laureate of Coney Island. I would feel enormous satisfaction in being regarded as the voice of the average American.

Michael Wilding

6061   You can pick out actors by the glazed look that comes into their eyes when the conversation wanders away from themselves.

Bob Willett

6062   He realized he was a failure when the waiter refused to serve him a businessman's lunch.

Geoffrey Williams

6063   Bark: This is a sound made by dogs when excited. Dogs bark at milkmen, postmen, yourself, visitors to the house and other dogs; some of them bark at nothing. For some reason dogs tend not to bark at burglars, bailiffs and income tax collectors, at whom they wag their tails in the most friendly manner.

Grace Williams

6064   We learn from experience. A man never wakes up his second baby just to see it smile.

John H. Williams

6065   The instability of the economy is equaled only by the instability of economists.

Tennessee Williams

6066   When I stop [working], the rest of the day is posthumous. I'm only alive when I'm writing.

Charles E. Wilson

6067   I thought what was good for the country was good for General Motors, and vice versa.

6068   The price of progress is trouble, and I must be making a lot of progress.

Earl Wilson

6069   Experience is what enables you to recognize a mistake when you make it again.

6070   The fastest way for a politician to become an elder statesman is to lose an election.

6071   You can say this for these ready-mixes—the next generation isn't going to have any trouble making pies exactly like mother used to make.

6072   A woman may race to get a man a gift but it always ends in a tie.

6073   Success is simply a matter of luck. Ask any failure.

6074   You may not be able to read a doctor's handwriting and prescription, but you'll notice his bills are neatly typewritten.

6075   Gossip is when you hear something you like about someone you don't.

6076   Somebody figured it out—we have 35 million laws trying to enforce Ten Commandments.

6077   Modern man drives a mortgaged car over a bond-financed highway on credit-card gas.

6078   Today's accent may be on youth, but the stress is still on the parents.

Edmund Wilson

6079   His style has the desperate jauntiness of an orchestra fiddling away for dear life on a sinking ship.

6080   There is nothing more demoralizing than a small but adequate income.

Harold Wilson

6081   The Right Honourable Gentleman has inherited the streak of charlatanry in Disraeli without his vision, and the selfrighteousness of Gladstone without his dedication to principle. [On Harold Macmillan.]

6082   One man's wage rise is another's man's price increase.

Sloan Wilson

6083   Success in almost any field depends more on energy and drive than it does on intelligence. This explains why we have so many stupid leaders.

Thomas Wilson

6084   Love is a talkative passion.

6085   It costs more to revenge than to bear with injuries.

Woodrow Wilson

6086   A nonentity with sidewhiskers. [On Chester Arthur.]

6087   Prosperity is necessarily the first theme of a political campaign.

6088   I used to be a lawyer, but now I am a reformed character.

6089   A digestive disturbance is a "turmoil in Central America."

6090 A conservative is a man who just sits and thinks, mostly sits.

6091 Every man who takes office in Washington either grows or swells.

6092 He is more apt to contribute heat than light to a discussion.

6093 All the extraordinary men I have ever known were chiefly extraordinary in their own estimation.

6094 Day of routine. Kept in my office till quarter of five on business that might have been finished before three if academic men were only prompt in movement and brief in statements. [As president of Princeton University.]

6095 The wisest thing to do with a fool is to encourage him to hire a hall and discourse to his fellow citizens. Nothing chills nonsense like exposure to the air.

6096 If you think too much about being reelected, it is very difficult to be worth reelecting.

6097 Conservatism is the policy of make no change and consult your grandmother when in doubt.

6098 An ineffectual attempt to put an elusive ball into an obscure hole with implements ill-adapted to the purpose. [On golf.]

6099 I am a vague, conjectural personality, more made up of opinions and academic prepossessions than of human traits and red corpuscles.

6100 A Yankee always thinks that he is right, a Scotch-Irishman knows that he is right.

6101 Gossip: sociologists on a mean and petty scale.

6102 When you have read the Bible, you will know it is the word of God, because you will have found it the key to your own heart, your own happiness and your own duty.

6103 The man with power but without conscience, could, with an eloquent tongue . . . put this whole country into a flame.

6104 Once lead this people into war and they will forget there ever was such a thing as tolerance.

6105 The use of a university is to make young gentlemen as unlike their fathers as possible.

6106 Every great man of business has got somewhere a touch of the idealist in him.

6107   The right is more precious than peace, and we shall fight for the things which we have always carried nearest our hearts—for democracy, for the right of those who submit to authority to have a voice in their own government, for the rights and liberties of small nations, for a universal dominion of right by such a concert of free people as shall bring peace and safety to all nations and make the world itself at last free.

6108   The sum of the whole matter is this, that our civilization cannot survive materially unless it be redeemed spiritually. It can be saved only by becoming permeated with the spirit of Christ and being made free and happy by the practices which spring out of that spirit.

Walter Winchell

6109   Bore: a guy who wraps up a two-minute idea in a two-hour vocabulary.

6110   Gossip is the art of saying nothing in a way that leaves practically nothing unsaid.

6111   Broadway is a main artery of New York life—the hardened artery.

6112   Nothing recedes like success.

6113   Broadway is a place where people spend money they haven't earned to buy things they don't need to impress people they don't like.

6114   If you break 100, watch your golf. If you break eighty, watch your business.

Duke of Windsor

6115   The thing that impresses me most about America is the way parents obey their children.

Richard Winnington

6116   What I am waiting for is a film about beautiful identical quintuplets who all love the same man.

Stephen Winsten

6117   We die before we have learned to live.

P. G. Wodehouse

6118   Why don't you get a haircut? You look like a chrysanthemum.

6119   The butler entered the room, a solemn procession of one.

6120   I could see that, if not actually disgruntled, he was far from being gruntled.

6121   It was one of those parties where you cough twice before you speak and then decide not to say it after all.

6122   She looked as if she had been poured into her clothes and had forgotten to say "when."

6123   Has anybody ever seen a dramatic critic in the daytime? Of course not. They come out after dark, up to no good.

6124   He was a man who acted from the best motives. There is one born every minute.

Thomas Wolfe

6125   Conceit is such a small thing, after all! Conceit is only mountain-high, world-wide, or ocean-deep!

Sir John Wolfenden

6126   Schoolmasters and parents exist to be grown out of.

Edna E. Wood

6127   She swallowed her pride, but it left a lump in her throat.

Grant Wood

6128   All the really good ideas I ever had came to me while I was milking a cow.

James Mason Wood

6129   Education today, more than ever before, must see clearly the dual objectives: education for living and educating for making a living.

Douglas Woodruff

6130   Why be disagreeable, when with a little effort you can be impossible?

6131   Nothing is easier in America than to attend college, and nothing harder than to get educated.

Leonard Woolf

6132   Patriotism is the finest flower of Western civilization as well as the refuge of the scoundrel.

Alexander Woollcott

6133   The audience strummed their catarrhs.

6134   The English have an extraordinary ability for flying into a great calm.

6135   Many of us spend half our time wishing for things we could have if we didn't spend half our time wishing.

6136   The scenery in the play was beautiful, but the actors got in front of it.

6137   There's nothing wrong with Oscar Levant—nothing that a miracle couldn't cure.

6138   All the things I really like to do are either immoral, illegal, or fattening.

6139   There is some cooperation between wild creatures. The stork and the wolf usually work the same neighborhood.

6140   The play left a taste of lukewarm parsnip juice.

6141   A hick town is one where there is no place to go where you shouldn't be.

6142   A broker is a man who runs your fortune into a shoestring.

Sir Henry Wotton
6143   An Ambassador is a man of virtue sent to lie abroad for his country; a news-writer is a man without virtue who lies at home for himself.

6144   Tell the truth, and so puzzle and confound your adversaries.

Herman Wouk
6145   Income tax returns are the most imaginative fiction being written today.

Frank Lloyd Wright
6146   Television: chewing gum for the eyes.

6147   Early in life, I had to choose between honest arrogance and hypocritical humility. I chose honest arrogance and have seen no occasion to change.

6148   If it keeps up, man will atrophy all his limbs but the push-button finger.

6149   A doctor can bury his mistakes but an architect can only advise his client to plant vines.

6150   When an attorney characterized Frank Lloyd Wright as America's greatest architect, Wright confessed to his wife that he could not deny it because he was under oath.

6151   The longer I live the more beautiful life becomes.

6152   New York: prison towers and modern posters for soap and whiskey.

6153   Automobiles: ferryboats coming down the street gnashing their teeth.

6154   Civilization: art and religion are the soul of our civilization. Go to them, for there love exists.

6155   Give me the luxuries of life and I will willingly do without the necessities.

John David Wright
6156   Business is like riding a bicycle. Either you keep moving or you fall down.

Lawrence Wright
6157   Man in all periods has been willing to walk miles for a drink, but not for a bath.

William Wrigley, Jr.
6158   When two men in business always agree, one of them is unnecessary.

Philip Wylie
6159   We're about to enter the age of flight before we've even developed a chair that a man can sit on comfortably.

Denis Bevan Wyndham-Lewis
6160   It is the proud perpetual boast of the Englishman that he never brags.

Judge Yankwich
6161   There are no illegitimate children—only illegitimate parents.

Thomas Russell Ybarra
6162   He owned and operated a ferocious temper.

6163   A Christian is a man who feels
Repentance on a Sunday
For what he did on Saturday
And is going to do on Monday.

Francis Yeats-Brown
6164   To me the charm of an encyclopedia is that it knows—and I needn't.

Edward Young

6165   At thirty man suspects himself a fool;
Knows it at forty, and reforms his plan;
At fifty chides his infamous delay,
Pushes his prudent purpose to resolve;
In all the magnaminity of thought
Resolves; and re-resolves; then dies the same.

6166   Some of renown, on scraps of learning dote,
And think they grow immortal as they quote.

6167   All men think all men mortal, but themselves.

F. Z. Young

6168   As the French physiologist Claude Bernard once said, "It is what we think we know already that often prevents us from learning."

Henny Youngman

6169   I've got all the money I'll ever need if I die by four o'clock.

Lin Yutang

6170   The humor of the Chinese people is seen in inventing gunpowder and finding its best use in making firecrackers for their grandfathers' birthdays.

6171   When a man is past forty and does not become a crook, he is either feebleminded or a genius.

6172   Happiness for me is largely a matter of digestion.

6173   I have a hankering to go back to the Orient and discard my necktie. Neckties strangle clear thinking.

6174   Plato's Republic does not begin, as some of the modern writers would have it, with some such sentence as: "Human civilization, as seen through its successive stages of development, is a dynamic movement from heterogeneity to homogeneity," or some other equally incomprehensible rot. It begins rather with the genial sentence: "I went down to Peiraeus yesterday with Glaucon, Ariston's son, to pay my devotion to the goddess, and at the same time I wanted to see how they would manage the festival, as this was the first time they held it."

6175   From the Taoist point of view, an educated man is one who believes he has not succeeded when he has, but is not so sure he has failed when he fails.

6176   There is still a belief that . . . to be uncomfortable is to be virtuous.

Israel Zangwill

6177   A man likes his wife to be just clever enough to comprehend his cleverness, and just stupid enough to admire it.

6178   The only true love is love at first sight; second sight dispels it.

Robert Zend

6179   People have one thing in common: they are all different.

6180   Being a philosopher, I have a problem for every solution.

Zeno

6181   Better to trip with the feet than with the tongue.

Edith Zittler

6182   The only way to stop smoking is to just stop—no ifs, ands or butts.

Émile Zola

6183   Perfection is such a nuisance that I often regret having cured myself of using tobacco.

PROVERBS OF
MANY NATIONS

6184   A man without a smiling face should not open a shop.

6185   To open a shop is easy; the difficult thing is keeping it open.

6186   Dogs show no aversion to poor families.

6187   It is about as hard for a rich man to enter heaven as it is for a poor man to remain on earth.

6188   You may change the clothes; you cannot change the man.

6189   If you do not ask their help, all men are good-natured.

6190   A man does not live a hundred years, yet he worries enough for a thousand.

6191   Misfortunes always come in by a door that has been left open for them.

6192   If you don't want anyone to know it, don't do it.

6193   Great politeness usually means "I want something."

6194   If a man does not receive guests at home, he will meet very few hosts abroad.

6195   When the guests have gone, the host is at peace.

6196   Mischief all comes from much opening of the mouth.

6197   Men mourn for those who leave fortunes behind.

6198   One man tells a falsehood, a hundred repeat it as true.

6199   Poverty is the common fate of scholars.

6200   If the poor man associates with the rich, he will soon have no trousers to wear.

6201   Children have more need of models than of critics.

6202   On the day your horse dies and your gold vanishes, your relatives are like strangers met on the road.

6203   If a gambler can reform, then there is a cure for leprosy.

6204   The fish sees the bait, not the hook.

6205   Come easy, go easy.

6206   A wise man makes his own decisions; an ignorant man follows public opinion.

6207   There are two sides to every question—the wrong side and our side.

6208   Answer not a fool according to his folly, lest thou also be like unto him. Answer a fool according to his folly lest he be wise in his own conceit.

6209   Every eel hopes to become a whale.—*German*

6210   In America an hour is forty minutes.

6211   A dragon stranded in shallow water furnishes amusement for the shrimps.—*Chinese*

6212   There are only two kinds of Chinese—those who give bribes and those who take them.—*Russian*

6213   Cider smiles in your face, and then cuts your throat.—*English*

6214   Motto of a modern coed: every man for herself.

6215   Coffee has two virtues: it is wet and warm.—*Dutch*

6216   A modern college is where two thousand can be seated in the classrooms and fifty thousand in the stadium.

6217   The man who expects comfort in this life must be born deaf, dumb, and blind.—*Turkish*

6218   When a cook cooks a fly he keeps the best wing for himself.
—*Polish*

6219   Who has not courage needs legs.—*Italian*

6220   Even the lion has to defend himself against flies.—*German*

6221   A man should live if only to satisfy his curiosity.—*Yiddish*

6222   Brilliant daughter; cranky wife.—*Dutch*

6223   If you deceive me once you are a scoundrel; if you deceive me often you are a smart man.—*Yugoslav*

6224   A rat that gnaws at a cat's tail invites destruction.—*Chinese*

6225   The Devil comes where money is; where it is not he comes twice.—*Swedish*

6226   What you dislike for yourself do not like for me.—*Spanish*

6227   A really rich man is careless of his dress.—*Chinese*

6228   When drink's in, wit's out.—*Scottish*

6229   The best way to get praise is to die.—*Italian*

6230   Never do anything standing that you can do sitting, or anything sitting that you can do lying down.—*Chinese*

6231   A dyspeptic is a man that can eat his cake and have it, too. —*Austin O'Malley*

6232   Every man thinks his own geese swans.—*German*

6233   The only real equality is in the cemetery.—*German*

6234   When a learned man errs he makes a learned error.—*Arab*

6235   He who has burned his mouth blows his soup.—*German*

6236   Never touch your eye but with your elbow.—*English*

6237   Every shut eye ain't asleep.—*Black American*

6238   Nobody's family can hang out the sign "Nothing the matter here."—*Chinese*

6239   A fat man is no good in war. He can neither fight nor run away. —*American*

6240   A father is a banker provided by nature.—*French*

6241   The first part of the night, think of your own faults; the latter part, think of the faults of others.—*Chinese*

6242   Fear gives intelligence even to fools.—*French*

6243   When a man fights, it means that a fool has lost his argument. —*Chinese*

6244   A sleeping fox counts hens in his dreams.—*Russian*

6245   Those who have free seats at the play hiss first.—*Chinese*

6246   Do not remove a fly from your friend's forehead with a hatchet. —*Chinese*

6247   If you seek friends who can be trusted, go to the cemetery.
—*Russian*

6248   When a dove begins to associate with crows, its feathers remain white but its heart grows black.

6249   A baby is an angel whose wings decrease as his legs increase.
—*French*

6250   If birds knew how poor they are, they wouldn't sing so sweetly.
—*Danish*

6251   Build and borrow,
A sackful of sorrow.—*German*

6252   Many a friend has been lost by a jest, but none has ever been got by one.—*Czech*

6253   When you go to buy, use your eyes, not your ears.—*Czech*

6254   A calamity that affects everyone is only half a calamity.—*Italian*

6255   It is easy to be generous with other people's money.—*Latin*

6256   Under capitalism man exploits man; under socialism the reverse is true.—*Polish*

6257   There is only one pretty child in the world, and every mother has it.—*From Cheshire County, England*

6258   Don't talk unless you can improve the silence.—*From Vermont*

6259   No call alligator long mouth till you pass him.—*Jamaican*

6260   Before I judge my neighbor, let me walk a mile in his moccasins.

6261   The situation in Germany is serious but not hopeless; the situation in Austria is hopeless but not serious.—*Viennese*

6262   Good is when I steal other people's wives and cattle; bad is when they steal mine.—*Hottentot*

6263   Greeks tell the truth, but only once a year.—*Russian*

6264   After shaking hands with a Greek, count your fingers.—*Albanian*

6265   A gypsy tells the truth once in his life and immediately repents.
—*Russian*

6266   Last night I thought over a thousand plans, but this morning I went my old way.

6267   Big thieves hang the little ones.—*Czech*

6268   There are no fans in hell.—*Arab*

6269   Don't buy the house; buy the neighbor.—*Russian*

6270   A good husband should be deaf and a good wife blind.—*French*

6271   When the fox preaches, look to your geese.

6272   If my aunt had wheels, she would be an omnibus.—*German*

6273   If my aunt had been a man she'd be my uncle.—*English*

6274   With enough ifs we could put Paris into a bottle.—*French*

6275   An income is what you can't live without or within.

6276   Do no good—and you will suffer no ingratitude.—*Arab*

6277   Spanish is the language for lovers, Italian for singers, French for
diplomats, German for horses and English for geese.—*Spanish*

6278   A fool, unless he knows Latin, is never a great fool.

6279   He who goes to law for a sheep loses his cow.—*Spanish*

6280   A lawyer's opinion is worth nothing unless paid for.—*English*

6281   If you lend, you either lose the money or gain an enemy.

6282   To be for one day entirely at leisure is to be for one day an
immortal.

6283   If you have had enough of your friend, lend him some money.

6284   Good parents, happy marriages; good children, fine funerals.
—*Chinese*

6285   Life is an onion, and one peels it crying.—*French*

6286   While the tall maid is stooping, the little one has swept the
house.—*Spanish*

6287   The loser is always in the wrong.—*Spanish*

6288   No one acts more foolishly than a wise man in love.—*Welsh*

6289   The greatest love is a mother's; then comes a dog's; then comes a
sweetheart's.—*Polish*

6290   If you were born lucky, even your rooster will lay eggs.—*Russian*

6291   Good luck beats early rising.—*Irish*

6292   A maiden marries to please her parents, a widow to please herself.—*Chinese*

6293   Before going to war say a prayer; before going to sea say two
prayers; before marrying say three prayers.

6294   There were two brothers who were smart and a third who got married.—*Polish*

6295   Bachelor, a peacock; betrothed, a lion; married, a donkey. —*Spanish*

6296   Medicine can cure only curable diseases.—*Chinese*

6297   Every miser has a spendthrift son.—*French*

6298   The miserable are very talkative.—*Hindu*

6299   Modesty is an ornament, but you go farther without it.—*German*

6300   When I had money everyone called me brother.—*Polish*

6301   Money has no ears, but it hears.—*Japanese*

6302   If you have no money, be polite.—*Danish*

6303   Money never goes to jail.—*Arab*

6304   No monkey ever laughs at another.—*West African*

6305   In the eyes of its mother every beetle is a gazelle.—*Moroccan*

6306   Diseases enter by the mouth; misfortunes issue from it.—*Chinese*

6307   The mule always keeps a kick in reserve for its master.—*French*

6308   The big fish eat the little fish, the little fish eat the water insects, and the water insects eat the weeds and the mud.—*Chinese*

6309   The mantis seizes the locust but does not see the yellow bird behind him.—*Chinese*

6310   I do not like noise unless I make it myself.—*French*

6311   Nobody don't never get nothing for nothing, nowhere, no time, nohow.—*American*

6312   Old birds are hard to pluck.—*German*

6313   Everybody knows better than anybody.—*French*

6314   The best company must part at last, as King Dagobert said to his dogs.—*French*

6315   A lucky physician is better than a good one.—*German*

6316   If the thunder is not loud, the peasant forgets to cross himself. —*Russian*

6317   If your neighbor has made one pilgrimage to Mecca, watch him; if two, avoid him; if three, move to another street.—*Arab*

6318   If you bow at all, bow low.—*Chinese*

6319   A politician is an animal who can sit on a fence and yet keep both ears to the ground.—*American*

6320   Them as has gits.—*American*

6321   Enthusiasm for a cause sometimes warps judgment.—*William Howard Taft*

6322   If you throw a stone in Prague, you throw a bit of history.—*Czech*

6323   Even the dog of a great man is proud.—*Japanese*

6324   When the prince wants a minister to die, he dies.—*Chinese*

6325   In politics a man must learn to rise above principle.—*American*

6326   At once is two hours and a half.—*Scottish*

6327   Who has, is.—*Italian*

6328   The best prophets are children and fools.—*French*

6329   Man can bear all things except good days.—*Dutch*

6330   A fool may ask more questions in an hour than a wise man can answer in seven years.—*English*

6331   Even the Emperor has straw-sandaled relatives.—*Chinese*

6332   To the ant a few drops of rain is a flood.—*Japanese*

6333   To a mouse, a cat is a lion.—*Albanian*

6334   The best part of repentance is the sinning.—*Arab*

6335   If I have no featherbed, I'll sleep on straw.—*German*

6336   If you scatter thorns, don't go barefoot.—*Italian*

6337   Whoever is rich is my brother.—*Russian*

6338   A rich man and an ashtray—the more they collect, the dirtier they get.—*Japanese*

6339   The foolish sayings of a rich man pass for wise ones.—*Spanish*

6340   When you are kissed by a rogue, count your teeth immediately. —*Hebrew*

6341   If you live in Rome, don't quarrel with the Pope.—*French*

6342   The Russian is clever, but always too late.—*Russian*

6343   Everything has an end, except a sausage, which has two.—*Danish*

6344   Keep quiet and people will think you a philosopher.—*Latin*

6345   Silence is the fool's wisdom.—*Spanish*

6346   Solitude is terrible even when drowning.—*Russian*

6347   Spinach is the broom of the stomach.—*French*

6348   A stick in the hand is better than a tongue in the mouth.—*Yiddish*

6349   When the stomach speaks, wisdom is silent.—*Arab*

6350   These three are always strangers: death, a son-in-law, and a nephew.

6351   Never give a sucker an even break.—*American*

6352   If you would avoid suspicion, do not lace your shoes in a melon field.—*Chinese*

6353   Great talker, great liar.—*French*

6354   He who steals a handful of gold is put in jail; he who steals a whole country is made king.—*Japanese*

6355   Travel is a foretaste of hell.—*Turkestan*

6356   The heaviest baggage for a traveler is an empty purse.—*German*

6357   Women always speak the truth but not the whole truth.—*Italian*

6358   A little truth helps the lie to go down.—*Italian*

6359   When you shoot an arrow of truth, dip its point in honey.—*Arab*

6360   Truth is an orphan.—*German*

6361   He who tells the truth must first have one foot in the stirrup. —*Turkish*

6362   When two do the same thing, it is not the same thing.—*Medieval Latin*

6363   If the unlucky man became a barber, men would begin to be born without heads.—*German*

6364   Virtue carries a lean purse.—*Japanese*

6365   Never trust a woman with a man's voice.—*French*

6366   If you are poor, though you dwell in the busy market place, no one will inquire about you; if you are rich, though you dwell in the heart of the mountains, you will have distant relatives.—*Chinese*

6367   The woman cries before the wedding; the man afterward.—*Polish*

6368   A whitewashed crow will not remain white long.—*Chinese*

6369   The rich widow's tears soon dry.—*Danish*

6370   Wives and watermelons are picked by chance.—*Greek*

6371   If you want peace in the house, do what your wife wants.—*African*

6372   Winter either bites with its teeth or lashes with its tail.—*Monten-egrin*

6373   No woman is too bashful to talk scandal.—*Dutch*

6374   When a woman has no answer, the sea is empty of water.
—*German*

6375   In youth we believe many things that are not true; in old age we doubt many truths.—*German*

6376   The only secrets women keep are those they don't know.
—*Yugoslav*

6377   When a beautiful woman smiles, somebody's purse weeps.
—*Italian*

6378   One yawn makes two yawners.—*French*

6379   Wherever there is a neck there is a yoke.—*Russian*

6380   Ask the young; they know everything.—*French*

6381   There are many loving parents in the world, but no loving children.

6382   The reason why parents love the younger children best is because they have now so little hope that the elder will do well.—*Japanese*

6383   A man without money is like a wolf without teeth.—*French*

6384   There are more fools among buyers than among sellers.—*French*

6385   You never lost money by taking a profit.—*American*

6386   Profit is better than fame.—*Danish*

6387   No man ever had enough money.—*Gypsy*

6388   A heavy purse makes a light heart.—*Irish*

6389   Where profit is, loss is hidden nearby.—*Japanese*

6390   The buyer needs a hundred eyes; the seller but one.—*Italian*

6391   Getting money is like digging with a needle; spending it is like water soaking into sand.—*Japanese*

6392   Hold back some goods for a thousand days and you will be sure to sell at a profit.—*Chinese*

6393   Without a shepherd sheep are not a flock.—*Russian*

6394   Live with wolves, howl like a wolf.—*Russian*

6395 If the rich could hire other people to die for them, the poor could make a wonderful living.—*Yiddish*

6396 It is less painful to learn in youth than to be ignorant in age.

6397 Mention money and the whole world is silent.—*German*

6398 When money speaks, the truth is silent.—*Russian*

6399 The closed mouth swallows no flies.—*Spanish*

6400 Everybody's business is nobody's business.—*English*

6401 The fish dies because he opens his mouth.—*Spanish*

6402 The busiest men have the most leisure.—*English*

6403 Bargain like a gypsy, but pay like a gentleman.—*Hungarian*

6404 Money swore an oath that nobody who didn't love it should ever have it.—*Irish*

6405 Money smells good no matter what its source.—*Latin*

6406 What do we live for, if it is not to make life less difficult to each other?—*George Eliot*

6407 God is a busy worker, but He loves help.—*Basque*

6408 The gem cannot be polished without friction, nor men perfected without trials.—*Chinese*

6409 What soberness conceals drunkenness reveals.—*Latin*

6410 A man is a lion in his own cause.—*English*

6411 Those who are happy do not observe how time goes by.—*Italian*

6412 Everyone pushes a falling fence.—*Chinese*

6413 One father is more than a hundred schoolmasters.—*English*

6414 He does not believe that does not live according to his belief. —*English*

6415 He that has the worst cause makes the most noise.

6416 Self-praise is no recommendation.

6417 He that seeks trouble never misses.—*English*

WISDOM FROM
THE BIBLE
AND THE TALMUD

6418   Jesus said to her [Martha], "I am the resurrection and the life; he who believes in me, though he die, yet shall he live, and whoever lives and believes in me shall never die."—*John 11:25*

6419   There is nothing new under the sun.—*Ecclesiastes 1:9*

6420   What is a man profited, if he shall gain the whole world and lose his own soul?—*Matthew 16:20*

6421   And what doth the Lord require of thee, but to do justly, and to love mercy, and to walk humbly with thy God?—*Deuteronomy 10:12*

6422   He that is without sin among you, let him first cast a stone at her.—*John 8:7*

6423   A feast is made for laughter, and wine maketh merry: but money answereth all things.—*Ecclesiastes 10:19*

6424   Where there is no vision, the people perish.—*Proverbs 29:18*

6425   It is naught, it is naught, saith the buyer: but when he is gone his way, then he boasteth.—*Proverbs 20:14*

6426   Let another man praise thee, and not thine own mouth.—*Proverbs 27:2*

6427   It is easier for a camel to get through the eye of a needle than for a rich man to enter the kingdom of God.—*Matthew 19:24*

6428   I have fought the good fight, I have finished the course, I have kept the faith.—*2 Timothy 4:7*

6429   None of us liveth to himself, and no man dieth to himself.
—*Romans 14:7*

6430   The sun will set without thy assistance.—*The Talmud*

6431   Three things are good in little measure and evil in large: yeast, salt and hesitation.—*The Talmud*

PEARLS FROM PERIODICALS

6432   People wouldn't get divorced for such trivial reasons if they didn't get married for such trivial reasons.—*Bridgeport Star*

6433   An optimist is a driver who thinks that empty space at the curb won't have a hydrant beside it.—*Changing Times*

6434   A conservative politician is one in office.—*Columbia Record*

6435   The paramount question before the country today is "How much is the down payment?"—*Judge*

6436   For most of us, life is what we make it, but for the pedestrian, it's if he makes it.—*Judge*

6437   "Handle this child carefully," the child specialist said to the mother. "Remember, you're dealing with a sensitive, high-strung little stinker."—*L. & N. Magazine*

6438   A perfect example of minority rule is a baby in the house.—*Milwaukee Journal*

6439   When in danger or in doubt
Run in circles, yell and shout.—*Naval Academy*

6440   Marriage originates when a man meets the only woman who really understands him. So does divorce.—*Ohio State Sun Dial*

6441   Chicago bellboys organize for bigger tips. They give or take no quarter.—*Dallas News*

6442   Heredity is what a man believes in until his son begins to behave like a delinquent.—*Presbyterian Life*

6443   Ignorance of the law does not prevent the losing lawyer from collecting his bill.—*Puck*

6444   To recur to the deliberate methods of our great chess players, we hear that one of them has bequeathed his next move to his grandson. —*Punch*

6445   It's strange that men should take up crime when there are so many legal ways to be dishonest.—*Sunshine*

6446   Theodore Roosevelt said a thorough knowledge of the Bible was worth more than a college education. A thorough knowledge of anything is worth more than a college education.—*Yale Record*

6447   Modern woman's fondest wish is to be weighed and found wanting.—*Arkansas Gazette*

6448   A distant relative can be very distant when he has money.—*Florida Times Union*

6449   "Never again" means until the next time.—*Toledo Blade*

6450   A raspberry will grow up, get ripe, come to town and go to all sorts of trouble just to get a few seeds lodged in your teeth.—*Life*

6451   An optimist can always see the bright side of the other fellow's misfortune.—*Richmond News-Leader*

6452   If, as a psychologist tells us, there is no such thing as pain, what is it some people give us.—*Knickerbocker Press*

6453   Overheard in a department store: "Be quiet, be quiet, and mama'll buy you a drum."—*Judge*

6454   A liberal is one who believes in more laws and more job holders, therefore in higher taxes and less liberty.—*Baltimore Evening Sun*

6455   A cynic rises to remark that homes never before were as comfortable and families so seldom in them.—*Seattle Times*

6456   Our view of an athletic man is the fellow who hires a small boy to cut the grass so he can play golf and obtain a little exercise.—*Portland News*

6457   A friend forgives your defects, and if he is very fond of you, he doesn't see any.—*Saint Louis Globe-Democrat*

6458   Flattery is obnoxious to all except the flattered.—*Wilmington Morning News*

6459   The objection to gardening is that by the time your back gets used to it, your enthusiasm is gone.—*Baltimore Sun*

6460   As soon as a farmer can afford to do so, he moves to the city, and then, as soon as he can afford it, he gets himself a country place.—*New York American*

6461   Nothing can be more frequent than an occasional drink.—*Ohio State Journal*

6462   An educated man earns more. And it seldom takes over ten years after graduating to get educated.—*Washington Post*

6463   Many have reduced it to life, liberty and the pursuit of golf balls.—*Arkansas Gazette*

6464   Scientists say that certain musical notes can prevent sleep. So can certain promissory notes, professor.—*Arkansas Gazette*

6465   A humorist asks why no costume has ever been designed for chess. Well, there is the two-pants suit.—*Detroit News*

6466   A specialist is one who has his patients trained to become ill only in his office hours. A general practitioner is likely to be called off the golf course at any time.—*Kansas City Star*

6467   Why is it a woman who constantly complains that she has nothing to wear has to have six closets to keep it in?—*Detroit News*

6468   Nothing irks a college student more than shaking out the envelope from home and finding nothing in it but news and love.—*Detroit News*

6469   A historian announces that women used cosmetics in the Middle Ages. Women still use cosmetics in the middle ages.—*Judge*

6470   When better predictions are made, sports writers won't make them.—*Judge*

6471   The inventor of the loudspeaker succeeded in getting a big sound out of a small voice. What is needed now is someone to develop a process for getting a big thought out of a small brain.—*Webster City [Iowa] Freeman-Journal*

6472   The hard part of making good is that you must do it over every day.—*Vancouver Post*

6473   Everything comes to him who waits for taxicabs on rainy days— except taxicabs.—*Judge*

6474   "Special pains given to beginners" is a statement in an ad of a music teacher. Few advertisements are that frank.—*Greenville [South Carolina] Piedmont*

6475   Sometimes a movie hero is one who sits through it.—*Newspaper Enterprise Association*

6476 Among the things we don't understand is how a mosquito can get along without any sleep.—*New York World*

6477 The mosquito bites the hand that feeds him.—*Financial America*

6478 Our ideal summer resort is one where the fish bite and mosquitoes don't.—*Philadelphia Public Ledger*

6479 They say a mosquito can fly ten miles. But it isn't the distance he flies that bothers us. It's what he does when he stops.—*El Paso Herald*

6480 The great misfortune of mankind is that only those out of office know how to solve great problems.—*Minnesota Star*

6481 Money used to talk. Now it whispers.—*New York World*

6482 A model for mothers is the Kansas woman who told the judge that she never struck her children except in self-defense.—*Springfield Union*

6483 There is the man who thinks and the man who thinks he thinks. The latter is the one who really enjoys life.—*University Missourian*

6484 Probably no man ever got so much out of a surgical operation as Adam did.—*Arkansas Gazette*

6485 Faster mail service seems a blessing until you examine what you get.—*Muskogee Phoenix*

6486 Golf liars have one advantage over the fishing kind—they don't have to show anything to prove it.—*Tampa Daily Times*

6487 Patriots used to shout: "Give me liberty!" Now they leave off the last word.—*Detroit Free Press*

6488 The only thing wrong with the world is the people.—*Toledo Blade*

6489 Hotel guests have been known to leave their room only because they couldn't get it into their suitcases.—*Judge*

6490 No man is a hero to a bill collector.—*Louisville Times*

6491 A study of the Presidential situations in some countries shows the rebels occasionally lead slightly in the early shooting.—*Detroit News*

6492 One of the world's greatest mysteries: Why can't the Scotch play a tune on a bagpipe?—*Florida Times-Union*

6493 One reason we are a great nation is because we have been unable to exhaust our resources in spite of our best efforts.—*Ithaca Journal-News*

6494 Is there not some Burbank who can cross the cranberry-bush with the sugarbeet?—*Minneapolis Journal*

6495   Rear Admiral: Official title given to backseat drivers in the Navy.
—*Life*

6496   An auto mechanic never fails to hear opportunity knocking.—*Life*

6497   This is truly a mechanical age. Even public officials are frequently machine made.—*Florence [Alabama] Herald*

6498   Everybody is tending to business this week, and news is scarce.
—*Harrison [Arkansas] Times*

6499   Guests at a nightclub were held up by bandits and robbed of all their money and valuables. The management of the club took the loss quite philosophically, realizing that these are days of keen commercial competition.—*Humorist*

6500   Revised: Ask dad—he owes.—*Life*

6501   Very few men wake up to find themselves famous. They generally dream they're famous, then wake up.—*Detroit News*

6502   Some people are born failures, some meet with misfortune, and some nurse a perennial desire to get something for nothing.—*Tacoma Ledger*

6503   When a fat person steps on a scale, he always experiences a sinking feeling.—*Life*

6504   Modern fiction, says critic, runs too much to love. Yes, and modern love runs too much to fiction.—*Wall Street Journal*

6505   The fire was put out before any considerable damage was done by the volunteer fire department.—*Portland [Texas] Journal*

6506   We have just heard of an angler in the last chronic stages who, while explaining the size of a fish he caught, had to get out of the bus to do it.—*Punch*

6507   Probably nothing appreciates less the publicity it gets than a poor fish caught by a President of the United States.—*Cincinnati Enquirer*

6508   Fish with hands have been discovered in the South Seas. These, it is believed, were developed telling other fish how big the fellow was they got away from.—*New York Evening Post*

6509   Does the button industry subsidize the laundries?—*Greenville [South Carolina] Piedmont*

6510   An expert says that 15 percent of the people play golf. Probably he meant 15 percent of the golfers.—*Nashville Tennessean*

6511   That new orchid called "Sophrolaelicattleya" makes it a little more difficult to say it with flowers.—*Boston Post*

6512   Einstein says nothing is unlimited. He should see the American's capacity for being fooled.—*Minneapolis Star*

6513   The reason ideas die quickly in some heads is because they can't stand solitary confinement.—*Associated Editors, Chicago*

6514   Our foreign relations seem to be poor relations.—*Toledo Blade*

6515   It's a wise fraternity man that knows his own clothes.—*Colorado Dodo*

6516   A loyal American is one who gets mad when an alien cusses the institutions he cusses.—*Huntington Herald*

6517   In Connecticut the people don't lock the barn door after the horse is stolen. They open a summer theater.—*Judge*

6518   One reason there is so much humor in the world is because there are so many persons who take themselves seriously.—*Philadelphia Inquirer*

6519   Betting is a means of getting something for nothing. Experience teaches us that it is usually a method of getting nothing for something.—*Punch*

6520   We are always happy in the spring, but still there is a certain feeling of sadness. It looks as if everything were coming back except us.—*Milwaukee Journal*

6521   The statesman who places the welfare of his country above that of his locality may go down in history—at the very next election.—*Arkansas Gazette*

6522   Men still die with their boots on but usually one boot is on the accelerator.—*Arkansas Gazette*

6523   A resort is a place where the natives live on your vacation until next summer.—*Columbia State*

6524   There's one consolation about both life and taxes. When you finish one, you're through with the other.—*Buffalo Evening News*

6525   Love is woman's eternal spring, man's eternal fall.—*Helen Rowland, Woman's Home Companion*

6526   A college education is a four-year plan for confusing a young mind methodically.—*Banking*

6527   Some current novels could be described as historically incorrect, but hysterically successful.—*Arcadia [Wisconsin] News-Leader*

6528   The first real touch of winter is the fuel dealer's.—*Virginian-Pilot*

6529   It often happens that when a fellow gets a job he stops looking for work.—*Standard Democrat*

6530   We read of a novelist who makes a practice of pausing before finishing a novel. Another good plan is to pause before beginning one. —*Punch*

6531   An apple a day keeps the doctor away—unless you get the seeds in your appendix.—*Iowa State Green Gander*

6532   A daily paper remarks that there are too many burglaries in this country. It does not state, however, what is the ideal number to have. —*Punch*

6533   Quite often when a man thinks his mind is getting broader it is only his conscience stretching.—*Marathon [Wisconsin] Times*

6534   Some people have tact, others tell the truth.—*Virginian-Pilot*

6535   Cemetery: a place filled with people who thought the world couldn't get along without them.—*Judge*

6536   Civilization is just a slow process of creating more needs to supply.—*Roanoke World-News*

6537   "You," said Adam, "are the first girl I ever loved." That's the way it got started.—*Peru [Indiana] Tribune*

6538   You can lead men to a conference but you cannot make them think.—*Arkansas Gazette*

6539   A bird in the hand is bad table manners.—*Wall Street Journal*

6540   Home is the place where you don't have to engage reservations in advance.—*Arkansas Gazette*

6541   The tragedy of the flea is that he knows for a certainty that all of his children will go to the dogs.—*Annapolis Log*

6542   America is a country where they lock up juries and let the defendants out.—*Burlington Daily News*

6543   Personally, we don't pretend to know the unfailing secret of success, but there are times when we are very much afraid that it is hard work.—*Dallas News*

6544   Loyalty is faithfulness, and effort, and enthusiasm. It is common decency plus common sense. Loyalty is making yourself part of an organization—making it part of you.—*Good Reading*

6545   A historian says that a game something like golf was played in A.D. 1004. This game is played still.—*Humorist*

6546   The difference between a poor man and a millionaire is that one worries over his next meal and the other over his last.—*Irish Digest*

6547   Nowadays a real football fan is one who knows the nationality of every man on the All-American team.—*Judge*

6548   Some weddings are supposed to be quiet affairs, but the only really quiet affair in the home is dad's birthday.—*Milwaukee Journal*

6549   The only farm relief that will ever really benefit the farmer will be to relieve him of his farm.—*Life*

6550   If men had no faith in one another, all of us would have to live within our incomes.—*Marion Star*

6551   It usually takes five years for a tree to produce nuts, but this isn't true of a family tree.—*Detroit Free Press*

6552   You can't tell. Maybe a fish goes home and lies about the size of the bait he stole.—*Syracuse Post-Standard*

6553   A reader asks if fish gain weight rapidly. This depends entirely upon who catches 'em.—*Detroit News*

6554   He who laughs last is probably the one who intended to tell the story himself a little later.—*Humorist*

6555   It's worth the taxi fare to feel you don't care what happens to the fenders.—*Judge*

6556   Some men are successful chiefly because they didn't have the advantages others had.—*Columbia Record*

6557   When two egotists meet, it is a case of an I for an I.—*Lahore Tribune*

6558   So far, no modern has invented an intelligence test to equal matrimony.—*Austin American*

6559   A hick town is a place where nobody ever saw a rich policeman.
—*Washington Post*

6560   Adam and Eve in the Garden of Eden could not complain how much better things were in the good old days.—*Troy Times*

6561   Some men live on credit, but the Scotchman pays as he goes. That is, unless he goes with somebody.—*Judge*

6562   A Scottish golfer, after fourteen years of retirement, has resumed the game. Evidently he found his ball.—*New York Herald Tribune*

6563   You had best try to save something while your salary is small. It is almost impossible to save after you begin earning more.—*Milwaukee Journal*

6564 June is the month of weddings and cooing. The billing follows. —*Atlanta Constitution*

6565 It's a sure sign of summer when a Scotchman throws his Christmas tree away.—*Denison Flamingo*

6566 If you save a little of your salary every week for ten years at the end of that time you'll be an exception.—*Judge*

6567 When a man makes an anonymous donation it simply means that he hopes people will find it out without his telling them.—*Life*

6568 A noted physician says that the best reducing system is described in four words: "No more, thank you."—*Sherman [Texas] Democrat*

6569 The best thing about a popular song is that it is not popular very long.—*Judge*

6570 You can't fool all the people all of the time, but the average politician is contented with a sizable majority.—*Detroit News*

6571 The wages of war is debt.—*Wall Street Journal*

6572 Sometimes when Fortune seems to be smiling upon a mere mortal, she's merely laughing at him.—*Pittsburgh Sun*

6573 The millennium will be here when principle wins a battle with expediency in politics.—*Greenville [South Carolina] Piedmont*

6574 A recent book is entitled "How to Spend Money." It has no doubt had a good sale in Washington.—*Florence [Alabama] Herald*

6575 The income tax collector seems to be our most successful fortune teller.—*Philadelphia Public Ledger*

6576 It may be brutal to shoot little rabbits; but seal-skin coats must be provided in some way.—*Marion Star*

6577 Fifteen percent of the people play golf, says an expert. If you call it golf.—*Wall Street Journal*

6578 Milwaukee girl, according to headline, "Found a Husband on the Golf Links." Nothing strange. That's where most of them are.—*New York American*

6579 The one and only argument against the adoption of English as the universal language is that so few of us really speak it.—*Columbus Dispatch*

6580 The man who saves money nowadays isn't a miser; he's a wizard.—*Columbus Dispatch*

6581 Liberty consists in giving everyone full right to mind everyone else's business.—*Life*

6582   About the time one learns how to make the most of life, the most of it is gone.—*Saint Louis Globe-Democrat*

6583   You save a lot of unnecessary conversation if you remember that people are not going to take your advice unless you charge them for it.—*Gopher Chatter*

6584   After you lose your membership in it, the younger generation seems pretty bad.—*Arkansas Baptist*

6585   There's nothing so annoying as arguing with a person who knows what he's talking about.—*Voice for Health*

6586   A rare book is one that comes back after you've loaned it out. —*Journeyman Barber*

6587   If the safety pin were invented today, it would have two transistors, a regulator, an off-and-on switch, and require a service check every six months.—*Bits and Pieces*

6588   Conscience is that still, small voice that tells you what other people should do.—*Bits and Pieces*

6589   When a man says he has a clear conscience, it often means he has a bad memory.—*Bits and Pieces*

6590   Conscience is that still, small voice
        That quells a wicked thought,
        Then adds this sequence,
        "Besides you might get caught."—*Supervision*

6591   A bore is somebody who goes on talking while you're interrupting.—*Sunshine*

6592   To entertain some people all you have to do is sit and listen. —*Ohio Grange*

6593   Just because nobody disagrees with you does not necessarily mean you are brilliant—maybe you're the boss.—*Construction Digest*

6594   He's the kind of guy who follows you into a revolving door and comes out ahead of you.—*Bits and Pieces*

6595   If you ever see an editor who pleases everybody, he will be neither sitting nor standing, and there will be a lot of flowers around him. —*Capper's Weekly*

6596   An executive is a man employed to talk with visitors so that the other employees can keep on working.—*Grit*

6597   An expert is someone called in at the last minute to share the blame.—*Wisconsin Journal of Education*

6598   A father is someone who carries pictures where his money used to be.—*Lion*

6599   Small boy's definition of Father's Day: It's just like Mother's Day only you don't spend so much.—*Australasian Manufacturer*

6600   If you can't think of any other way to flatter a man, tell him he's the kind who can't be flattered.—*Construction Digest*

6601   A real friend is a person who, when you've made a fool of yourself, lets you forget it.—*Bits and Pieces*

6602   We're trying to enlarge our circle of friends to include people we like.—*New Yorker*

6603   The Lord loveth a cheerful giver. He also accepteth from a grouch.—*Church Bulletin*

6604   Use everything as if it belongs to God. It does. You are His steward.—*Houston Times*

6605   A gossip is a person who will never tell a lie if the truth will do as much damage.—*Owenton [Kentucky] News Herald*

6606   He who relates the faults of others to you will relate your faults to the other fellow.—*Grit*

6607   Housewife's lament: Keeping house is like threading beads on a string with no knot at the end.—*Capper's Weekly*

6608   People who don't know whether they are coming or going are usually in the biggest hurry to get there.—*Bits and Pieces*

6609   Inflation hasn't ruined everything. A dime can still be used as a screwdriver.—*Sunshine*

6610   If insurance rates get any higher, it'll be easier to pay cash for the car and finance the insurance premiums.—*Current Comedy*

6611   Lawyers are the only people in the world who can write a 10,000-word document and call it a brief.—*Rough Notes*

6612   A manicurist married a pedicurist and they waited on each other hand and foot.—*Kreolite News*

6613   If you think a woman driving a car can snarl traffic, you ought to see a man pushing a cart in a supermarket.—*Journeyman Barber*

6614   Modesty is that certain feeling that others will discover how wonderful you are.—*Argus Poster*

6615   It's peculiar how a dollar can look so big when it goes to church and so small when it goes for groceries.—*Grit*

6616   If you're dog-tired at night, it may be because you growled all day.—*War Cry*

6617   What we call understanding is the beginning of knowing that we do not know.—*Miami Herald*

6618   Most of us like people who come right out and say what they think—unless they disagree with us.—*Grit*

6619   Never neglect the opportunity of keeping your mouth shut. —*Missouri Pharmacist*

6620   Oratory is the art of making deep sounds from the chest seem like they are important messages from the brain.—*Grit*

6621   The trouble with being a parent is that by the time you're experienced, you're unemployed.—*Kreolite News*

6622   The toughest thing about raising kids is convincing them that you have seniority.—*Quote*

6623   A pessimist is a person who is seasick during the entire voyage of life.—*Grit*

6624   Two pessimists met at a party. Instead of shaking hands, they shook heads.—*Chicago Tribune*

6625   Small boy to friend: It may be unconstitutional, but I always pray before a test.—*R & R Magazine*

6626   Nothing gives a man more leisure time than always being on time for appointments.—*Construction Digest*

6627   A reformer is one who insists on his conscience being your guide. —*Parts Pup*

6628   The worst thing about retirement is to have to drink coffee on your own time.—*CPA Journal*

6629   No man is as important as he sounds at his alumni banquet. —*Wall Street Journal*

6630   If a man stands with his right foot on a hot stove and his left foot in a freezer, some statisticians would assert that, on the average, he is comfortable.—*Oral Hygiene*

6631   If at first you do succeed, try something harder.—*Bits and Pieces*

6632   A modern employer is one who is looking for men between the ages of 25 and 30 with 40 years' experience.—*Changing Times*

6633   The trouble with success is that the formula is the same as the one for a nervous breakdown.—*Executives' Digest*

6634   Teacher: Not only is he the worst behaved child in my class but he also has a perfect attendance record.—*Anderson [South Carolina] Independent*

6635   The local doctor says he doesn't believe in unnecessary surgery. He won't operate unless he really needs the money.—*Quote*

6636   If motorcar makers could build their motors so they would run only as fast as the drivers could think—what a nationwide traffic jam we would have.—*Construction Digest*

6637   Two halves make a hole, and the fullback goes through.—*Notre Dame Juggler*

6638   What is better than presence of mind in a railway accident? Absence of body.—*Punch*

6639   Death and taxes may be the only certainties in life, but nowhere is it written that we have to tax ourselves to death.—*Nation's Business*

6640   Patrick Henry should come back and see what taxation with representation is like.—*American Flint*

6641   A teenager is a person who gets up on a Saturday morning and has nothing to do, and by bedtime has it only half done.—*Rough Notes*

6642   My teenage daughter is at that awkward age. She knows how to make phone calls, but not how to end them.—*Modern Maturity*

6643   Most people who flee from temptation usually leave a forwarding address.—*Australasian Manufacturer*

6644   You're getting along in years when you don't dare to resist temptation for fear you won't get another chance.—*Quote*

6645   "Thinking," said the little boy, "is when your mouth stays shut and your head keeps talking to itself."—*Arkansas Baptist*

6646   When you hear, "Now this is just off the top of my head," expect dandruff.—*Quote*

6647   Thrift: A moss-grown obsession of those primitive men whose accomplishment was to create the United States of America.—*Fifth Wheel*

6648   A tip for those going abroad: In an underdeveloped country, don't drink the water; in a developed country, don't breathe the air.—*Changing Times*

6649   If you think you have someone eating out of your hand, it's still a good idea to count your fingers regularly.—*Balance Sheet*

6650   No matter what other nations may say about the United States, immigration is still the sincerest form of flattery.—*Pathfinder*

6651   No one needs a vacation so much as the fellow who has just had one.—*Bits and Pieces*

6652   I feel sorry for someone who has to win at everything.—*Snoopy*

6653   You can't reduce by talking about it. You have to keep your mouth shut.—*Grit*

6654   Among the best home furnishings are children.—*Banking*

6655   Some gals don't want to marry go-getters. They're looking for already-gotters.—*Powergrams*

6656   The easiest way to change a woman's mind is by agreeing, disagreeing, or saying nothing.—*Quote*

6657   It is unfortunate that so many citizens are demanding something for nothing. It is even more unfortunate that they are getting it.—*Grit*

6658   About the only moral exercise many a person gets is shadow-boxing with his conscience.—*Cincinnati Enquirer*

6659   New caddy: Oh, Mister, I'm afraid you lost your ball. It went down that little hole there by the flag.—*Octopus*

6660   Actions speak louder than words—but not so often.—*Farmer's Almanac*

6661   A consultant is a man who saves the firm almost enough money to pay his fee.—*Octopus*

6662   Man that is born of a woman hath but a short time to live, and is full of misery.—*Book of Common Prayer*

6663   An Englishman who is laughed at thinks it's because his tie is crooked.—*Beachcomber*

ANONYMOUS
EPIGRAMS

6664 The difference between a conviction and a prejudice is that you can explain a conviction without getting angry.

6665 A man can't argue with the woman he loves.

6666 Somehow or other he blundered into magnificence. [About the architect of All Souls College, Oxford.]

6667 The atomic bomb is here to stay. But are we?

6668 Children are natural mimics—they act like their parents in spite of every attempt to teach them good manners.

6669 The art of being a parent consists of sleeping when the baby isn't looking.

6670 Parents used to strike children to discipline them. Now it is usually in self-defense.

6671 Small boy: If I'm noisy they give me a spanking . . . and if I'm quiet they take my temperature.

6672 Speculate when you have more money than you need; not when you need more money than you have.

6673 If we could only see ourselves as others see us, we would never speak to them again.

6674 He murmured, as he left the committee table,
"How tranquil must have been the Tower of Babel!"

6675 Marriage, which makes two one, is a lifelong struggle to discover which is that one.

6676 Overheard: I married her because we have so many faults in common.

6677   Failure is the path of least persistence.

6678   A professor is a man whose job it is to tell students how to solve the problems of life which he himself has tried to avoid by becoming a professor.

6679   Church bulletin board; Work for the Lord. The pay isn't much, but the retirement plan is out of this world.

6680   Among the books with unhappy endings are checkbooks.

6681   If ignorance is bliss, why aren't there more happy people?

6682   Madam, I'm Adam.

6683   I am an atheist, thank God!

6684   Suburb: the bedroom of a metropolis.

6685   The father of liars took the first cold shower.

6686   To marry a woman for her beauty is like buying a house for its paint.

6687   As I was laying on the green
        A small English book I seen.
        Carlyle's Essay on Burns was the edition,
        So I left it laying in the same position.

6688   A bore is one who, when you ask him "How are you?" tells you.

6689   A boy is an appetite with a skin pulled over it.

6690   The brain is a part of the human mechanism that begins to function at birth and stops when its owner gets up to make an impromptu speech.

6691   If you hear an owl hoot "To whom" instead of "To who," you can make up your mind he was born and educated in Boston.

6692   The ancient Hebrews had a goat on which all the sins were placed, so the holding company idea isn't new.

6693   The main difference between Swiss cheese and Camembert is that the ventilation is a little better.

6694   Give a politician a free hand and he will put it in your pocket.

6695   There is no such thing as a cheap politician.

6696   A good politician is one who has prejudices enough to suit the needs of all his constituents.

6697   A liberal politician calls it share-the wealth; a conservative calls it soak-the-rich.

6698   Every four years in the United States is the year of the Big Wind.

6699   Possession is nine points of the law and self-possession is the other one.

6700   A preposition is a very bad word to end a sentence with.

6701   They are proud in humility, proud in that they are not proud.

6702   A criminologist says that jails are a prolific source of crime. That should be a warning to avoid them.

6703   The problem of the middle class is trying to save while spending as much as the rich do.

6704   A professor says that married men are much more inventive than single men. They have to be.

6705   All husbands are alike, but they have different faces so you can tell them apart.

6706   A hypocrite is a man who carefully folds his *New York Times* around his tabloid before starting home.

6707   Every man is, or hopes to be, an idler.

6708   The early North American Indian made a great mistake by not having an immigration bureau.

6709   A pitiful figure: a truck driver with an inferiority complex.

6710   When there is too much stall in installment, a boom has gone too far.

6711   There is no limit to either intelligence or ignorance.

6712   The same person invented the telephone booth and the breakfast nook.

6713   Journalism has two patron saints: Ananias and Nell Gwyn.

6714   The life of man: school tablet, aspirin tablet, stone tablet.

6715   Out in the country, life is what you you make it, but in the city it too often is what you make.

6716   A flea and a fly in a flue
        Were imprisoned, so what could they do?
        Said the fly, "Let us flee,"
        Said the flea, "Let us fly,"
        So they flew through a flaw in the flue.

6717   An epicure, dining at Crewe,
        Found quite a large mouse in his stew.

Said the waiter, "Don't shout,
And wave it about
Or the rest will be wanting one, too!"

6718   There was a young man of Devizes,
Whose ears were of different sizes;
The one that was small
Was of no use at all,
But the other won several prizes.

6719   The bottle of perfume that Willie sent
Was highly displeasing to Millicent;
Her thanks were so cold
They quarreled, I'm told
Through that silly scent Willie sent Millicent.

6720   It is easy to know and do right. When in doubt, simply do whatever you least want to do.

6721   Despotism tempered by assassination: that is our Magna Charta.

6722   Salt is what makes things taste bad when it isn't in them.

6723   Sarcasm is the sour cream of wit.

6724   Satisfaction is a state of mind produced when you witness another person's discomfort.

6725   A person who is satisfied with what he has and what he hasn't is happy.

6726   I could wish that in the next era of civilization the monkeys may get on top and begin shooting scientists into space.

6727   Scientists are men who prolong life so we can have time to pay for the gadgets they invent.

6728   The five B's of middle age—baldness, bridgework, bifocals, bay windows and bunions.

6729   All work and no play makes jack.

6730   The horse and mule live thirty years
And nothing know of wines and beers.
The goat and sheep at twenty die
And never taste of Scotch or Rye.
A cow drinks water by the ton
And at eighteen is mostly done.
The dog at fifteen cashes in
Without the aid of rum and gin.
The cat in milk and water soaks

And then in twelve short years it croaks.
The modest, sober, bone-dry hen
Lays eggs for nogs, then dies at ten.
All animals are strictly dry:
They sinless live and swiftly die;
But sinful, ginful, rum-soaked men
Survive for three score years and ten.
And some of them, a very few
Stay pickled till they're ninety-two.

6731   Too many people are ready to carry the stool when there is a piano to be moved.

6732   When a woman really loves a man, he can make her do anything she wants to do.

6733   Good luck is a lazy man's estimate of a worker's success.

6734   Money doesn't always bring happiness. A man with ten million dollars is no happier than a man with nine million dollars.

6735   Good night; sleep tight
Don't let the mosquitoes bite.

6736   A communist is a guy who says everything is perfect in Soviet Russia, but stays here because he likes to rough it.

6737   Old cinema films are sold as junk. Some of them, of course, started like that.

6738   What is worse than a flute? Two flutes.

6739   European nations cannot understand our foreign policy. Well, that makes us even.

6740   I'm glad the sky is painted blue:
And the earth is painted green:
And such a lot of nice fresh air
All sandwiched in between.

6741   Necessity is the argument of those who have no good reasons.

6742   Oboe: an ill woodwind that nobody blows good.

6743   Some so-called open minds should be closed for repairs.

6744   Hobby: hard work you wouldn't do for a living.

6745   There are more time-saving devices and less leisure in American homes than ever before.

6746   If you have the right to complain when there is nothing to complain about, you are living in a democracy.

6747   He that lives on hope has but a slender diet.

6748   Travelers say that the Eskimo is a perfect host. He never lets callers who have dropped in for the evening guess that the last few months of their stay are beginning to drag a little.

6749   Women have a keen sense of humor. The more you humor them the better they like it.

6750   When a big-game hunter disappears, something he disagreed with ate him.

6751   A husband is simply a lover with a two days' growth of beard, his collar open and a bad cold in the head.

6752   A luxury is anything a husband needs.

6753   Stand still and silently watch the world go by—and it will.

6754   Conscience: the thing that acts when everything is feeling good.

6755   A conviction is that splendid quality in ourselves which we call bullheadedness in others.

6756   Courtship: a man pursuing a woman until she catches him.

6757   Experience is a hard teacher, and there are no graduates, degrees, or survivors.

6758   An apple pie without some cheese
        Is like a kiss without a squeeze.

6759   Some dance floors are so crowded you can't tell who your partner is.

6760   It may be bad for the child to give it a swift smack occasionally, but what a good thing it is for the mother!

6761   Family ties are stronger at Christmas—and louder.

6762   The height of irony is to give father a billfold at Christmas.

6763   We suppose a sword swallower gets his start with green peas and a knife.

6764   The Eleventh Commandment: mind your own business.

6765   Committee: a group of men who keep minutes and waste hours.

6766   A man is known by the company he avoids.

6767   For the dental association we suggest the slogan "Be true to your teeth or they will be false to you."

6768   The eagle does not catch flies.

6769   Heavenly Father, bless us,
And keep us all alive.
There's ten of us to dinner
And not enough for five.

6770   It is fortunate that diplomats generally have long noses, since usually they cannot see beyond them.

6771   When a diplomat says yes he means perhaps; when he says perhaps he means no; when he says no he is no diplomat.

6772   The age of discretion is reached when one has learned to be indiscreet discreetly.

6773   Dachshund: a dog and a half long and a half a dog high.

6774   The dog is the only animal who has seen his God.

6775   Fame is chiefly a matter of dying at the right moment.

6776   Father: a kin you love to touch.

6777   Figures don't lie, but liars figure.

6778   Flattery: hearing from others the things you have always thought about yourself.

6779   A naturalist says that ants move faster in summer than they do in winter. Of course. The don't have to hurry to picnics in winter.

6780   Absence makes the heart grow fonder—of somebody else.

6781   A friend is one who dislikes the same people that you dislike.

6782   Friendship increases in visiting friends, but more in visiting them seldom.

6783   Genealogist: one who traces back your family as far as your money will go.

6784   An oyster is a fish built like a nut.

6785   What a wonderful bird the frog are—
When he stand he sit almost;
When he hop, he fly almost.
He ain't got no sense hardly;
He ain't got no tail hardly either.
When he sit, he sit on what he ain't got almost.

6786   There is a famous family named Stein—
There's Gert, and there's Epp, and there's Ein;
Gert's poems are bunk,

Epp's statues are junk,
And no one understands Ein.

6787   A wise old owl lived in an oak,
The more he saw, the less he spoke;
The less he spoke, the more he heard;
Why can't we all be like that bird?

6788   Than an oyster
There's nothing moister.

6789   Never miss an opportunity to make others happy even if you have
to leave them alone to do it.

6790   Optimism is the state of mind which believes matrimony will be
cheaper than the engagement.

6791   If it wasn't for the optimist, the pessimist would never know how
happy he isn't.

6792   Every cloud has a silver lining and even an old suit of clothes has
its shiny side.

6793   A university professor is a person whose words are so long they
paragraph them.

6794   Money puts the prop in propaganda.

6795   The world seldom asks how a man acquired his property. The only
question is, has he got it.

6796   Only Americans have mastered the art of being prosperous
though broke.

6797   Publicity is easy to get. Just be so successful you don't need it, and
then you'll get it.

6798   It is never too late for a woman to keep an appointment.

6799   The Puritan through life's sweet garden goes
To pluck the thorn and cast away the rose.

6800   The great unwashed. [Rabble.]

6801   Genius has limitations; stupidity is boundless.

6802   A monologue is a conversation between a realtor and a prospect.

6803   Everybody loves a fat man until he sits down in a bus.

6804   You never hear of a man marrying a woman to reform her.

6805   Remorse is a sign that it wasn't quite as pleasant as one expected
it to be.

6806   Get a name to rise early, and you may lie all day.

6807   One swallow doesn't make a summer, but it breaks a New Year's resolution.

6808   In many ways the rest of a man's days depend upon the rest of his nights.

6809   Trying to solve the country's problems with Congressional oratory is like trying to untangle a traffic jam by honking your horn.

6810   Sometimes it looks like the world beats a path to your door if you produce better claptrap.

6811   A wise man knows everything; a shrewd one, everybody.

6812   Everyone is crazy but me and thee, and sometimes I suspect thee a little.

6813   Pickpockets motto: every crowd has a silver lining.

6814   Some nations are said to have too much gold. Still, if you have to be afflicted with something, we don't know but that we would like gold as well as anything.

6815   Hear no evil, see no evil, speak no evil, and you'll never be a success at a cocktail party.

6816   Is our government sound? asks a contemporary. Yes, mostly, we should say.

6817   A grapefruit is a lemon that had a chance and took advantage of it.

6818   One must be perfectly stupid to be perfectly happy.

6819   The skin of the hippopotamus is two inches think. With a face like that he needs it.

6820   History is something that never happened, written by a man who wasn't there.

6821   Snoring is sleeping out loud.

6822   Abolish sleep, as suggested, and destroy the only few hours man lives above reproach.

6823   A small town is a place where a telegram is opened with prayer.

6824   An adult is one who has ceased to grow vertically but not horizontally.

6825   Several thousands of people in this country cannot read or write. They devote themselves to writing our popular songs.

6826   Second wind: what a speaker gets when he says, "In conclusion."

6827   No speech can be entirely bad if it is short.

6828   Alimony—the cash surrender value of a husband.

6829   A good speech has a good beginning and a good ending, both of which are kept close together.

6830   In spring nature gives all vegetation the green signal.

6831   A statesman thinks he belongs to the nation, but a politician thinks the nation belongs to him.

6832   Platitudes are the Sundays of stupidity.

6833   A stenographer is a girl who learns to type on your time while she is waiting for a chance to get married.

6834   Stupidity would be very charming if it only had better manners.

6835   Sweets to the sweet have made much business for dentists.

6836   Tabloid: a newspaper with a permanent crime wave.

6837   Talent is an infinite capacity for imitating genius.

6838   A woman, generally speaking, is generally speaking.

6839   The higher taxes go, the sharper the voter grinds his ax.

6840   A tax cut is the kindest cut of all.

6841   A woman reaches for a chair when she answers the telephone.

6842   Television: radio with eyestrain.

6843   Abstinence makes the head grow clearer.

6844   Time is something that we ain't got nothing but.

6845   If you think you think, ask yourself what is the greatest thought you ever thought, then listen to the silence.

6846   The good die young—
Here's hoping you live to a ripe old age.

6847   May all your troubles be little ones. [To a bridal couple.]

6848   Here's to you, as good as you are,
And here's to me, as bad as I am;
But as good as you are, and as bad as I am,
I am as good as you are, as bad as I am.—*Old Scotch toast*

6849   It is well to put off until tomorrow what you ought not to do at all.

6850   A woman's tongue is her sword and she never lets it rust.

6851   Traffic sign in eastern village: "Slow, no hospital."

6852   In a subway you not only learn to think on your feet but on other people's.

6853   Truth crushed to earth will rise again; but a lie will do the same thing.

6854   No man has ever become famous who had a twin brother.

6855   Sign at a factory gate: Anyone who likes work can have a whale of a good time here.

6856   All the world's a stage, but most of us are stagehands.

6857   It is not necessary for a writer to be crazy, but it is useful.

6858   A reckless driver is seldom wreckless long.

6859   When you listen to her eat, she sounds like a soprano.

6860   There is no use telling a hair-raising story to a bald man.

6861   He told a story about a peacock and it was a beautiful tale.

6862   He took a picture of the Grand Canyon and asked the film developer to make a life-size enlargement.

6863   A flower in your jacket button hole will make you feel important all day long for only a dollar.

6864   He had been married about twenty awed years.

6865   One psychiatrist said to another, "You're fine. How am I?"

6866   He never opens his mouth unless he has nothing to say.

6867   She had not spoken to her husband in five years because she didn't want to interrupt him.

6868   He was on the phone for fifteen minutes, but he had not said a word as he was talking to his wife.

6869   Although he carved his name on his desk in the eighth grade, he never became famous.

6870   In the old days you waited patiently two hours for a stagecoach, but now you gripe if you miss the first section of a revolving door.

6871   Then there was the moron who thought a mental institution was a college, but found that in a mental institution you have to show some improvement before you get out.

6872   The California booster said the state was great in every way except for occasional bad weather that blows in from Nevada.

6873   He was not a yes man, because when his boss said no, he said no.

6874   As the mother rabbit said to the baby rabbit, "You were pulled out of a magician's hat, so stop asking where you came from."

6875   The tree is no sooner down, but every one runs for his hatchet.

6876   Rainy days will surely come
Take your friend's umbrella home.

6877   It has often been asked what this nation stands for, and the question is easy—too much.

6878   The United States is a country of quiet majorities and vociferous minorities.

6879   An American university is an athletic institution in which a few classes are held for the feebleminded.

6880   He took only $250 to have dinner at a fancy restaurant, but he was not expecting to leave the waiter a large tip.

6881   Here lies old thirty-three-and-a-third percent,
The more he got the more he lent,
The more he lent the more he craved—
Good Lord, can such a man be saved?

6882   No more lessons, no more books,
No more teacher's sassy looks,
No more Latin, no more French,
No more sitting on a hard board bench.

6883   Velocity is what you let go of a hot frying-pan handle with.

6884   Take-home pay is what you owe after deductions.

6885   A good many foreigners think the eagle on the American dollar is the bird of paradise.

6886   A doorknob is a thing a revolving door goes around without.

6887   In God we trust; all others must pay cash.

6888   Jack Sprat could eat no fat,
His wife could eat no lean,
And so between the two of them
They licked the platter clean.—*English nursery rhyme*

6889   Economists now say we move in cycles instead of running around in circles. It sounds better, but it means the same.

6890   A scientist says: Roast beef made England what she is today.
Moral: Eat more vegetables.

6891   To err is human; to remain in error is stupid.

6892   Exactness is the sublimity of fools.

6893   She had her face lifted, but it fell when she got the bill for repairs.

6894   Gentleman: a man who can disagree without being disagreeable.

6895   A bachelor is one who enjoys the chase but does not eat the game.

6896   Strange how much you've got to know
        Before you know how little you know.

6897   Alaska: nothing but miles and miles of miles and miles of land.

6898   A Los Angeles landlord was arrested and charged with robbing
        people who were not his tenants.

6899   Our laundry has just sent back some buttons with no shirt on
        them.

6900   The law protects everybody who can afford to hire a good lawyer.

6901   Pedantry: stupidity that reads a book.

6902   A legend is a lie that has attained the dignity of age.

6903   Half a loaf is better than no time off.

6904   We are told most of the food on the stage during a play can be
        eaten. The idea may eventually be copied by more restaurants.

6905   There, little luxury, don't you cry—you'll be a necessity by and by.

6906   Any man who agrees with his wife can have his way.

6907   Man is the only animal that eats when he is not hungry, drinks
        when he is not thirsty and makes love at all seasons.

6908   All men are born free, but some get married.

6909   Pessimist: one who, when he has the choice of two evils, chooses
        both.

6910   Marriage is a romance in which the hero dies in the first chapter.

6911   People with good memories seldom remember anything worth
        remembering.

6912   If a man can remember what he worried about last week, he has a
        very good memory.

6913   A man who boasts only of his ancestors confesses that he belongs
        to a family that is better dead than alive.

6914   A person never knows how wonderful it was to be born poor until after he makes money.

6915   The moron thought an octopus was an eight-sided cat and couldn't understand why a black dog was called a greyhound.

6916   The Sultan got sore on his harem
And invented a scheme for to scare 'em;
        He caught him a mouse,
        Which he loosed in the house;
(The confusion is called harem-scarem.)

6917   There was a young man of Herne Bay,
Who was making some fireworks one day;
        But he dropped his cigar
        In the gunpowder jar.
There was a young man of Herne Bay.

6918   There was a young lady of Flint,
Who had a most horrible squint.
        She would scan the whole sky
        With her uppermost eye,
While the other was reading small print.

6919   There was an old party of Lyme,
Who married three wives at one time.
        When asked, "Why the third?"
        He replied, "One's absurd,
And bigamy, sir, is a crime!"

6920   The newspaper society notice said that out of fifty guests at the party, more than thirty had been married to the same man for more than thirty years.

6921   Speaker in the Canadian Parliament: I smell a rat. I see it in the air. And, by the grace of God, I'll nip it in the bud.

6922   A fern is a plant that you're supposed to water once a day, but when you don't it dies, but if you do it dies anyway, only not so soon.

6923   An optimist is a doctor who looks after your eyes.

6924   A pessimist is a doctor who takes care of your feet.

6925   You can fool some of the people all of the time, and all of the people some of the time, but the rest of the time they will make fools of themselves.

6926   There was a young lady of Niger,
Who went for a ride on a tiger.

> They came back from the ride
> With the lady inside
> And a smile on the face of the tiger.

6927 Frustration: when you have ulcers but still aren't a success.

6928 There was a young fellow of Perth,
Who was born on the day of his birth,
   He was married, they say,
   On his wife's wedding day,
And he died on his last day on earth.

6929 There was an old man of Tralee,
Who was bothered to death by a flea,
   So he put out the light
   Saying, "Now he can't bite,
For he'll never be able to see."

6930 A great many prominent family trees were started by grafting.

6931 The exchange of Christmas presents ought to be reciprocal rather than retaliatory.

6932 A literary critic is a person who finds meaning in literature that the author didn't know was there.

6933 Many people who emphatically protest that they are putting all their cards on the table usually put them there face down.

6934 The real problem of your leisure is to keep other people from using it.

6935 Sales resistance is the triumph of mind over patter.

6936 Few men really want justice; what all mankind prays for is mercy.

6937 Too many people don't care what happens, as long as it doesn't happen to them.

6938 If you can't make a man think as you do, make him do as you think.

6939 An adult is one who has stopped growing except in the middle.

6940 Experience is one thing you can't get for nothing.

6941 When a man repeats a promise again and again, he means to fail you.

6942 The meek may inherit the earth, but they'll cease being meek as soon as they come into their inheritance.

6943 We are an idealistic people, and we'll make any sacrifice for a cause that won't hurt business.

6944   The person that always says just what he thinks at last gets just what he deserves.

6945   The greatest service that could be rendered the Christian peoples would be to convert them to Christianity.

6946   You are what you think, and not what you think you are.

6947   A sufficient commentary on human nature is that a mob never rushes madly across town to do a needed kindness.

6948   Never be as funny as you can be.

6949   Many women have a nice sense of rumor.

6950   For every woman who makes a fool out of a man, there is another woman who makes a man out of a fool.

6951   Middle age is ten years older than you happen to be at the time.

6952   Middle age is that period in a man's life when he'd rather not have a good time than have to get over it.

6953   There was an old fellow of Trinity
        Who solved the square root of Infinity,
            But it gave him such fidgets
            To count up the digits,
        He chucked Math and took up Divinity.

6954   A is an apple, sour and green,
        Working in Tommy but cannot be seen.

6955   Sign in secondhand store: We buy old junk. We sell antiques.

6956   No matter how bad a child is, he is still good for an income tax exemption.

6957   Autumn: that wonderful season when father has exhausted all his barbecue recipes and the family can eat indoors in comfort again.

6958   The only time modern youngsters don't know all the answers is during school hours.

6959   To win the praise of a man, first praise him. When he tells others what you said he will have to tell how important you are to make it sound impressive.

6960   In a lot of homes, antiques are merely furniture that's finally been paid for.

6961   The three R's of life: it's Romance at 25; Rent at 35; and Rheumatism at 65.

6962   Some lies are so well told one would almost have to be a fool not to believe them.

6963   By the time you're rich enough to sleep late—you're so old you wake up early every morning.

6964   The newspaper error said Colonel Randolph was a bottle-scarred veteran.

6965   Anything which parents have not learned from experience they now learn from their children.

6966   What the United States needs is less paternalism in Washington and more in American homes.

6967   Pawnbroker: a person who asks you to see him at your earliest inconvenience.

6968   A pedestrian is a man whose son is home from college.

6969   A pedestrian is a man who has a car and a grown-up daughter.

6970   Pessimist: one who sizes himself up and gets angry about it.

6971   A pessimist is a person who stops by the meat market before he goes hunting and has a chicken sent home.

6972   Philosophy: a filter turned upside down, where what goes in clear comes out cloudy.

6973   Free verse: the triumph of mind over meter.

6974   There's no fool like the fool who thinks he is fooling you.

6975   Policeman: a never-present help in time of trouble.

6976   Money is honey, my little sonny,
        And a rich man's joke is always funny.

6977   Anyone who has to ask the cost can't afford it.

6978   Entrances are wide; exits are narrow.

6979   Even the best plan degenerates into work.

6980   I seen my duty and I done it.
        You seen your duty and you done it noble.

6981   In Japan the award for quality and productivity is the Deming Prize. In the United States it's an antitrust suit.

6982   There is no crisis to which academics will not respond with a seminar.

6983   What a scarcity of news there would be if we all obeyed the Ten Commandments.

6984   Success often comes from taking a misstep in the right direction.

6985   Success is not so much what you are but rather what you appear to be. Appearance is reality.

6986   Management is the art of getting other people to do all the work.

6987   Work is the price you pay for money.

6988   Money does make all the difference. If you have two jobs and you're rich, you have diversified interests. If you have two jobs and you're poor, you're moonlighting.

6989   IRS—Infernal Revenue Service.

6990   A nickel goes a long way now. You can carry it around for days without finding a thing it will buy.

6991   The rich may not live longer, but it certainly seems so to their poor relations.

6992   I live by the Golden Rule: he who has the gold makes the rules.

6993   Wealthy people miss one of life's greatest thrills—paying that last installment.

6994   It is better to be miserable and rich than it is to be miserable and poor.

6995   If absence makes the heart grow fonder, how some people must love their church.

6996   Before I start my speech I'd like to say something.

6997   Don't worry if your job is small,
          And your rewards are few;
          Remember that the mighty oak
          Was once a nut like you.

6998   Advice to loose talkers: build a better mouth trap.

6999   Advice to doctors: always write your prescriptions illegibly and your bills plainly.

7000   Don't worry: everything comes out in the wash, including the buttons.

7001   Don't hesitate to give advice: it passes time and nobody will follow it anyway.

7002   A little flattery now and then makes husbands out of single men.

7003   There are three kinds of friends: best friends, guest friends, and pest friends.

7004   It was so hot the other day that I saw a hound chasing a rabbit, and they were both walking.

7005   She's such a good cook that even the holes in her doughnuts taste better than anybody else's.

7006   What this country needs is more ex-Senators and ex-Congressmen.

7007   A help-the-needy committee met at luncheon today and resolved to have another luncheon.

7008   Faith will never die as long as beautiful seed catalogues are printed.

7009   You never realize how fortunate you are until you see how many things your friends haven't given you.

7010   Marrying for money is a hard way to earn it.

7011   Take care of the pennies and the dollars will take care of your heirs and their lawyers.

7012   The king was in the laundry
        Washing out his shirt;
        The queen was in the kitchen
        Sweeping up the dirt;
        The maid was in the parlor
        Eating bread and honey;
        Along came a neighbor and
        Offered her more money.

7013   A schoolgirl version: "I pledge a legion to my flag, and to the republic of Richard Stams, one nation invisible, with liberty and justice far off."

7014   A cynic says that double jeopardy, which we hear so much of nowadays, is when your doctor calls in a consulting physician.

7015   Elephants and head waiters never forget.

7016   A true conservative is one who can't see any difference between radicalism and an idea.

7017   They laughed when I sat down at the piano—I had forgotten to bring the stool.

7018   They laughed when I picked up the violin; they didn't know I was from the installment company.

7019   They laughed when I said I could not tell a joke, but they stopped when I told it.

7020   They laughed when they saw him put iodine on his paycheck; they didn't know he had got a cut in salary.

7021   My friend laughed when I spoke to the waiter in French, but the laugh was on him; I told the waiter to give him the check.

7022   The waiter laughed when I spoke to him in French; no wonder, he was my old professor.

7023   Girls who chatter don't much matter.

7024   Jonah was proof that you can't keep a good man down.

7025   He didn't seem to care whether a black speck in his pudding was a fly or a raisin.

7026   The height of laziness is getting up at five o'clock in the morning so you'll have more time to loaf.

7027   He's so cheap he uses the same calendar year after year.

7028   Her critics said she was so old she knew the Big Dipper when it was just a drinking cup.

7029   He is so tall that he stands on a chair to brush his teeth.

7030   She's so old, she's forgotten who she is and there's no one living who remembers her.

7031   She is so thoughtful, every time she throws a cup at her husband she takes the spoon out.

7032   An absent-minded professor sent his wife to the bank and kissed his money good-by.

7033   He thought a buttress was a female goat.

7034   Calvin Coolidge was so silent, he was always worth listening to.

7035   We don't get ulcers from what we eat but from what's eating us.

7036   When you're right, no one remembers; when you're wrong, no one forgets.

7037   Harvard offers education à la carte, Yale a substantial table d'hôte, Columbia a quick lunch and Princeton a picnic.

7038   We always remember those who have done us a favor—when we want another favor done.

7039   The equator is a menagerie lion running around the middle of the earth. Climate lasts all the time but weather only a few days. The government of England is a limited mockery.

7040   A man who marries twice commits bigotry.

7041   The king wore a robe trimmed with vermin.

7042   The watchwords of the French Revolution were Liberty, Equality, Maternity.

7043   A metaphor is something you shout through.

7044   A vegetarian is a horse doctor.

7045   He spent a small fortune to cure his halitosis only to find his friends didn't like him anyway.

7046   A volcano is a sick mountain.

7047   Women are getting men's wages now—but then, they always were.

7048   Even a waiter finally comes to him who waits.

7049   Wall Street: a thoroughfare that begins in a graveyard and ends in a river.

7050   A wise man may look ridiculous in the company of fools.

7051   Wisdom is divided into two parts: (1) having a great deal to say, and (2) not saying it.

7052   After man came woman—and she has been after him ever since.

7053   If you want to change a woman's mind, agree with her.

7054   There's only one way to handle a woman, but no one knows what it is.

7055   Next to the dog, the wastebasket is man's best friend.

7056   He said as soon as he realized it was a crooked business, he got out of it, but he didn't say how much.

7057   An apple a day keeps the doctor away, but an onion a day keeps everyone away.

7058   When her accountant husband proposed, he said, "I'd like to make a joint income tax return with you."

7059   Money talks, but it also stops talk.

7060   A great city, a great solitude.

7061   Figures don't lie, except political figures.

7062   Talk is cheap, except when you hire a lawyer.

7063   Talk is cheap because the supply always exceeds the demand.

7064   Where ignorance is bliss, 'tis folly to take an intelligence test.

7065   No man knows if honesty is the best policy unless he has tried both.

7066   If half the world doesn't know how the other half lives, it's not the fault of the confession magazines.

7067   A little nonsense now and then
Is relished by the wisest men.

7068   Television: it is a medium of entertainment which permits millions of people to listen to the same joke at the same time, and yet remain lonesome.

7069   Acupuncture doctor on phone: Take a safety pin and call me in the morning.

7070   I sometimes doubt the goodness
Of that everlasting bore,
Whose love embraces mankind
But skips the man next door.

7071   Keeping peace in a large family requires patience, love, understanding and at least two television sets.

7072   The first thing you learn during a hospital stay is that you're not fully covered by your insurance or your gown.

7073   To err is human, and to blame the mistake on somebody else is even more human.

7074   A schoolteacher asked the children to define the word advice. "Advice," said a little girl, "is when other people want you to do the way they do."

7075   Civilized nations are ones that simply can't endure wrongs or injustice except at home.

7076   What a pity to be born a rascal and be handicapped by a conscience!

7077   A coward is a man in whom the instinct of self-preservation acts normally.

7078   I wouldn't live forever,
I wouldn't if I could:
But I needn't fret about it,
For I couldn't if I would.

7079   If Diogenes returned today, he would be looking for an honest summer resort circular.

7080   Half the world knows how the other half ought to live.

7081   Our laundryman has the wisdom of a Solomon. When he can't decide to whom a certain shirt belongs, he splits it in half.

7082   The cat is in the parlor, the dog is in the lake;
The cow is in the hammock—what difference does it make?

7083   If man sprang from monkeys he ought to spring once more and make it a safe distance.

7084   An airport is where you go to waste time waiting that you're going to save flying.

7085   Antiques are things one generation buys, the next generation gets rid of, and the following generation buys again.

7086   The army private's jacket was okay, but the pants could be taken in about an inch around the armpits.

7087   If you have a cheap car, it breaks down. If you have an expensive car, it malfunctions.

7088   It's harder to keep your chin up after you've got more than one.

7089   Ed's a regular churchgoer. Never misses an Easter.

7090   I know a guy who's so conceited that on his birthday he sends his parents a telegram of congratulations.

7091   When a man won't listen to his conscience, it may be because he doesn't want advice from a total stranger.

7092   The cost of living keeps going higher—but it's still a bargain.

7093   A drug is that substance which, when injected into a rat, will produce a scientific report.

7094   One of the nicest things about being bald is that when company comes all you have to do is straighten your tie.

7095   It's so hot in Texas that I saw a bird pulling a worm out of the ground—with a pot holder.

7096   It's so hot down there that they're boiling the water—to cool it off.

7097   The average temperature in our apartment is seventy degrees—fifty in the winter and ninety in the summer.

7098   Homework is what gives a youngster something to do while he's watching television.

7099   No patient should have to leave the hospital until he's strong enough to face the cashier.

7100   Hospitality is the art of making people want to stay without interfering with their departure.

7101   Housework is what a woman does that nobody ever notices unless she doesn't do it.

7102   Doing nothing is the most tiresome job in the world, because you can't quit and rest.

7103   Intuition is what tells a wife her husband has done wrong before he thinks of doing it.

7104   Weiler's Law: nothing is impossible for the man who doesn't have to do it himself.

7105   Chisolm's Law: anytime things appear to be going better, you have overlooked something.

7106   Biology defines life as "the metabolic activity of protoplasm." But there are times when it seems even worse than that.

7107   A loser is a guy whose junk mail comes marked postage due.

7108   Love is only for the young, the middle-aged, and the old.

7109   Marriage isn't a battle that somebody is supposed to win.

7110   Never be so busy bringing home the bacon that you forget the applesauce.

7111   You always remember a kind deed. Particularly if it was yours.

7112   Any man who says he can read a woman like a book is probably illiterate.

7113   Sign in finance company window: Loans—for those who have everything but haven't paid for all of it yet.

7114   If you have to borrow money, borrow from a pessimist. He never expects to get it back anyhow.

7115   Sign in a loan company window: Now you can borrow enough money to get completely out of debt.

7116   Sign in a Fort Lauderdale restaurant: If you are over 80 years old and accompanied by your parents, we will cash your check.

7117   Morning is so nice they ought to make it later in the day.

7118   Late arrival at concert: The usher said they're playing the Fifth Symphony. That means we missed the first four!

7119   As the prig is bent, so is the snob inclined.

7120   Optimist: a man who goes into a restaurant with no money and figures on paying for his meal with the pearl that he hopes to find in the oyster he plans to order.

7121   Things are pretty well evened up in this world. Other people's troubles are never as bad as yours, but their children are a lot worse.

7122   More than fifty percent of Americans wear glasses, which gives you some idea of how important ears are.

7123   Abraham Lincoln had difficulty getting an education, but what do you expect from a guy who didn't play football, basketball, or baseball?

7124   If at first you don't succeed, that makes you just about average.

7125   Carrots are positively good for the eyes. Have you ever seen a rabbit with glasses?

7126   Nothing stretches slacks like snacks.

7127   One of the best ways to lose a friend is to tell him something for his own good.

7128   When it comes to giving, some people stop at nothing.

7129   Gossip is when you must hurry and tell someone before you find out it isn't true.

7130   The more interesting the gossip, the more likely it is to be untrue.

7131   The rush hour is when traffic is at a standstill.

7132   Don't be discouraged if your children reject your advice. Years later they will offer it to their own offspring.

7133   We get our parents so late in life that it is impossible to do anything with them.

7134   Wouldn't it be wonderful to be as brilliant as our children thought we were when they were young, and only half as stupid as they think we are when they're teenagers?

7135   How can a society that exists on frozen dinners, instant mashed potatoes, packaged cake mixes, and instant cameras teach patience to the young?

7136   Patience often gets the credit that belongs to fatigue.

7137   He who sings his own praise is seldom asked for an encore.

7138   A housing development is where they cut down all the trees and then name the streets after them.

7139   September is when millions of bright, shining, happy, laughing faces turn toward school. They belong to mothers.

7140   Forget what people think of you. You're people. What do you think of you?

7141   The best face-lift is a smile.

7142   Plenty of people are willing to give God credit, yet few are willing to give Him cash.

7143   Success is being able to hire someone to mow the lawn while you play tennis for exercise.

7144   If at first you don't succeed, you'll get a lot of advice.

7145   Summer is when the kids slam the doors they left open all winter.

7146   Conversation is the art of telling people more than you know.

7147   It has reached a point where taxes are a form of capital punishment.

7148   Internal Revenue Service man, to Sherlock Holmes: You make a lot of amazing deductions.

7149   My uncle is an optimist. He just asked the Internal Revenue to take him off their mailing list.

7150   Teacher's note on report card: Your son excels in initiative, group integration, responsiveness, and activity participation. Now if he'd only learn to read and write!

7151   It seems a little ridiculous now, but this country was originally founded as a protest against taxation.

7152   I can teach it to you, but I can't learn it for you.

7153   Kids aren't interested in putting their shoulders to the wheel these days—all they want to do is get their hands on it.

7154   It's always hard to get teens to hang up things—coats, towels, jeans, shirts—and especially the telephone.

7155   A great oak is only a little nut that held his ground.

7156   A Texan bought a ten-gallon hat, but he had an eleven-gallon head.

7157   A minute is never long enough for those who ask you if you can spare one.

7158   No one is more exasperating than the guy who can always see the bright side of our misfortunes.

7159   Could she be carrying her vegetarianism too far? She won't even eat animal crackers.

7160   You are overweight if you are living beyond your seams.

7161   Everybody likes a good loser—provided it is the other team.

7162   The one ambition in the life of a paper napkin is to get down off a diner's lap and play on the floor.

7163   College teaches men much more than some persons think. Many graduates have been offered major-league contracts.

7164   A more expensive article doesn't cost more, but it takes a few more installments to pay for it.

7165   Then there was the absent-minded professor who went round and round in a revolving door because he couldn't remember whether he was going in or coming out.

7166   An absent-minded professor found he had forgotten something when he left home, but he couldn't remember what it was.

7167   One moron took a bicycle to bed so he wouldn't have to walk in his sleep and the other one took a hammer so he could hit the hay.

7168   Advice is what the wise don't need and the fools won't take.

7169   He lives in an apartment overlooking the rent.

7170   The best way to tell a woman's age is not to.

7171   The best argument for everlasting peace is that it would enable us to finish paying for past wars.

7172   Winter is when your car won't start running and your nose won't stop.

7173   Mama Bear to Papa Bear: This is positively my last year as den mother!

7174   When a true genius appears in the world, you may know him by this obvious sign—that the dunces are all in confederacy against him.

7175   Sign on a car driven by an Indian in New Mexico: Love America or give it back.

7176   Nothing makes temptation so easy to resist as being broke.

7177   Most of us would be delighted to pay as we go if we could just catch up with paying for where we've been.

7178   Medical science has progressed to the point where the human body, with proper care, will last a lifetime.

7179   When a dietician recommends something you like, she adds that it should be eaten in moderation.

7180   A taxpayer is a government worker with no vacation, no sick leave, and no holidays.

7181   The trouble with giving advice is that people repay you.

7182   If you don't learn from your mistakes, there's no sense making them.

7183   It may be true that most people can't stand prosperity. But it's also true that most people don't have to.

7184   Usually the first screw to get loose in a person's head is the one that controls the tongue.

7185   Think twice before you speak, especially if you intend to say what you think.

7186   There's something to be said for living in Russia at that; you'd never lose an election bet.

7187   The only way we can attain perfection is to follow the advice we give to others.

7188   Childhood is the time of life when you make funny faces in the mirror. Middle age is the time of life when the mirror gets even.

7189   The reason some people won't suffer in silence is because it would take all the pleasure out of it.

7190   The fool who's soon parted from his money must wonder why that's supposed to make him different from everybody else.

7191   If you think no evil, see no evil, and hear no evil, the chances are that you'll never write a best-selling novel.

7192   The trouble with staying home from work is that you have to drink coffee on your own time.

7193   A good education enables a person to worry about things in all parts of the world.

7194   Always laugh heartily at the jokes your boss tells—he may be giving a loyalty test.

7195   The animal trainer at the circus who bravely climbs into the cage full of lions impresses everybody except the school bus driver.

7196   You can always spot an educated man. His views are the same as yours.

7197   How much it adds to human grief
          That witty speech is often brief!
          How true it is—and what a pity!
          That lengthy talks are seldom witty.

7198   Adolescence is that period when children feel that their parents should be told the facts of life.

7199   Social success is the infinite capacity for being bored.

7200   A mind that is always open may let in a lot of nonsense.

7201   After you've heard two eyewitnesses' accounts of a motor accident, you begin to worry about history.

7202   A reckless driver is one who passes you on the road in spite of all you can do.

7203   What did people do with their spare time before the radio and television?

7204   Each New Year is an adventure into which we must go.

7205   If we profited by our mistakes, we would all be millionaires.

7206   A bachelor is a rolling stone that has gathered no boss.

7207   A necessity is something you can't get along without but do, and a luxury is something you ought to get along without but don't.

7208   Sign on the windshield of an old, beat-up jalopy at a used car lot: Price $2,300. Rebate $2,100.

7209   She shifted her brain into neutral and let her tongue idle on.

INDEX

Business (continued)
3484, 3765, 3783, 4046, 4269, 4318,
4463, 4489, 4512, 4542, 4555, 4761,
5648, 5675, 5680, 5829, 5861, 6106,
6114, 6156, 6158, 6184, 6185, 6400,
6498, 6581, 6943, 7056
Businessman, 4024
Business school, 1340
Busy, 1042, 1835, 2446, 2501, 2755,
3372, 3470, 3854, 4519, 6402, 6407,
7110
Butcher, 4109
Butler, 3447, 6119
Butter, 4053
Butterfly, 1865
Button, 1943, 6509, 6899, 7000
Buttonhole, 5999
Buy, 1822, 2483, 2835, 2972, 3115, 3869,
3952, 5540, 5587, 5830, 6253
Buyer, 6384, 6390
Buy low, 271, 3104, 8990
Buzz, 2446

Cab, 183
Cabbage, 405, 3266, 5171
Cabots, 622
Caesar, Gaius Julius, 776, 1176, 2041
Cake, 2337
Calamities, 406, 1286, 6254
Calculators, 702, 4156
Calendar, 7027
California, 97, 358, 6872
Call, 2200
Calm, 381, 1511, 2886, 4168, 4971, 5040,
6134
Calories, 3955
Cambridge, 659
Camels, 407
Canada, 621, 646, 655, 1412, 1548, 3500,
3671, 5662
Canadian, 367, 1798, 4035
Candidate, 684, 2511, 3489
Candles, 2337
Candor, 3763, 5843, 6618, 6933, 6944,
7185
Cannibal, 747
Cannon, 715
Cannon, Jimmy, 1403
Can opener, 4192
Can't be done, 2423, 5037
Capable, 1941, 4830
Capacities, 1946, 5444
Capital, 1345, 1848

Capitalism, 963, 2271, 3360, 3743, 4825,
6256
Capitalist, 3880
Capital punishment, 1647, 7147
Captain, 4145
Car, 4330, 4371, 4421, 6077, 6522, 6610,
6636, 7087, 7153, 7172, 7208
Cards, 551, 1381, 2723, 5154, 5836, 6933
Care, 6937, 7025
Career, 1851
Careless, 3263, 6227
Cares, 3245, 4918
Caricature, 5772
Carrots, 7125
Carry on, 4662
Cars, 3766, 6969
Cash, 6887, 7142
Cast, 4739
Cat, 2193, 3066, 3121, 3682, 3768, 5225,
5343, 5384, 6224, 6333, 6730, 6915,
7082
Cataleptic, 3389
Catastrophe, 3020
Catechism, 4143
Caterpillar, 1865
Catsup, 141
Cattle, 6262
Catty, 4452
Caught, 4591, 6590
Cause, 85, 270, 1632, 2205, 3080, 3157
Caution, 5955
Celebrity, 100, 3550, 3779
Celery, 2480
Celibacy, 865, 2739, 4991
Cemetery, 652, 1037, 1218, 2413, 6233,
6247, 6535
Censorship, 4750, 4756
Censure, 5137
Ceremony, 5018
Certain, 534, 1615, 1744, 4700, 4942,
6639
Chair, 1894, 5224, 6159, 6841
Challenge, 6631
Chance, 1148, 2068, 2543, 4010, 5516,
5737, 6370, 6817
Change, 155, 210, 279, 475, 560, 779,
957, 985, 1225, 2033, 2180, 2892,
3231, 3255, 3424, 3456, 3645, 3814,
3954, 3856, 4195, 4407, 4559, 4663,
5026, 5109, 5503, 5719, 5783, 5798,
6097, 6188, 6656, 7053
Chaos, 3096, 6042
Character, 268, 522, 638, 866, 1155,
2435, 3087, 3094, 3125, 3195, 3273,

ABOUT THE AUTHORS

Herbert V. Prochnow is a former president and director of The First National Bank of Chicago and has held a number of high-level government and consulting positions. He was a financial columnist for the *Chicago Tribune* for several years, and has written numerous books on economics, banking, and public speaking.

Herbert V. Prochnow, Jr., a graduate of Harvard Law School, is a Chicago banker. He is the author of various business articles and a book on banking, and has collaborated with his father on the earlier editions of *The Public Speaker's Treasure Chest, A Treasury of Humorous Quotations, The Toastmaster's Treasure Chest,* and *A Treasure Chest of Quotations for All Occasions.*

28 DATE DUE $DAYS$

MAR 0 8 2005			
	WITHDRAWN		
GAYLORD			PRINTED IN U.S.A.